Llyn Ogwen
Milestone Buttress
Helyg
Llyn Clyd
Y Garn
Tryfan
Llyn Idwal
Llyn Bochlwyd
N
W
E
S
Llyn Peris
Devil's Kitchen
Nan Peris
(Old Lanberis)
Llyn Cwn
Glyder Fach
Llyn Caseg-fraith
Glyder Fawr
Snowdon Mountain Railway
HALFWAY STATION
A 4086
Pass of Llanberis
Llynnau Mymb
Halfway House
Ynys Ettws
Llyn Cwmffynnon
Afon Nant Peris
CLOGWYN STATION
Cwm Glas Mawr
Pen-y-Gwryd Hotel
Nantygwryd
Llyn Du'r Arddu
Llyn Glas
Pen-y-Pass
Crib Goch
A 498
Llyn Coch
Glaslyn
Llyn Teyrn
Nant Cynnyd
Llyn Nadroedd
SNOWDON/ YR WYDDFA
SUMMIT STATION
Llyn Llydaw
Cwm Dyli
Llnau Dlwaunedd

JULIAN & CLARE HARTWELL
MARTYRWELL
CHERITON
ALRESFORD
HAMPSHIRE SO24 0QA
Tel:01962 771273

FAR, FAR, THE DISTANT PEAK

FAR, FAR, THE DISTANT PEAK

The Life of Wilfrid Noyce

Mountaineer, Scholar, Poet

Stewart Hawkins

CURBANS BOOKS

Copyright © Stewart Hawkins 2014
First published in 2014 by Curbans Books
37 Courtyards, Litle Shelford, Cambridge, CB22 5ER

Distributed by Gardners Books, 1 Whittle Drive, Eastbourne,
East Sussex, BN23 6QH
Tel: +44(0)1323 521555 | Fax: +44(0)1323 521666

The right of Stewart Hawkins to be identified as the author of the work has been asserted herein in accordance with the Copyright, Designs and Patents Act 1988. All rights reserved. This book is sold subject to the condition that it shall not, by way of trade or otherwise, be lent, resold, hired out or otherwise circulated without the publisher's prior consent in any form of binding or cover other than that in which it is published and without a similar condition including this condition being imposed on the subsequent purchaser.

British Library Cataloguing in Publication Data
A catalogue record for this book is available from the British Library.

ISBN 978-0-9574043-0-4

Typeset by Amolibros, Milverton, Somerset
This book production has been managed by Amolibros
Printed and bound by T J International Ltd, Padstow, Cornwall, UK

To Romie and Ro

CONTENTS

List of Illustrations		vi
List of Maps		vii
Foreword		xi
Introduction		xiii
Chapter One	Early Days	1
Chapter Two	St. Edmund's	7
Chapter Three	Charterhouse	13
Chapter Four	Early Years in the Mountains	25
Chapter Five	Cambridge	45
Chapter Six	Service in World War II	71
Chapter Seven	Climbs in the Himalaya 1943-45	86
Chapter Eight	The Years 1946-50 – Settling in	125
Chapter Nine	The Years 1950 to 1954 – Getting Established	145
Chapter Ten	Everest 1952-53	158
Chapter Eleven	Everest Aftermath	208
Chapter Twelve	Himalaya and Karakoram 1957-60	218
Chapter Thirteen	The Years of Fulfilment 1955-62	258
Chapter Fourteen	The Pamirs 1962	291
Epilogue		304
Appendix A	Publications and Documents	311
Appendix B	First Ascents by Wilfrid Noyce	314
Appendix C	Bibliography	316
Appendix D	Wilfrid Noyce and Polio	320
Appendix E	A Pamir Pilgrimage	323

LIST OF ILLUSTRATIONS

The Family Tree of the Noyce and Kirkus Families   xvi

Facing page 110

1. Wilfrid Noyce aged six, and Jocelyn Ronald Noyce aged four, 1923.
2. Wilfrid, Jocelyn and Rosemary Noyce, 1931.
3. Wilfrid, Jocelyn and Rosemary (later Rosalind) Noyce, 1927.
4. Right: In his first term at Charterhouse, October 1931.
5. The Manods, North Wales – Noyce's first mountains.
6. Bryn Hyfryd, the Noyce family summer home at Ffestiniog.
7. An extract from Noyce's diary in his last year at school.
8. Wilfrid and Jocelyn Noyce at the Simmons' house at Hurtmore.
9. The Weekite house photograph – summer 1932.
10. Charterhouse 1935. Frank Fletcher teaching the Classical VI. Noyce is in the back row at the end on the right.
11. Leading on Belle Vue Bastion, Tryfan 1935.
12. Leading on Tryfan 1935.
13. Leading on Lliwedd 1936.
14. At Newton's Farm, Girton, 1936.
15. Noyce at the Close, Girton, 1936.
16. 2/Lt Wilfrid Noyce KRRC, 1941.
17. Noyce on Trisul, 1943.
18. Signal Intelligence Officers at the WEC, Delhi July 1944.
19. David Gould on summit of Chamian Sankar, Garhwal 1943.
20. With the Dhotiyals, Garhwal, 1943.
21. Gyalgin near summit on first peak, 1943.
22. With Gunturia in Garhwal, 1943

Facing page 206

23　Aircrew Centre, Kashmir – Noyce going up to dig out ponies on the Zoji La, 1944.
24　Aircrew Centre – Noyce with a pupil on the Kazim Glacier, 1944.
25　Srinagar, Kashmir – Picnic group Florence Castle, Wilfrid Noyce, John Hansbury, Gordon Macdonald.
26　Wedding Day 12th August 1950.
27　Tenzing Norgay with Rosemary, Wilfrid and Michael Noyce, Godalming, 1957.
28　Jeremy and Michael Noyce Badgers Hollow, Godalming, 1960.
29　Family group at Hurstmere 1957, Rose Binney, Lady Noyce, friend of Lady Noyce, Rosalind, Jeremy, Rosemary, Michael.
30　Noyce on Mount Everest, 1953.
31　Noyce with Anullu at Camp IV on Everest, 1953.
32　A scene of desolation, the Swiss tents on the South Col, 21st May 1953.
33　Noyce and the Sherpas on the Lhotse Face, 1953.
34　Charterhouse Climbing Meet, Cwm Glas, April 1955.
36　Signing an autograph for Stephen Pearne at a Young Persons' Literary evening, Guildford 1954.
35　Displaying mountain equipment at a village fête, 28th June 1959.
37　With Carthusians on Tryfan, January 1957. From left to Right, D. Mallock, A. Roberts, A.Rabeneck, A. Young and D. Meggs with Wilfrid Noyce and Angus Graham on Adam and Eve.
38　Noyce on the scree with John Hunt, Pik Garmo behind.
40　Robin Smith and Wilfrid Noyce on the summit of Pik Garmo, 24th July 1962.
39　The Wilfrid Noyce Memorial bench at Grayshott.
41　The Accident.
42　Jeremy Noyce at the memorial to his father and Robin Smith, Garmo Valley, Tajikistan, 29th September 2009.

LIST OF MAPS

The Mountains of North Wales	Front endpaper
The Himalaya and Lake District	Back endpaper
The Alps around Zermatt	41
The Mont Blanc massif	65
Noyce's sketch map of his Trisul journey	89
Sketch map of the second trip to Garhwal	94
Map showing the area of activities of the Aircrew Centre	103
Eastern Sikkim showing Pauhunri and Noyce's route	117
The Road to Katmandu	165
The approach march to Everest	171
Routes to the summit of Everest in 1953	177
Machapuchare and the Annapurna Basin	222
Map of Gilgit, Nagar and Hunza	239
The route to the summit of Trivor	243
Sketch map of the High Atlas	279

ACKNOWLEDGEMENTS

To Dr Reginald Hall for his advice and assistance on the appendix on Wilfrid Noyce and polio.

To The Religious Society of Friends in Britain for permission to print Wilfrid Noyce's record of service with the Friends Ambulance Unit.

To the Royal Geographical Society (with IBG) for the use of their Everest archives.

The Weekite house photograph of 1932 is reproduced by kind permission of the Headmaster and Governors of Charterhouse.

The extracts from **Menlove, the life of John Menlove Edwards** are reprinted with the kind permission of Jim Perrin.

The extract from **The Spirit of Adventure** is reprinted by kind permission of Colin Mortlock

The extracts from **With Friends in High Places** are reprinted with kind permission of Mainstream Publishing.

The extracts from the **RSI Journal** are printed with kind permission of the Secretary, Royal Signals Institution.

The extracts from the **Malvern Gazette** are printed by kind permission of the Editor, Newquest.

The extracts from the **Surrey Advertiser** are printed with kind permission of the Editor.

The extract from the **Herald for Hindhead** is printed with kind permission of The Editor, **Tindle News**.

Extracts from **Ascent of Everest, Life is Meeting** and **Red Peak** are printed with kind permission of Hodder and Stoughton

Extracts from **The Emperor's Codes** are reprinted by permission of Peters Fraser & Dunlop (www.petersfraserdunlop.com) on behalf of Peters Fraser & Dunlop, Drury House 34-43 Russell Street London WC2B 5HA

Most of the illustrations have been kindly provided by the Noyce family. Those listed below are printed by kind permission of the persons or organisations indicated.

The Manods, North Wales, Noyce's first mountains, Stewart Hawkins

Bryn Hyfryd, the Noyce family summer home at Ffestiniog, Stewart Hawkins

The Weekite house photograph – summer 1932, Charterhouse

Charterhouse 1935 Frank Fletcher teaching the Classical VI, *Country Life*

Signal Intelligence Officers at the WEC, Delhi July 1944, Hodder and Stoughton

Aircrew Centre – Noyce with pupil on Kazim Glacier, Eileen Jackson

Aircrew Centre – Noyce going up to dig out ponies on Zoji La, Eileen Jackson

Srinagar, Kashmir. A picnic group with Florence Castle, Eileen Jackson

With Carthusians on Tryfan, John Herington

Charterhouse climbing meet, Cwm Glas April 1955, Richard Hills

Noyce and Hunt on Scree, Graeme Nicol

Robin Smith and Wilfrid Noyce on the summit of Pik Garmo, Alpine Club

The Wilfrid Noyce Memorial bench at Grayshott, Stewart Hawkins

Jeremy Noyce at his father's memorial, Garmo Valley, Stewart Hawkins

The Accident, Google Earth

The maps with the following exceptions are from the Noyce archives.

The endpapers were designed by Martin Shoesmith

The maps of Zermatt and Mont Blanc were kindly provided by the Swiss Federal Topography Office

FOREWORD BY STEPHEN VENABLES

On the evening of 10th May 1988, with two Americans and one Canadian companion, I completed a new route up the East Face of Everest and stepped out, exhausted, onto the wind-scoured plateau called the South Col. We were the first people to reach this bleak spot from Tibet, but we were acutely aware that many, many others had been here before us, climbing from Nepal. One of the very first was Wilfrid Noyce. During a critical stage of the 1953 Everest expedition it was he, with Sherpa Anullu, who was selected to make the first, hugely symbolic, push to the Col, final staging point for the summit itself. Afterwards, describing the forlorn, tattered remains of the tents left by the previous year's Swiss attempt, Noyce wrote one of the most evocative passages in Everest's long literature, in **South Col** – his engagingly personal complement to John Hunt's official expedition account, ***The Ascent of Everest.***

Unlike the author of this biography, I never knew Wilfrid Noyce, but as a young teenager I was certainly aware of the famous mountaineer who had so recently been killed in the Pamirs. At Charterhouse I was briefly in the same German class as his son Jeremy. I was interested in mountaineering and owned a copy of Noyce's anthology ***The Climber's Fireside Book***; and every day, walking through the South African Cloister on the way to Music School, just beyond the sad collection of Boer War memorials, I would pass two stone plaques commemorating victims not of war but of the mountains, both of whom had taught at the school. One was dedicated to George Mallory, who died on Everest in 1924. The other was for Wilfrid Noyce – 'mountaineer, scholar, poet'. Later, having taken up climbing myself, I learned more about Noyce – the early pioneering rock climbs with Menlove Edwards, the lightning fast alpine ascents with the famous guide Armand Charlet, the wartime explorations in Sikkim, then Everest, Machapuchare, Trivor and that final ill-fated climb in the heart of Central Asia.

As a climber, he seems to have moved with enviable ease and grace, bordering at times on the nonchalant. As a writer, he was always fascinated by the emotions and motivations underpinning his chosen activity, fascinated by his surroundings, generous in description of his companions. On Everest he was clearly one of the strongest climbers in the team. Had Hillary and Tenzing not succeeded, he would probably have been next in line for a summit attempt. But that they did succeed and he suppressed personal ambition in gracious celebration of the team's collective achievement.

Everest did not dampen his enthusiasm for high mountains. He continued to visit the Himalaya and triumphed with the first ascent of Trivor, one of the giant seven-thousanders of the Karakoram. But, as this book reveals so clearly, he was much more than just a climber. He was a talented all round sportsman, a formidable scholar and, above all, a writer with interests that ranged far beyond the sometimes arcane world of mountaineering. Italy was a particular passion and the main focus of his research when he took the bold step of abandoning the security of his teaching post to become a full time writer. The tragedy is that he died soon after starting this new adventure, so full of promise. But he left the books, the story of great climbs and a life which, as Stewart Hawkins explores in this biography, was an inspiration to many, many other people.

INTRODUCTION

I hadn't meant to write this book – or any book for that matter. However, I had done several missions in Central Asia for the European Union TACIS programme (Technical Aid to the Commonwealth of Independent States) and I was very aware that Wilfrid Noyce had died with Robin Smith on Mount Garmo in 1962 when they were with Sir John Hunt on the Soviet British Pamirs Expedition. From Malcolm Slesser's book **Red Peak** I knew that the Russians had built a memorial to them in what is now Tajikistan, not far from where they died.

I was one of the large number of young people whom Wilfrid Noyce inspired with a love of high hills. He taught me French at Charterhouse, was our Senior Scoutmaster and introduced me to the mountains. Most of this book has been written within sight of the Ecrins in South-East France.

I felt that it would be an expression of thanks and appreciation to Wilfrid Noyce to visit the memorial and to see its condition. When I set about finding the location of the memorial, I talked to members of the 1962 expedition and they were very helpful. Graeme Nicol, the doctor on the expedition, in the course of our discussions said, "Are you going to write a book about Wilf then?"

That was not in my plan but I thought about it and discovered that a publisher had considered asking Alan Hankinson that self-same question but it finally emerged that no biography of Noyce had apparently yet been written. The story of the visit to the memorial with Wilfrid's younger son Jeremy and two other friends is recounted in an appendix.

Noyce was forty-four years old when he died and managed to fill those years with a sustained level of achievement that would have kept others going for twice as long. As a schoolboy I spent a fair time with the Noyces but rarely did one get an inkling of what Wilf had done before he arrived at Charterhouse to teach in 1950. He was far too modest to say anything other than to acknowledge that he had been at the school as a boy and had done some exciting climbs.

The Noyce family members have been very supportive in this quest and Rosemary, Wilfrid's widow, gave me access to the family records. Rosalind, Wilfrid's sister, has provided considerable information and I have worked with Jeremy on his father's slides for some of the illustrations.

I would also like to acknowledge the help of Wilf's Everest colleagues, George Band and Mike Westmacott, his companions in the Pamirs, Ian McNaught-Davis and Graeme Nicol, and other climbing companions, Richard Brookes and Colin Mortlock.

I would also like to thank Pauline McCausland, the archivist at St Edmund's school, and Margaret Mardall, the Recorder, and Catherine Smith, the Archivist at Charterhouse. The archivists at King's College, Cambridge were very helpful and I very much appreciated the assistance of Major Alan Edwards at the Intelligence Corps museum.

Eileen Jackson provided a number of pictures of Noyce's activities with her husband in Kashmir and a number of Old Carthusians, Richard Hills, Tim Mimpriss, Peter Norton and John Herington provided anecdotes and photographs. John, Helen Chalmers and Anne Boit read the text and I am very grateful for their comments. Geoff Milburn spent many days editing the text, and provided excellent guidance on style and presentation.

Steve Dean and Jim Perrin, both acclaimed biographers of mountaineers, and Trevor Braham, chronicler of the Alps and Himalaya, were generous with their advice. Peter Martin, lately Mayor of Godalming, was very helpful with access to the borough library and archives, and Colin Leakey provided considerable background on the relations of the Noyce and Leakey families. I am most grateful for the support of Martyn Berry, joint editor of **Speak to the Hills**, and he, Marcia Newbolt, and Colin Leakey corrected a number of inaccuracies. While I have tried to avoid them, nonetheless any errors that still remain are entirely my responsibility

The library teams at the Alpine Club and the Climbers' Club have been very supportive and I appreciated the hospitality of Jeremy Hinchcliffe, the Balliol College librarian, while I was reading the Noyce letters held there. My special thanks are due to Jimmy Cruickshank, the biographer of Robin Smith, for his suggestions and information that throws additional light on the the final accident. My colleague of the Arabian mountains,

INTRODUCTION

John Harding, provided very good guidance on the tortuous business of publication and I am also grateful to Jane Tatam of Amolibros for her vital and sustained support in getting this book into print.

Finally my thanks are to my wife, Sandra, for her tolerance and patience. She has never failed to be supportive and encouraging.

Curbans
Alpes de Haute Provence
May 2013

Family Tree of the Noyce and Kirkus families.

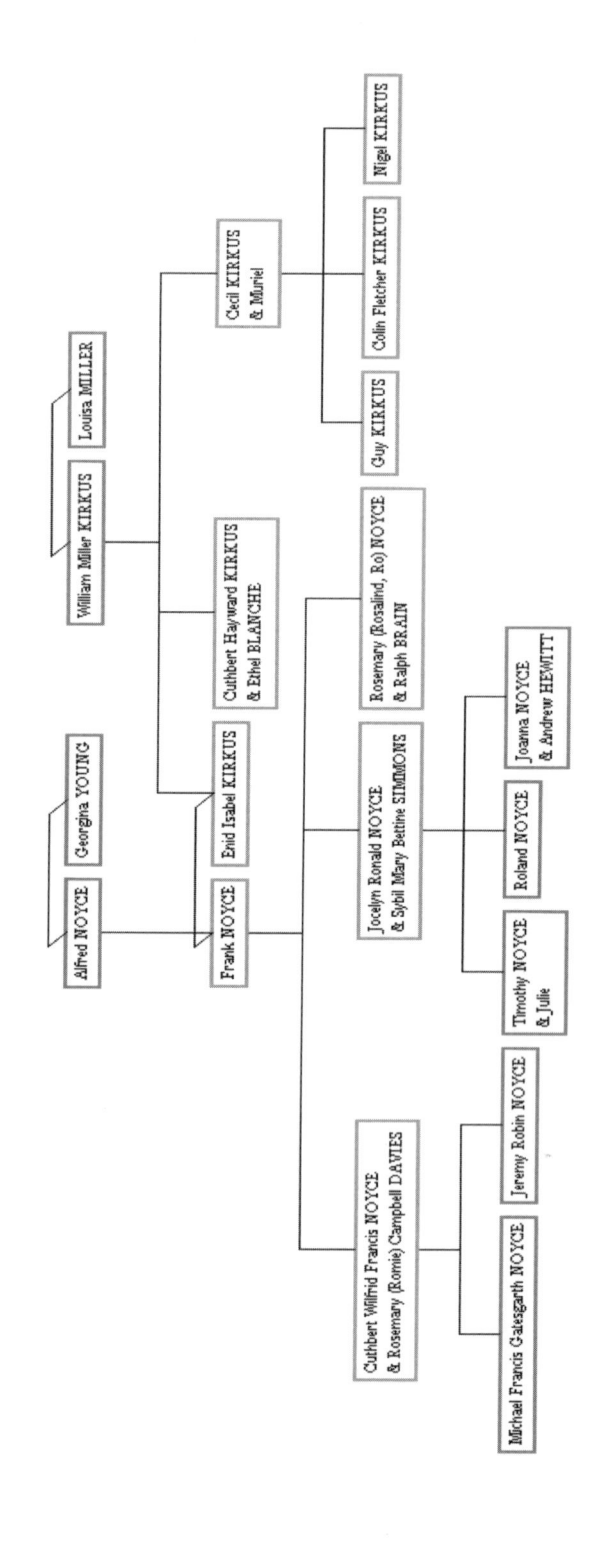

CHAPTER ONE

EARLY DAYS

It is 21st May 1953: imagine the excitement, two tiny figures in blue anoraks break the skyline above the South Col at 26,000ft (7,925m). The other members of the expedition who are anxiously looking upwards watching Wilfrid Noyce and the Sherpa Anullu from their camps in the Western Cwm raise a mighty cheer. It is a huge boost to morale and the final assault of Everest is on!

The British Mount Everest expedition, led by Colonel John Hunt and supported by a large number of British companies and institutions, was up to that point foundering. The painstaking organisation, elaborate preparations and extensive acclimatisation had brought the expedition and its attendant Sherpa porters through the challenges of the lower part of the mountain, the Icefall and the Western Cwm. Climbers and stores were positioned high on the mountain and they were now trying to cross the Lhotse face to ascend to the South Col, a windy plateau from which the final assault on the summit could be made. It had not gone well. The expedition was losing momentum and morale was declining. Four climbers with supporting Sherpa porters had been assigned to make the route across the Lhotse face. Colds and flu forced three to descend and this left George Lowe, one of the two New Zealanders on the expedition, up there with one Sherpa porter. Reinforcements were sent up but even after twelve days efforts were still foundering.

John Hunt decided that it was now or never and on 20th May he asked Wilfrid Noyce, who had often climbed with Hunt, and Charles Wylie, a major in the Gurkhas, and secretary of the expedition, to take some Sherpas up to Camp VII, at 24,000ft (7,300m) and to go on afterwards up to the South Col. When they got to Camp VII they were very tired and most of them were exhausted, so consequently they all spent the night there in some discomfort. The facilities there were limited, it was crowded, the climbers did not have enough to eat. The following day most of the Sherpas were uneasy and did not want to go on, so Noyce, to whom fatigue and exhaustion were total strangers, said, *"I'll take Anullu,"* one of the best Sherpas there, and the two of them, equipped with oxygen, set off. After one or two daring moves they found a route over the Geneva Spur and down to the South Col and this instantly changed the whole psychology of the expedition. *"We were thinking we're going to fail and founder: but now he's made it so we can go ahead."*[1] When he returned to Camp VII, Noyce and Anullu were *'relatively fresh and for Noyce it was "one of the most enjoyable day's mountaineering I have ever had"'.*[2] It was a very important role psychologically at this point on the expedition and without a doubt this paved the way for ultimate success.

Who was this unassuming man who inspired so many with a love of the mountains and showed them how to achieve beyond their expectations? Most of his year was spent teaching the glories of the French and German languages to adolescents in the middle and senior forms of an English public school. From the age of seven, however, he wanted to be in the mountains to get to the top of whatever hill or mountain on which he found himself. In addition the same drive and determination brought him considerable academic distinction both at school and at Cambridge. This drive for excellence, as we shall see, was not for glory or riches but for his own personal fulfilment. He was one of the last of the elegant generations of mountaineers who climbed mountains for their own sake and for their humanising and regenerative effect. He eschewed the idea of competitive climbing and regarded skiing as purely a means of locomotion. The present commercialisation of the mountains, in particular Everest, would have horrified him and he would have found the present pursuit of fame and fortune in ever more hazardous situations unacceptable. To Wilfrid Noyce the mountains were sacred and were there for the delight and respect of man and to enable him to link with nature. For his own personal satisfaction, he always wanted to get to the summit and to admire the view.

Like so many of the mountaineers of his generation he was also able to convey his emotions and sensations in the hills in well-fashioned prose and poetry, illuminated by scholarship and supported by experience, so that readers and his pupils such as myself were delighted and inspired by the spirit of his words.

To his contemporaries he appeared to come from a patrician

background, with his public school and Cambridge education but his antecedents were much more modest. The Noyce family was originally from Hampshire around East Dean and Tytherley, and the records of the county covering several centuries mention Noyces with varying degrees of distinction. Alfred, Wilfrid Noyce's grandfather, was born in 1852 and married Georgina Young, born two months earlier. He was employed as a Railway Porter and eventually lived at Dean House, Alderholt, near Salisbury. Wilfrid's father, Frank, was the eldest son of Mr. Alfred Noyce, and was born in 1878. He was educated at Bishop Wordsworth's School and at Salisbury School and his early promise was evident. The records of the Oxford Local Examinations in 1895 show that he has *'shown sufficient merit to be excused from responsions'* – the pre-requisite examination then, in Latin, Greek and Mathematics for admission to the universities of Oxford and Cambridge. He went as a scholar in Mathematics to St. Catherine's College, Cambridge in October 1897.

One of Frank's friends at Cambridge was Cuthbert Kirkus from Liverpool and during the vacations he used to go home with Cuthbert, who had a brother Cecil and a sister Enid. Cuthbert's father, William, was a member of the Liverpool Stock Exchange and they lived in Sefton Park, a part of Liverpool that still retains its distinction. William Kirkus rented for some years a house called Bryn Hyfryd on the edge of the town of Ffestiniog in North Wales where the Kirkus family spent holidays. After he left Cambridge Cuthbert went into insurance and during the 1914-18 war served in France as an officer in the Royal Garrison Artillery until he was killed on 31st July 1917. Cecil was educated at Sedburgh School and eventually became an automobile engineer with his own thriving business.

Cecil developed a great love for the hills at Ffestiniog and fortunately his wife Muriel also shared this passion. They had three sons Colin, Nigel and Guy. Colin the eldest was introduced to the hills from Bryn Hyfryd and his first ascent was Manod within sight of the house. Cecil and Muriel later regularly rented a cottage in the Vale of Llangollen for three or four weeks in the summer, encouraging further their sons' love of the hills.

Frank Noyce took the examinations in 1901 for the Indian Civil Service, the most rigorous and selective filter of the time. His daughter recalls him saying that he still had nightmares about them thirty years later. It was solid examinations for a fortnight. He arrived in India in

December 1902 and was assigned to the Madras Presidency. He clearly was very taken with Enid Kirkus and the correspondence with her developed into courtship. He came home for his first home leave in 1911 and spent nearly eighteen months in England during which time he married his sweetheart Enid Kirkus and they returned to India to the Revenue and Agriculture Department at Simla, now known as Shimla.

Simla was the summer capital of India. It is at 7,000ft (2,300m) in the foothills of the Western Himalaya. From the year 1864, during the months of April to October, the entire apparatus of government was transferred there. This involved a day's train ride to the base of the hills at Kalka and then a bone-shaking ride of eight or nine hours in a tonga or curricle drawn by successive pairs of ponies. The Noyces, however, were fortunate in being based there permanently for the next four years.

The life of a member of the ICS in India, however, was comfortable and gracious but lacking most of the modern conveniences of flush toilets and running water. The few wives that accompanied their husbands out at this time were made of stern stuff to cope with all the vicissitudes and hardships of Indian life. The Warrant of Precedence established a clear pecking order on every official and social occasion and a dim view was taken of any contraventions. Enid Noyce had to learn quickly and even as a new bride she was accorded the honour of Senior Lady at private functions for six months. An official's wife could devote herself almost exclusively to the social and official support of her husband and a large number devoted themselves also to good works. Enid Noyce, for example, founded The Lady Noyce School for the Deaf and Dumb in Delhi, which still bears her name.

On the domestic front as the lady of the house, the *memsahib*, not only was she expected to accompany her husband to various events, but also to supervise a considerable number of staff, there was the *khitmagar*, the chief bearer, or butler-valet, who looked after the *sahib* or the master of the house, and he assisted the memsahib in the supervision of the servants – and perhaps remembered wistfully the sahib's bachelor days. One important component of the sanitation was the 'thunder-box', which was serviced by the *mehtar*, or sweeper who was almost invisible in the way he carried out his functions of removing what was called, rather primly, 'the night-soil'. There were cooks, cleaners, gardeners, the *dhobi* who did the washing, the *chowkidars* who watched the house at night, and others all in a hierarchy of functions and castes with their own specific roles.[3]

Frank Noyce was transferred back to the Madras Presidency in December 1916 but returned in Simla in June 1917 on assignment to the central Revenue and Agriculture department. Enid Noyce was back on familiar ground for her first confinement and Cuthbert Wilfrid Francis Noyce was born on the last day of the year, possibly in the Portmore Nursing home, which flourished at least until the beginning of World War II. Still on that site now is the Portmore Government Girls Senior Secondary School. Wilfrid was baptised in Simla with the name Cuthbert in vivid recent memory of his uncle who had tragically died five months previously in Flanders.

The house that the Noyce family occupied in Simla in their later years, when Sir Frank Noyce was a member of the Viceroy's Council, was called 'Inverarm', a large and splendid mansion which is now the home of the Himachal State Museum.

The children would be looked after by an *ayah*, or children's nurse, who was usually an unmarried girl and who showed great fondness and loyalty to her charges. She might neglect them sometimes in pursuit of amorous adventures, but would, with the other staff, just as easily spoil the children with clandestine gifts of sweeties from the bazaar. These were of doubtful content and were probably both of unhygienic manufacture and bearers of all kinds of disease. Such children were brought up by the servants and developed very good relations with them as well as with Indian children of their own age. Like all children they learned to communicate with each other very quickly and would quickly understand and later speak Hindustani, the vernacular language, as a matter of course. For most of the time they were thus able to communicate with all the locals of whatever status or caste they were. They saw their parents only when the social and official rounds permitted. Hindustani, or now perhaps more properly Hindi or Urdu, was the means of communicating with the Indians. This lingual acquisition by the young Wilfrid was later to stand him in good stead on many occasions. Brother Jocelyn Ronald was born in 1919 and when Wilfrid was five they came to England in July 1922 when Frank Noyce was posted as the acting Trade Commissioner for India in London for nine months.

The Noyces went to England in the company of an old friend, Mabel Hutchesson, who had been working as a midwife in India. They intended to leave the boys in England as it was time for Wilfrid to start school and so they established Mabel in a house, Hindhead Chase in Grayshott, to provide a home for them as they would not be able to get back to India even in the school holidays. Later on the Noyces moved the establishment to Ensleigh, a larger house across the road, where other children of the servants of Empire could stay during the school holidays and in the case of day-boys and day-girls, they could live there during both holiday and term-time.

During the next three years Wilfrid, and later Jocelyn, went to a local pre-preparatory school, St. Ursula's in Grayshott. Enid Noyce would come home from India most years and the boys would spend their summer holidays with her at Bryn Hyfryd.

Enid Noyce came back to England in 1926 for the birth on 7th September of Rosemary, later known as Rosalind, whom she left in the care of 'Hutch' when she returned to India a year later. Rosalind remembers that there were always about three or four children who stayed there in term time and twelve to fourteen in the holidays. *"There were two groups,"* she recalls, *"one of older boys and girls which included her two brothers, and the group of younger children which I was with."*

Wilfrid and Jocelyn appear to have spent their Easter and Christmas holidays with Hutch all through their childhood, until they received holiday invitations from a wider range of friends at preparatory school and Charterhouse. Rosalind, that much younger, was with Hutch until Sir Frank and Lady Noyce returned from India on retirement in 1937 and bought Grayshott House, not far from Ensleigh.

The Noyce brothers had a fatherless childhood, apart from the nine months that they were in London. Parental care was remote and they saw their mother only during the summer holidays. The years in boarding schools provided them with considerable support but certainly Wilfrid, while very much his own man, still appears to have looked for relationships to provide role models, support and, at times, counsel.

Notes

1   George Band Conversation with author 18.11.2008
2   John Hunt *Ascent of Everest* p.166
3   John Masters, *Bugles and a Tiger,* p.138 & seqq

CHAPTER TWO

ST. EDMUND'S

At the age of five or six the children of the 'servants of Empire' were taken from the care of the ayahs and the governesses in the carefree colonial environment and sent back to Britain to the care of uncles and aunts, who perhaps only enjoyed the courtesy title, and other guardians to ensure that they should not be too spoilt. The uncle and aunt guardianship was a lottery, some children loved it, while others hated it. In the case of the Noyce boys, and later their sister, it seems to have been a very happy regime at Grayshott with Mabel Hutchesson.

After two or three years of this they would enter a preparatory school where the ideas of conscientious study, competitive games and robust Christianity were inculcated. Needless to say they were single-sex and the only moderating female contact was in the shape of the matron and perhaps one or two lady teachers for the junior forms. Starting in a boarding institution at this early age is much easier than at thirteen or fourteen. One becomes habituated to the lack of privacy, the communal nature of most activities and the need to accommodate the irritations of others' habits much more easily.

Enid Noyce had come home from India early in 1926 to see Wilfrid enter St. Edmund's Preparatory School at Grayshott, near Hindhead, for the summer term, when he was eight and a half. She also wanted to be with Mabel Hutchesson for the birth of daughter Rosalind later in the year.

St. Edmund's was founded in 1874 at Hunstanton St. Edmund on the coast of the Wash in East Anglia when the number of preparatory schools was increasing rapidly to satisfy the new public schools. It was a family affair, like many of them, with the academic side being the responsibility of the husband, usually a classical scholar, and the domestic arrangements being managed by the wife. The Reverend John and Mrs. Morgan Brown followed the pattern and regarded the pupils as an extension of their family and inculcated in them the family values of intellectual effort and hard physical activity with a strong religious background. Cyril, the son of John and Frances Morgan Brown, gained a first in Classics at Oxford, took over when his father retired and, as the school grew, asked his brother-in-law Wilfrid Richmond to become a partner in the school. This collaboration was of short duration.

By 1899 the school had outgrown the premises in Norfolk and the search for new premises was guided by the young Mrs. Morgan-Brown's health requirements. Hindhead was recommended as being the 'Little Switzerland of Surrey'. It had plenty of open spaces as well as distinguished inhabitants such as Sir Arthur Conan Doyle, the creator of Sherlock Holmes, who was the first president of the Hindhead Golf Club.

Very quickly the Morgan-Browns decided on a house, built in 1870 on the edge of the village of Grayshott in rolling and wooded land, which by 1899 had been let to a middle-aged playwright, George Bernard Shaw. The negotiations were completed, the buildings had been comprehensively altered and the school moved in during the summer holidays of 1900. The original house forms the central part of the school and other buildings and land have been added over the years to the twenty-three-acre site.

In 1902 yet another family member, Ivo Bulley, a cousin of Cyril's wife, joined the school as an emergency replacement for a master who had gone down with measles. Although he did not have a university degree, he was invited to stay on. However, the First World War intervened and he went to the army. He returned after the war and married Cyril's daughter who by then had a key position in the school administration.

When Wilfrid Noyce entered the school, Cyril Morgan-Brown had handed over the active management of the school to his main partner, Ivor Sant, the deputy head, a classicist who supervised the academic side and Ivo Bulley, who after the war had done an external London University degree. Bulley, who was not favoured as a successor to Morgan-Brown as he was not a classicist – or an Oxbridge graduate – but could teach Common Entrance candidates their Greek irregular verbs, was nonetheless recognised as a very competent administrator. Eventually in 1930 he became a partner and in 1933 became headmaster.[1]

However, from the time he joined the school he provided an alternative approach to those who thought classics and the winning of scholarships to the public schools, usually classicists, were the essential objectives of a good preparatory school. Team games were important, cricket, rugby and football, but Ivo Bulley had a light-hearted view of games and promoted paper-chases, war-games and other unorthodox outdoor activities.

It would appear that Sant and Bulley were key influences in the young Wilfrid's time at St. Edmund's. Sant recognised the intellectual promise and established the base on which the future successes at Charterhouse and Cambridge were realised. Bulley with his unconventional approach to sporting activities provided encouragement for the young Noyce's interest in hills and mountains that was indulged during holidays at Bryn Hyfryd. During the first holiday from St. Edmund's Noyce was allowed to climb his first mountain, Manod, which was all of 2,166ft (660m) and is visible from Bryn Hyfryd.[2]

Talking to contemporaries of Wilfrid Noyce at St. Edmund's, it seems to have been a very happy school. *"It was a hard school – not very easy, but it was an excellent education. It was hard work to keep up with the group."*[3] There was very firm discipline but the boys seem to have enjoyed the life there. One was expected to take part in everything that was going – including boxing. There was even a golf-course. There were very happy memories of St. Edmund's and particularly of Ivo Bulley, the headmaster. Rosamund Bulley, his wife, was a great character. She could still vault over a five-bar gate at eighty![4] The Robertson-Glasgow brothers, both on the staff at that time encouraged and taught the boys golf. They both left the school later, one to help set up another preparatory school and the other, 'RC', became a very well-known sports journalist in the 1950s and 1960s.

In May 1926 eighty-one boys were in the school in seven classes or forms. Wilfrid went into the bottom form I for his first term and showed very early signs of academic promise, collecting the first crop of many prizes that he was to receive in his academic career, with an overall Honours prize as well as awards for French, English and Latin and general form work. The prizes were all works of 'improving' literature, such as *A Tale of Two Cities*. The following term he was moved up to form IIb and was nearly a year younger than the oldest boy in the form. At the end of this term he came fifth in form and collected a *True Story Book* for Honours and *Flat Iron for a Farthing* for French.[5]

He continued his rise up the school, holding his own academically with boys who were much older, and adding Divinity to his prize subjects. Boys who were potential scholars to the public schools often spent two years or more in the top form and Wilfrid for his two years there was comfortably near the top all the time collecting prizes for Classics and Divinity and general Form Work. He does not appear to have received a prize for Mathematics! The top form was orientated towards getting scholarships, usually by means of exhibiting an impressive knowledge of Latin and Greek grammar and syntax. The author recalls that in 1951 Charterhouse was still expecting candidates for scholarships to translate a piece of English verse into fluent and erudite Latin elegiac couplets. Wilfrid, with his classics, obtained the third Foundation scholarship to Charterhouse in June 1931.

It would be unfair, however, to present the young Noyce as a 'swot'. He participated in other activities and games and athletics coming second in the eighty-yard sprint at the end of his first year. In the 1927 summer holiday competition his painting, a 'fleet of painted ships upon a painted ocean' was judged a 'very good effort' and the best of Class 1. In his last year, 1930-31, he was active in the six-a-side football and a 'hard-hitting bout' of boxing is recorded. *'Noyce has a fine reach but never makes the best use of it; he must hit straighter!'*[6] He played fives. He was captain of the school second cricket eleven and appears to have been an indifferent batsman but a competent bowler.

From his own writing it is clear that even at this age Wilfrid's heart was in the hills and the heights. In the holidays he was to be found exploring the mountains around Ffestiniog, the Moelwyns and the Manods with routes of increasing difficulty, and eventually climbed Moel yr Hydd *'a rock climb from which I breathed thankfully for escape'*. His cousins, Nigel and Guy Kirkus, *'already bitten with the rock-climbing madness'*, came to Bryn Hyfryd on one holiday and took him on *'more educated scrambles'* and tried *'to find more energetic patches on the north ridge of Tryfan'*. For Wilfrid *'the idea of climbing rocks for themselves came slowly'*. As he wrote later about this period:

> *Guy talked, and well; he was also a person to admire, for his own feats and for his admiration of the feats of Colin, the eldest. To Guy, rock-climbing was natural and great because Colin climbed. And to us it must be all the greater. We could see Guy and appreciate his skill and strength. We could not see the heroes whom he named and with whom he would not compare himself. Natural enthusiasm grew with knowledge of him, with sighting far off the scene of exploits (the black Devil's Kitchen hole for instance), and with*

hearing their tales. It became a point of honour to study First Ascents and 'Standards' on rock faces of which we knew nothing, and to classify our own doings round Ffestiniog as we believed they would be classified by the 'Guide'.

The twentieth century is reckoned one of mechanical skill. What skill, thought I on those days, is worth anything beside this that I am doing – my breath steady and my limbs sturdily plodding, the sun around and all nature by to smile at me only? Superb egoism that would make the winds even a bellows simply to my glorious activity, the hills a gymnasium of beauty. But what were the winds indeed but powers, to make my appetite crisper and my tramp firmer? Or for what was the rock on the hill, but to spur me to see whether I could get up it? And in my own loves I found I had a good precedent: in the example of men of my admiration.

So went the reasoning; little of it in those days that was not self-concerned, and we had not come to know the second of the "two Verities, yourself and the hill you climb." It remained as a background faintly with us, assumed and not recognised. The terminology of the school sports was misleading and made us only the keener for technical accomplishment. I came to long more and more for the first 'real' rock climb, for the introduction into the sport by the high-grade expert.[7]

It was the joy of physical exertion and of being in the heart of nature that already enthused him in those early years. This would develop into an unstoppable rhythm of fluid, balanced movement that became the hallmark of his later successes.

A manuscript fragment on the page of an exercise book, '*A relic of about 1930*' shows his feelings at that time about mountains.

When I grow old and tired and grey,
When youth has left me you will still remain,
   Silent, majestic, white…

Far in the valley while the evening breezes
Caress your snowy brow – sunset aflame,
I'll dream in sorrow as a yearning seizes my body,
   To return to you again.

But when at dawn, a flame of crimson wakes you
And, in the hush of sunrise, not a sound
   Breaks the unearthly stillness.
You'll receive me, borne by faint zephyrs
   Softly from the ground.

Notes

1. See Bernard Palmer, *Willingly to School, a History of St. Edmund's Hindhead,* 2000
2. *Wilfrid Noyce, Mountains and Men p.12*
3. John Garton Ash, *Telephone conversation 9.1.2009*
4. Mrs. Coggin, wife of Peter Coggin, St. Edmund's 1933-38, *Telephone conversation 9.1.2009*
5. St. Edmund's School Archives
6. St. Edmund's School Records
7. Wilfrid Noyce, *Mountains and Men pp 13-14*

CHAPTER THREE

CHARTERHOUSE

Wilfrid Noyce left St. Edmund's in July 1931 and started at Charterhouse in the September and entered Weekites, one of the eleven boarding houses, each, with one exception, accommodating fifty to sixty boys. The housemaster was fifty-year-old Hugh Jameson, who had been teaching at the school for twelve years. While the headmaster sets the tone of a school, it is the housemaster who influences the immediate environment of the boys and provides most of the pastoral care and advice. Noyce appeared to take his entry to Charterhouse in his stride and was placed in the Special Remove with the other Foundation Scholars. He was second in class in his first term and collected his first prize at Charterhouse. He did well in Greek and Science, but was, however, twenty-third equal out of twenty-five in Mathematics. In French somewhat surprisingly he appears to have been mediocre. A Weekite house photograph of 1932 shows a very determined Noyce looking at the camera from the back row.

In his second year he had already chosen the classicist route and was in Form Va Classical, This was a very good year academically; he was awarded a Senior Scholarship, worth then £96.10s. per annum. He was also top of his form. His mediocre performance in Maths being offset by being top in Classics and Science and third in English. In French he was still somewhere in the middle of the pack. He received the form prize as well as the Classics and Biology prizes.

Form Va Classical was in the charge of Gibson, a scholar of Christ's College, Cambridge with a first in the Classical Tripos. Of him Richard Eyre, who was at the school in the early forties wrote:

> *As a teacher, Gibson could not fail to draw boys on to share something of his own passion for truth, for the discovery of* rerum

> causa. *He had undoubted technical ability as a classical scholar: yet from so full and wide-ranging a mind did his teaching arise that the Classics seemed often to be one vehicle amongst several which might serve to convey his rich fund of ideas. The scholarship was there: but, perhaps not surprisingly, it went unmarked. Gibson had goods to offer which could not be obtained elsewhere, and it was these which caught the attention and acted magnetically.*[1]

The next year brought more specialisation in the Classical Under VIth. The academic success continued and Noyce was very clearly top of the form ahead of all his peers by a considerable margin. There were school examinations at the end of the year in ten of the key subjects and Noyce achieved 826 out of 1,000. His nearest rivals were Edgar Palamountain who received 796, and Richard Greene 741. Palamountain subsequently had a distinguished career in industry and Greene an equally illustrious career in the law. Noyce received the Form, Classics and History prizes and his two rivals each received the Second Form and Classics prizes. His form master this year was V. S. H. Russell, 'Peter', a very capable and enlivening teacher of the classics, whom the author (of this book) remembers with affection and considerable respect. I shared the shock of all those who witnessed his sudden death during the 'Charterhouse Masque' on Friday 6th July 1956.[2] I recollect his description of the rather lurid socks of a fellow pupil as 'exclamatory hose' – a pun on a feature of Greek grammar, which was appreciated greatly by the class.

Wilfrid Noyce, by then a colleague, wrote the obituary of his old form master.[3]

> *A first-rate school-master? Yes. A conscientious J.P.? Yes, he was that too. A scholar, a wonderfully sensitive musician, a profound and widely-read theologian? He was these as well, and yet how little of him do these attributes give! Even if I think back to the days when he taught me, I can do little more than paint in the unimportant detail which is not the person. I recall the reserve and difficulty of speech, which made him unapproachable at first: then the wise thought that used to come stumbling out too fast for words, certainly too fast for us to absorb it; the infectious enthusiasm for authors long dead as if they were living now; the explosion (there is no other word) of laughter at a nice touch of the incongruous; above all the sense, slowly awakening in our last*

> *two years, that here was someone treating us as persons in our own right. These are the things a boy remembers.*

and further on …

> *Just as it is impossible in a few strokes to paint his portrait, so it is possible and easy to see features from it, reflected in many facets, among those who loved him here at Charterhouse, who learned from his wisdom on the Bench, or who came back again and again to visit him, long after they had left the school. If all these have carried from him into their lives something that they count as precious, that is the best posterity he would have asked.*

During this year in recognition of his status as a 'good chap' Noyce was invited to join the School Fire Brigade. This was a select group who among other activities were called upon to assist with the extinguishing of any fires in the event of one breaking out on the school premises. It was disbanded in 1936.

In his fourth year Noyce moved inexorably into the Classical VIth, which in those days, and probably until after the Second World War, was the ablest branch of the VIth Form. His contemporaries found themselves in the same form as the boys of the year ahead. The latter were in their second year in the Classical VIth and provided increased competition.

The headmaster was traditionally the form-master of the Classical VIth. Frank Fletcher, as an undergraduate at Balliol, with his brothers had been introduced to mountaineering and had started his climbing in the Alps with A. D. Godley, a member of the Alpine Club and later the Public Orator at Oxford and author of much humorous verse. He was a keen mountaineer and: '*in body, as in mind he sought high and arduous places*'.[4] The death of his philosophy tutor, Nettleship, from exposure on Mont Blanc in his third year (1892) was a considerable blow both emotionally and intellectually. However he continued to climb in the Alps for many years.

In addition to being a great headmaster, Fletcher was a great teacher.

> *Not all fine scholars – and his scholarship was superlatively fine – are good teachers, and of those that are, some make their name as teachers as much by dramatic performance as by teaching.*

> *But no man was less of an actor than Sir Frank: his power as a teacher came straight from his intellect and from his heart; and it was the integrity of both, his lucid mastery of what he taught and his keen desire that those he taught should understand, that made us eager to learn from him. He remembered always that the personal object comes first after the verb to teach, the boy before the subject, and while the interest of the work absorbed him, he neither forgot his pupils' inexperience nor underestimated their capacity to learn.[5]*

Frank Fletcher was able to engage and nourish the desire to study of his sixth form;

> *In his sixth form at Charterhouse classical composition was no weary route march on the level, but an exciting attempt (led by him personally) on some Everest whose lovely summit seemed in that clear air delusively attainable. To read with him the Agamemnon of Aeschylus, the Republic of Plato, or the Book of Job was a revelation such as Chapman gave to Keats. As one looks back on the distant panorama of the classics through the haze of many years in the busy world, the books that one read with Frank Fletcher stand out clearly and sharply from all the rest, forever floodlit by his personality. That feat of teaching can only be achieved by genius.[6]*

Frank Fletcher himself expressed his great joy in teaching the Classical VIth.

> *But it is really worthwhile, and has its rewards when a teacher feels he has succeeded in interpreting for a boy what he meant to say and in showing him how to express it more clearly, when he sees a boy beginning to catch the pleasure of creating something for himself which any form of composition may give. But there is surely no form of teaching more pleasant than to read with appreciative boys some of the great works of English or Greek or Latin literature, to introduce them to Hamlet or Lear or the Agamemnon or either Oedipus or the Epistles to the Corinthians or the second or fourth or sixth Aeneid. It is as delightful a task at sixty-five as at thirty-three.[7]*

A. L. Irvine shared the Classical VIth with Frank Fletcher for twenty years and their influences were complementary.

> *I have frequently discussed their teaching with Carthusians of their time; and the conclusion that I have reached is that if one were to ask each of their pupils, "To whose teaching do you owe more, Sir Frank's or Irvine's?," The votes would be pretty evenly divided.*[8]

'Uncle' Irvine was more down to earth and at times was felt to be pedantic in his teaching of the classics.

> *First he taught his pupils to appreciate the sounds and rhythms of ancient literature. An early stickler for the reformed pronunciation of Latin, he never let a false phoneme pass any more than a false quantity. Poetry deserved to be recited, as in antiquity, and with feeling as well as accuracy. Secondly, he insisted that when translating in school we should not go on to the next sentence until we had found exactly the right word, which was an invaluable linguistic and critical training.*[9]

Being together with the boys of the 'upper bench' provided an additional stimulus and Noyce finished the year third and interestingly came second in Divinity. He edged away from Palamountain and Greene who were seventh and tenth respectively and collected the second Gordon Whitbread prize 'for the encouragement of the study of Classical Literature' founded in 1884, and a Talbot prize, worth £2 in books, based 'upon the results of the annual Examination in Classical Subjects, Divinity, History and Essay'. (It was £10, when I received one twenty years later.) The same summer younger brother Jocelyn, who had entered Weekites in 1933, was awarded a scholarship.

In September 1935 Noyce returned to school, already becoming part of a mountaineering legend. Noyce was now in the senior year in the Classical VIth and, in spite of his heavy responsibilities as Head of House and later as Head of School, stayed at the top of the form. He had had a very good summer in the Alps and had been in the Lakes with Menlove Edwards for whom his feelings were deepening. His last year at school was a triumphant period. He was Head Monitor of Weekites and he was awarded a classical scholarship to King's College, Cambridge.

A contemporary in Weekites was Paul Simmons, known by all as

'Ted', and over the years Noyce and Simmons had become very good friends. The Simmons family lived just up the Hurtmore road a few 100 yards from the school so it was very accessible for visits at weekends. Both Noyce brothers spent holidays from school with the Simmons, when they were not in the mountains, as their parents were still in India. Part of the attraction must have been Ted's sister Bettie who eventually married Jocelyn Noyce and the Simmons and Noyces remained close. When John Hunt and David Cox were writing about Wilfrid Noyce in 1993 they quoted,

> *A recent letter from Paul Simmons, a contemporary colleague at Charterhouse, makes it clear that, although in no way assertive, he soon emerged as a natural leader who was the obvious choice to be head of his house and head of the school. He was a fine scholar and a good all-round athlete, but the qualities which are particularly emphasised in this letter are, "his austerity towards himself, his moral courage and his lack of fear."*[10]

From early on Noyce wrote letters, notes and poems and kept a diary. A number of his companions on later expeditions observed that he was always writing in his spare moments in his inimitable handwriting which scarcely changed over the years. Already at this age he could be present in body but his thoughts would be very distant; words and verse came readily to him and were usually committed to paper with a well-worn pencil.

At Christmas 1935 he wrote:

A Star

Black arms are warring
Grey mantle: one bright spark
Twinkles, winks, dies to us.
Sulphur and brimstone
Hurling through space
Tiny we see thy light:
Tiny seems good on earth;
Yet vast thou art
Good too is heavenly.
Dimly we see thee,

Falser lights blurring,
Look down – and stumble,
See, the limits hide thee,
Only ghost shadows.
"Whither eternity?
What can that do for thee?
Mind thou those wild arms."
Fools, that we struggle
Blurred in our own mist
Striking each other
Reaching for thee.
Star thou of Bethlehem,
Blind not our dusky eyes.
Christmas: O open them.
Perfect one Jesus,
Loving thee, look how we
Hate our own selves
Hate all around us,
Cold grow and desperately
Numb to God's self.[11]

Already a strong philosophical and spiritual element in Noyce's personality was emerging and this developed more and more over the years.

When Noyce went back to school in January 1936, he already had won his scholarship to King's College Cambridge; he had just had a very successful week in North Wales with Menlove Edwards and David Murray-Rust. During his last two terms he was determined to enjoy all that Charterhouse had to offer. He had settled in as Head of his house in the winter term and was now looking to introduce new ideas within the house such as a book committee for the House Library, improvements in the Sick Room and abolishing the payments made by monitors to their study fags. He was maintaining his position in class and participating very fully in school activities. Early in the term he and all the Head Monitors breakfasted with Robert Birley, who had taken over from Frank Fletcher in September 1935. Birley had been appointed at the age of thirty-two and was the school's first non-classical headmaster. Frank Fletcher was also present on this occasion.

Noyce spent considerable time with his friends who were usually in the same house, such as Ted Simmons, James Marriott, Richard Greene or Graham Dunbar. They all had their places at Oxford or Cambridge or in a profession and were able to participate in an active life outside the classroom. There was some physical exercise almost every day for them. In the Lent term, ironically called the Long Quarter, hockey, which had recently been introduced into the school, was the major sport and Noyce improved his play in 'shootabouts' with Simmons and Marriott and played regularly for his house. He was also a reserve for the school 1st XI. Running, whether on his own or in company, was a regular activity and he was in the school cross-country team. When they ran against Wellington College, Noyce was slightly peeved that Coggins, who had been at St. Edmund's and was now at Charterhouse, and Barbour, both two years his junior had come in before him.

Jocelyn and Noyce sometimes would go back to Ensleigh, their home from home at Grayshott, at weekends. There they would play golf at Hindhead or at St. Edmund's or just enjoy being away from school. The diary suggests that at times Noyce was under some strain. His relationship with Menlove Edwards was deepening and he was working on the Tryfan Guidebook at the same time. Edwards took him out to lunch at the Lake Hotel in Godalming on Sunday 9th February. He had a *'good time'*. A few days later Noyce records, *'Good day. Fives in afternoon. Put the weight a bit, hockey game, a run with Graham. Lit*[erary] *& Pol*[itical Society lecture on] *Chinese art.*[12]' He took very seriously his responsibilities in the house particularly in matters concerning individuals.

His diary is full of this type of comment, *'Good day. Corps in afternoon & cold but amusing if futile. Tea with Mrs H*[odgson†]*. Very good run with Graham & it in moonlight. Felt good.'* He records his sadness and disappointments as well as the times when he is feeling happy. However his moments of gloom did not last long. The presence of friends was important, although he could enjoy a long run or walk on his own.

Fives is a winter game of two varieties, Eton and Rugby. Charterhouse plays Eton fives which originated with a group of boys using their hands to hit up a hard ball, like a golf ball in the buttresses and niches of Eton College chapel. Whoever failed to get the ball up lost the rally and a point for his team. Now it is played by two teams of two in specially created fives courts and the rules have been formalised. In the spring the

---

† Col P. E. Hodgson was the School Bursar.

boys started athletics training in readiness for the summer and Noyce in addition to his running used his strength to advantage in putting the shot.

Noyce's relationship with the Corps was ambivalent. The parades for NCOs were a bore and he describes them as fatuous on more than one occasion. He clearly enjoyed some of the big occasions, recording *'good fun and a good view'*[13] with the Corps Guard of Honour on Saturday 25th January lining the streets of Godalming for the proclamation of King Edward VIII. But the summer inter-house tactical competition, the 'Arthur Webster' was *'that arch folly'.*[14] However, he did take his Corps responsibilities seriously and they stood him in good stead when he was called up for the Army.

When he heard that he was going to Germany with the hockey team he wrote: *'They're re-arming. Heaven preserve the world from childishness, if not from wickedness.'*[15] He thought considerably about Christianity. At one point he writes *'The Lecture on Guildford Cathedral converted me.'*[16] He also attended the lecture given by the Biology master, Stork, on 'Christianity and War' one Sunday morning. His inclinations were towards pacifism and he was developing an altruism out of the muscular Christianity that the School engendered and this became more evident as he got older.

Noyce had good relations with masters of all generations. As he had effectively been brought up without a father, Sir Frank Noyce did not retire until Wilfrid was at Cambridge; the association with older men gave him reassurance and support that was not available from the family. Certainly Ensleigh had been established as a home from home under Mabel Hutchesson, but it lacked the father figure. Relations with Murray-Rust were particularly close, but he spent considerable time with Harry Iredale who had come to the school in 1930 and was rather older. He would visit him frequently and they would walk together. Noyce would also go with him to the school mission in Southwark.

In all the sports Noyce strived always to do better. He always noted when he could have done better, and there was a determination to do better next time, whether it was cross-country running, tennis, athletics, hockey, cricket or fives. The same applied to his form work, and his shortcomings he did not tolerate easily. His diary is full of self-critical comments.

There was a good relationship with the masters that taught him. He sought the advice of Russell on House matters and found the visits and teas with 'Uncle' Irvine, as he was known to generations of Carthusians, *'great fun'*. Fun was very much part of Noyce's life and he always sought to extract enjoyment and happiness out of any activity.

Joe Stork, the head of Biology, who had been teaching at the school since 1926, took a great interest in the development of hockey and organised a tour in Germany in April 1936. Noyce, Simmons and Greene were included as part of a strong contingent from the classicists and sixth form. Claud Wright, another member of that group, and Noyce's predecessor as Head of School, recorded:

> *At Easter 1936 he, with B.C. Lee took a Carthusian team to Germany to participate in a school and club hockey festival. Except for stern warnings from the Foreign Office to be discreet in what we said about German politics – Hitler had re-entered the Rhineland a fortnight before we started – we were led on a light rein, if any. We stayed first in Cologne, where Joe slipped off the gangway of our host's houseboat into the Rhine (not seriously wet) on the way to the first of very many vinous evenings. We played two matches, morning and afternoon, on most days for a week or more and our hosts seemed to try to disable us with hospitality in the evenings. Perhaps Joe and Bertie Lee kept more of an eye on us than we suspected, for we won every match but two, which we drew.*[17]

Stork left Charterhouse at the end of that summer term to become Headmaster of Portsmouth Grammar School and then in 1942 Headmaster of the Royal Naval College, Dartmouth, until he retired in 1955. Claud Wright combined a career in the Ministry of Defence and subsequently the Department of Education with being President of the Geological Association in 1956-58 and later winning a number of prizes for his contributions on geology and palaeontology.

When Noyce became Head Boy in his last term, he was a little nervous at first and the prospect of the various meetings at School level he found daunting. He appears to have been happy enough with the Library meetings but those with the School Monitors and the Games Committee were more testing. They were the boys with real responsibility for their houses and school-wide activities. In between times Noyce was preparing his entry for the Elder Prize. This was awarded annually for Classical composition. This was one of the prizes he did not get, which did not seem to bother him.

Besides an enormous amount of outdoor activity, particularly tennis in the summer term, Noyce found time to maintain his other interests. He was writing poetry – *'wrote a poem the other day on a dream. Haven't shown it to anyone.'* – and was working on the climbing guide for Menlove Edwards. His interest in Michelangelo was becoming a passion. This was nurtured further by a school art lecture and he acquired some prints of which he wrote on 20th February, *'Still gloating over the Michelangelo prints, which I think are of the most wonderful thing in the world.'* In the summer term he was writing a monograph on Michelangelo, the forerunner of his poetical biography of the painter.

At weekends when he was not out with his friends and their families there might be visitors and Geoffrey Winthrop Young, who lived not far from Godalming, and Geoffrey Bartrum, a fellow-member of the Climbers' Club, took Noyce out for a *'nice lunch and pleasant conversation, though rather unfruitful'.*[18] Bartrum came over again four weeks later with Menlove Edwards. They had some *'small talk about guide'* before Noyce left to join his friend James Marriott at the Marriott home in Bagshot for a tennis tournament.

There was a harvest of distinctions; he received the Alick Tassell prize, just recently founded in 1933, of £100 'to be awarded annually by the Headmaster to the best Classical Scholar of the year', a School Exhibition of £80 for four years at Cambridge, the first Talbot scholarship 'tenable at Oxford, Cambridge, Dublin or Durham University, and payable in four yearly instalments, each of about £18', and was first for the Gordon Whitbread prize.

A poem written at Charterhouse in 1936:

The Escape

Paths that must centre in the dark
On the inscrutable ahead:
Blindfold to stumble, where a spark
Glimmers pin-pricked the way we're led;
   Glimmers but faintly, for we know
   It is not ours, the way we go

Wherefore to seek outside? I must,
Must doff that self, and feel at one
Man's fever-throb to man, as dust
Pulses and swims under the sun.
   So in her eyes I seemed to see
   Succeeding self, eternity.

So, thought to o'erleap myself, so then
Lit by one circled beam-shot light
Atoned in her, at one in men
Pervade divinity through night
  So looked, and looking in me saw
  Such light as was not there before.

It was a fast moving, active and successful final year.

Noyce left Charterhouse at the end of July 1936 and went to the Alps with David Murray-Rust and Richard Hope. He did more work on the Tryfan guide with Menlove Edwards in the August and prepared to go up to King's College Cambridge for the Michaelmas Term starting in October 1936.

Notes

1 Obituary *The Carthusian December 1959*
2 The Pageant of the History of Charterhouse, performed every five years
3 *The Carthusian December 1956*
4 George Turner, pupil of F. Fletcher at Marlborough, Headmaster, Charterhouse 1947-52 Sermon in Charterhouse Chapel 20.11.1954 *The Carthusian March 1955*
5 George Turner 20.11.1954
6 Hon. Mr. Justice Pearce *The Times* cited in *The Carthusian March 1955*
7 Frank Fletcher *After Many Days p.262*
8 R. L. Arrowsmith, Charterhouse Master, *The Carthusian 1967*
9 L. P. Wilkinson *The Carthusian July 1967*
10 *Alpine Journal 1993 p.67*
11 Unpublished dated 25.12.1935
12 Diary entry for 12.2.1936
13 Diary entry for 25.1.1936
14 Diary entry for 27.5.1936
15 Diary entry for 3.3.1936
16 Diary entry for 20.3.1936
17 *The Carthusian 1937*
18 Diary entry for 7.6.1936

CHAPTER FOUR

EARLY YEARS IN THE MOUNTAINS

When Wilfrid and Jocelyn were at St. Edmund's, Enid Noyce would come home from India most years and they would spend the summers at the family house, Bryn Hyfryd, at Ffestiniog, tramping over the familiar Manods and the Moelwyns. They also ventured farther and farther afield in the Welsh hills, going over to Tryfan and the Idwal Slabs. Their cousins, Nigel and Guy Kirkus guided by them in more adventurous ascents, *'educated scrambles'* as Wilfrid described them. Guy, whom Wilfrid admired for his strength and skill on the crags, was inspired by eldest brother Colin who was one of Britain's eminent rock-climbers at that time. The desire and enthusiasm for greater challenges on the mountains was growing.

In the Easter holidays of 1934 when Wilfrid was sixteen he was introduced by Guy to real rock-climbing and for this his boots were bought specially, according to Colin's specifications. He took the bus up from Bettws y Coed to the bleak Ogwen Cottage for his first encounter with the dragonish Mrs. Jones. Guy joined him the following morning and they left for Tryfan.[1]

Tryfan is for some the iconic Welsh mountain as it rises in a rock ridge right up from the Ogwen Valley like a dark lion maintaining guard over the Glyders to the south. It stands almost on its own and is immediately identifiable. It used to be one of the great rock-climbing nurseries and provided a range of climbs with many that were not only interesting but challenging.

They went for the first of very many times up Heather Terrace then up the North Buttress to the summit. That day they also climbed Gashed Crag, *'A slippery slab above the Gashed Crag I could not climb, but found "the Boots" scrabbling in a hot determination not to leave me stranded like fish on a line.*[2] He appears to have spent the rest of the holiday on his own scrambling and walking and observed thirteen years later '*that the crossing of Glyder Fawr (it was most important to go right to the cairn), the Snowdon Horseshoe and back in gym shoes on a day of falling snow and mist, would try me too hard now*'.[3]

The summer holiday that year was with his cousin Colin and they stayed at the Idwal Youth Hostel. The first evening they did Monolith Crack, for a long time reputed to be the hardest climb in North Wales. Already intense feelings were being evinced as he climbed, '*The thought current bubbled out in pattering accompaniment to hasty breathing; in its exactness, impossible to recapture and unprintable*'. He then '*wrote an ecstatic postcard to* [the family at] *Ffestiniog*'. Colin also led him up the Direct Route on Glyder Fach, and Holly Tree Wall. It was, however, on Crib Goch Buttress that Noyce made his first lead under Colin Kirkus's very capable and thoughtful guidance. Noyce observed the balance and rhythm of Kirkus's movements and sought to emulate them and so developed his own fluid way of climbing.

Noyce had fallen in love with the Welsh hills which had become his native heath and he revelled in the physical exertion in the familiar scenery in a way that he could not on the Helsby outcrops in Cheshire or the trivial chalk pits at Cambridge. In August 1934, he climbed on Craig-yr-Wrysgan and is supposed to have done a *Very Difficult* but later could not remember exactly where he went. He felt that the Scottish hills where he was in the autumn were still too large for him to feel truly in harmony.

The hills had become so much part of Wilfrid Noyce's life that a holiday without them scarcely counted. His sister tells the story of when they had a day on the beach:

> *I don't remember this, but Mum used to tell me that there was one occasion in Wales. It was my birthday, and it was to be my day, so I wanted to go to the seaside and we went down to the sea, but Wilf wanted to drive back by way of the mountains so that we could see the mountains and he kept saying, "What do you want to do? Oh you want to build a sand-castle; come on we'll build a sand-castle; that's it. Now can we go to the mountains?" "No, not yet." "Oh what else do you want to do Ro? Sail your boat? We'll sail your boat. Now can we go to the mountains?" And finally we got apparently to drive around by the mountains on the way*

home. So he was quite well into them by then. I must have been quite young. He must have been 15 or 16 by then. Oh yes. I don't recall it but I do recall Mum telling me.[4]

At this time also he '*hunted and collected high names*', and specifically famous mountaineering personalities. He met Dr. Visser, a redoubtable explorer of the Karakoram and Himalaya, who introduced him to General Bruce, the leader of the British 1922 Everest Expedition, a big man with big enthusiasms, who despised the 'rocknasts' and encouraged him to go much higher. *"The Himalayas, the biggest thing, that's what you want… go all out for it. Rocks are practice. I couldn't take you myself, too old – but Braddles will take you – wonderfully good at starting people."* And so in the Easter holidays in 1935 he stayed with Major Gedley Bradley who lived at the Bryn Tyrch hotel at Capel Curig. Bradley was a member of the Climbers' Club and had a number of first ascents to his credit. They motored gently out to the crags, had some good climbing – and Bradley was quite content to be led – and then returned to tea by the fire in the late afternoon. The manner of this was not entirely to Noyce's taste; he would have preferred to be in a cottage or tent, more part of the landscape, and not cut off from the mountain environment. This yearning was to remain with him until the end. After a week David Murray-Rust came to stay at Bryn Tyrch and was a more adventurous companion for the second week, ready for escapades in all weathers. Like Frank Fletcher, he gained a First from Balliol and worked as a research fellow with Sir Harold Hartley in electrochemistry. Although a brilliant career as a researcher was open to him, he was motivated by a desire to communicate science to young people and he became a master at Charterhouse in 1931, at the age of twenty-seven. He formed a close climbing friendship with Wilfrid Noyce, although he did not teach him. This was the start of a long association of Wilfrid, and indeed the Noyce family, with the Murray-Rust family. When David's son Peter was born in 1941 Noyce was invited to be a godfather, and a very good one he was.[5] Later Murray-Rust used to come to the Noyces' house at Grayshott and joined them on a holiday in the Lake District in the summer of 1935.

Murray-Rust had for a considerable time been a pacifist and after he married Frances Kendrick in 1939 they both became Quakers. He became headmaster of the Quaker school at Sidcot in 1946 and was there until 1957. Peter, who like his father was a Balliol chemist, has continued the family Quaker tradition and believes that his father had a considerable influence on Noyce with his feeling for the spiritual and his robust practical humanitarianism.

They managed The Holly Tree Wall and Long Chimney on the Terrace Wall, two respectably difficult climbs. On occasions they went on up to the summit of Glyder Fawr in the evening, sometimes taking in the Central Arête as a variant.

David Murray-Rust went home at the end of the week and at Easter there was no room at Bryn Tyrch so Noyce was allowed to stay in the Climbers' Club hut at Helyg as a prospective member of the club although he was still too young to become a full member. His expectations were high given that *"Helyg was hallowed with the mighty names of mighty men"*. On Good Friday morning the members emerged from under their blankets and Wilfrid at breakfast asked to be *"taken up something good"*. He ended up leading another climber up Ivy Chimney on Milestone Buttress, scarcely 'difficult' and it proved to be an enormous disappointment. His enthusiasm for steep and challenging climbs was frustrated with the average easy-angled climb on the Welsh crags. However relief was at hand.

> *The majority decided to go down to Capel in the evening, for beer at the hotel. They changed to sport coats and flannels, and asked if I would care to come. But I would stay, in the hope of talk with Menlove Edwards, who had come up; the best rock-climber of all, Guy had said, along with Colin Kirkus and Jack Longland. I watched him as they were eating: a tattered coat over broad shoulders, woolly hair curled back from a face rounded and firm, childlike but for eyes that were old and the jutting chin that forced a fold before the lower lip. They had gone now.*
>
> *"Tea?" The talk had started.*
>
> *We went on, about climbing. What of the cliff of d'ur Arddu, photographed on the kitchen wall? And the face of Scafell with Central Buttress, where you need the rope slings? Of course, the upper part of the Pinnacle face would go some day, said Menlove. No one had dared it yet. At present we were frightened of an exposure of more than a few feet; needed a jug-handle every so often, and then were frightened of having nothing to come back to. Standard of nerves would go up, so that we could go on much longer.*[6]

Menlove fed the dreams and aspirations of the young Noyce, already a competent climber, thanks to his cousins. And now listening to the greatest practitioner of all, it was a heady evening for a young man, who was already having enormous academic success, to enjoy the undivided attention of a living legend.

The following day, Easter Saturday, Noyce says he was half-startled at Menlove's suggestion that they should climb together. *"We'll go over, look at some small cliffs in the Llanberis Pass. Get a lift."* Charles Robb, on his way to climb on Lliwedd, took them round.

> *At Pen y Pass we met Geoffrey Winthrop Young, driving forth the legions of the Easter party to the rocks. I had been reading his* On High Hills, *in an enchantment, the best account yet written of mountain experience. I had not dared to hope for this, the first of many meetings. Words were exchanged, a promise given to come in for tea.*[7]
>
> *"I always go to a cliff where there's a downhill path, if possible," said Menlove. We started down the Llanberis Valley.*

They reached Clogwyn y Grochan and made the first ascent of Long Tree Gate which was graded Hard Severe in the 1955 guide.[8]

> *The bottom pitch looked hard, rock not too good. I thought Menlove awkward as I looked up at him. It was steep certainly, but there were great holds, all over the moss-covered ledges. And he could surely jam. Myself couched on the soft grass below, neck twisted up, it was easy for me to shout encouragement. He struggled up the bulges, slowly pulled out to a tree for a belay, tied on and held the rope for me. I had seen the holds, I could do it. But when used they seemed all wrong. The wretched foothold-that-was-to-be hung somewhere round my hip.*
>
> *"Hold tight."*
>
> *Luxury of a rest on the rope, but a luxury soon turned to pain, for my arms weakened.*
>
> *"Let me down."*
>
> *Somehow – I had not seen it – the blood had got out of a finger, congealed quickly with the dirt. So up again. "I really have got the holds this time," I shouted. But the same hold looked more greasy, and the higher one as far away. That move I had*

thought to do, it was impossible now. I was too tired. I must go down.

"Can you lower me?"

There was more blood on the hands, a sign of clumsy climbing, and a shameful need to ask for a pull from the rope.

"You climb and I'll pull, both together."

Feeling and enjoyment swam back at the top of the pitch. When I was at rest, the mountains had the chance, which they always took, of peeping through the covering of self-struggle. The world till now had been beating exhaustedly with my own heartbeat. Now I was at peace with them. It would have been hard to define their rôle at this time in my climbing. More than a scenic background, they were expected to reflect the climber's reaction in their own moods, calm of sunset or the speed of the chase. Now when I had failed, they began to show through a little more for what they are, beings beyond and behind me, unfeeling and considerably uncaring for my struggles.[9]

Afterwards they did another first ascent up on Coed Trwsgl – Rough Wood in Welsh – later renamed Scramblers' Gate and not quite so challenging being merely a Medium Severe. When they stopped for tea on the way back at Pen y Pass, Noyce was mildly shocked that 'the heroes' had done no more than 'Route II and enjoyed it'. He saw the *striking contrast: Geoffrey Young's superb head in the aristocratic style…Menlove, by contrast, as he used to say, who disliked southern speech and ways, but who came under the spell. "Geoffrey's a decent old thing," he said and went on to tell how he disagreed with him on almost everything.'* Winthrop Young at that time was fifty-nine years old and Menlove not quite twenty-five!

The following day Menlove and Noyce were given a lift by Stuart Chantrell to Pen y Gwryd. They went down the Llanberis Pass to Carreg Wastad and did the first ascent of Dead Entrance, Very Difficult, a gentler expedition after the previous two days.

On Easter Monday as no transport was offered they went for something nearer Helyg. *"A cliff near the road,"* said Menlove. They walked along to Tryfan, and round to Milestone Buttress, where the lines of nail scratches are visible from far away. It is some fifteen minutes from the Bangor road; but Menlove wanted something new and he had an eye for the untrodden, and said that nobody had the energy to look round the corner where the steeper rock held more moisture and vegetation, both uncomfortable features of any climb. Here was a green and greasy groove that split the whole face. They had to traverse into it at half-height, the last section involved Menlove jumping on to a turf ledge with Noyce perched safely behind a big block out of sight.

> *"...am going to jump into the crack, hold the rope." I braced, aware shamefully of my inexperience at holding anybody, supposing this turf ledge were to fail. He did jump: at least I think he did. The turf ledge failed. It was a justifiable gamble, since the worst that could happen was an uncomfortable pendulum swing below. This happened, as I know from the sudden jerk on my shoulders, then "Let out more rope," from below. I had been pulled forward, jammed against the boulder, but the voice that rose was almost unruffled. Menlove rose from the depths unmoved, ready to try again. He tried again and this time landed safely. His excavations had revealed holds and he struggled up, muddy in socks, the greasy narrows of the main crack, inviting me to struggle after, but this went quickly. Then, like lords, we lolled on purple couches of heather, over bread and chocolate and oranges, and laughed like lords. But no more grass or grease. I must be taken to something clean, like Belle Vue Bastion on the Terrace Wall above.*

This was the first ascent of Soap Corner, later named Soap Gut by Squint Start.[10]

Menlove, rather a purist, comments on the climb:

> *Route is pleasant; of very doubtful standard owing to No. 2's unhappy ideas about the use of grass. CWFN did his best to spring-clean the place, and little of the original climb now remains. The point marked X is where the leader dangled on the rope, and just above there No. 2 set about to rub the rocks down.[11]*

Menlove agreed to go to Belle Vue Bastion – on condition that Noyce led.

> *That was not the bargain. I could not. "Yes you could. You'd like to." Undoubtedly. To lead Belle Vue Bastion at a tender seventeen, to lead the rock corner which had defeated pioneers of the North*

Buttress direct. It was impossibly good. At any rate one could look at it and come down.

Noyce led under Menlove's guidance and watchful eye.

The rain arrived just as we did below the buttress. "Better rest here at the bottom," Menlove said… "It is very peaceful to rest before effort." I wondered why I should run even the small risk to get up a rock. What is it? I did not know. Better to admit that we have in us a kink, all of us, I thought, and pray it may be harmless.

The Bastion is a jagged corner of wrinkled rock which steepens up. It is exposed throughout and the leads are not short. It was well known long before its first ascent in 1927.

The hardest point is on the second pitch, 30 feet above the second man, an upward move to the left and on to a foothold whose moulding is difficult to see. Nothing is below, before the boulders. The rock after the shower was slightly greasy, even to socks. Down a little, I thought, and steady. Try another hold. A little grab, and draw up, quickly. Got it. Got it quicker than expected, foothold not too bad. Menlove said that was the worst bit. Tensed breathing, Now the 'Grove of Bollards' and lovely rest watching those same far hills. Menlove came up in boots, slowly and carefully. "The last bit you'll find piano playing," he said. And very pleasantly it was.[12]

The 1949 Guidebook describes Belle Vue Bastion as Just Very Severe in Rubbers, a major lead for any seventeen-year-old. Noyce reflected later that he then concluded – dangerously – that climbs described as Very Severe required fitness and confident ignorance of the psychological differences to overcome them. Again at that point he reflected on how he would introduce his son to the mountains: when staying with Bradley earlier, he felt it would be better to start his son's acquaintance with the hills by staying in a tent or farm cottage as part of the landscape. He would also *'hope to lead him slowly, among far hill ridges and mists, away from guidebooks until he had reached the years of discretion. The temptation, against which the Abraham brothers gave quaint warning, to find out the greatest in difficulty and try it, is to the young irresistible.'*[13] This was written originally in 1947 some years before there were any Noyce sons.

After this amazing weekend Noyce went back to Bryn Tyrch. The following weekend Menlove returned and on the Sunday effortlessly took Bradley and Noyce up the Chimney Route on Clogwyn d'ur Arddu, one of the fiercest cliffs in Snowdonia. It faces north and is only visited by the sun very early or very late in the day. The sombre appearance, steep angle and hard shape give it a grandeur unsurpassed in Wales and rivalled by few crags in the British Isles. Noyce again;

> *The cliff was beautiful and terrifying in steepness. But we got up not too hardly, Menlove in boots and we scrambling in rubbers, in surprise that it could be done. The top overhang was a difficulty to clinker nails. It seemed that for an age he hung from one hand, lassoing and stirruping himself with the other. Then he was up, in a cocoon of muddy rope – and another Very Severe was added.*

Menlove Edwards appears to have been clearly affected with this young, brilliant, vigorous, capable, very handsome and agile young man and as the year went on he was more and more conscious of a deeper emotion. Noyce certainly had an admiration for Edwards that went close to hero-worship if not infatuation in the same way as adolescent schoolboys had 'pashes', as we used to say at Charterhouse, on distant figures or close friends. This sort of homosexual emotion was not uncommon in the exclusively male environment of an English public school and to some extent was a stage that a number of boys passed through. Some took longer to grow out of it and in the 1930s at Oxford and Cambridge, particularly the latter, being largely male preserves, homosexual relationships flourished in spite of the legislation.

Following the casual meeting at Pen y Pass, when he was back at Charterhouse Noyce started to write to Geoffrey Winthrop Young asking for his advice and wanting to 'talk climbing'. He was soon asking if he could change 'Mr Young' to 'Geoffrey'. Winthrop Young noted on one of the letters he received from Noyce, '*The Charterhouse climbing boy whom I tried to steady down.*'[14]

Bradley invited Noyce to join him at Grindelwald in the Bernese Oberland in August 1935. G. R. Speaker joined the party; he was a member of the Climbers' Club and was later the Club Guidebook Editor. At Grindelwald it was raining. So they took the train through the Eiger up to the Jungfraujoch to the luxurious hotel carved into the mountain. From his bedroom Noyce had his first amazing view of the sudden new world of crest and cornice close at hand and antlike figures trailing over the ice-field. The Jungfrau is above to the right and the Mönch behind. In the cold, slow Alpine dawn they went out on to the south-west ridge of the Mönch, technically not a difficult climb but requiring care; the snow melting on ice, on the descent, was a new and terrifying hazard. The midday heat following the chill of the dawn was a new experience.

The Mönch was the only major peak that first summer. They spent several long days on the crags of the Engelhörner, and over towards the Grimsel Pass Brenda Ritchie led Noyce and another up the Klein Gelmerhorn, *'a tapering pinnacle of square solid rock with the feel of a Lakeland buttress and the surroundings of sunlit Alpine snow-field. A perfect day; but as General Bruce had said, not the complete thing'.*[15]

After the exhilaration of a first Alpine season the summer holidays were crowned with a complete family holiday in the Lake District. They gathered at Scale Hill Hotel, by Crummock Water, where they bathed and played. *'British hills, to be loved best, need the companionship of friends who are loved.'*[16] Wilfrid and his brother Jocelyn walked up Great Gable *'trying our hardest not to race'*. They found Menlove Edwards eating an orange on Honister, having some time previously tried to sail to Norway in a leaky fishing dinghy. The Noyce-Edwards team was back in business; they concentrated on Scafell and Pillar Rock, depending on the family's requirements for the car.

Noyce admits that perhaps climbers are extraordinarily selfish and unperceptive, and fortunately the family was equally extraordinarily unselfish. *'These were, for a boy, the most purely enjoyable days possible, of simple physical pleasure in the company of a tip-top leader and great friend.'*

A great deal of climbing was done. Menlove climbed in boots, Noyce in rubbers, except on Scafell's Central Buttress. They did Routes I and II on Pillar, Eagle's Nest ridges, Sepulchre and Innominate Crack, then as a climax Central Buttress. After the four hard hours on this last they had to *'run all the way back, not to be over-late for the patient car'*.

He was ecstatic about the ability to be a fly on a vertical wall.

> *The side wall of the Flake Crack seemed to lean more and more above us, as though it were moving against the sky; while Menlove struggled in boots to climb the top flake direct, and, failing, to fix stirrups so that I could climb over and past him. In this place it*

is normal for the second to use his belayed leader as a ladder, and grip the sharp top to safety. Astride the flake he helps the leader up through a tangle of confusing rope. The rest seemed easy.

Then the weather broke; however, A. B. Hargreaves, an early pioneer of the Lakeland and Welsh crags, had said that the north-west on Pillar Rock was a wet-weather boot climb.

It must be done, therefore. First up in rain, I thanked God for the squared holds. We descended the North Climb, by repute easier. Perhaps it was the reaction from the ascent; I failed feebly at the North Climb hand-traverse, descending, wet and dirty; struggled twice and sat at the bottom looking dully at the rain and unfriendly grey grass. Say that you love the hills as the poet loves his lady. Yet your way has failed; it is shameful. You are young and petulant. But you cannot stop loving.

Three days later Menlove was leading on Botterill's Slab, on Scafell, when his arms gave out three-quarters of the way up, groping on slimy holds. He was safe but had to stop. Noyce ran round and dropped a top-rope so that Menlove could complete the climb. As second, Noyce watched Menlove feeling and scraping on the wet rock, wondering, '*as his thigh numbs against the grass, until he forgets almost what he would do if the leader did fall*'.

Shortly afterwards Edwards, whom the Climbers' Club had commissioned to write guidebooks to the North Wales crags, invited Noyce to collaborate with him. By this time his emotions for Wilfrid were very strong and he wanted to spend as much time as possible with him. Menlove also talked of doing the South Face of Mont Blanc, which was a significant ambition of British climbers at the time. David Murray-Rust remembers talking with Wilfrid about this project and being uneasy. Perhaps fortunately it did not happen.

Noyce supposes that this climbing frenzy is inevitable for a boy just starting – he had only been rock-climbing for less than eighteen months – and had been tutored by the most eminent climber of the day. His accomplishment of difficult climbs had been recognised and he was beginning to make a name for himself. He was still a schoolboy, still in the world of competitive sports, of winners and losers, highest scores and fastest runners, but on the threshold of a sport that, in theory at any rate, did not count winners but only recognised personal skill, endurance, determination and resolution.

> *Mountaineering technically appears a cousin, if distant to games. It might follow, therefore that it is important, who has done the hardest climb. The attitude is that, unwittingly often, of those who have been unsuccessful at games, and who find that by pushing their abilities they can win the casual repute of the climbing world; from whose company I could not utterly exempt myself. In that spirit many must have studied guidebooks, ticked off climbs and marked rises in standards. That spirit creeps into school and university clubs.*

(This was certainly evident at the first Charterhouse school meet that Noyce held in April 1955 at Cwm Glas. Again the emotions felt by the seventeen-year-old Noyce were relived by us in the company of Noyce and his redoubtable friends, David Cox, Jo Kretschmer and John Hansbury.)

1936 started for Noyce at Bryn Tyrch with David Murray-Rust and Nares Craig, who was a contemporary in Weekites. With them also was a certain Merrit. On the fine day of 2nd January they went over to Tryfan and did Milestone Buttress, Staircase and Gashed Crag. Noyce records that '*Nares is good*' and that Merrit was a weight for Murray-Rust leading Gashed Crag. Menlove Edwards joined them that evening. The following day they went over to Idwal Slabs on Glyder Fawr and climbed Charity and Hope and Noyce led Merrit up the Central Arête. '*Nares is very daring and he's very cheerful about things.*' On Saturday 4th January, a cloudy day, they went to Tryfan and did the South Arête. Penelope Seth Hughes joined them and enthusiastically took notes all the time. They came down the chute and found it much quicker! There was a blizzard on the Sunday and as the weather deteriorated they climbed Pinnacle Rib on Tryfan but had to give up taking notes. Later in the day Noyce went for a walk with Edwards and his diary records '*What am I doing?*'

Despite the continuing bad weather Noyce and Craig went round to Lliwedd on 6th January and in the rain and mist looked at Heather Shelf but did not climb it. The following day they found Route II on Lliwedd very hard but '*conquered*' it. They were greeted with snow and mist at the summit. Returning to Bryn Tyrch, Noyce worked on the guidebook. Edwards did not go with them on 8th January so Noyce and the others went over to Llanberis Pass and tried The Nose on Dinas Mot, a Severe climb on which the rain and wind defeated their attempts. At this time Noyce admits he had a greater feeling of closeness to Edwards.[17] The next day the weather was still very bad but they managed to climb Grooved Arête on Tryfan. Noyce made notes on the climb and got very wet. The guidebook was progressing but slowly. The rain had stopped for their last day and they went over to Idwal and did Route V, then two Severe climbs, the Original Route on Holly-Tree Wall and Javelin Gully, the hardest climbs that week.

Before leaving on 11th January, Noyce went on a scramble with Edwards in the fine weather then they went back on the train and had *'conversation on deep things'*. Clearly at this time the relationship with Edwards was causing Noyce some concern. He records. *'Has anything come between us? Or was there any thing before?'* They had lunch and tea together at Birkenhead. *'A very pathetic scene. It made me cry.'* Noyce went on to stay in Sefton Park with his Kirkus grandparents as his grandmother was ill.

His sadness lasted all through the service at Liverpool Cathedral on the Sunday morning and his walk in the afternoon. It may have been relieved a little when his Uncle Cecil (Kirkus) came to tea. The following day he took the train back to Grayshott for a few days at home. He enjoyed some golf at the Hindhead course with Nares Craig and Jocelyn, 'Joce', who later preferred to use his second name Ronald, before returning to school on 21st January 1936, the day King George V died, and Edward VIII succeeded him.

In the early months of 1936, the original infatuation of Noyce with Menlove became real affection and Noyce may have been put at a disadvantage. Noyce confides to his diary in February 1936 *'Hockey then tea with Rust. He seems to know my relation with Menlove. Good.'*[18]

In the Easter holidays of 1936 Noyce returned from the school hockey tour to Germany and the following day, Thursday 16th April, with Jocelyn headed off to North Wales, this time as guests, with Menlove Edwards, of Geoffrey Winthrop Young at Pen y Pass. David Murray-Rust was there also. The first day they went round the Snowdon Horseshoe. Snowstorms gave way to sun and warmed their otherwise cold lunch on the Snowdon summit. Saturday was fine and Noyce at Edwards's encouragement led The Nose Direct on Dinas Mot. David Murray-Rust writes:

> *Menlove was a climber without especial grace (quite different in this to Wilfrid) but he was immensely strong and confidence-giving. He was also utterly patient, either in the lead or on those occasions when he was encouraging Wilfrid to attempt a lead. I only once remember him being near to irritation. Wilfrid was to lead a hard-ish climb – it was the Nose of Dinas Mot. The weather was not awfully good and a third person, a friend of Wilfrid's, wanted to join on the rope. Menlove thought a third man would slow the party, so as to cause Wilfrid to wait about and get cold. The chap did join and all was well, but he was unwelcome.[19]*

Murray-Rust cites this as an example of Menlove's caring good-nature but Jim Perrin, the biographer of Menlove Edwards, suggests that, as this was when the emotions of Edwards toward Noyce were at their most passionate, Menlove wanted Wilfrid all to himself!

> *The infatuation – for it was apparently initially one-sided – probably began as that which a boy that had come through the English public school system could easily have conceived for a gifted and original figure from a world to which he ached to belong. Noyce would have been put at a disadvantage by it, and perhaps rendered more susceptible to Menlove's advances, but nonetheless, adolescent homosexual conduct or fixation is not to be wondered at in any way. It is a standard phase in many an individual's development, whether suppressed or expressed. The single-sex public school system tend[ed] to retard development out of the phase (if in the case of the individual it is just a phase), so that the recipient of such an education may take part in homosexual practice throughout school and university (in the Thirties the latter were still predominantly male institutions) and still make a heterosexual adjustment later in life...*
>
> *In the case of Wilfrid Noyce, we have Menlove's poetic testimony that there was an initial imbalance of affection, but whatever degree of truth there is in this, it would have been inextricably bound up with Wilfrid's view of Menlove's status as a climber.*
>
> *Wilfrid was a kind and sympathetic character and the likelihood is that once he had got to know Menlove and been received into his confidences, he would have begun to feel sorry for him and, after*

some soul-searching (which would quickly have been dispelled or even ridiculed after he arrived, later in 1936, at King's College, Cambridge), would have been prepared to show Menlove the desired physical favours.[20]

His pupils at Malvern did not believe that Noyce was homosexual *'although we did know which masters were!'*, to quote an Old Malvernian, and certainly when he was later at Charterhouse there was never any suggestion of him having any homosexual inclinations.

Jocelyn and the others went up The Cracks, a slightly less challenging climb. Noyce comments, *'Joce is so good.'* They all went on by the upper buttress to the summit. Some climbers finish a rock-climb and descend to the bottom to do another as quickly as possible and rarely go to a summit. Noyce from very early on would always go to the summit, certainly at the end of the day, to make the very most of the mountain experience and to revel in the view.

The following day, 19th April, they all went round to Glyder Fach and Murray-Rust was to lead Jocelyn Noyce up Oblique Buttress. It was a Severe and Murray-Rust was doubtful. He shared his doubts with Edwards:

> *I had great confidence in his judgement, not only of his own capacity, but also of others – including myself. Once he and Wilfrid were to climb a Severe on Glyder Fach – The Direct Route. I was to lead Ronald Noyce, Wilfrid's brother, up a milder Severe, the Oblique Buttress. I asked Menlove whether I could lead it (I had never led a climb before that I hadn't seen); he gave obvious thought to the matter, then said, "Yes you can do it all right; there is one difficult bit near Severe, but you'll do it." He was quite right, and because he had judged my capacity correctly, he helped me, vicariously, to climb at my best. There was nothing dare-devil or irresponsible about him – certainly not when the safety of others was in question.*[21]

The others went to Lot's Groove, graded Very Severe, and Noyce did not lead this. He notes that he did this one *'on a rope'* led by Edwards. Afterwards they went up to a snowy summit and enjoyed *'a grand view'*. Edwards went off at that point for two days.

Two others joined the group on 20th April, a Miss Lemare and G.

R. Speaker. Together they went over Bristly Ridge on Glyder Fach and came down by the Gribin. They were late home because they had finished with The Flake Climb.

The weather did not hold on the following day and so the party waited before tackling the North Buttress on Tryfan. They got as far as Terrace Wall then descended in a snowstorm. Edwards joined them again in the evening. In the morning it was snowing but it cleared to give a glorious day and the party set off for Cwm Silyn. There they climbed Outside Edge despite the residual snow and ice. Once again they enjoyed very good views.

On 23rd April they went over to Tryfan's Milestone Buttress and tried to get up inside the final chimney of the Central Block. They had to come out and Joce, who was holding Noyce, had sore fingers and so they had another abortive day. For their last day they had very good weather and excellent climbing. Murray-Rust led them up Terrace Wall, with the exception of Joce, who could not climb that day. Then Noyce led Edwards on the first ascent of Long Chimney Direct on Milestone Buttress. He called it *'an outstanding climb'*.

He was back to Ensleigh for a few days, doing work on the guidebooks and studying Michaelangelo. It was then back to school for his final term.

In July 1936 Wilfrid Noyce left Charterhouse and spent part of the summer in the Alps, in the Saas Fee area and later round Zermatt in a group led by Richard Hope which also included David Murray-Rust. The combination of good weather and the meeting in the huts of Swiss climbers *'who seemed to be hewn out of the same rock as the mountains'* and the contrasts of the snow and the valleys provided an experience that was only surpassed by that in the Himalaya.

> *We lay one evening on an alp looking over to the fairy clouds that draped the tented spires of the Dom's satellites. It was a still sunset. David Murray-Rust said: "To think we shall have to write another post-card home to-morrow, We had another lovely day yesterday." That was the crux. Our experience was too utterly different from anything we had known before. The hope to communicate it was absurd.*

They then crossed into the Mattertal by the Nadelgrat, *'tent ridge of snow between the Sudlenspitz and the Nadelhorn[22]'*, and the following day went over an easy pass to St. Niklaus, whence they took the train

The Alps around Zermatt.

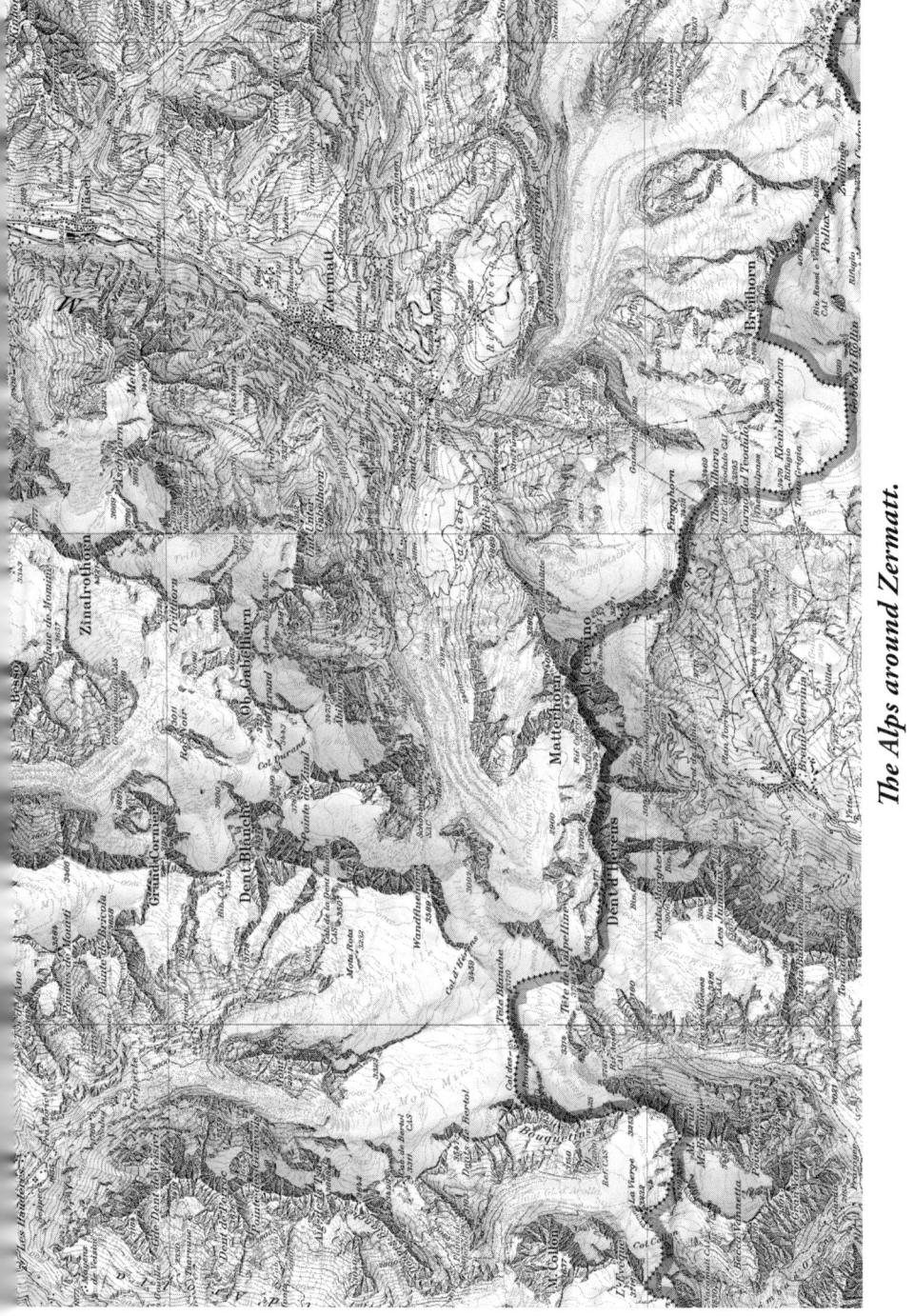

to Zermatt.

As a self-led group they did not need guides, and besides they had been told that there was a well-beaten track up the Matterhorn. Wilfrid was asked to lead and fortunately, *'the glow-worm light of another party guided us in humble mood to the track… The rest was joy; the ridge soared towards the isolated, incomparable summit.'* Here they found a solitary German munching his bread and apple. *'He seemed guardian of the mountain.'* The descent was not quite so easy and the precipices on the north face reminded them that this was very different from *'the tiny cliff fragments of Britain'*. Remembering what the General had said, they recognised that they were nowhere on the mountain ladder. However, they had climbed the Matterhorn and that mattered.

Returning to England, in the August, he worked with Menlove Edwards on the Climbers' Club guidebook to Tryfan. This was a period of intense, disciplined climbing. They climbed the routes on the mountain, old and new, and measured them with precision. They tramped happily up to the Heather Terrace every morning from their tent in the bilberry hollow under the east face and in the course of their labours at the end of August and the beginning of September they added a number of new routes.

> *They wrote the book squatting over mugs of cocoa in the evening light. Noyce would write up a climb, then pass the description to Edwards. It would come back with almost every phrase rejected or corrected. One golden evening Noyce's cousin Colin Kirkus, who had just been up one of the buttresses and down another, sat smoking, in shorts, outside the tent. Menlove smoked too. "You're the only person I take a cigarette off, Colin." But the habit grew on him later.*[23]

They did the first ascent of Steep Bit on Gashed Crag on 24th August, North Side Route on the 27th, Girdle Traverse of Terrace Wall three days later, Yew Buttress on 1st September and Scars Climb on the following day. Soap Gut and Hangman Gut were climbed for the first time on 4th September. One of the more notable climbs they did was the Munich climb. A Bavarian party had attacked the north wall of the South Buttress on 1st July 1936 and had had the impertinence to use iron pegs to hold themselves to the rock. As a matter of national honour for the purists they needed to be removed and it became another first ascent by Edwards and Noyce. They finished the details of Terrace Wall with a crawl up Scars Climb. *'At the bottom was R. V. M. Barry. I envied his long looseness and the ease with which he seemed to caterpillar up Central Route. I wondered if all the climbers I did not know climbed as well as he, for he seemed of another and more aggressively proficient school.'*[24]

They took a break from Tryfan and went over to Glyder Fach opposite, to climb Lot's Groove then succumbed to the temptation of Great Slab on Clogwyn d'ur Arddu. They returned to Helyg to wind up their fortnight's work. Menlove did the final composition and unselfishly put Wilfrid's name always first – both on the first ascents and on the frontispiece – although he himself did the major work. The guidebook to Tryfan appeared in 1937.

In the late twenties and early thirties, the climbers from Liverpool, Manchester and Birkenhead, such as Colin Kirkus and Menlove Edwards, with their training on the local Helsby Crags were setting the pace for first ascents and the development of climbing techniques on the Welsh crags. In the mid-thirties it was Noyce and members of the Oxford University Mountaineering Club (OUMC) John Hoyland, David Cox, who became a long-term climbing partner of Noyce, and Robin Hodgkin of the Oxford Nobel-prize winning family, who were setting the climbing agendas and expanding their activities to the Alps.

In October 1936 Wilfrid Noyce went up to King's College, Cambridge, where his reputation as a fine mountaineer had already preceded him.

Notes

1 Wilfrid Noyce, *Mountains and Men p.14*
2 *Ibid p.15 et seqq.*
3 Gym shoes on the Horseshoe in good weather are not a good idea. In snow they are madness!
4 Rosalind Brain, Conversation 6.10.2008
5 Dr. Peter Murray-Rust, *Conversation 21.11.2008*
6 Wilfrid Noyce, *Mountains and Men p.21*
7 *Ibid p.21*
8 Peter Harding, Llanberis Pass, Climbers' Club Guidebook series edited by C. W. F. Noyce 1955, p.48
9 Wilfrid Noyce, *Mountains and Men p.22 et seqq.*
10 J. M. Edwards and C. W. F. Noyce, Climbers' Club Guide to Tryfan, 1949 Edition, Editor H. E. Kretschmer

11 Jim Perrin, *Menlove p.115*
12 Wilfrid Noyce, *Mountains and Men p.24 et seqq.*
13 *Ibid p.19*
14 Letter from Marcia Newbolt (née Winthrop Young) 3.5.2011
15 Wilfrid Noyce, *Mountains and Men p.29 et seqq.*
16 *Ibid p.25*
17 Wilfrid Noyce, *Diary entry 8.1.1936*
18 Wilfrid Noyce, *Diary entry 19.2.1936*
19 David Murray-Rust cited by Jim Perrin, *Menlove p.131*
20 Jim Perrin, *Menlove p.130*
21 David Murray-Rust cited by Jim Perrin, *Menlove p.131*
22 Wilfrid Noyce, *Mountains and Men p.29*
23 Geoffrey Sutton and Wilfrid Noyce, *Samson p.36*
24 Wilfrid Noyce, *Mountains and Men p.50*

CHAPTER FIVE

CAMBRIDGE

When Wilfrid Noyce entered King's College, Cambridge as a classical scholar on 6th October 1936, he had a brilliant academic record and was already recognised as a leading member of the new generation of mountaineers. He was by now a member of the Climbers' Club and a very welcome new member of the Cambridge University Mountaineering Club (CUMC).

Cambridge in the late 1930s was in ferment while the national economy was struggling out of depression. On the continent Fascism was extending its limits and large numbers particularly among the intelligentsia in Cambridge and Britain generally felt that Communism was the only possible way of countering it. Pacifism had a strong hold and there was little enthusiasm for taking a strong line with the Fascists.

Noyce had strengthened his association with Geoffrey Winthrop Young who, with his wife Len, lived at Gomshall near Guildford and their daughter Marcia recollected later that, '...*till war scattered us all, he became part of our extended family. Poems and accounts of expeditions came and went. At that time our homes were not far apart; Wilfrid cycled over, and we went to the wonderful birthday parties at Grayshott.*'¹

In King's at that time was the distinguished economist, Professor Arthur Pigou, described in L. P. Wilkinson's **Kingsmen of a Century** as the patron saint of King's climbers. He had created and overseen the building of a fine house, Lower Gatesgarth on Buttermere in the Lake District in 1910. It was designed to enable the guests to enjoy outdoor activities in all weathers and benefit from excellent facilities... to receive the wet garments and to revive body and soul in stimulating and comfortable surroundings. He was a man of substantial means and hosted generations of lovers of the hills, from expert climbers and marathon fell-walkers to ordinary mortals, besides lending the house to more than twenty honeymoon couples over the years. He also encouraged and sponsored young and promising climbers. Pigou held great house-parties for his friends and protégés. Geoffrey Winthrop Young, H. V. Reade, H. E. L. Porter, Raymond Bicknell, Harold Raeburn, Claude Elliott, the headmaster of Eton, and many others were among the regular guests. Pigou himself was a competent mountaineer, having led guideless parties safely up big ascents in the Alps over a number of years until a heart defect at the age of fifty restricted his activities. He liked his protégés to be intelligent, not intellectual, athletic and handsome, and Noyce met all these criteria.

Pigou's initial meeting with Noyce may have seemed casual, as part of collecting a party for the Lakes in the January but it would appear that Pigou felt strongly that Wilfrid should be vigorously encouraged in his mountaineering. Of all Pigou's young friends, Wilfrid was the one who meant the most to him. They became very close friends and, although he did not teach Wilfrid, he took a fairy god-fatherly, but critical, interest in his mountain endeavours.

David Murray-Rust had an aunt, Miss Alice Hibbert-Ware, a naturalist, particularly ornithological, who went to live in Girton in the early thirties. Soon after, in 1932, Louis Leakey and his wife Henrietta Wilfrida ('Frida') Leakey moved into The Close, the house opposite that of Miss Hibbert-Ware and they all became firm friends. Louis Leakey was the famous palaeontologist who made a number of anthropological discoveries in Kenya. Murray-Rust was a frequent visitor to his aunt, and came to know the Leakeys very well. Part of the attraction may have been Frida's friend from her days teaching at Benenden, Frances (Jeff) Kendrick, whom David eventually married in 1939.

In 1936 Frida had two young children, Priscilla (1931) and Colin (1933) but by then she was divorced. After overcoming the shock of separation from Louis she became very much involved in local affairs. She was invited to be the chairman of the parish council and founded the Infant Welfare Centre, later known as the Girton Baby Clinic. She also became involved in the Hostel for Basque Children for which Pampisford vicarage was taken over, and The Close was becoming the focus of a great deal of social activity. Murray-Rust introduced Wilfrid Noyce to Frida Leakey in his first term at Cambridge. This was the start of a very long association between the Leakey family and the Noyces. Noyce was frequently at The Close for Sunday lunch, which was a great social occasion, and he would sometimes bring his undergraduate friends. Frida also had a number of friends in the academic world and these were regular visitors. The politics of most of these visitors could be described as left-leaning and some of them became Communist. The Close was of sufficient size to allow a nursery school to be established on the premises. A governess did the teaching assisted by parents, who very often were part of the university. Charlotte Sinker was a pupil, while her father Sir Paul Sinker became the first head of UNESCO. Jake Waddington, another pupil, was the son of Conrad Waddington, a Fellow of Christ's College who became after the war, Professor of Animal Genetics at Edinburgh. Jake himself became famous as an astrophysicist at the University of Minnesota where he discovered the first evidence of heavy ions in cosmic rays. Hugh Heywood, the Dean of Gonville and Caius College was secretary of the Basque Refugee Committee and was godfather to Colin. Another pupil was Rosalind Turner, the daughter of a professor. She married Robert Runcie, the future Archbishop of Canterbury, when he was Dean of Sidney Sussex College. Another visitor to The Close was Arthur Rook, a contemporary of Noyce at Charterhouse, who was at Trinity and went on to become President of the British Dermatologists. Frances Cornford, the poetess, was also a friend of Frida and Noyce may have met her son John, on a visit to Britain in late 1936, before he returned to the Spanish Civil War and his death near Cordoba on 28th December 1936.

The Close was very much a source of support and comfort for the undergraduate Noyce and he became a close and valued friend of the family. Colin and Priscilla Leakey spent considerable time with him and Colin related later that he regarded him very much as an elder brother. There was a continuing correspondence right throughout Noyce's life and he kept Frida informed of his activities and would ask for her advice on many occasions. In 1939 when war was declared, Noyce was camping with the Leakeys and Jeff and David Murray-Rust in North Wales.

Noyce could not avoid taking part in the CUMC meet in the December at Helyg, in North Wales. Here he was in a different role to that which he was accustomed. He was one of the more experienced, *'the shepherds were few and the sheep many'.*[2] as he wrote later, and found the new discipline of instructing and leading others in the mountains even more enriching and satisfying. The meet itself was very heavily subscribed to the extent that the 'guides' became permanent staff and the others were in two groups and each group did six days. No day was without its climbs and the weather appears to have been uniformly bad. However they did manage a climb to the top of Caernarvon Castle.

Those two weeks were clearly hard work. Noyce said that he needed a holiday after that. 'Home' at that time was Ensleigh, at Grayshott, where he had spent holidays from school and where his sister was still living. His parents, however, were still in India as Sir Frank Noyce did not retire until April 1937.

It was to Lower Gatesgarth that Noyce repaired after Christmas and he joined in all the activities with gusto. His academic conscience was salved by intending to read Herodotus while on the train and do Greek composition in the evenings. He raced round the lake in rain, did a first ascent of the Birkness Front of Eagle Crag and demonstrated his tolerance of hardship by swimming in the lake. Menlove Edwards was also a guest at Gatesgarth on this occasion. Like Edwards, Pigou appears to have been rather besotted by Noyce and as a consequence one highly embarrassing incident on the holiday came about because of this. Noyce's birthday was on New Year's Eve, and after dinner, a lavish meal prepared by Gatesgarth's resident housekeeper, presents were given to him. Professor Pigou, as host, gave his first. It was a Leica camera, the top of the range, complete with various filters, a set of lenses of differing focal lengths, cleaning materials, a case, and film. When it came to Menlove's turn to offer up his gift, rather hesitantly, a little hurt perhaps, he handed over a smaller package. Noyce opened it. It was a Leica camera – the basic model – just that.[3]

One of the more amusing features of these parties was the grading of effort and merit based on the army system, but with more wit. Silver medals were awarded, with due solemnity, for outstanding feats. The Brass Medal for Distinguished Incompetence was presented on all occasions deserving it.[4]

In Cambridge life Noyce's intellect, sociability and originality were recognised by his election to The Apostles, the Cambridge elite, intellectual, secret society. The membership was largely from King's and Trinity colleges although certainly not exclusively. They were original thinkers and anti-establishment by tradition. When the society was founded early in the nineteenth century the object was to undermine the dominating position of the Church of England in university life. Those who had been Apostles as undergraduates and wished to remain associated became honorary members or 'Angels' and indeed a number such as Ludwig Wittgenstein, the philosopher, became Angels when they were Senior Members of the University, without having been admitted as undergraduates. At various times there were more Angels than Apostles. They met on a Saturday evening in a member's room to hear and debate members' papers, usually long into the night. In the 1920s they appear to have been a carefree, even frivolous, group, according to Sir Jack Longland, the distinguished educationalist, celebrated mountaineer and long-time chairman of the BBC radio programme *My Word*. In the 1930s, the mood had changed and the discussions were mainly political in view of the growth of Communism and Fascism and veered towards the anti-imperialist and liberal anti-authoritarianism.

At that time the main influences were Maynard Keynes, the economist, of whom it was said that as bursar of King's College he put the chapel up as a guarantee for a loan, and Ludwig Wittgenstein. Arthur Pigou was not elected to the Apostles partly because Keynes was not keen on having other economists in the society. Bertrand Russell, elected 1892, the acerbic philosopher and atheist, and George Macaulay Trevelyan, elected 1895, Fellow of King's and Regius Professor of History 1927-40, and a number of other dons continued to influence the society in Noyce's time. Noyce himself does not appear to have been a very active member of the Apostles. According to the minutes of the Society he attended only one meeting, on 4th June 1939:
'
The Society met in Kirsch's rooms in Trinity (elected 13.11.38). Kirsch was moderator. The subject was: 'Is There an Element of Altruism in my Choice of Job?[5]

Of the nine present three voted in the affirmative and the other six, which included Noyce, disagreed.

Looking at the subjects debated at other times and the comments in the minutes of the debate that Noyce attended, it is difficult to take the Apostles very seriously even at this time.

'Can we have too much faith for Happiness?	*25.11.39*
To be or not to be?	*27.2.37*
Must we be bullied by Economics?	*5.6.37*
Has Nature a Nature?	*27.11.37*[6]

It was clearly a powerful network with members, honorary members and Angels. The annual dinners were well attended with thirty or so round the table but Noyce was never among them.

The Apostles were repelled by Nazism and many of them sympathised very much with Communism and even became party members: some went further and became Soviet agents, notably Guy Burgess and Anthony Blunt, while others became disillusioned, particularly after the Molotov-Ribbentrop pact in 1939. The Republican side in the Spanish Civil War (1936-39) particularly claimed the loyalty of many Apostles who raised money and provided assistance.

Another Apostle at that time was Victor, later 3rd Lord, Rothschild. He had come up to Trinity in 1929 and was a Prize Fellow of Trinity from 1935 to 1939. During World War II he was a colonel in the Intelligence Corps and was awarded the George Medal as a key figure in bomb-disposal. After the war he became Head of Research for Royal Dutch/Shell. Other members were Eric Hobsbawn, the Marxist historian, and Alan Hodgkin, the biophysicist and Nobel prize winner for Medicine.

In February 1937 H. H. Sills, Assistant Tutor at King's wrote to the Tutor D. H. Beves saying that, '*Carney, Boyd, Noyce and Scott-Malden would like to be entered for the John Stewart of Rannoch Classical Scholarship (University).*'[7] The list was duly submitted but only Carney and Scott-Malden won scholarships.[8]

Noyce was also one of four who worked with Arthur Pigou, as treasurer, to adopt temporarily a German Jewish boy who was waiting to join his mother in Palestine. They got him out of Berlin, sent him to King's College Choir school, and sent him to his mother before the war started.[9]

His climbing exploits were not confined to the mountains and hills. On one occasion Noyce was unable adequately to explain to the magistrates why he had been found on top of a lamp-post on Guy Fawkes night (because it's there?)! He did not, however, join the *Night-climbers of Cambridge,* mainly members of the CUMC who maintained their skill in term-time by scaling the spires and towers of Cambridge, and recalled, '*It is true that my only roof climb was a licit one up King's Chapel, on the early morning of King George VI's Coronation,*† *to remove an effigy of Edward VIII slung between two pinnacles.*'[10] When later he told this story he recalled that the Dean was very hesitant about asking him and was on his knees praying until he descended with the offending article.

---

† 12th May 1937

The Dean, The Rev. Canon Eric Milner-White was a man of courage nonetheless, having been awarded the DSO in the First World War. He was also the Dean who started the Festival of Nine Lessons and Carols in King's College Chapel on Christmas Eve. Subsequently the Council of the College at their meeting on 6th November 1937, *'Agreed to fix four stone corbels in the angles of the chapel turrets (to prevent climbing) at a cost of about £32.'*[11]

In June 1937 Noyce gained a first class in the Preliminary Classics part of the Tripos and continued his prize-winning with a book prize worth £2.10.0, based on results of the College or Tripos examinations. It was for those who did not receive a more prestigious Glynn or Cooke prize.[12]

At the end of July Menlove Edwards, in order perhaps to maintain their relationship, invited him to work on the second edition of the Climbers' Club guide to Lliwedd, the cliff on one of the ridges of Snowdon. They explored the Far East Buttress and climbed in the Central Gully. They had hit a difficult patch *'the swoop of the slabs, seemed to run briquette fashion (like books in a shelf, and easy to take out near the centre), scared me. I knew I must fall. We roped down and I did the top part under protection.'* In 1938 Edwards did the first ascents of Central Gully, The Clam and The Squiggle with F. D. R. Dodd, which Noyce says, *"must have been his finest feat"*.[13] Edwards continued work on the Guidebook on his own and it was published in 1939 under both their names, Edwards insisting that Noyce's name be in front of his. *'An absurd order of our names'*, commented Noyce.

After the Central Gully climb, Noyce left to join Arthur Pigou in the Swiss Alps and to meet Hans Brantchen, a noted Alpine guide. They trained initially in the Bernese Oberland and then in the Valais went to the Younggrat of the Breithorn, climbing it from the Riffelalp hut. There was soft slushy snow over ice on the ridge and they had been beaten to it by three Germans. Brantchen's *amour propre* was dented, his patriotism took over and they overtook the Germans and crossed a steep ice couloir to gain the summit ridge. This undulating ridge led to the summit. The descent was an anticlimax through sticky snow as they reached the Gandegg and crossed the Gorner glacier in the heat.

They climbed the south face of the Weisshorn, a climb made notable by Geoffrey Winthrop Young and Josef Knubel. It was almost unexplored and they set out to take the most direct route:

> *The face itself, once reached, was a thing of ribs and shallow couloirs – never hard enough to stop us long, always hard enough for caution, with the two sky-line ridges converging above. Much has been written in comparison of face and ridge climbing, from the angle of pleasure. They are pleasurable both, we can only say that, for different reasons. A suggestion on the summit to Hans that we should try the ridge type of pleasure by descending the Schalligrat or north ridge was sedately squashed by him. I was told, small-boy-like to keep something for next season, and not be greedy.*[14]

Noyce describes the ascent of the Zmutt ridge as, '*surely the most satisfying of all possible Alpine climbs, with the soaring airy arête to the suspended summit*'. This and the Viereselgrat of the Dent Blanche they did and enjoyed the view of '*the col that hangs itself, like a sheet on a clothes-line between the Dent d'Hérens and the Matterhorn*'.[15]

The next day Noyce spent reading **Paradise Lost** at the Schönbuhl Hut while looking with the other eye at the huge cirque of cliffs around it. The day after, early in the morning, they went quickly over the Col Tournanche. The rock-climbs seemed to him to be less severe than in Britain but nonetheless with greater exposure. Comparisons with British crags no longer seemed appropriate and he became used to the long, continuous and narrow, but safe, paths in the Alps. Good rope discipline was essential as there was ice in the cracks. Then there was the joyful relief as they descended the other side down on to the glacier.

A few days later they did the north ridge of the Dom which Noyce regarded as a '*rather artificial rock climb with easy snow close by its side*'.

Returning from Switzerland, Noyce joined the family holiday at the Royal Hotel, Capel Curig, where he did a bit more work with Menlove Edwards on the Lliwedd guide[16] and in September the two of them were at the Pigou house at Buttermere. Ronald Noyce and other friends joined them. There was great swimming in Crummock Water and Buttermere and a new climb was made on Eagle Crag up in Birkness Combe. On 19th September a large group set out and at Styhead Pass Ronald and a couple of friends went over to the Napes to climb. Noyce and Edwards headed straight on for Scafell. They looked at the first-aid equipment at the pass and wondered if they should ever need it! "*People so seldom fell.*"[17]

Noyce recounts what happened next:

We arrived under Scafell, lunching on the Mickledore ridge and looking back over at the cliffs. On the right is the main rock face of the mountain, steep and hard of texture. It was fairly dry. On the left, as we saw it from the Pikes direction, was the Mickledore face, a short bulge of some 250 feet, seeming to overhang in its lower section. It was black to look at, and moisture dripped from its base. Mickledore Grooves, the nearest climb to the right, should be dry enough, we said. Colin [Kirkus] did them in socks. The first section had awkward corners, a little wet, and I took a shoulder. It landed us on the main slab of the climb, a huge tilted thing pointing us up to the right, into a steep corner at the top of which were friendly grass ledges. It was the long run-out, perhaps 120 feet. Menlove belayed his rope on a minute-looking knob. I started. It was still a little wet, and the socks' edges crinkled at times over the holds. The moves were to be done quickly, cat-like. At each I wondered whether it would be easy to get down, if I wanted to. The rope below lengthened. I was at last in the corner, on the first and less comfortable ledges. A party above, on the easy ground, called down to ask us, were we all right. Of course we were. But I shall need a lot of beer this evening, I shouted. For safety, I struggled at hitching the rope round a rock spike. I must look out – the sock might slip. Gently jerking and pulling, I did coax the rope around, with enough out to last to higher ledges. It looked not altogether too steady, the spike, but it must be used, just in the frail hope of further protecting the last few feet.[8]

Jim Perrin takes up the narrative:

Then the turf moved, slid, accelerated, hurled into space and Noyce with it, the earth wheeling, smacking him into ledges, Menlove struggling to take in the vital few feet of rope that would keep him from the ground, bracing himself; a savage jolt, flesh ripped from his palms as the rope ran, then silence, Noyce swinging limply below, only feet above the scree, his face shattered, bleeding. Two strands of the balloon-cable had parted – perhaps nicked as they pulled from the spike – but the knot and the third strand held. Menlove roped down, cradled the injured boy's head, expertly stopped the bleeding. Help came, the body was carried down. There was difficulty about transport in the valley, but when they got to Whitehaven Hospital, an emergency operation was carried out on the head, and after being unconscious for three days, Noyce opened his eyes and pulled through. Had he been climbing with anyone else but Menlove, he would have died. He fell 180 feet and was desperately injured, but he was climbing with a man of enormous physical strength who was also a doctor. He saved him in the fall and sustained him after it.

David Murray-Rust had a most interesting view of Menlove's role in the aftermath of the accident:

*There was something immensely powerful about Menlove (conventional observer, brought up conventionally, might have called him a "weak character" because of his abnormalities, but they would have been wrong); and this power was not just physical. The extreme instance was at the time of Wilfrid's near-fatal accident on Scafell. First, Menlove by his competence and strength probably saved Wilfrid's life on the mountain. But later the real test came. Wilfrid was lying unconscious and very near to death in hospital. Menlove refused to leave his bedside during all this time; and I am quite sure that in some way Menlove's support – his **willing**, as it were for Wilfrid to live – was the critical factor in that coming about. I am certain that both Wilfrid's father and mother recognised this and, through their gratitude, accepted Menlove's friendship for Wilfrid, for I am sure that Frank Noyce would have felt in ordinary circumstances that it was a friendship he wouldn't approve of.*[19]

Noyce himself recounts:

It is apparently noted more often by racing motorists than by climbers that events immediately before an accident slip the memory. There has not been time to imprint them. I remember nothing from that last belay to the pain, three days later, when I started to dim consciousness in Whitehaven hospital: nothing but a distant chaos of lights and voices and jolts and operating tables.[20]

He awoke only after the first skilful patching of the bleeding face; an eye and the jaw had been knocked out of shape and the face was not pretty to look at. As both Noyce and Edwards were well-known climbers the accident was reported nationally:

The Times 20th September 1937

> *Undergraduate's Fall On Scafell – Life Saved by Friend*
> *Mr. Wilfred Noyce, 19, an undergraduate at Cambridge and son of Sir Frank Noyce, of Endsleigh, Grayshott, Surrey, was admitted to hospital at Whitehaven yesterday suffering from fractures of the jaw and nose, as the result of a fall in the Lake District. With Dr. J. M. Edwards, of Rodney Street, Liverpool, he attempted the difficult Mickledore Grooves climb, near the top of Scafell. They were roped together and Noyce had nearly reached the top when a piece of rock around which the rope was belayed broke away. Noyce fell, but Dr. Edwards saved his life by clinging to the rope. His injuries were caused by the rope swinging as he fell and dashing him against the rock face.*

His progress was followed closely by **The Times**:

The Times 23rd September 1937

> *News in Brief*
> OPERATION UPON MR. W. NOYCE
> *Mr. Wilfrid Noyce, son of Sir Frank Noyce, who is in Whitehaven Hospital as the result of a climbing accident on Scawfell, has been operated upon, and his condition yesterday was stated to be satisfactory.*

John Hunt, leader of the successful Everest expedition in 1953, and a regular Alpine companion of Noyce subsequently commented, '*A failure to fix a belay after a long run-out on the East Buttress of Scafell in 1938 may well have been responsible for the seriousness of the accident in which Menlove Edwards saved his life.*'[21]

Following the accident he convalesced at Gatesgarth for a couple of months until his facial bones had knitted sufficiently to enable the plastic surgeons to start their work. He had leave of absence from King's and in the terminology of the College he was *degraded a year*.[22] This enabled him to have as much sick-leave as required but he maintained attendance in college. He nonetheless was elected Treasurer of the CUMC for 1937-38.

The surgery to rebuild Noyce's face was carried out by Sir Harold Gillies, the New Zealand-born surgeon who developed grafting techniques for the badly injured in World War I and subsequently developed many techniques of plastic surgery at the Queen's, later Queen Mary's Hospital in Sidcup. He had read medicine at Gonville and Caius College, Cambridge and won Blues for rowing and golf. His cousin Archibald McIndoe joined him in 1930 and the latter became very famous for his plastic surgery on very badly injured RAF airmen in World War II.

The lack of vigorous physical activity imposed by convalescence enabled Noyce to reflect on his situation. He was clearly in no way discouraged by the brutality of his fall.

> *It interested me that I never had any idea of leaving the hills, or even, in all honesty, cliffs, after this accident. I knew somehow that height would hold the same, and no more, terrors for me in the future.... The hills around were the same, but I was somebody else. I was, among other things, an invalid, looking up at them from a bed. It would take long to clamber up them; longer still to think of climbing them. I should never climb them in quite the same way. But the hills were there, the faces of those were there who had supported me through it all, to whom I had been grateful everlastingly for their silence and uncomplaint. Together they would impose a more becoming humility.*[23]

During his convalescence Noyce was entertaining an elderly man at home who had the vigorous speech of someone much younger and the 'knowing air of a picture collector, a connoisseur, one who has argued art through life and knows the ways'. This art collector heaped scorn on the idea that mountains were beautiful. He said that the only reason Noyce thought that they were beautiful was because he felt good when he was up there and had done the climb. It was totally subjective:

> *Poets will take to anything large and mysterious and untried. They started off now on power stations and skyscrapers. Anything will do.* and later, *I remember, one sunrise, they dragged me out of the hut to see Mont Blanc. It was just not real – a huge cardboard-looking thing, lop-sided wedding-cake effect. There were some nice wispy*

clouds about, that the Italians might use to set off a Madonna, and some great orange things looking like lush Veronese. Photography, of course, would have been worse than useless to capture them. But there was no beauty in the mountain itself.[24]

Noyce reflected,

I confess his remarks struck hard. It was only after two hours thinking that I found any reply. By then, unhappily, he was gone.

I should have answered that they are not new, but have from the beginning wakened something in me that was asleep. I have had the feeling that I have been here before. Mountains are also especial to me in that they combine two rules of our life, of effort and awe. The effort produces friendship and co-operation, which are the sole human certainties; the awe is salutary in face of a Nature we can never hope to control or comprehend. So it is with the sea. So it is with the hills. We forget them in our everyday doings, as we forget friendships and awe. But they are behind, watching, lurking with our friends somewhere between ourselves and divinity.

Having said this to myself, I was inclined to ask what it meant. Did all answers to questions lead simply to another interrogation mark? The demon voice was at the back of me, hunting and haunting, probing passions in which it had no business, no legitimate business whatever. I stamped, petulant. The greatest things, I said, are great because they are too large to be put into words. And I was comforted for a while.[25]

Noyce wrote quite a number of poems at this time. 'Sentinels of Buttermere' was written in October 1937.

Where the grey old crows go wheeling,
In the birch-tree beds to lie,
Where the sunset's sword comes stealing
Through the hills, through a dimming sky

Where the mists cling draped to the mountains,
A quiet walks on the lake,
Where a hand laid over the fountains
Gives, sleepy, the echoes they make.

Far, Far the Distant Peak

Where the winds from all points come seething,
Storm top on top to burst;
Where streaked as the lightnings go writhing,
Pale lips of the cloudlings are pursed.

Here, greyed by October's beating
Are the guards of our sacred land;
Here, dust to the dusk stars pointing,
The watchers of Buttermere stand

They are cloaked in the sunset of bracken,
They look down on the trees by the shore;
They are Lords of that loveliest pattern
Man never shall alter more.

Through the winter, the whirlwinds may clatter,
May cover their shoulders in snow,
Where the rain on those windows will patter
So happy, unannounced, below.

In summer, their joy is in the valley:
The tree-tops are sprinkled with red.
And cloud legion on legion will rally
To gather the cool of its bed.

While they stay, there will ever be beauty:
Brown leaves that go hugging the bank,
Shadowed aisles, where the beeches stand haughty,
Mossy balls where the creepers curl rank.

Should they go, then our glory is vanished:
The wild fern from the field where it blows,
The primrose's grave beauty is banished:
We are gone, where our loveliness goes.

Men have played there through all their ages,
They have gathered the stones from the beach,
They have learned, with the wisdom of sages,
What the streams and the pinewoods can teach.

*They shall learn: while those hills stand over
Their inheritance never can fade:
They shall love: for that God is their lover
Who saw good all the creatures he made.*

Another love of Noyce's was Italy, the Italian language and literature and in the early part of 1938 he went to Rome to improve his Italian and view ancient sites. Later on he took an interest in early nineteenth-century travellers in Italy. Two poems date from then.

In the Baths of Caracalla

*You sturdy Latians, were you then so great,
And must your long life's toil oppress us now?
Were works that stand athwart the laws of fate
All for the smoothing of the Emperor's brow?
You mingled mighty with contemptible,
Knew others' way of life but not your own;
And when you'd show yourselves kind souls, and placable,
You build a stable for a thousand men.
This, then, the Cyclops that gave birth to us,
This the blank page on which our lives are writ;
This, rolled in words to man sound sonorous
That still-born creature, reft of sense or wit.
   Dear God almighty, grant that we regret
   If, doing great things, small ones we forget.*

Before the Apollo of Veii

*1.
What could you tell,
Child of strange days, that have known
Old orders of things?
Wielded a spear that was your own,
Fashioned what brings
Joy to the power of the throne,
A sceptre to Kings.*

2.
Only your eyes
Laugh at my pleading; you give
Vacant replies,
And the fire of your blue and your gold
Dances and dies
As a tale that we heard, when of old
Tellers were wise.

3.
Look, they are closed,
Lips that had quivered alive,
Closed for a while;
Yet shall they open, shall strive
Joy to beguile,
Giving, for all we would give
Only a smile.

And in Italian:

The Temple in the Woods
(A first attempt, not too serious)

Il tempietto
delle silve
E il tempietto
di nostr'amore.

Potente dio
di nostr'amore
Come ci piace
Quel tempietto

(There is a temple in the woods
We call the temple of our love.
Good lord of lovers, God above,
How sweet's the temple in the woods!)

Noyce returned from Italy and went up to the Lakes with brother

Ronald and they walked extensively over the hills. It was a dry period and would have been very good for rock-climbing but at that time he did not feel the urge to climb crags and mused on the enjoyment of mountains without the need to climb to the top. It may have been an acceptance of his temporary weakness or a reflection on the views of less summit-seeking poets, who enjoyed the hills at every level:

> *The more men see mountains, and the more desire for them compels strong limbs to clamber up them as high and as hardly as they can, the more difficult it is to realise that they may be enjoyed through mere looking or strolling.... . The climber rampant has not time to enjoy more than the sensations of alternate intense movement. and tiredness, with the pleasure, which we must allow him, of ticking off the peaks and precipices of achievement. He has his reward. But he must confess, in matters of appreciation, the justice of poor Ruskin's harshly criticised invective against greased pole acrobats.*[6]

Noyce said once to one of my contemporaries at Charterhouse that walking to the top of the Worcestershire Beacon gave him as much pleasure as being on a Himalayan peak.

Noyce used the 1938 CUMC Easter meet to ease himself back into climbing. It was a big group, forty-one and they needed both Helyg and the nearby Tal y Braich to accommodate them all. He was organising the novices and introducing them to the delights of Tryfan and the Glyders. 'Ronald, my brother, a stalwart and essential pillar of the meet: ardent for clefts, until he became wedged in the cleft of the Monolith Crack and had to be pulled out backwards. It was a good meet.'[27] Ronald was Secretary of the CUMC in 1939-40.

In the summer term of 1938 Noyce was in Cambridge and was editor of the journal *Cambridge Mountaineering* for that year and was elected President of the CUMC for the year 1938-39.[28]

In the July Noyce went back to the Bernese Oberland to join Hans Brantchen again. They had the idea to traverse the Eiger, Mönch and the Jungfrau, a most ambitious plan. In the event they were able to do the Mittellegi, '*whose sharp crest we trod almost in fear that the snow and boulders we loosed would bombard the church and chalets below*'. Mist and snow prevented them from going on to the Mönch and they had to take the train up to the Jungfraujoch.

The north-east ridge of the Jungfrau had not been climbed since the big rock fall of the year before and they were uncertain whether it would be possible. They proceeded cautiously, and the ridge was as perfect as it looked, *'the shoulder as worthy of embrace'*. In the early dawn they were at the rock fall:

> *A huge tower had simply been sliced in half, the unwanted rock being dumped dirtily on the glacier below, not far from the Jungfraujoch. We were forced out for three or four hundred feet over the Wengern chalets, Hans again crashing down boulder after boulder seemingly on top of them. It was refreshing to be back off the dark face and on rocks that did not tremble even before they were touched. The higher arête was more than a compensation. Such Alpine ridges are of an aloof airiness with which Britain has nothing to compare. To tread a crest like the Jungfrau's, that gives the ice-cream curve of cornices to vary with finger-work on gradually warming slabs, with mauve slowly fading to pink and pink to gold over all Switzerland – this rather than the climbing of the faces is perhaps the most characteristic of Alpine fields of pleasure. So taken with it was I that day, that I fell shamefully on my stomach through one of these small twisted cornices and saw, later in the day, from the glacier, the gash where my hind and four quarters had dangled themselves abruptly over either side.*[29]

Later, from Grindelwald they went up gently over the north flank of the Mönch to the Concordia Hut on the Great Aletsch glacier, redolent of Leslie Stephen and John Tyndall, the eminent nineteenth-century mountaineers, both of whom had sheltered in the nearby Faulberg cave before a hut was built in 1877. From the hut they crossed the glacier, a long walk, and then traversed by a rock rib on the eastern Finsteraarhorn face. This consisted of steep red blocks, poised one above the other, each threatening to be the last before an impassable chasm that divided them from the parent mountain. They then descended to Grindelwald by the Strahlegg Valley watching a storm gather from the north. It was a long trip and even Hans Brantchen mused on, *'how many paces they had walked that day'*.

Noyce and Brantchen looked at the Eiger face that overhangs Grindelwald and watched a combined party of Germans and Austrians probing their way up it. There was a storm and it was thought in the valley that they had perished, but the party got to the top and were safe.

They thought that the Wetterhorn was more for them as the ledges were wider and the tilt of the face milder. They changed early on into Kletterschuhe and went slowly from one terrace to another. Their main problem was finding the route; each chimney petered out in an impossible overhang. Two-thirds of the way up they were encouraged by the sight of a rusty piton that had been left by an earlier party. This was different to a Welsh cliff. The size and the uncertainty of what was above were on a different scale. However the rock was dry and broken but clean and gripped well. The mist arrived but they were out on the gable side of the Scheidegg Wetterhorn:

> *This shoulder of the Wetterhorn overlooking Scheidegg is boned with rock and can, as we found, be muscled with ice. There remained some 500 feet to its summit. In purgatorial crampons I could swear, with more of emphasis and less of piety than Dante's overburdened sinners, that "I can no more." There is very little in mountaineering more unpleasant than the wearing of crampons when rock juts through the ice and when feet are tired enough to dig the points with a will through baggy trousers – perhaps only wet bamboo precipices in Garwhal can compare. From the shoulder the top of the Wetterhorn proper still looked something like Everest viewed from the Base Camp. We toiled towards it, still in crampons. But Hans had spied a side couloir that led directly down towards the Gleckstein hut: we would indeed have been benighted if we had tried to continue. Joyfully we abandoned the crampons, were down somehow, and at last on the long pleasant stumble in the dark to Grindelwald.*[30]

At the end of August 1938, feeling more confident, Noyce went over to Chamonix to climb with Armand Charlet, perhaps the doyen of the Chamonix guides, another introduction from his fairy godfather, Arthur Pigou. He steeled himself for this meeting by walking through Chamonix and observing the people and the surroundings. The *'elaborate professionalism, its School and the towering red rock of the Aiguilles'* were unnerving:

> *Armand appeared to me the acme of that Chamonism I was beginning to dread: karabiner and kletterschuhe, smart white ski*

jacket, athletic knee breeches (to mock my old plus-fours), tanned face and short hair, with an air of certainty about him.

Noyce suggested that they try the Mer de Glace face of the Grépon. Charlet agreed rather dismissively and by the time Noyce had unpacked and got himself up to the Montenvers hotel, Charlet was already there, ready to go.

They set off for the Tour Rouge hut and Noyce made the mistake of keeping the rope slack between them. Charlet went faster, Noyce went faster, and so he arrived at the hut, panting – a lesson learned! The following morning after a 4.30 start Charlet went straight up, paying little attention to Noyce: if the coils slackened he just went faster. As they entered the couloir the rocks became harder and the angle steeper. They stopped for food at the Niche des Amis and then went on over the top of the Aiguille du Rocher.

Charlet had by now assessed his client and became less distant and more conversational, although Noyce's replies came with difficulty between pants. At the foot of the final crack Charlet put on Kletterschuhe, saying that they were not necessary for Noyce. Noyce recalled:

> *The final crack is very much the hardest passage of the climb. The granite is still red and rough, but a solid little line of overhang against blue sky is all that can be seen of it. I belayed Armand and craned out from the wall to watch his kletterschuhe scrabbling. Then, but only at the third attempt, he was out of sight, merged into the blue itself; and I must be up after him, wrestling with a few inches of rough rock against a bare skin. Exaltation, loneliness and despair. But I was up, suddenly and comically, rubbing my nose against the metal madonna that receives her penitents upon the summit of the Grépon. A speechless Armand had festooned her with coils. He was dissatisfied with his first unsuccessful efforts in the crack, and had chastised himself as a corrective with self-imposed silence. It was 7.35 a.m., and for two hours we lay idle.*[31]

From the top they saw two Englishmen roping down from the Great Gendarme. Suddenly their ice-axes clattered down to the Nantillon glacier. Charlet chaffed Noyce about his compatriots. They roped down and Noyce went too fast, to show how good he was, and scorched his

The Mont Blanc massif.

chest. There was an ironic pleasure for Noyce when Charlet, in a slither, dropped his own ice-axe at the glacier. They detoured to retrieve it and reached Montenvers at noon.

Charlet had climbed and explored over the whole of the Mont Blanc massif and had developed a number of his own routes. The next expedition was one of these. Conditions were uncertain but it would need the co-operation of a good client for success. Noyce was enthusiastic and Charlet was persuaded. As Charlet became more relaxed with his new client, so Noyce began to take his responses beyond the 'yesses' and 'noes' and to speak the French he had been learning for years.

They went up to what is now the Charpoua Refuge. He realised also that they might be doing something adventurous that they did not wish to share with their hut companions. As Charlet cooked over his little Meta stove he discoursed on the great routes and Noyce was a ready listener.

They started at 1.30 from the refuge and went over the moraine and then across the flat glacier. They were making for the couloir between the Pic sans Nom and the Aiguille Verte. They climbed quickly and Noyce worked hard to keep up; the gradient became steeper and he continued to keep the rope slack. Steps were cut, or rather nicks in the snow and they stepped on these. Can Charlet keep this speed up? Noyce never asks if he can – he just keeps going. Then over a series of rock ribs and they are out on the Aiguille sans Nom rocks just below the Brèche. It is dawn.

The rocks above looked warm and inviting. They were cold and they moved one at a time chipping ice from the cracks. The higher they climbed, the more friendly the face of the buttress became. It merged to a ridge and then to spikes and then to *'one, absurd, defiant splinter, the Pointe Petigax, summit of the Aiguille sans Nom. It was the Aiguille I had never trodden but in dream; no lingering on its sharp tip, and no easy passage.'* Charlet shouted out that they needed to keep to schedule. It was an agreeable but slow climb in the sun to the top of the Aiguille Verte. *'the long line of Valais peaks rose to greet us, like old friends who smile. We sat and ate, as humans do in front of scenery too great for their grasping. The time was about 8.0 a.m.'*[32]

Noyce would have liked to prolong the pleasure and continue on the summits, but Charlet, in common with other guides with whom Noyce climbed later, was disinclined to go beyond the agreed summit and wanted to head homewards. It seemed to Noyce to be almost a trade-unionist approach. They descended by the Whymper Couloir with very few stones coming at them. '*But it seemed a poor place compared with the jagged ridge beside it, and the lower slopes oozed stickiness.*' They reached the Couvercle Refuge at 11 and had a very good lunch. From there they went back across the Mer de Glace, past les Moulins, where they listened to the water bubbling below the ice, to the Montenvers hotel.

The climax of this first season in Chamonix was the ascent of Mont Blanc, the massif that sprawls over the meeting point of France, Switzerland and Italy, the monarch of them all. They started after lunch from Montenvers and went up the Mer de Glace past the Requin hut, over the Géant glacier and on up in worsening weather to the bivouac at the Col de la Fourche, where they spent more of the night than they planned. At 2.00 the weather became worse and they stayed put.

At 10.00 they had to make a decision as they had not provisioned for a long period of bad weather.

Charlet suggested that they should at least look at the Brenva ridge. In fact they left at 11.30 and descended to the Brenva glacier and went up to the Col Moore.

> *Of the ridge proper, all that remains in memory is a rapid scramble on rock, with an occasional frothy plunge. The terrors of A.E.W. Mason's ice arête disappeared when I was up to my knees in it. It was a pleasure to reach the harder ground of the séracs and have steps to cut. We got through them first time. I had long ceased to regard Armand as a 'rocknast' only; but his ice technique and mountaineering ability here increased my respect tenfold. For we were wrapped in mist and a mild blizzard had blown our way, blotting out everything.*[33]

They reached the Col de Brenva and then the long plod to the Mont Blanc summit which they reached at 15.00. Then they went down through the mists very quickly to the Vallot Observatory and then to the Aiguille du Goûter hut where there was a large contingent from the Swiss Alpine Club. They were determined to get to the summit on the morrow.

The hut was crowded and there was little space and '*the majority slept on the floor and sang to keep out the draughts. The most memorable bed-fellows were three American students, who asked Armand how long it would take to reach the top. He said three hours. They looked at each other, very tough in Rugby sweaters and ski-caps, "Right; in two and three-quarter hours we are up that mountain."'*

They watched the others go off. It was very cold and there had been a heavy snow-fall. They stayed in the hut all day hoping for better weather to go back over the top to Mont Maudit. Soon the parties returned. Nobody reached the top, not even the Americans. The following day dawned fair and Noyce and Charlet went up again to the summit, where they were surprised by a voice. A French scientist had dug himself in, with his wife, and had spent the week studying snow conditions at 4,800 metres. He said that, *'He had slept through most of the storm very warmly.'* He also recommended it as a course of action for mountaineers!

They continued on over Mont Maudit and Mont Blanc du Tacul, where Noyce recollected some fine ice gargoyles. They ran, to Noyce's horror, through the crevasses of the Géant ice-fall and reached Montenvers as the sun was struggling through dark clouds. They looked up. *"That,"* said Armand, *"is the end of the season for some time."* And it was so.

In early September Noyce joined the family for a holiday in Guernsey. He wrote to his tutor, Nathaniel Wedd, *'We also are at the sea-side at the moment, shrimping & making sand castles.'*

However to reassure him in view of all this mountain and family activity he adds:

> *I have had a glorious time revelling in those things I had long wanted to have a go at. The Iliad more or less passim & chunks of the Republic. Also Theocritus & Callimachus to set those off, and in Latin those thrilling letters of Cicero's from 49, he hedging and turning tail ignominiously with each letter. I'm about to make a dive into Lucretius . I hope I can keep it up, as for him, when it comes to reading about atoms & systems (in which too, it is difficult to believe) I always sigh for someone intelligible like Horace. The fate of the prophet !*[34]

He was back to Cambridge for the Michaelmas term. In December the CUMC had their winter meet at Helyg and once again Noyce was introducing novices to the mountains. He did, however, during that time manage to make the first ascent of Truant Rib on Craig Yr Ysfa with D. M. Craib.

At Easter 1939 the CUMC held their meet close to Ben Nevis. Noyce had climbed Gardyloo Gully with three companions and they had reached the top of Raeburn's Arête when a boulder was dislodged and fell on Noyce's leg, breaking it. They spent a frozen night on the ledge. One of them set the bone correctly and they waited until the rescue party, with Jackson Murray of the Scottish Mountaineering Club, started at 7.00 in the morning. Murray organised the descent carrying Noyce's stretcher and he was brought to Fort William Hospital. Mercifully nobody was frostbitten.

In the summer term, Noyce, as captain of the college tennis team, was not able to participate fully in the matches but his devotion to the Latin and Greek authors earned him a first class in the Classical Tripos Part I.

With the threat of war there was no opportunity to go to the Alps and Noyce was preparing to return to Cambridge for his fourth year. However, on the day war broke out, on 3rd September 1939, he was in camp in North Wales with Frida Leakey, her two children, Priscilla and Colin, and David and Jeffy Murray-Rust. The Murray-Rusts were by now Quakers and all of them were friends of Arthur Pigou who with Winthrop Young had been powerful figures in the Friends Ambulance Unit (FAU) in the First World War. Influenced by them, Noyce appears to have been a pacifist, at this point, if not a Conscientious Objector, and he joined the FAU at Edgbaston and was sent to the training unit at Manor Farm in October 1939. For the last two weeks of November 1939 he worked as Deputy Leader of the afternoon shift in Bethnal Green Hospital, dealing with casualties, dressings, the transport of patients and the manufacture of various dressings. He was also very keen on gym. His FAU record notes:

> *Driver:- (No Test) – Some experience*
> *Cooking:- Slight experience*
> *Interpreter: French (Good), Italian (Good)*
> *Hobbies:- Mountaineering, Travelling (Secretary Cambridge Mountaineering Club: Member of Alpine Club): Tennis (Capt of King's): Squash*

Under the heading *'Social Work'*, it notes: *Schoolmaster – very keen*.[35]

He left the FAU and returned to Cambridge just before Christmas and started to work towards a Modern Language Tripos. In June 1940 he was awarded a First in the Modern Languages Tripos Preliminary Examination Part II.

He now had firsts in both Classics and Modern Languages, as well as a wide range of contacts among those who were to play important parts in government and the services in subsequent years, and a reputation for speed and endurance in the mountains.

Notes

1. Letter from Marcia Newbolt 3.5.2011
2. Wilfrid Noyce, *Mountains and Men p.51*
3. Jim Perrin, *Menlove p.146*
4. *Wilfrid Noyce, Mountains and Men p.53*
5. *Apostles Minute Book. 4.6.1939.* King's College Library, Cambridge. KCAS/3/1
6. *Ibid*
7. *Tutor's letter book 1918-1945.* King's College Library, Cambridge. KCAC/4/3
8. *Cambridge University Calendar 1938-39*
9. Obituary, Annual Report of the Council, King's College, Nov. 1962
10. Wilfrid Noyce, *Cambridge Mountaineering 1956*
11. *Council Minutes 6.11.1937.* King's College Library, Cambridge. KCGB/5/1/4
12. *Ibid*
13. Wilfrid Noyce, *Mountains and Men p.54*
14. *Ibid p.33*
15. *Ibid p.33*
16. Geoffrey Sutton and Wilfrid Noyce, *Samson p.38*
17. Wilfrid Noyce, *Mountains and Men p.54*
18. *Ibid p.55*
19. Jim Perrin, *Menlove p.153*
20. Wilfrid Noyce, *Mountains and Men p.55*
21. John Hunt & David Cox, *Wilfrid Noyce 1917-1962: Some Personal Memories* AJ 1993 p.67
22. *Senior Tutor Register Book 1918-1938.* King's College Library, Cambridge. KCAC/4/1/2
23. Wilfrid Noyce, *Mountains and Men p.55*
24. *Ibid p.58*
25. *Ibid p.58-60*
26. *Ibid p.62*
27. *Ibid p.63*
28. Wilfrid Noyce, *Cambridge Mountaineering 1946*
29. Wilfrid Noyce, *Mountains and Men p.35*
30. *Ibid p.37*
31. *Ibid p.40*
32. *Ibid p.43*
33. *Ibid p.45*
34. Wilfrid Noyce, letter to Nathaniel Wedd of 8.9.1938
35. Library of the Society of Friends (LSF) : TEMP MSS 876 : Personnel cards

CHAPTER SIX

SERVICE IN WORLD WAR II

Wilfrid Noyce had returned to Cambridge just before Christmas 1939 and in June 1940 he was awarded a first in Part II of the Modern Languages Tripos. By this time events at Dunkirk had overpowered his pacifism and according to his sister he decided that he should do some 'proper soldiering'. His early holidays in Ffestiniog and his continuing attachment to the Welsh mountains led him to the Welsh Guards and he received his call-up papers *'in the middle of harvest'* on Brynrorsedd ridge in North Wales. Consequently on 12th September 1940, he entered the Guards Depot at Caterham for basic training. When the author of this book returned to school, during National Service, for a climbing session with The Mallory Group (the school mountaineering club) Noyce recalled the time at the Depot when all he had to do was to live up to the shine on his immaculately polished boots. Also in the Welsh Guards depot at this time was another mountaineer, David Gould, who was a climbing companion in India later in the war. After basic training, Noyce was transferred to the Welsh Guards Training Battalion at the beginning of January 1941. Following the officer selection boards and recognition of his three years in the Charterhouse Officer Training Corps (OTC) he was posted on 27th March 1941 to 162nd Officer Cadet Training Unit (OCTU) at Perham Down, Bulford, on the edge of Salisbury Plain.

On 9th May 1941 he was transferred to 103 OCTU also at Perham Down, which trained officers for the Royal Armoured Corps and on 19th July passed out in the middle of the squad with a 'B' grade and appointed to an Emergency Commission in the King's Royal Rifle Corps (KRRC). Emergency commissions were for those who were not planning to make a permanent career in the service. On 27th July he moved again to 1st Motor Transport Battalion, KRRC, at Chiseldon, near Swindon.

Near Perham Down was the village of Cholderton and in April 1941 Noyce wrote:

Cholderton in Wiltshire[1]

I'd like to sleep at Cholderton
and never wake again
unless it were to sunbeams
or beat of April rain.

I'd like to step its acres
and have its friends for mine,
to drink my pint of evenings
and stay abed till nine.

For if I lived at Cholderton
I never could be sad
unless the cow came factious
or hay-time drove me mad.

But ah! Wherever man is
he moans his hay and cow,
and if I went to Cholderton
I'd fare as ill as now.

On 13th August he was sent back to Cambridge, this time attached to the 10th Battalion KRRC (The Rangers). A Major John Hunt, also a keen mountaineer, was the second-in-command, and this was the beginning of a very long association and friendship. With them he moved up to Thetford, in Norfolk, a large flat expanse of training area well-known to generations of soldiers, until the beginning of December when he was released from 10 KRRC and seems to have gone back to Cambridge. While he was there he gave a talk to the CUMC entitled 'Reminiscences'. During this period he suffered an alarming loss of weight, and on 28th January he was sent before a medical board in Cambridge and was graded 'C'. This meant that ordinary soldiering was no longer for him. Fortunately there were alternatives.

By 1942 the war in the Far East was intensifying and Britain needed to strengthen her intelligence activities in face of the Japanese. Many of the British Japanese speakers, diplomats and businessmen had been rounded up and interned by the Japanese and so there was a great urgent need to create Japanese speakers. John Tiltman, the head of Bletchley Park's military section, the main centre for UK and allied decryption and decoding, consulted the School of Oriental and African Studies (SOAS), in London University. They reckoned that it took five years to train someone properly and two years was the minimum required to achieve any decent level of Japanese. So another solution was sought. Tiltman had himself learnt Japanese in a few months and thought that something similar could be achieved with suitable students and a teacher such as Captain Oswald Tuck.

Tuck had served in Naval Intelligence in World War I, and had been Assistant Naval Attaché in Tokyo. He had retained his deep knowledge of the Japanese language and Japanese ways, which were very different from ours. Although by now he was aged sixty-five, Tiltman asked him if he could teach young students enough Japanese to break codes in six months. He indicated that he could turn out Japanese speakers in four months. He accepted Tiltman's invitation and at the same time they recruited through the various networks, which included particularly the heads of the Oxbridge colleges, the brightest classicists and modern linguists for interpretation and cryptography work. These were plucked from their studies at Oxford and Cambridge and gathered together for courses at Bedford in the Gas showrooms at Ardour House.

One of the Fellows of King's was Patrick Wilkinson, a classicist, also an Old Carthusian, who at the beginning of the war was recruited into code-breaking at the Government Communications Headquarters at Bletchley Park. It is believed that he arranged for Noyce to be recruited into the organisation. On 2nd March 1942 Noyce entered the world of Intelligence. He was sent to N° 4 Intelligence School (Inter-Service Special Intelligence School) in Bedford for the Japanese course. This was part of the Bletchley Park organisation and it lasted as an Intelligence School until well into the 1990s in various forms in London and elsewhere.

Also at Bedford was another new student of Japanese, Ian Grimble, who subsequently became a writer, broadcaster and great publicist for Scotland and Robert Burns. Noyce and Grimble appear to have been billeted with a local family in Bedford, the Gridleys who lived at 2 Putnoe Lane. Noyce seems to have got into the bad books of the mother. Apparently he grew vegetables in the garden of the house and he went round after the horse that pulled the milk float in order to get the manure. He used to take one of the children with him and perhaps not surprisingly their mother did not altogether approve. Noyce and Grimble became very good friends and both eventually served in India.

John Hunt was very interested to use the mountains as a means to prepare and toughen soldiers, to develop a greater fitness and team spirit, as well as to experiment in mountain warfare, particularly for his Armoured Corps. He ran a training camp based at Helyg, the Climbers' Club Hut, in North Wales in the last two weeks of May 1942 and recruited Wilfrid Noyce and other distinguished climbers, such as Alf Bridge and C. F. Holland as instructors.

Noyce, however, had until then regarded the mountains as a pure, almost sacred, element and one that should not be associated with such profane activities as military training. He felt that the idea of coaching unsuitable and reluctant pupils over fell and rock appeared repugnant. It was somehow disloyal,

> *...to the Cambridge ideals to be night-operating over the Carnedds or doing a battle inoculation course up the little valley under Gallt yr Ogof. I could not get over the oddity, nor stop regretting that mountains must be dragged into what we consider the bloody business of war.*

And later,

> *Those whom "a priori" I expected to continue disliking the thing beamed suddenly into unexpected appreciation. The first day I had on my rope a sergeant-major, a major and a lieutenant. The sergeant-major, in ill-nailed boots and on his belly, had struggled triumphantly as far as the Belle Vue Terrace on the North Buttress of Tryfan. He said: "Do you think it's possible, sir, to hate a thing and enjoy it at the same time?" I answered that I thought it was.*

Noyce's experience as an instructor was growing. He had been instructing on the CUMC meets and now John Hunt was using that teaching experience combined with the technical skills of a great mountaineer. As a 'hostilities only' soldier Noyce found it hard to appreciate the value of mountains to the professional soldier, '*...to a* *purist, unnatural that mountaineers should partake anything tainted with the smell of the dirt track.'* He recognised that John Hunt wanted to create an enthusiasm for the mountains among non-mountain-minded people and he used the means that they were used to.

Hunt reciprocated the compliment when he wrote:

> *I was, however, more than fortunate in my instructors. Among them were such able leaders as A. W. Bridge and Lieutenant C. W. F. Noyce, both of whom joined the School for part of the Course. In addition, instructors were lent by a rock-climbing Troop of a Commando billeted in the neighbourhood, and among them no less a celebrity than C. F. Holland (Lance-Corporal), who was with our ropes on several occasions. From Capel Curig, M. G. Bradley and the Aitchesons père et fils, came out to assist on one day, so that we did not lack for willing and well-qualified assistants.*
>
> *On the 21st evening we had a minor excitement, when two Instructors sent out to place clues for a Compass Route, failed to return by 9.30 pm. Noyce and I set out carrying food, blankets, and first aid kit, and made for Moel Siabod, in case the compass bearing between that summit and a small lake to the west of it might have led them into trouble on the crags. We failed to rouse any response to our shouts and whistle blasts in the moonlight, and on return at 2 am, found that they had come in only one hour after we had started!*[2]

Before the army course, Noyce indulged his penchant for climbing alone. Early in May 1942 he climbed, solo, Curving Crack on Clogwyn d'ur Arddu which had first been climbed by Colin Kirkus and Alf Bridge together. It was a very tough and hazardous climb he wrote:

> *I wrestled hotly to the top of the Curving Crack, in a fear and a sure vowing that I would never be guilty of the like rashness again. On the grass above, I lay in the sun. I had done – what? I had done something that only I could tell. Something foolish, something I must not repeat, but something that I felt still to have been "worth" the doing.*

However Noyce was clearly not too discouraged. An entry in the Helyg hut book at about the same time records:[4]

> *May 7th 1942 TRYFAN Up Grooved Arête lower part to Terrace Wall. Sunny. Up Old Long Chimney down Terrace Wall Variant. Up New Long Chimney down Old Long Chimney. Up Belle View Bastion. Down Terrace Wall Variant, over Bristly Ridge and Glyders. Down Devil's Kitchen. Up Hanging Garden Gully.*
> *IDWAL SLABS*
> *Up central Rib and up Cinderella. Down Holly Tree Wall and up Cinderella's Twin and down Lazarus. Down Tennis Shoe.*
> *EAST WALL*
> *Girdle Traverse and down Grooved Wall. Up Ash Tree Wall, down by Tennis Shoe.*
> *Heather Weakness, etc. Up Rake End Chimney. Up Heather Wall but defeated on last pitch so down Heather Weakness.*
> *C.W.F.N.*

This was some 4,500 feet of solo climbing at Severe grade or harder and a considerable walk entirely on his own.

At that time there were important railway installations at Bedford and on 30th July 1942 there was a German air raid thought to have been targeting the railway station. They appear to have missed the station but hit 2 Putnoe Lane and the house was destroyed and Michael Anthony (7) and Judith Sheila (4) Gridley were both killed. The parents survived but Noyce was *'injured by enemy action*[5] and was admitted to St. Peter's Emergency Medical Service (EMS) Hospital, Bedford. The following day he was transferred to EMS Hospital, Arlesey, in Buckinghamshire. Rosalind, Wilfrid's sister, remembers that Ian Grimble *'came to our house and reported going to see Wilf in hospital. He himself was not badly hurt but he said that Wilf had been given morphine and greeted him with utmost cheer and said that he felt absolutely wonderful as a result of this morphine.'*

On 14th August Noyce was discharged from hospital and prepared for his imminent embarkation for India from Liverpool on 27th August.

Out of his six months at Bedford he had been otherwise occupied outside the course for at least one of them. Notwithstanding he had acquired an impressive facility in Japanese and cryptography to be of immediate and effective service on arrival in India.

Noyce was sent to what was called, opaquely, the Wireless Experimental Station (WEC) and attached to 'A' Indian Special Wireless Group. From then on Noyce and Grimble maintained a steady correspondence. The centre was based at Ramjas College, which was formerly part of Delhi University, set on the top of a hill a few miles south of Delhi Annand Parat, 'hill of happiness', was difficult to approach and thus very suitable as a secure site. The hill was rocky with excellent buildings but badly situated for radio reception. *'One walked up to an open gateway to a large, bare quadrangle, surrounded by solid-looking buildings.'*

The WEC had been set up earlier in the war to intercept and interpret signals from Japanese headquarters, units and ships, signals intelligence or 'SIGINT'. There were other intercept stations in India set-up under the WEC, at Ranchi and at Bangalore. WEC was officially 164 Signal Wing RAF and in 1943 was commanded by a Group-Captain Ewens. It was a fully integrated centre and had five sections, collating and evaluating signals intelligence, traffic analysis, breaking and translating Japanese Army and Army-Air-force codes, radio interception and administration:

> *This was a nerve centre of intelligence from military wireless sources against Japan. Well over a thousand are believed to have inhabited it, at its height, made up of Intelligence Corps (the real Wireless Experimental Centre, India Command); RAF from 166 Signals Wing; Women's Auxiliary Corps (India); Indian airmen, many from the far south of India, perhaps with Malayalam or Tamil mother tongue; West African Signals, from what are now Ghana and Nigeria; occasional British ATS, and more than one WAAF officer; and, of course a host of Indian Army NCOs and men. There were many civilians too, not least the Sikh postmaster, and Habibullah, the Pathan fruitseller, and last but not least the cycle shop at the gate, our lifeline off duty at a hire of one rupee eight annas a day.*[6]

The equipment improved greatly as the war progressed. Initially they had standard RAF and army equipment and

> *the receiving antennae were primitive, mainly vertical wires festooned from horizontal lines between eight or more 120-foot steel masts.... While the intercept operators, at that time mainly Royal Signals, were quite outstanding, their output was adversely affected by the high noise level and poor maintenance.... One of these operators, a Corporal Idi Amin, of the King's African Rifles*

(KAR) was later to become quite notorious in Uganda.[7] He was at that time however an excellent NCO.[8]

The masts were eventually replaced by very strong 160-foot steel masts made from standard Indian telephone pole sections. These were aligned for specific coverage and covered the entire Japanese occupied area of South-East Asia. They also withstood typhoon winds of 160 mph, unlike the standard army masts which were completely demolished by such storms.

The communication system was equally poor at the start but a new transmitter station was erected and high-powered transmitters from Marconi and RCA were installed in 1943 so that there was a good link with Washington. The Intelligence Section used Hollerith machines for primary sorting and then sent those intercepts which could not be decoded locally either to the UK or the US. The cryptographers at the beginning used Enigma drums picked up in the Western desert and some recovered from a German plane that had crashed in the Himalaya.

Wilfrid Noyce was part of the new draft of cryptoanalysts who arrived at the end of 1942 and beginning of 1943. On 1st October 1942 he was promoted War Service Lieutenant, still KRRC, as *'there were no second lieutenants in WEC,'* and was subsequently appointed Intelligence Officer on 1st January 1943. He was in Section C which was commanded by a regular officer, Lieutenant-Colonel Peter Marr-Johnson, who had been attached to the Far East Combined Bureau (Intelligence) in Hong Kong in 1940 in a capacity so secret that even his colleagues in the organisation did not know about it. In 1941 he had run the Special Liaison Unit in Singapore handling 'Special' for the Commander-in-chief. Later he worked for General Wavell in Java and following a spell in Washington he took charge of the WEC 'C' Section. Most of his staff found him distant and not very accessible, which perhaps was not altogether surprising in view of his highly secretive past. He ran a tight ship and had little time for war-commissioned officers. In spite of this, or perhaps because of this, the section was very successful.

Hugh Skillen, who wrote **Knowledge Strengthens the Arm,** about intelligence in WWII, and was in command of the Maintenance Workshops at WEC, remembers the Boys' Club. The members who were mainly products of the Bedford Japanese course, *'were very high-class translators'*. He remembered particularly Wilfrid Noyce and Hugh

Lloyd-Jones, a classicist from Westminster, who after the war returned to Oxford to graduate with Firsts in Mods and Greats (Classics) and, as one of the most original classical scholars of the era, became Regius Professor of Greek at Oxford from 1960 to 1989. He was knighted in 1989 and eventually died in October 2009.

In the team was Maurice Allen, some nine years older than Noyce, a graduate of LSE and already a Fellow of Balliol. He joined the Royal Signals in 1940 and after a spell in the Middle East came to WEC. He ended up as Lieutenant-Colonel in 1944 and after the war had a distinguished career in the IMF and the Bank of England.

Noyce shared a room with a Wilfred Smith and seems to have settled in very well. In his spare time he went on long walks. Another man, Darlow *'…blows silent cigarette smoke at me but is placidly compliant. Bell works hard and is rather good value. The rest of the mess – a tiny one – is rather fun.'*[9]

He mentions that it is *'Hard work. But I have never felt so important – without justification again – since Charterhouse.'*

Noyce was very conscious of his father's service and influence in India and he resumed and strengthened the many links his parents had with the country. The Ikramullahs' 'Ikram' was in the Indian Foreign Service and in the 1950s became head of the Pakistan Foreign Service. He and his wife Soghra were a great help to Noyce for some of his later expeditions. There were also the Roys[10] and the Tymms. It was not long before, in 1937, that Sir Frank Noyce had retired after some thirty-five years in India. Lady Noyce herself had founded what is now known as the Government Lady Noyce Senior Secondary School for Deaf and Dumb. For her charity work she received the Kaiser-i-Hind Gold Medal in the 1937 Coronation honours. Wilfrid's Headmaster at Charterhouse, Frank Fletcher, was knighted and Lord Baden-Powell, Chief Scout, was appointed to the Order of Merit at the same time!

Noyce wrote subsequently of his father:

> *It was…not till I found myself, during the war, in the Army in India, that I formed some estimate of his influence. The most astonishing result of his work lay for me in the number, both of Indians and British, who claimed him and my mother as their personal, even their best friends. He had won Indian hearts by his persistence in regarding them as human individuals, to be helped and trusted. This was his own invariable rule, whatever*

might be the Government policy of the day. This attitude he had demonstrated publicly in his handling of Nationalist Members, and privately by a wealth of contacts. He had won them too by the strong sense of humour that lightened his firmness. Jokes about his handwriting are still current. And the story was gleefully told how a reference was made once in the Assembly to the "portly figure of the Honourable Member." My father had replied that, alas, it must be confessed that "there is a Destiny that ends our shapes". It was therefore because they so loved him that the Indians respected the strength of his opinions about India's future, and his grave forebodings at the possible result of a too early grant of independence.[11]

Sometimes the association with his parents' friends was more duty than pleasure, particularly when they felt possessive about him. Lady Esmé Roy who entertained them and perhaps looked after them more than they wanted, seems to have been exigent in her requests to them. He wrote to Grimble:

Second: Esmé, I am writing because it really is too bloody silly this friend monopoly business and I ought to have made the position clear before. It is my fault and I am afraid it has thrown a lot of strain on you in my absence. I am telling her that even if I didn't like the people I go to see I should have to see them for parental reasons. As it is I have seen less of them than I ought, owing to her. I see now that the Delhi "one man's house is another man's prison" has worked on me: perhaps things appear in clearer perspective here. But again I have managed to leave you with main baby. The Literary Society sounds a terror![12]

By early February 1943, when the Japanese finally gave up their fight for Guadalcanal, the Allied code-breakers were still trying to break into the high-level Japanese codes. The Japanese Army's Water Transport Code, or *senpaku angosho 2*, a four-figure enciphered code known as 2468 since this appeared as the first group, or 'discriminant', of each message, was under attack at various centres. Noyce appears to have taken the lead and with Allen realised that the first letter of the third group was not random. The third group in the 2468 received at Delhi was the repeater group or indicator. As in the main naval systems, this gave the starting point of the additive which was added to the encoded message. The breaking of this Water Transport Code in March 1943, was the first significant penetration into high-level Japanese Army code.

Similar work had also been going on at Arlington Hall, an entirely military establishment and the US equivalent of Bletchley Park. The Japanese Water Transport Code was broken there in April 1943, with no apparent co-ordination between the two teams. Joseph P. Richard received the Legion of Merit for his work. Wilfrid Noyce was promoted Acting Captain on 1st May 1943. This code was more important than its name suggests: it was used to communicate key information such as details of troop movements, and highly valuable data on logistics, orders of battle and, frequently, the strategic intentions of the Japanese government.

Within a very short space the Central Bureau of Intelligence was able to read the Water Transport Code without difficulty and did so until the end of the war. It may be helpful to understand a little of how code-breaking was carried out and the following is taken from Michael Smith's book ***The Emperor's Codes:***

> *With the squares we could recover the additive starting places of all messages and immediately sorted them by book and page, but we found that the row and column co-ordinates on the additive pages were in mixed random order. This meant that in order to write out the messages with the enciphered groups in the correct position above each other, they had to find two or three that started with the same row and column. They slid one message along the top of a second until subtracting a known likely code group in one message gave an additive that, when it was added to the enciphered group below it in the second message, left them with another known and commonly used code group in the second message.*
>
> *After several possible additives had been found other messages in the same row or column could be tried so that other row and column digits could be placed and more messages using them added. Non-linguists could start and recover much of a page, starting with the dendai or message number group followed by a number group, which always occurred one third of the way in to the message as transmitted. Since the Japanese Army knew that the beginnings of a message were its weakest parts, they cut them into several parts and sent them in a rearranged order. I think*

this procedure baffled Washington and gave the Japanese Army high-level traffic security for almost a year and a half after the war started.[13]

Within weeks, Central Bureau (of Intelligence) was able to read the Water Transport Code without difficulty and did so until the end of the war. Perhaps more importantly as a result of the work done by Richard, Noyce and Allen, the Allied code-breakers knew how the Japanese signallers enciphered the additive indicators for their high-level codes and ciphers. Delhi was already producing decodes which provided details of military units embarking on troop transports for the various areas occupied by the Japanese, and the knowledge gained through breaking it was being used to attack the other high-level military codes.

This constant pressure for results caused considerable strain on the members of WEC. At the time that he was doing the vital work with Maurice Allen in March 1943, Noyce writes:

It is beginning to look as if I shall be here some time. I wish you were here too. There seems to be no way of telling how long we may last. I want you if you can do it to find out from the powers that be how long they think it will last (of course I want it to last as long as possible: and if only you could get down). But Bell has had to go on leave from overwork and it is a certain amount of strain now. From that and I suppose selfishly I begin to think of the hills.[14]

He had already asked Grimble to recover his climbing boots from the cobbler who was stretching them and… '*Another thing that wants doing to them if Dildar* [his servant] *can manage it is to wet the soles (so that the nails rust in finally).*'

In May 1943 he managed to get a month of leave to go up to Garhwal, where he wanted to explore Trisul, 23,630ft (7,198m) a peak on the edge of the Nanda Devi sanctuary. He returned to WEC on 14th June.

It has been suggested that shortly after this Noyce left India temporarily and was attached to Special Forces in Europe. There he is said to have operated radio communications with the Resistance in Normandy and later with the Partisans in Italy.[15] His military record gives no corroboration of this service. He returned to Delhi in spring 1944 and shortly after took a month's leave to explore more mountains in Garhwal, returning to the WEC finally on 26th June 1944.

A good description of life in the WEC at that time was recorded by Michael Kerry, a young Pilot-Officer, who was trained in Japanese and code-breaking in the relaxed and rarefied atmosphere at the School of Oriental and African Studies in London and Bletchley Park in 1944 and found WEC something of a culture shock.

> *The trouble with the WEC was that it was much more militaristic than Bletchley Park. It was such a contrast. Four of us went out in June 1944, all of us RAF officers. We were equipped for the Boer War with drainpipe shorts and pith helmets. So we bought some new khaki shorts, which were fine, and some new hats which as it turned out later were not. We arrived at the WEC and were shown into Peter Marr-Johnson's office. He said he did not like the RAF and he liked them even less improperly dressed, and told us to get out. We puzzled over this and eventually realised that the new tan hats we had bought were in fact 'Bombay bowlers' as worn by Indian civil servants.*[16]

Despite being in the RAF, Kerry was put to work on high-level army codes.

> *I sat opposite Wilfrid Noyce, the mountaineer, who was a very nice chap but had a very battered face. He had fallen off a number of mountains and must have had India-rubber bones. A great character in the section was Hugh Lloyd-Jones who became Regius Professor of Greek at Oxford. We worked on army messages, mainly using the 7890 code and carrying daily reports of strengths of things like weapons, rations, sickness. It was quite hard at times working with indistinct photographs of captured codebooks in a temperature of 117 degrees (47°C). There was no air-conditioning and an Indian woman was employed purely to sit by a great big woven straw door, khaskhas tatti, throwing handfuls of water over it every few seconds to keep the temperature down.*

The Army and the RAF, unlike the Royal Navy, were very protective of their female members and did not send them to the far-flung corners of the empire. So life at WEC was agonisingly celibate in contrast to Bletchley Park and indeed very abstemious. Kerry recalled:

A friend of mine who took his sex life very seriously pursued an Indian servicewoman but that was it, and I can't remember very much drinking or alcohol. When we weren't working on anything current we worked normal daytime hours and at six o'clock you went off to your little bungalow, you each had a bearer, and he served you with tea. Once a week, every Wednesday, we had a curry lunch and took little horse carts or ghari into Delhi to have tea.

Sir Michael Kerry, KCB, QC, who had a distinguished career as a public servant and retired as HM Procurator General and Treasury Solicitor, recalled that Noyce:

Was very pleasant to work for but was not particularly chatty and since we obviously moved in different circles in the mess I learnt very little about him as a person...

Sometime in August Wilfrid was posted to a mountain training unit in Kashmir much to the envy of all those who remained in the heat of Delhi.[17]

After nine months in Kashmir, Noyce was recalled to the Wireless Experimental Centre in May 1945 and spent July and August in Delhi. He celebrated the end of the war in the Far East by losing his identity card. His army record recalls:

...8 August Reprimanded by Col. E. R. Riddley, MBE, Officer Commanding Delhi Area, on 8.8.45 for neglect to the prejudice of good order and military discipline in that he on the afternoon on 9.7.45 whilst cycling in the Delhi Area lost his identity card.[18]

This does not appear to have impaired his army career significantly and the following month he was given twenty-eight days' leave. This enabled him to go up to Sikkim where he had his eyes on Pauhunri 23,385ft (7,100m) on the Sikkim-Tibet frontier. This was a solo expedition, with no European companions and again Noyce planned to live as much as possible off the country. He left Delhi on 8th September 1945 and returned on 11th October. He was in Delhi for a month and then went down to Bombay and embarked on 21st November. He finally arrived in England shortly before Christmas 1945.

Notes

1. First published *Encounter*
2. John Hunt *Climbers' Club Journal (CCJ) 1942 pp 22,24*
3. *Wilfrid Noyce, Mountains and Men p.150*
4. Climbers' Club, Helyg Hut Book, entry for 7.5.1942
5. Army Form B199A for Officer n° 198356
6. Michael Smith *The Emperor's Codes p.162*
7. President Idi Amin Dada, President of Uganda 1971-79
8. Major T. Gray *Royal Signals Institution Journal Vol 18-2 (1987)* cited by Hugh Skillen *Knowledge Strengthens the Arm p.424*
9. *Wilfrid Noyce, Letter to Ian Grimble 29.2.1943* (sic)
10. Sir S. N. and Lady Esmé Roy
11. *Wilfrid Noyce, St. Catherine's College Society Magazine 1949 pp.29-30*
12. Letter to Ian Grimble from Aircrew Centre 13.9.1944
13. Michael Smith *The Emperor's Codes p.175*
14. *Wilfrid Noyce, Letter to Ian Grimble 23.3.1943 from A' Indian Special Wireless Group, 12 ABPO.*
15. Email from Colin Leakey 19.2.2011 describes visit in 1948 with Noyce to his hide-outs in Forges-les-Eaux and Florence
16. Michael Smith *The Emperor's Codes pp.230 & seq*
17. Sir Michael Kerry to the author 28.2.2011
18. Army Form B199A for Officer n° 198356

CHAPTER SEVEN

CLIMBS IN THE HIMALAYA 1943-45

Wilfrid Noyce heeded General Bruce's advice to him as a teenager and took the opportunity while he was in India to organise three climbing trips to the Himalaya. He made use of his connections with the Himalayan Club and was helped by their representative in Garhwal on two of the occasions. The Club and its members were also generous in lending equipment.

The expeditions were relatively modest affairs, consisting only of two or three climbers and a few locals as porters and guides. They lived as much as possible off the country and had tinned rations for the higher altitudes. Their success was dependent very much on the Sherpas and porters with them and Noyce's early upbringing in India and knowledge of Urdu gave him an easy relationship with them.

He was in the Himalaya on a further occasion for nearly nine months as Chief Instructor at the Aircrew Rehabilitation Centre in Kashmir.

Garhwal 1943 – Trisul

In May 1943 Noyce went up to Garhwal, in the Central Himalaya with the objective of climbing Trisul, 23,630ft (7,198m) on the south-western edge of the Nanda Devi sanctuary. It was also some 8,200 feet or 2,500 metres higher than Noyce had ever been before.

David Gould, who had gone through the Welsh Guards Depot with Noyce and was in India with the Gurkhas, joined him and Tony Smyth, who was with the RAF, hoped to be with them with two Sherpas. In addition to their ill-matched equipment they all wore solar topees.

Unfortunately Smyth, when he joined them in Garhwal was starting a bout of malaria and had to stay behind at Ranikhet. They loaded up the coolies at Baijnath and headed north. At the first camp they opened the bundles with some trepidation and pitched the tents. Nothing seemed to be missing. Noyce wrote, '*Trisul at last showed gradually pink to gold, glorious and inaccessible; it would have been worth coming so far to see only that.*' The next day they reached Debal on the Pindar River and appear to have rested there a day. They looked at the tents; one had a hole in it, the other two were sound. Smyth's Sherpas caught them up there. The local porters were Dhotiyal who were '*…all cheerful, small, and full of smiles over vast heaps of chapattis and hookah of an evening.*' The only kit that they had was a bundle of rags – '*yet any of them could produce a needle, for instance, from nowhere.*'

Gould meanwhile recruited two chaps for the army and turned them over to the local Gurkha recruiting sergeant. Noyce had misgivings, '*tearing the innocent, the happy, away from sight of Trisul to go adopting the prone position in a Karachi barrack.*'

The march on up through Lohajang and Wan, for Noyce, '*…was pure wonder: the peony arranging its snow delicately to match the glaciers of Nanda Ghunti, Trisul's henchman.*' This first trip to the Himalaya was making a huge impression on him.

They arrived at Wan at 9.30 on 19th May and the forestry officer recommended a hut at Bhuna underneath the Western ridges of Trisul. As they had no maps, '*…it was a wonderful stroke meeting him, as we have no adequate maps and can't see what there is to climb and explore.*' They thought it would be an easy walk to Bhuna. They were dismayed to find that it was a 4,000-foot (1,220m) climb and having appealed to the porters started at 14.20 in the afternoon. The impressive forests of huge cedars, deodar trees interspersed with mauve and cream peonies compensated for the rigours of the climb to the ridge. A rapid 1,000-foot descent to the forest plantation brought them to Buna at 18.50. They did not find the supplies they had hoped for at Buna so on 20th May Noyce took three porters down to Suttol. They managed to find a few potatoes. After a long conversation in '*…foul Urdu, their's being dialect anyway*'. *They had not heard of Hitler or the war – that I did gather,*' there was no atta, only dal[†] so two of the porters stayed behind. Noyce and Karak Singh went back up to Bhuna, '*…a hell of a sweat, cursing the hut-guardian all the way.*' Noyce then admits to a side of his character that is not easily perceived:

[†] Pulses (dried beans, lentils and peas).

I'm incredibly bad at being angry, I spend vast periods cursing myself for stumbling, etc: get thoroughly bad-tempered – then am forcedly nice to other people – till I burst. But then comes a downhill stretch, swinging along, the pack now feels all right, the peonies and rhododendrons smile, this seems the nearest thing to heaven.[2]

To add to the discomfiture they discovered a 'foreign' tent at Bhuna. It was a large and leisurely party but they did give Noyce a useful map.

They reached the next camp on 21st May, just below the col at Bagcho Kharak on the edge of the snow at 12,200ft (3,3716m). This became their Base Camp for the initial approach to Trisul. At this point Gould developed mountain sickness. Although very fit and strong, he had never been high, and the sickness, if it is going to strike, does so between 3,500 and 4,000 metres. Here the Dhotiyals were sent down as they were bare-footed and the snow and rock was misery for them. They had reached this point by borrowing shoes and gym shoes, but this was the limit. They agreed to return after two days for the return carry.

On 22nd May, leaving Gould in camp, Noyce, with the Sherpa Gyalgen who had already been on Everest headed on up and reached the Trisul ridge. At 15,600ft (4,752m) Gyalgen suggested that there was nowhere to camp further along the ridge. They levelled a patch and pitched the tent. Gyalgen, as a professional Sherpa, busied himself with everything and Noyce sat or lay on the slope, irritated that he had brought no books, tobacco or cigarettes. A huge white and yellow eagle wheeled above them.

The following day they set off at 6.45. The ridge was icy and Noyce slipped several times but Gyalgen was slow but competent. They were at the top of the first peak 17,000ft (5,200m) at 9.15. They roped up. Ahead of them was a series of pinnacles separating them from the peak of Chananian Sankar. They continued and went up a corniced ridge up to the top of the first pinnacle. At 11.30 Noyce left Gyalgen and went on to the highest pinnacle, climbing on rock to the top. The return was 'foul' with slush and Noyce's topee fell off and they had to descend a snow couloir to get it. Noyce commented, '...*it is, of all maddening headwears, the one least to be worn on a climb; besides, it marked me as the Englishman in India looking his most ridiculous.*'[3] When they reached camp David Gould was still not acclimatised and they had failed to climb Trisul.

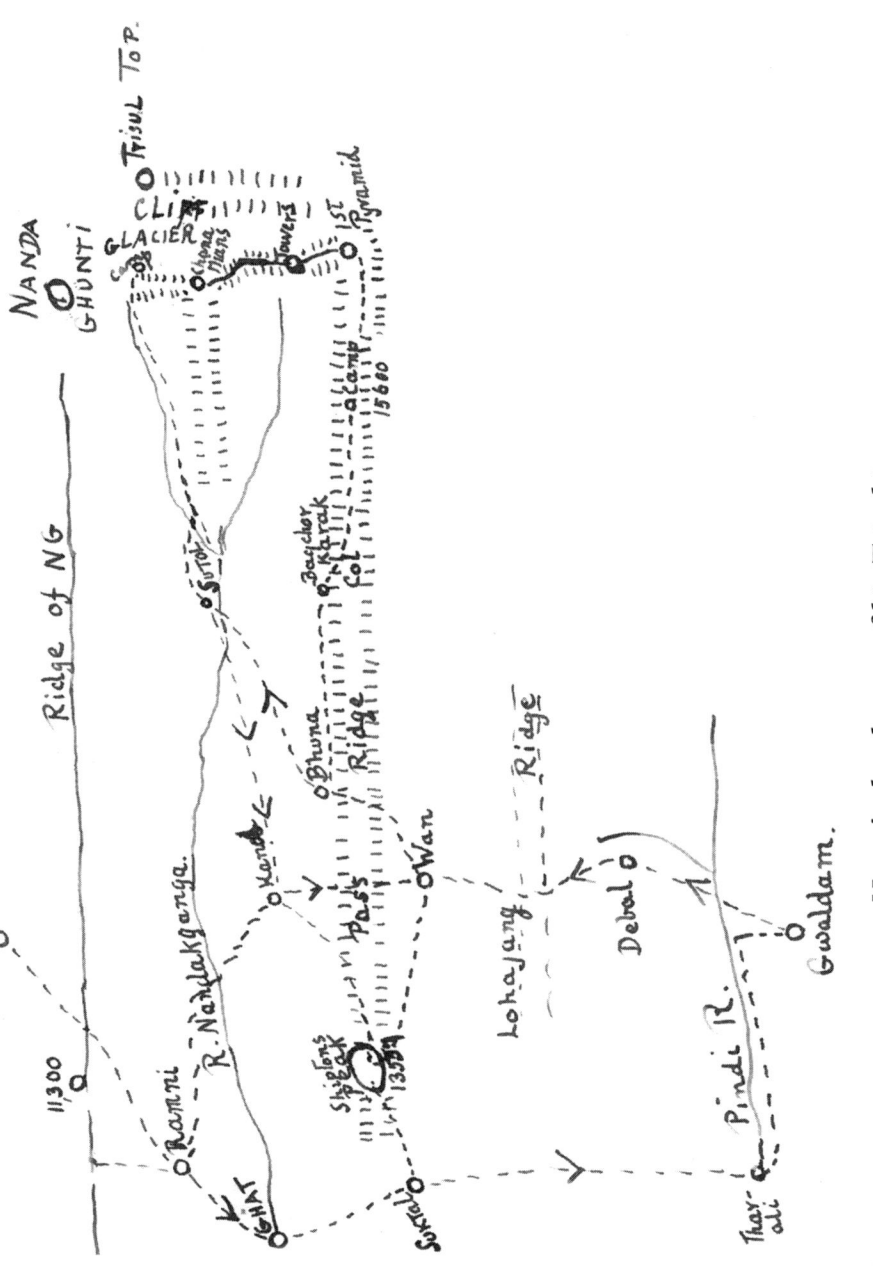

Noyce's sketch map of his Trisul journey.

On 24th May the Dhotiyals came back and took the loads down and Gould went with them. Noyce went back up to the col and followed the ridge back down to Bhuna, taking in a 14,000ft and a 13,500ft peak on the way. He was attacked by an eagle and beat it off. When he got there his foot, which had been burned by the sun and healed, then hit a rock and was now very sore.

Two days later they made their way up the valley between Nanda Ghunti and Chananian Sankar towards Trisul. It was pleasant walking initially and then became thick bamboo forest. There was scarcely a path and a guide was essential. *'Can't think how the porters managed with loads, tent poles, etc.'* They found an idyllic camp site at 9,600ft (2,900m), shaded by trees and with water where the rest of the party joined them at 13.30. The sheep was slaughtered in the traditional manner by cutting the jugular. They cooked the blood, *'which was delicious'*, they put the beast in the fire until the skin came off easily and Gould and Noyce had the heart, liver and kidneys for dinner. The porters then had a large share of the rest.

They continued up the valley the following day through undergrowth, climbing steeply. They found a good camp-site, looking down the valley and after supper Noyce went higher to reconnoitre the route. He notes: *'Bad temper all day, partly because I have messed my camera film, partly undergrowth.'*

They reached the ridge leading up to Chananian Sankar with a splendid view of Nanda Ghunti on the left, Trisul at the centre, on the edge of the Nanda Devi sanctuary. They went up the ridge and camped at 13,900ft (4,233m) from where they could see the rather stony and grubby Trisul Glacier. It was 10.40. When they had eaten, Noyce went down and explored the head of the glacier and the 10,000-foot west face of Trisul.

On 29th May the day started badly; the hot water for cocoa was knocked over and they forgot the rope. They continued up the ridge which got steadily trickier. Gould then slipped and fell but Noyce held him. They continued and at about 15,800ft (4,800m) the altitude caught up with Gould. They thought they were some 700ft below the peak. Noyce went on and found the peak only 200ft farther on – barometric pressure playing tricks – and went back to get Gould. It was the first Himalayan summit for both of them, exactly ten years before the first ascent of Everest. Gould was tired and suffering from headaches so they decided to go back. They descended by a steep snow couloir and arrived at the camp at 14.00. The guide and porters were there and they continued on to the Base Camp. At which point Noyce's foot appeared to be much better.

The next day they started through the jungle in pouring rain and eventually found shelter under a rock where they made camp. Another sheep was purchased which cheered everyone up and they all ate very well. Noyce wandered farther along the path, '...*a dream world indescribable of trees and flowers, and birds and steep hillsides – the stream happy and bubbling now.*'[4]

They went back to Sutol on 31st May and they paid off the guide. They set off early on 1st June for Kanol, west of Sutol. '*Trisul hung cloudlike and cloudgirt, with the sun behind him. Almost the most wonderful thing I have ever seen.*' Then it was on to Wan, where Gould left Noyce to return homeward on 2nd June. '*David has been great fun as companion, and the whole expedition far happier and more successful (so far) than we could have most wildly hoped.*'

Noyce told his porters to go to Kanol where he would meet them later and went off on his own to climb 'Shipton's Peak', 13,557ft (6,400m) north-east of Wan which Eric Shipton had climbed before the war.

The following day, 3rd June, Noyce set off with the porters to go north-west towards Ramni. He was entirely in the hands of the Dhotiyals who looked after him very well and their leader, Nagya, was a very good cook '...*and would make an excellent servant*'. Noyce now refers to them as '*the lads*'. It was a more relaxed period. The porters had their days off but Noyce always found a peak to take in, not as high as Trisul but with good views, 'Up through rockier scenery, very like Cynfal near Ffestiniog'.

There was time to appreciate the peonies, buttercups and the Himalayan oaks, looking like English elms, and to swim in the Gohna Lake. They left Ramni on 7th June and went down to Ghat and there met one of Tony Smyth's Sherpas, who had come not only for a tent, which he did not get, but also the altimeter and ropes, which he did. He also invited Noyce to join him – which he had to turn down. They went on together to Suktal where they camped.

On the morrow Noyce continued with his porters and they went on down the valley. There was a point at 10,990ft (3,350m) on the ridge to the east which had to be explored, as a final fling. On the way down he was caught by torrential rain and arrived in camp soaked. Fortunately, the lads had collected masses of wild strawberries!

They reached Tharali the following day. Noyce felt very tired. His foot was still giving a little trouble and he had to wear only shoes as his boots had been put too close to the fire and one had burned! Tharali was the beginning of civilisation as indicated by the tin roofs and a small post office. Farther on down, at Gwaldam, they found a bungalow occupied by three lady teachers from the Christian College at Bareilly. There Noyce made contact, beard and all, '...*pleasant indeed, not young or knowledgeable'.* They gave him tea out of a teapot! He responded with a gift of a tin of sausages and celery soup.

> *After that wandered up into the woods and found a most charming shepherd with flute on which he played for me. Alas no camera. Down to rice and berries, most luxurious supper, and a present of scones, sent by the ladies! After dark wandered to the woods by moon, wondering how everything could conceivably be so lovely. Thick clouds shot with light over the hills, wind in the deodars. So to bed, after one of the loveliest days of all.*[5]

On 11th June they left for Garur and then went up in the afternoon to Kansani, a hill-station, where they camped near the road. The following morning they crammed on to the bus to Ranikhet. They arrived at 13.15. He '...*made a mess of paying off the Dhotiyals, as David had overpaid them and had to climb down with some ignominy.'*

On 13th June he took the bus down to Kathgodam.

> *Arrived to find train full, but taken in hand by fatherly assistance officer, and had bunk. Dinner on train, to my thinking most luxurious: universally condemned by my neighbours as unfit to eat. And so the plains. How inadequate one feels to talk to people – "Had a good time?" "Lovely, thank you."*[6]

Garhwal 1944 – Simsaga

Noyce's second Himalayan trip was a year later and it was a gamble with the monsoon, but he was happy to accept the rains as an alternative to the Delhi heat. The objective was to explore the area around Sundardunga and Simsaga peak in Garhwal. It was east of his climbs the previous year.

On 24th May Ian Grimble, and Geoffrey Rawlinson, met Noyce at Delhi station. They were also met there by a Brigadier Glenny carrying test tubes and specimens who asked them to collect specimens of insects at above 16,000ft (4,860m), where there was no visible means of support for them. Rawlinson promptly took charge of the insect gathering.

They reached Ranikhet where Mrs. Browne, the local secretary of the Himalayan Club, again provided advice and assistance with provisions, equipment and porters, despite having been in hospital for most of the year with a broken leg. They waited most of the following day for their luggage to arrive from the train then packed the loads for the porters, who had already turned up. That night they had the first encounter with the bugs that bite. Noyce tried to sleep in a sleeping bag on the lawn but was forced inside by voracious insects.

On 26th May the bus and the porters arrived at 6.00 and they set off finally at 7.00. At Someshwar they left the bus and started to walk to Bageshwar, up a long valley to a saddle with rhododendrons and fir trees. Bageshwar was still a valley or two away and they continued for a distance and camped some twelve miles from Someshwar. Starting early the following day they reached Bageshwar at 8.00 and found the Dak Bungalow down by the river.

They decided that they would use the Dak Bungalows where possible to save their own supplies of food. The network of Dak Bungalows was originally established under the Moghuls to provide night-stops for the postal or Dak runners who carried messages throughout the country. Subsequently they were used by other travellers as rest-houses where they would find meals and accommodation. As they were by a river, Noyce could not resist a bathe.

> *A horrible saint, covered with white sand, objected to my bathing nude. He then bathed himself, uttering horrible cries. We were reluctant to breakfast off eggs fried, tho' Ian liked the contrast. Anyway it was a superb bathe.*[7]

They then carried on up the valley and camped short of Kapkot. It was cooler and there were no predatory insects. Grimble tried his chanter – but not a sound came out! The following day, 28th May, they continued up the river valley and arrived at Kapkot in time for breakfast, then pushed on to Loharket which, at 5,700ft (1,730m), was high above the river and quite a sweat to reach. The Dak bungalow was available and had a *'colossal meal of rice and vegetable, and tea and tea and tea and tea'*. At the shop in Loharket, they bought some sugar and cigarettes for the

Sketch map of the second trip to Garhwal.

porters. They wondered whether they had enough food for Sundardunga but reckoned they could get a sheep up there if necessary. The following day they went up to a pass at nearly 9,500ft (2,900m). This gave them their first view of the snows. From there it was a 3,000-foot descent to the tumultuous torrent of the Pindari River and the beginning of the Sundardunga Valley. At the bottom they went on a couple of miles farther and stopped to camp under a threatening sky.

It rained all night and the morning of 30th May was misty. It cleared gradually and the peaks at the end of the deep valley made a magnificent sight. With the mists swirling around them they seemed to be at 30,000ft (9,000m). They started at 7.00 and contoured round the inlets and gullies and reached Jaitoli at 13.00, too soon to camp. Despite the almost continuous rain they pushed on and came to a torrent at 16.00 and camped. Grimble put his kilt on and *'swathed in a Scottish misty dampness sniffed the air, as my grandfather had sniffed it* [at Ffestiniog] *and said, "This is the place." It reminded us too well of home. A great hatred of the sun and a longing for the coldest and dankest spaces of the world is likely to come upon British exiles in hot places.'* Grimble slept in the small and leaky tent, having found his spot under a rock too misty.

The valley path became more difficult. The map was wrong and instead of getting to Sundardunga, 10,700ft (3,250m) at breakfast time, having started at 6.45, they reached it at 15.00. They camped in pleasant pasture land. Rawlinson and Noyce did some reconnoitring up the valley towards Sukeram and Grimble bought a sheep so that they had *'sumptuous liver and kidney and heart – a huge gorge it seemed after no meat for a week'.* Once again it rained in the night.

The following day Noyce and Rawlinson did a reconnaissance farther up the valley. The rain started and they found shelter under a rock, *'…where Rawlinson produced his diary and composed "Thoughts under a Boulder at 12,000ft". A determined person,'* wrote Noyce. Later they found a colossal boulder providing great shelter on a steep valley side at 13,000ft (3,950m). They decided to make this their advanced base. They climbed another 600ft hoping to see the Sukeram Glacier and returned to the camp at 16.00. Grimble cooked more of the sheep but unfortunately upset the pot of wild rhubarb.

On 2nd June they eventually sent two porters back to Sundardunga to bring food back up from Loharket. The rest continued up to the advanced Base campsite which they reached at 9.45. The route was partly in a snow-filled valley where they had to cut steps for the less well-equipped porters – some were in tennis shoes. After breakfast on mutton they said farewell to Grimble who had to go back down. Three porters went with him as the main carrying was now finished. Rawlinson and Noyce went up towards the peaks on the south side of the valley. They reached a ridge and emerged out of cloud into the sun. They were at 16,000ft (4,860m) and the south rim of the Nanda Devi basin was across in front of them, *'white with the most beautiful of hills'*. Exhilarated they raced back to camp in an hour but unfortunately the porters had failed to find the mutton hidden in the snow and so they ate rice and raisins for supper. Rawlinson was too tired to eat much.

They started gently on 3rd June at 9.00 and took the path to the glacier snout, all dirty and unstable, then went up the lateral moraine on the right. There was grass just below it and there they set up two tents and had a restful afternoon as the snow came and they spent the time writing. That night there was more snow and thunder and the smaller tent in which they had both been sleeping had collapsed. Early the following morning it was fine but as they started at 10.00 the mist came down. They crossed the Sukeram Glacier and followed a moraine in what they believed was the direction of Simsaga. They reached a small col at about 16,500ft (5,000m) in mist and snow. Rawlinson got out a Japanese Tommy cooker and started to boil some rice but after fifty-five minutes it was not cooked but they ate it just the same! From this point they could see the whole of the Southern Rim and the peaks that they wished to explore. They were able to plan a higher camp and to look at possible routes up Simsaga after which they returned to camp just after the porters arrived with wood and the snow then started again.

The snow had stopped by the morning. Two porters, Gunturia and Kalba, were kitted out to go with Noyce and Rawlinson and they all left at 9.30, in mist, and reached the small col at 13.00. They continued up and reached an altitude of 17,050ft (5,200m) at 14.15 and there they decided to camp and made a snow platform for the tent. The Dhotiyals came on slowly, being unused to such heights but assisted in establishing the camp. They then went back down to bring up more food the following day in case a higher camp was needed.

The problem facing the climbers was how to get from the *'glacier on to the plateau supporting the sweeping Simsaga ridge'*. The concern was that they had done no reconnaissance. Rawlinson went to sleep at 18.00 and had scarcely eaten, so Noyce was left alone to survey the mountain when the mist cleared later in the evening, and was uncertain whether their approach would work.

On 6th June they got off at 6.15. It was hard frozen snow and they made good progress until they got to the line that they had seen. They found a way round to the plateau under some seracs and by 8.00 they were under the real ridge. It was a laborious haul up to the top of the ridge, which they reached at 9.30 and from here the top seemed very close. Fifteen minutes later they started, in snow waist-deep along the ridge, then noticed a rock line which went from the upper glacier to right under the summit. The snow made for an easy crossing of the glacier until they reached the small *'bergschrunds guarding the final face'*. Breathing through the heavy snow was difficult and *'…in an odd mental complete aberration I suggested leaving behind the rope – 150ft and certainly very heavy, and carrying most of it round me – Geoffrey very scornful. We stopped for glucose. He ate nothing all day, swallowed occasional bits of glucose.'* The bergschrunds repulsed them the first time and finally Noyce tunnelled in and got above them and moved towards the rocks, clearing snow and chipping steps. The rocks were worse, being plastered with snow and only sticking out in places. They reached the right-hand lower summit at 13.00:

> *By now the old mist closed and snow for the rest of the afternoon. Peep over summit, an appalling drop into mist valley below, and a swaying misty ridge, which we had thought a walk, connecting with main summit. Ridge only 150 yards but brittle and slight cornice both sides, and always going in. Much swearing – and I committed dreadful incompetencies to deserve it. Geoffrey said he saw the other peak to the right, which we feared higher, just below us. Arrived top nearly 14.00 – and off pretty anxiously, axes started to sing and thunder in the distance.*[8]

They descended the other side of the rocks, Rawlinson sliding quite a bit of the way. The tracks of their ascent were largely already obliterated in the continuing snow. They stopped once or twice on steep and uncomfortable snow to collect the necessary insect specimens and reached the camp at 17.45 noting that the two porters had returned. The snow stopped and the mist cleared – it was very calm. Rawlinson heated water and Noyce ate a sardine. Then they packed up the camp and went down to Camp 1 arriving at 19.30, a long fourteen-plus hour day.

They had been very lucky with this climb. The weather had been reasonable and they had found a route quite quickly, despite having seen the mountain only three times through the mist and cloud. Neither Noyce nor Rawlinson had crampons, unthinkable now, and they ended up with painful, pumpkin faces from the effects of the sun, snow and wind. In addition they were less than two weeks from Delhi and had hardly acclimatised. It was a remarkable achievement.

On 7th June they went down to the Base Camp under the boulder and had an easy day. The following day they went up to Maiktoli, north of Sundardunga, just under the Southern Rim, and camped. On 9th June they continued and reached the moraine which they followed until they found a suitable boulder at 12.45 at the head of the glacier and moraine. There they camped as Noyce had stomach-ache and Rawlinson's face was very painful. 10th June was Rawlinson's last full day and they made an Alpine start under the moon and reached the col between South Maiktoli peak, 19,430ft (5,900m) and the Maiktoli peak, 21,800ft (6,625m) on the Southern Rim at 9.00. While Rawlinson collected bugs for Brigadier Glenny around the col, Noyce continued up the south peak to about 18,400ft (5,600m). He descended and together they went down to Camp I. The porters by this time had reached them and so they packed up and moved quickly down to Maiktoli, where they regaled themselves and '*ate lordly of bully beef and rice – first since 9 a.m. – and looked up towards our col – which we named Rawlinson-Noyce for want of a better one.*'

The next day Rawlinson left at 9.00 with two porters who were to come back from Sundardunga with more provisions. Noyce had easy day and on 12th June left with Gunturia and Kalba for the South Maiktoli peak. They reached 16,000ft (4,860m) and had just made camp when it started to snow. The porters went back down and Noyce spent an anxious night listening to thunder and avalanches.

On 13th June Noyce woke at 3.30 and set off at 4.30 on a very cold moonlit morning. To keep warm he had to keep moving. It was a long slog up the final slopes, skirting the crevasses, and he reached the summit of Maiktoli at 9.15. It was a narrow ridge with a sheer drop to the Sundardunga Valley and astonishing views all round, the peaks of Nanda Devi, Nanda Devi East, Maiktoli and Simsaga and beyond, possibly Trisul.

He descended in cloud to the col then reached the camp, just before 11.00, where the two porters Gunturia and Zudgir were arriving from below. The three of them struck the tent and continued down reaching Maiktoli at 13.25.

They carried on down to Jaitoli then went up the Pindar River to reach Dwali on 16th June; then rather than stop there Noyce pushed on, preferring to keep moving, to a campsite one and a half miles farther on, at 10,700ft (3,250m). It had become cloudy and a little rain fell – not a good omen. On 17th June they got off at 9.30 and arrived at the last water at 12.30 just under the moraine and set up camp. It started to rain and they retired to the tents. At 13.15 Noyce set off up the moraine to do a reconnaissance at which point the rain started again. He turned back at 15.10 at 13,600ft (4,130m) when it started to snow. He eventually got back to camp at 16.10 where everything was already soaked. By 18.00 further operations had become impossible. The porters wisely took refuge in a cave while Noyce stayed in his tent.

After a night of rain and spending the entire time dodging the drips Noyce woke at 6.30 on 18th June and left at 8.40 for the Pindari Needles. He climbed over new snow, with avalanches booming from the cliffs all round, to a col between the smallest, which he called 'Little Finger', and the other, larger needles. The crossing of the first larger needle was difficult and eventually Noyce arrived at another col below the biggest needles at 12.30. He tried these and was stopped by a wall of loose rock that would have been difficult even with ropes. Back down to the col and up the Little Finger with 400ft of *'really good rock climbing'* to the top at about 15,400ft (4,680m). The snow then started again and he returned to the base of the needle where he had left rucksack and ice-axe and then it was on down by a different way – another adventure.

Noyce arrived at camp at 16.00. It was still raining and snowing and they packed the tent and set off for the comparative luxury of the Phurkia Dak Bungalow where they arrived at 18.30.

19th June. After a breakfast of chapattis and porridge at 5.45 Noyce set off, again on his own, at 6.30 for the glacier. It was dirty with plenty of crevasses and he reached the second ice-fall. He realised then that he should not have gone so far on his own, and turned back at 12.20 at 14,600ft (4,440m). On his way down he felt that, after the 'lethargy' of the day before, he was so fit and rather than going straight down he followed the contour of the valley and enjoyed the meadows and the yellows and blues of the flowers, the birds, especially swallows, and the buzzing of the bumble bees, arriving at Burkina at 16.35. The sun was out so he had a bathe in the stream '*...which made me feel far better, and a real hero.*

A tremendous thankfulness, after the last climb, that I have been allowed so much, and been kept so safe. Bed by 8.30, over the Ring and the Book.'

On 20th June the trek back started. Meanwhile on his way to a small diversion up the Dwali Valley, a tributary of the Pindar, he met some US airmen on their way to Pindari. The Dwali Valley was jungle lower down then very stony higher up providing cavernous shelters for shepherds and their flocks. He reached the highest shelter at 12.55 from which he could see high peaks. On the way down he discovered that he had lost his watch. He returned to the last point where he had looked at his watch then started down again – and found the watch looking up at him from a dock-leaf; '...*there must be a divinity protecting people who are idiotic with their belongings,*' he reflected.

They continued down to Dhakuri and the chowkidar of the bungalow appeared and said that neither Rawlinson nor Grimble had paid their dues. As their names were not in the book, Noyce paid. In fact the other two had paid but to an old man – who clearly did not pass the money on!

That evening Noyce had supper with his porters, the Dhotiyals, and later the children of the village and was able to learn more about their way of life. The Dhotiyals, like the Sherpas, who are Bhotias, are from Nepal and apparently of lower status. As porters they received a lower wage, one rupee and eight annas a day, as opposed to up to five rupees a day for a Sherpa. Unlike the Sherpas they will not eat with the sahibs, nor will they drink tea from the same pot as the sahibs, or water from a water-bottle 'polluted' by others, even when very thirsty. With a mixed group of porters the Sherpas would always cook and provide personal services, but when they had gone the Dhotiyals quite happily and competently took over. Their religious scruples are reinforced in the winter which they spend with their families in their villages and the priests have a greater hold on them. When they are away in summer they maintain strict religious observances. They require fire to make their chapattis daily and thus are unhappy above the snow-line. They were normally bare-footed and this made it hard for them in snow so Noyce provided footwear when he could. They were porters and still are for Himalayan expeditions and in 1944 200 of them were with the Fifth Indian Division in the campaign in the north-east of India after the Battle of Imphal. They were not as adaptable as the Gurkhas who had accompanied General Bruce on early Himalayan expeditions or the Sherpas one associates mainly with Himalayan exploits now. Noyce believed that the Dhotiyals were quite as good as the others for the lower expeditions. His lead porter Gunturia was very good in all aspects of the operation and looked after Noyce very well.

Noyce, himself, developed a very high regard for the Dhotiyals. He expressed a deep feeling for the lead porter:

> *I have fallen completely in love with Gunturia, and with all Dhotiyals in their degree. I would do him any good: what can I? Absurd to lift him out of the truly happy and carefree life which he has won – an orphan from a Nepal village – for himself. Absurd to lead him to the plains. Better to salute him in passing, and buy him a new hookah – for theirs broke.*[10]
>
> *I had not believed it possible to feel affection so strong, suddenly, for so improbable a person and one with whom I could converse but so brokenly.*[11]

Again Noyce had set out on this trip to see if he could live off the country in the way the locals did. It had brought him into closer contact with them. The group ate dal porridge, atta and bought rice, sheep and *sabzi*, greens, as they went. This was supplemented by tins of cheese and jam. In the high camps and on climbing days they used tins of bully beef and sardines.

Aircrew Mountain Centre, Kashmir

The period in Kashmir was a different experience for Noyce. It was an opportunity to develop his instructing skills and to encourage in others his own enthusiasm and pleasure in the mountains. By July 1944 he was bored with life in Annand Parbat so was delighted to accept the invitation of Tony Smyth, now a Wing-Commander and the doyen of RAF mountaineers in India, to be the Chief Instructor at the Aircrew Centre which he was setting up in Kashmir.

He was bidden to go to Srinagar, the capital of Kashmir. He took the train to Rawalpindi, local transport to Murree then walked the four miles to the RAF station at Lower Topa, which was the initial muster point for the Centre. The authorities there knew nothing about him. He was dismayed by the camp:

'Everything about it centres you to the camp, the football, dance, tennis, concert, tombola, raffle, cinema...an infinite list,' he wrote to Ian Grimble on 23rd August.

> *Today walked into Murree this morning (it's astonishing, the sensation of being able to walk again) & quite pleasant pine country. Earliest bus on 25th and the equipment is going up on the 27th. So now: my main duty seems to look when I arrive less like a skeleton than it seems I look now. The instructor cannot arrive in the feebleness which the train journey produces!*

Clearly the hours worked and oppressive climate in Delhi left the code-breakers in the same condition as the aircrew.

The actual Rehabilitation Centre base was to be at Ganderbal some ten miles north-east of Srinagar, in the Vale of Kashmir. Noyce and Smyth went up to Srinagar on 26th August and on to Ganderbal, 'the Base Camp', a collection of house-boats on a small quiet stretch of water. Noyce was astonished and impressed at the amount of equipment that had been collected. There were ropes, ice-axes and boots with clinker nails, that were unobtainable in Delhi. The equipment was stored on shore and it included everything "*to make life creature-comfortable in the mountains*". They had quantities of American mountain rations, including chewing gum and cigarettes. For expeditions American shelter-halves were to be used. It was an idyllic spot, surrounded by green fields and orchards with snow-capped mountains in the background.

The main activity camp was established in tents at Sonamarg, at 9,000ft (2,700m), some fifty miles north-east of Srinagar in the valley of the Sind, a tributary of the Jhelum. It is twelve miles short of the Zoji La, the pass into Ladakh, or Little Tibet. This was an important thoroughfare for the caravans of dzoes, a cross between a cow and a yak, and mules into Ladakh and beyond. At that time it was also used as a secondary supply route for military supplies for China.

Their initial tasks were to investigate the possibilities for rock-climbing and mountaineering. Two mountaineers also serving in the RAF, Gordon Whittle and Harry Tilly, who were already in Kashmir, had done some reconnoitring and found some suitable areas. These Noyce explored with them and discovered a number of unexplored valleys and unclimbed peaks, entirely appropriate for the programme. They found an ideal area for rock-climbing, the Thajiwas Valley and they established a camp there

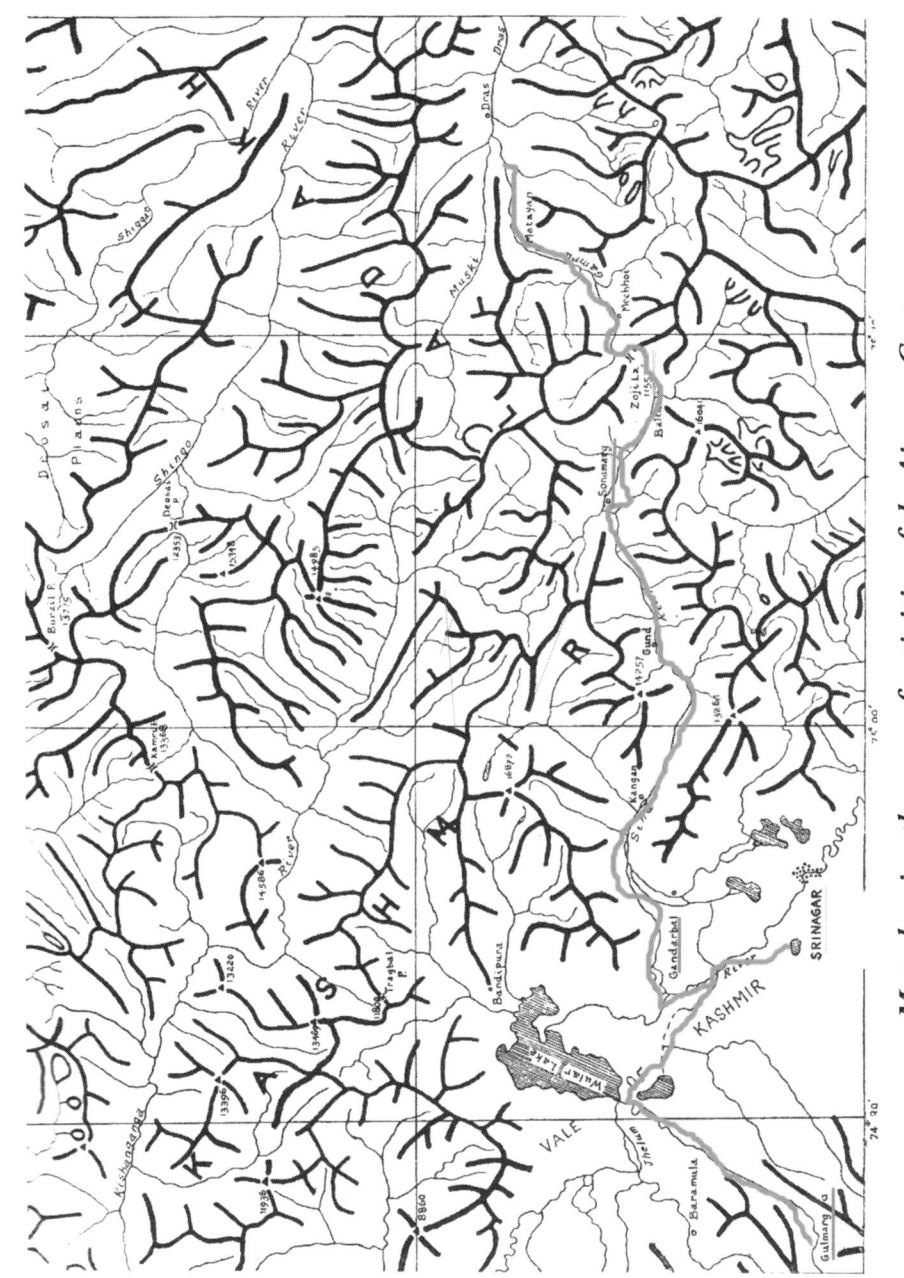

Map showing the area of activities of the Aircrew Centre.

at 11,000ft (3,700m) in a big marquee as the main base for activities. It was an hour's walk from the 'best buttress' and an hour and a half from the nearest glacier.

Noyce comfortingly, as ever, compared the area with his Welsh Hills and familiar parts of the Alps and his correspondence kept him in close touch with home.

The instructors had planned the routes and the expeditions and awaited with some anxiety the first arrivals. They were uncertain whether the diet of hard physical activity in the mountains was what was expected or desired by the crews. Noyce had still his own reservations on using the mountains as part of the war effort, as he had had in North Wales in 1942.

The courses were for eleven participants and lasted three weeks. At the beginning of the course they were weighed and subjected to a 'pack test' for five minutes to check their fitness and capacity. They were also weighed at the end. The members of the first course had all been drafted and appear to have arrived expecting a relaxing holiday on the houseboats on Dal Lake. The instructors had to tread carefully in order to reconcile the objectives of the Centre with the preconceived notions of the early participants. There were very few volunteers on the next three courses. The remark heard on rock, *"to think that people do this for fun"*, was typical of a number. Notwithstanding *'the crews played up remarkably well to our plans. The Nichinai, Saribal and Amarnath valleys were explored with the shelter-halves, sometimes in wintry weather and they also went over the Zoji La to Dras, the first village in Ladakh, where they met Tibetans and Ladakhis.'* The enthusiasm grew with the camps, the expeditions, the cooking, the marmots and a greater appreciation of the mountain scenery and those who gained a living there. By the end of September Noyce wrote,

> *Feel much more optimistic about airmen's reaction to hills after this last show. We really must not push our ideas at them: let them come with general stuff.*

By the fifth course, which consisted of those who enjoyed the mountains, but were not necessarily climbers, a policy had developed that the courses should provide for both climbers and trekkers. Whittle and Tilly would take parties into the drier and higher Ladakh. Tilly with two Australians climbed a peak of 17,061ft (5,150m) near Amarnath,

Whittle and Stokoe found 'Cumberland Peak' of 17,150ft (5,200m). Noyce himself with a party went into Ladakh in September to a side-valley to the south of Matayan. From a meadow camp below the glacier he and another instructor reached 17,400ft (5,300m) on a 17,871ft peak.

As the season advanced the powdery snow on the higher ridges made the use of shelter-halves more hazardous, but some of the 15,000ft (4,500m) peaks around the Thajiwas Valley were still accessible. The exploration possibilities were huge and Noyce compared them, in an article in the *Alpine Journal* vol. LV, to the Alps in the early golden days. *'Very roughly if you take 3,000 feet off the height of a Kashmir peak, you seem to get its equivalent for conditions in the Alps.'*

Noyce maintained all this time a prolific correspondence and acknowledged parcels of books and letters received from Delhi and Britain. He writes to Ian Grimble *'letter from Mrs Gridley,* [his and Grimble's landlady in Bedford, who lost both her children in the bombing.] *She would be remembered. A small son now and they're still at Bedford.'*[12]

Vacant of ideas. Yesterday raced on, when the others went back to a hill above: sunset beat me by 5 minutes. But I just gawped at the still frosty unreality of wonderful peaks, seen by me alone and what do they mean to me? What also does it mean to me that you couldn't be here to share it, and would it have been less unearthly, of another world?'

To know of only two Verities, yourself and the hill you climb. So I loitered the last few feet, wishing they would go on.[13]

On both the mountain courses that Noyce had instructed all ranks mixed in together. In both cases it worked very well. He is moved to write, *'I think you of all people broke down the last bit of snobismus in me – the feeling of 'officers & men' which I ought to have got over in the Guards, but clearly hadn't. It's gone now. And if ever it remained two most loveable serjeant instructors and helpers here would dispel it.'*[14]

The Thajiwas camp closed on 9th November and Sonamarg was cut off by a heavy snowfall on 12th November. A party under John Hansbury, an RAF sergeant instructor, had been in Ladakh and had great difficulty in coming over the Zoji La pass back to the Sonamarg camp. Shortly after that they dismantled the camp and retreated to Srinagar.

> *First of all, on the 12th the snow came. Came all afternoon to Sonamarg & much of the night we spent sweeping snow off the tents & repairing cracked tent-poles – which went like matches. I haven't seen such a weight in so short a time.*
>
> *So we are cut off by road & started taking down tents before the next fall. Tony Smyth got a truck up to within 2 miles on the 14th – & overturned it. We had a party over in Ladakh & on the 15th he and I went to Baltal, the first stage & made the Zoji La pass, which is 11,578 feet. We found them back [sic] under my very nice sergeant friend, John Hansbury, but having had fearful difficulties in the crossing, 2 horses slipped down an ice slope in to the river & had to be left, 2 more sank exhausted. And the lads had to be bullied on. They got in at 11.15 & of course the stuff was at the top of the pass – just under, on the stream. So I stayed on with JH at Baltal, & the last 3 days we have been up. To our astonishment 3 of the horses left had survived 2 nights at what must have been bitter temperature, and icy wind even at midday: and these are now over at Machoi on the Ladakh side & cut off for the next 15 days; the other one was dead in the stream. We brought some baggage down that day, the sleeping bags were what Tony had been anxious about: these last 2 days we have been tunnelling through a whopping snowdrift, which is piling up. Cold & it's hard to keep pace with the snow, but got all things except one, which couldn't find.*
>
> *Got back to Sonamarg this evening, and found the whole pay question for cooks and various wallahs for these months & for the last trek ponies had been left, so a frantic session & backsheesh haggle. Tomorrow we go down to Nasimbagh, & then after 3 months back to Srinagar.*[15]

Subsequently Hansbury was awarded the British Empire Medal.

The mountain camp at Sonamarg, after a hesitant start with a 'shanghaied' group, proved to be a great success in terms of climbing achievements, the return to fitness and the all-round development of the participants. Many found a love for the mountains and an enthusiasm for going high. Some because they had no previous knowledge of mountains, but with familiarity came pleasure and the desire to explore, while others wanted to extend their mountain experience. There were a quite a few who came back as instructors.

Noyce took the opportunity to create a guide to the Sonamarg area, the publication of which appears to have been a considerable challenge. He spent the rest of November and December at 24 Rest and Leave Camp, Nasimbagh, Srinagar. During this time, at the suggestion of his two flight-sergeants Noyce stayed with a Mrs. Castle who ran her house for troops on leave:

> *And well worth it, it was, for the 10/- a night that officers pay in the rising scale. Funny to be sitting in chairs again, and even more wonderful to have a radiogram, & Jack Jackson[16] (Lancashire & real gold) music keen, and the 5th, 6th, & 7th Beethoven – besides Tchaikovsky which was insisted upon by one member of the party. I realise that music is getting in among me, because I missed it so much the last 3 months & so enjoyed lying on the floor listening to it. But I'm like Aunt Julie in Howard's End, I just go on listening beatifically wondering how it can be so good.*[17]

Noyce was in regular contact with home: his parents had moved to London. Noyce wrote on 26th November to Grimble, '*Got a letter from Daddy that he is broadcasting at 8.15 Indian time on the 20th and on the 22nd. A pity. Do you know of anyone hearing it?*'

It was recognised, however, that skiing was a more obvious medium by which to introduce people to the mountains. It had a more pleasurable image. Gulmarg, 'Flower meadow', was some twenty-five miles west of Srinagar and was a favourite summer resort for those fleeing the heat of the plains. In the winter the only occupants were the *chowkidars*, the wardens. The Ski Club of India held Christmas and Easter meets in Gulmarg and had built a hut some 1,200ft higher at Khillan. The Mountain Centre would occupy the Garden School in Gulmarg – but they were unsure how habitable it would be, and they would eventually take over the Khillan hut.

Noyce wrote,

> *I am not sad to be here: truck brings you as far as Tangmarg below, whence a hot pull with load up to Gulmarg. They have taken the Garden School, which is a little beyond the Gulmarg saucer, in the woods. At present we're pretty primitive, only 4 of us here, no lighting or latrines. Put on the skis at once & spent afternoon & evening under tuition of a South American pilot officer – seems a nice chap – practising walks, turns, runs – and falls – in the garden.*[18]

Smyth prepared the buildings with a hardy Kashmiri contractor who could put up with the cold, and ordered the equipment, including 100 pairs of skis from Canada. Some of the instructors, however, including Noyce, had to learn on ones made in India. He felt strongly that skis were a means of locomotion and had the same feeling towards ski-racing as he did to race-climbing. By the end of November he was allocated a room with a spare bed: but this was occupied just before Christmas by Captain Charles Bagot, 'ski champion of India', who had been recruited as chief ski instructor.

He maintained regular contact with his friends in Delhi and at Christmas 1944 he wrote to Ian Grimble in Delhi,

I sent down, addressed to you, a parcel containing one bedspread, 4 Pashmina (woven ibex wool) scarves, & one red gauze object. It's an awful job for you the distribution. The bedspread is for Esmé,[19] the scarves are for yourself, Sir S. N.,[20] Sir John,[21] and Ikram. The red gauze object is for Soghra.[22]

Noyce's thoughts also turned to home, he wrote on 23rd December to Grimble,

Well, here is Christmas & I suppose as you say it is better in the hills. Companions are right enough (my W. O. and Flight-serjeant had to go) but it's still the Christmas of drink and horseplay a bit, & I have come more to agree with you than ever I did that Christmas is very much truly a thing of private firesides. Doing a job that satisfies much of me; the only real hardship I suffer from the war is being deprived of home & in that at least I am sharing with the front-liners.

Noyce went up to Khillan after Christmas to get some practice skiing before the courses started. On 30th December:

Heavy snowfall. Up to Khillan and plough around. The weather always skiable but not necessarily racing skiable. It's a comic assortment or cross-section of British Indian population…but only for a short time, & the hills will return to quiet.

The first ski course arrived on 4th January. There were nursery and practice slopes around Gulmarg; the Ski Club had cleared three intricate and steep runs through the 1,200ft of wood below Khillan. There were no ski-lifts and the normal way of getting to the top of a run was on a pony. Noyce eschewed the accepted approach, *'I'm acquiring a reputation – as an eccentric – for never riding a pony up and for carrying my own skis.'* The course programme was for one week on the Gulmarg slopes and the second week on the three Khillan runs; the third week was still based at Khillan but spent on more ambitious outings on the mountain of Apharwat, 13,592ft (4,131m), which might involve long hours on skis. Variations in capacity and skill kept the programme flexible and what the instructors prized most of all was enthusiasm rather than prowess. A key man in creating this enthusiasm was R. L. Holdsworth who instructed for the first six weeks at Khillan. He was greatly appreciated by those on the courses. There were still, however, some who took time to come to terms and resented being sent by government, even to *'do a thing for which most would give their eyes'*. Some would have spent all their time on the practice slopes, others painted and others just enjoyed looking at the mountains and clouds.

Noyce took over Khillan from Holdsworth and was surprised by how much the individuals were able to achieve in the three weeks, without forcing an unenjoyable pace. He admits that a number became more proficient on skis than him! *'On Apharwat and in the woods "pitches" of any steepness were found and taken straight.'*

Gradually spring came and the snow changed from powder to the more soggy variety and they had to ski early in the day or in the late afternoon. On 28th February 1945 there were huge avalanches. They tried to classify them using Seligman's *Snow Structure,* but they did not fit any category. There was a high wind and it started to blow down the mountain. The *chowkidar*, whose brother had been killed in the 1936 avalanche thought that we should evacuate to Gulmarg, which they did immediately. The hut was put out of bounds.

Noyce wrote later, *'…I don't believe I did ever tell you of Ronald suddenly appearing, being quite near an avalanche which descended over the marg* [meadows] *& wiped the Red and Blue runs, & of us all decamping to Gulmarg…. It was like home getting back here again.'* Ronald remarked on arrival, "I came up for leave, not to cope with this sort of thing." The letter also included a little vignette of Ronald and a glimpse of their relationship: *'He's on a course at Karachi. Good at getting on with people, drinks well in the mess, placidly contentified – we have got strangely little* *to say to each other in a way, though the bond of sympathy goes deeper than that. Fine to see him, & have him with me.'*[23]

When conditions improved at Khillan in early March Noyce and his team moved back and continued the courses. By this time there were many more volunteers on the courses and a greater initial enthusiasm for mountains to build upon. Tony Smyth had left the Centre in February to reconnoitre a site for another Mountain Centre in Sikkim. The terrain and weather conditions in Sikkim were unsuitable at that time for skiing but he sent a report to Delhi proposing a climbing camp there and recommended that Noyce go up with an advance party in April 'to start things off'. Charles Bagot was appointed Commanding Officer of Khillan and Gulmarg. Ronald Noyce went up to the Centre again at the beginning of March to enjoy a final two weeks' skiing with his brother.

The correspondence Noyce maintained with Britain and Delhi was prolific. And the Noyce family maintained the connection with Menlove Edwards, keeping a protective and generous eye on him. On 7th March Noyce wrote,

> *I have had Mrs Edwards' letter. The whole thing is utter disaster. Daddy says M[enlove]. wrote him, saying he'd "got into a bad mess" & would he help him out.' Also wanted my diary. It's much worse when he's a mental doctor himself & knows what it is all about. I do think though myself that it's a thing that time and a good peace and our presence may ultimately help. O dear, but what meanwhile? Prison bars.*

And later,

> *Letters from Menlove and Daddy. Menlove writes much more sanely, and Daddy gives the good news that he is to be released, from the hospital, and to live for a time with Stuart Chantrell, a friend. Daddy has been extraordinarily good and in helping him with funds: a good outlet for my surplus wealth.*[24]

He also records then that one of the great supports in Delhi, Lady Esmé Roy was leaving. She entertained well, although Noyce was not a natural party man, and sent various 'comfort' parcels up to him in Kashmir. He received a 'most lordly cake' as a parting gift.

The snow conditions were deteriorating further by mid-March,

1 *Above left: Wilfrid Noyce aged six, and Jocelyn Ronald Noyce aged four, 1923.*

2 *Above right: Wilfrid, Jocelyn and Rosemary Noyce, 1931.*

3 *Below left: Wilfrid, Jocelyn and Rosemary (later Rosalind) Noyce, 1927.*

4 *Right: In his first term at Charterhouse, October 1931.*

5 The Manods, North Wales – Noyce's first mountains.
6 Bryn Hyfryd, the Noyce family summer home at Ffestiniog.

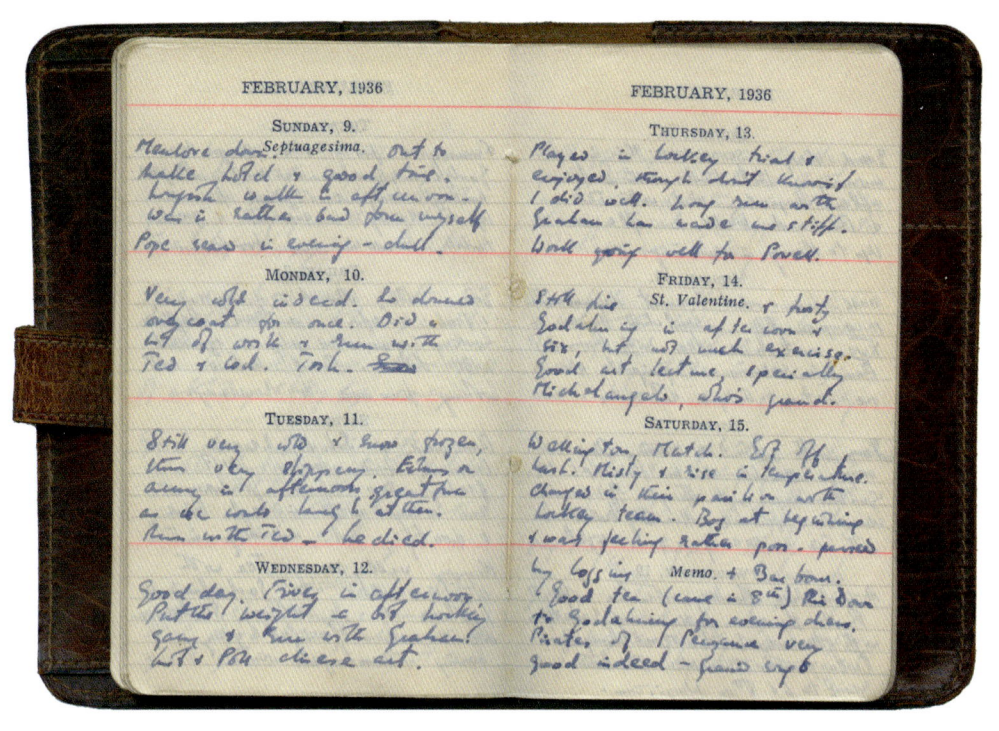

7 An extract from Noyce's diary in his last year at school. Note the mention of lunch with Menlove Edwards.

8 Wilfrid and Jocelyn Noyce at the Simmons' house at Hurtmore.

WEEKITES   SUMMER 1932.

Back row :— C.F. Rolo : O.P. Simmons : M.F. Burness : A.C.S. Julins : G.G.D. : C.M. Craig : C.W.F. Noyce.
G.E. Mosley : R.E. Heaton : P.D.A. Clarke : R.H.A. Lee : N.I. Dalgliesh : D. Caddy.

2nd Row :— C.S. Rolo : T.A. Scrutton : J.S. Bell : M.S. Godson : J.A. Trapman : R.D. Bowen : S.P. Coulson :
E.J. Knapp : M.A. Clarke : O.C.S. Lamb : A.W. Godfrey : M.L. Taylor : J.R. Briggs : R.E. Greene.

3rd Row :— F.R. Ward : L.M. Swinbank : D.M. Mulgan : J.R.M. Pilling : I.R.S. Gordon : K.H.F. Bower :
D.W. Iyer : E.T. Channell : D.C. McPherson : D. Powell : J.G. Hooper : T.F. Smith : T.J. Gooch.

Sitting :— J.T. Burness : J.C. Moss : W.F. Moss : H.P. Jameson Esq. : J.D. Lambert : Self : A.J.M. Smythe.

Sitting on ground :— J.D. Clewes : R.J.K. Burnham : D.G. Hannah : M.S. Gordon : J. Pharoside :
A.R. Skeggs : G.E. John : M.D. King.

9 Far left, top: The Weekite house photograph – summer 1932. Noyce at centre back. Paul 'Ted' Simmons is second from left in back row.

10 Left: Charterhouse 1935. Frank Fletcher teaching the Classical VI. Noyce is in the back row at the end on the right.

11 Top left: Leading on Belle Vue Bastion, Tryfan 1935.

12 Top right: Leading on Tryfan 1935.

13 Right: Leading on Lliwedd 1936.

14 Top left: At Newton's Farm, Girton, 1936.

15 Top right: Noyce at the Close, Girton, 1936.

16 Left: 2/Lt Wilfrid Noyce KRRC, 1941.

17 Below: Noyce on Trisul, 1943.

18 *Signal Intelligence Officers at the WEC, Delhi July 1944. Wilfrid Noyce is third from left in front row.*

19 *David Gould on summit of Chamian Sankar, Garhwal 1943, note the solar topee.*

20 *With the Dhotiyals, Garhwal, 1943.*

21 *Gyalgin near summit on first peak, 1943.*

> *...a fall of "brown snow" making the whole mountain a dirty yellow colour & sticky, hot, avalanchy. Ski Club members are beginning to arrive for the Easter Meet, making the "affairs of Khillan" more of a full-time job and we are not sure even how long we shall be allowed to stay. It's fun though trying to run the place,*

and further on, disdainful as ever of sickness,

> *As for feeling better: I have apparently been having jaundice this past fortnight – in fact since Ronald came. Did feel a bit dithery on the practice slope for 2 days, but by the time the Doc saw it had cleared sufficiently... I carried on – in fact climbed Agharwat twice with no ill-effect. Silly but I feel jolly lucky to have got off so lightly.*[25]

All this time the future of the Mountain Centre and Noyce himself were under discussion both in Delhi and at the headquarters of British Forces in Asia in Ceylon. Noyce clearly was enjoying his role and hoped that the Centre would continue or at least he could go to Sikkim. He was, however, still having doubts about it, *'I don't know what to do or think or judge best. Could I honestly go on with this with a clear conscience?'* He was getting enthusiastic letters from Professor Pigou, his Cambridge sponsor, saying what a grand job he was doing and urging him to continue. In a letter to Ian Grimble on 21st March he quotes a letter from Geoffrey Winthrop Young,

> *I expect you are doing the <u>better</u> work in your present job. No, in war, one has to go where one is sent, and it's no use comparing the relative danger or demerit of jobs as they are allocated to one. That's just luck, or providence, for those of us who don't intrigue or wire-pull. Yours is a good work and worth doing for itself as well as for future guidance. I'd stick to it ... Tony Smyth probably wants you badly. But I don't know why I give you all of this of myself, I always <u>do</u> seem to, but as Marcia says one of the joys of having a friend is that he is a person one <u>can</u> let off steam to, and who doesn't mind.*

Marcia was Geoffrey Winthrop Young's daughter and earlier in the month had written to Noyce to say how happy she was.

At the same time he announced, *"My job as old man of the mountain is ended: whether or no for good I don't know. Now I have taken opportunity to ship down to Srinagar for the Guide – and try to help organise equipment for Gordon Whittle, who has taken over the job on the Himalayan Committee."* He was still hoping, however, that there would be a job either at Sonamarg or in Sikkim.

A week later, as he wrote to Ian Grimble, he was expecting the arrival of Watson, an officer from Delhi, to inform them whether the Centre was to continue in Sonamarg or Sikkim. In the event Watson did not come, but Noyce talked to one Squadron-Leader Symonds *'who accompanied Tony to Sikkim. He has just come from Delhi & says the WEC authorities have asked for me back.'* Noyce's contact in Ceylon HQ *'...can't help because of the terms of the original agreement (with Brigadier Harris I suppose) under which I was allowed to come. The situation has of course altered a good deal since then. It looks as if the thing to do might well be to come down & say so in person to the high-ups.'*

He became more and more pleased with his role and with the success of the operation. Course 5 was really the first course with mainly volunteers and had set a new level of expectation for the instructors which became more and more justified. He wrote on 28th March,

> *I'm really bucked with the aircrew skiers – some of the later bunches are as nice as course 5 & extremely efficient. Took a party up the mountain yesterday, down the other side to Limian & a long slog back. They took it without a murmur, a 10½ hour day, & one actually went in for the races to-day.*
>
> *I have caused a flutter by not going for the races today. Made up my mind after the Christmas ones & it only needed sticking to. Different people get different things out of skiing: to me it's largely a means to an end (as a form of locomotion) a means which must be mastered, as I want to teach others to master it, to get to the end. And on this spring snow sometimes it's delightful. But ski-racing if you take that view is a crime like climb-racing.*

Despite his modesty and antipathy to ski-racing, the strong impression is given that Noyce by then was a very competent skier.

At the beginning of April there were still no clear decisions and he was advised that the original agreement would stand. He was not banking on Sikkim, which in any case was not likely to be before June 1945.

He wrote to Grimble on 4th April, inter alia, '*The Doc tells me your knowledge of Gaelic is remarkable considering the time. That's really pleasing. We had, by the way, a Scotch [sic] lad who persisted quite a long time in skiing in a kilt: but even he flagged.*' Then later, from the main base, Nasimbagh, Srinagar,

> *…took the last course down from Khillan this morning. But as I said I'm so lucky here that if there is anything really wanting doing I shall do it and indeed I am too lucky. I don't see but how some Nemesis must be waiting round the corner to strike soon.*
>
> *Well, the last crew is down, no more ski instructing a while, but looking back on it, there have been some good times and surprisingly good people. I think at last I was beginning to get the hang of putting it over.*

Noyce stayed in Srinagar until the end of April and he made efforts to advance his **Guide to Sonamarg.** He was refused permission to print it in Srinagar. The enterprise he had entrusted it to, Vasant Art, were not able to import the proper paper for the guide. He then sent it down in its half-finished state to Co Cooke, printers in Delhi. He asked Ian Grimble to see Cooke and to involve Gordon Whittle who by now was back in Delhi and had become a member of the Himalayan Committee.

On 13th April he writes,

> *Life has been brightened further by two very beautiful pictures of Marcia, for which I've managed to find a travelling frame, and a telegram from Rosemary announcing that she has got scholarships at both Oxford and Cambridge, and chose Oxford, chiefly I think because she was so taken with L.M.H. [Lady Margaret Hall] & the classical don in particular.*
>
> *I too am very glad its Oxford, but wrote off at once beseeching her natheless to give up classics. Not that it will have effect. I feel at present there's almost not <u>time</u> for classics, & that she would get most out of languages or English. But I am most awfully bucked about the scholarship. A letter from Daddy at the same time sounded doubtful about whether she would even get in.*

Noyce's independence of thought comes through again. He clearly was not sorry to have given up his Classics in favour of Modern Languages.

In his last letter to Ian Grimble from Srinagar, '*Mummy, Rosemary & her friend really are going up to Prof's* [Pigou] *in August. Things should be quieter then. The war in Europe is over.*' And he expressed guilt for enjoying the cool climate of Kashmir while others, particularly IG are in the heat of Delhi. '*Kashmir is beautiful: I would you were here, golly how much I wish it.*'[26]

He had, however, now instructed, in a formal sense, on two mountain meets. He had developed these skills in an informal but very important way with the novices on the meets of the CUMC in North Wales and Scotland. The first formal occasion was on John Hunt's Mountain Warfare School, in North Wales. In the case of the CUMC, they were all enthusiasts, in the Mountain Warfare School there were military objectives. In Kashmir there were those who were drafted, mainly at the beginning, and the enthusiastic volunteers. The objectives were to rehabilitate and enthuse the participants and to enable them to enjoy the recreational opportunities provided by mountains. The approach was gentle and liberal. Coercion would have defeated the objectives and the personalities of the instructors and the enthusiasm of those who already enjoyed the mountains brought the others along with them.

That experience may not have been the choice of all the participants but many more than one would expect would feel it was a beneficial period both physically and morally and one they would remember with pleasure.

> *For the opening of the hill gateway to men of the services Aircrew Mountain Centre deserves a very high mark. At the risk of spoiling hills – a risk run by William Shakespeare at every School Certificate examination – it showed men mountains and their recreational power. They, like Shakespeare, are large enough to defy such a risk. It brought the horse to water and resisting the possible kick, demonstrated that the water was good. It takes much wisdom in the horseman to see which horse needs the drink, and the problem of selecting the thirsty could not be solved by wholesale methods. Their number may be greater than we first suspected. But it does not include all men.*[27]

Wilfrid Noyce was recalled to the Wireless Experimental Centre in Delhi in May 1945 and was wondering if he would get another opportunity to get into the mountains before returning to Britain.

Sikkim 1945 – Pauhunri

By September 1945 hostilities were over and so Noyce was able to squeeze in another summit before he returned to Britain. He had reached 20,000ft on Simsaga and now wished to go even higher and had his eyes on a peak, Pauhunri, of 23,385ft (7,127m), on the Sikkim–Tibet border. He invited Angtharkay, a Sherpa of considerable experience to join him.

Angtharkay was born and brought up in Khumbu, in Eastern Nepal and later moved to Darjeeling. His first expedition was to Kanchenjunga in 1931. He was with Hugh Ruttledge, Eric Shipton and Frank Smythe on Everest in 1933; in 1935 he was with Eric Shipton and Bill Tilman on the Everest reconnaissance. On the last occasion he had with him Tenzing Norgay, on his first trip to Everest. Eighteen years later, Tenzing reached the summit of Everest on 29th May 1953 with Sir Edmund Hillary. In 1938 Angtharkay was on Everest again with Tilman, Smythe and Shipton when he was Sirdar for the first time.

Noyce had no European companions this time but he could not have had better support. He was, however, for the first time, worried if he was fit enough and that he was not suffering from any ailments.

After various changes of date, finally on 8th September he took the train from Delhi to Calcutta feeling that, *'the "lone-handedness" does increase my mettle, and make me determined to do it if it can be done'*. In Calcutta he booked the Grand Hotel for his return and discovered more equipment, which happened to be stored at the museum, and realised he need not have brought so much from Delhi.

Then, feeling immensely grateful for all those who had helped him, he took the night train from Calcutta to Siliguri, some 275 miles north, where the Himalaya rise vertically from the plain. He arrived in the early morning of 10th September. He took a taxi to the first landslip on the road to Gangtoks and walked the half-mile round it on a jungly precipice. His truck from Gangtok was on the other side and he reached the Sikkim border post at Rangpo at 12.45, where *'to my astonishment, I found passes, native policeman and salute, and everything set'*. Shortly beyond Rangpo there was another landslide and another truck beyond it which eventually got him to Gangtok. Angtharkay arrived shortly afterwards. They were greatly encouraged by a moderately rare view of Kanchenjunga, the third highest mountain in the world, 28,200ft (8,587m) and Pandim 21,950ft (6,684m) to the north-west on the Nepal–Sikkim border.

Sikkim is a country of steep valleys and rivers and the towns are either in the valleys – like Rangpo, or on the crests like Gangtok. The roads run along the valleys and the high towns are usually approached by a steep and sinuous road. In 1945 the roads were, at best, difficult beyond Gangtok and they would have to walk the rest of the way to Pauhunri. They had loads for seven porters, one of whom was a small woman who went bare-footed with a colossal pack, *'making me ashamed of my manlihood'*.

They set off on 11th September, at 10.00, in sun and cloud and went up to the Penlong La, at 6,240ft (1,900m), then down to the Teesta Valley and along over a huge landslide to Dikchu at 2,010ft. The leeches had started to attack and there were mosquitoes. Not surprisingly Noyce was very concerned that the mosquitoes were malarial.

The following day they started along the flat of the Teesta Valley then climbed up to Mangang, with views of cliffs and waterfalls that became more impressive as they made their way up to Singhik, 4,480ft (1,364m), and the Dak Bungalow. They rested there and Noyce wrote letters and was worried that he would succumb *'ignominiously'* to some disease. He was *'still in a funk'* about mosquitoes and malaria but Angtharkay said it was the last place for mosquitoes so he left the net there. Then over the next two days they battled with landslides and leeches and reached Lachung.

Noyce went to look at the village of Lachung. Prayer-flags and inscriptions and everyone was eating the large red local apples; Noyce thought that they were very, very hard. *'Many small children demanding backsheesh – who on earth has taught them?'* and they did not look very healthy with sores around their mouths.

On 15th September when the mist rolled back they had a view of an 18,000-ft (5,500m) peak opposite. They left Lachung and went up a track bordered by hedges and flowers. By mid-morning the rain started. The porters put on matting over their heads and loads and *'looked like beetles'*, the track became a quagmire and they arrived at Yumthang Rest House and it carried on raining all afternoon.

Angtharkay produced pineapple fritters for supper. He was a very capable cook and produced a wide range of dishes. On arrival he always attended to the needs of his sahibs, with tea and food, before taking his own boots off. It always impressed Noyce how the Sherpas, after a long hard day, would still dig platforms, erect tents and make tea before taking a rest themselves.

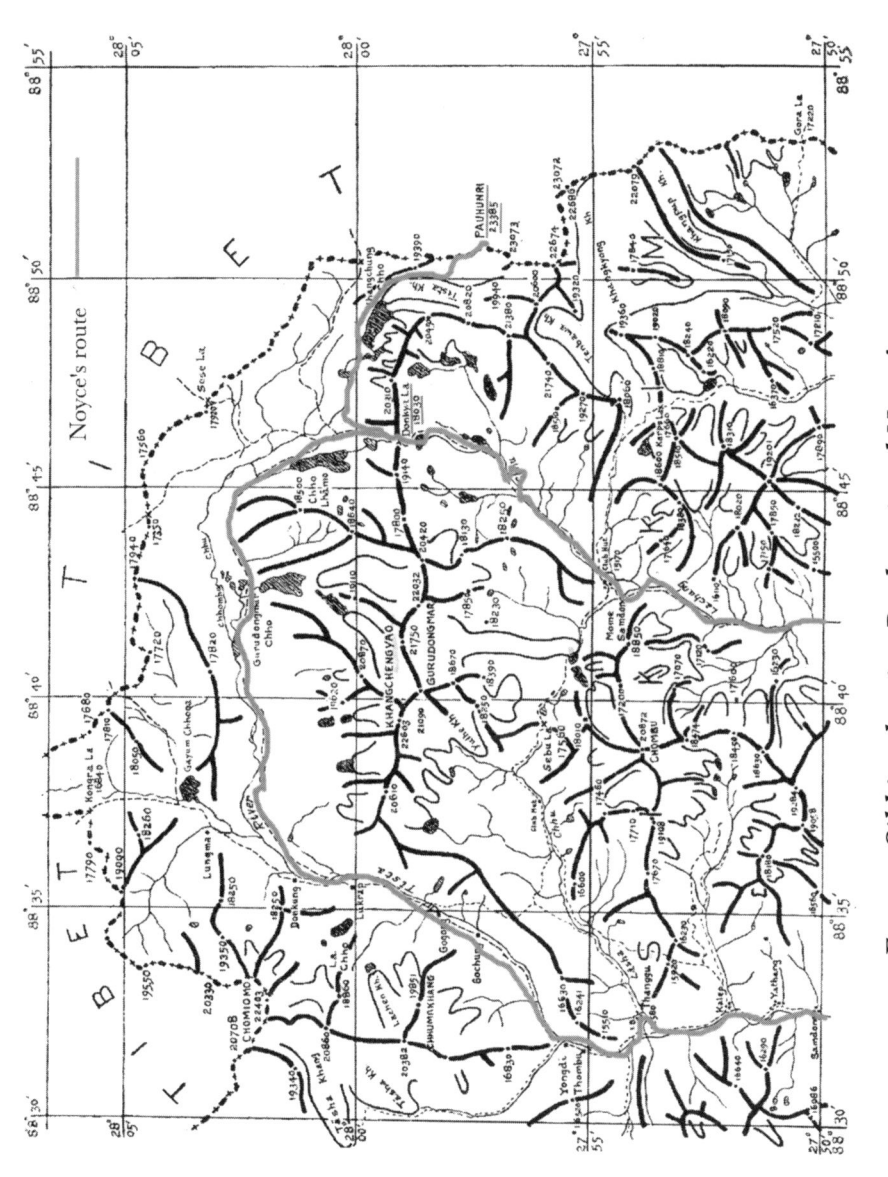

Eastern Sikkim showing Pauhunri and Noyce's route.

The following day they reached the tree-line and stopped to cut wood which they added to their loads. The last part was over boulders and very slow and Noyce was more and more conscious of his lack of acclimatisation. Here they met Tibetans with a yak and arrived at Mome Sandong 15,170ft (4,620m). It was a hamlet of a few shepherds' cottages, used mainly by Tibetans. Noyce took over one of them. Angtharkay immediately got a fire going, even with wet wood, and provided tea. Later he got some milk from a shepherd and produced Ovaltine!! There was still mist and drizzle but the flowering gentians provided a bright spot.

17th September dawned sunny and warm, a first. This was an acclimatisation day. Noyce bought some wine from a goatherd for two rupees, to keep for a celebration. After tea Noyce went off to reconnoitre on his own up to 16,000ft.

The following day Noyce started ahead of the others, to go slow, and to see what the weather was about to do. At 11.00 the snow came and he continued slowly with a view of Gurudongmar 22,032ft (6,708m) on his left. Then he met a snow-storm as he went higher. There was a gap in the clouds and Pauhunri was visible and he finally reached the rocky pass of Dongkya La at 18,030ft. (5,491m). At this point Noyce recognised that he needed more time to acclimatise. He was ten days out of Delhi and already higher than the summit of Mont Blanc 15,792ft (4,808m). He returned to camp in the rain, cold and sleet and there were scones and Tibetan tea to greet him.

The rain during the night made Noyce wonder if they should find an alternative to the Dongkya La route. However, it was a bright morning but as they were lunching, black clouds and snow arrived. In the face of horizontal snow they arrived at Dongkya La summit with Noyce in the rear. On the descent on a snowy path, Noyce was ahead, and the country to the east levelled off into the rolling plain of Tibet – quite a difference to what they had just passed through. The porters were carrying huge loads and to those they had added bundles of wood.

> *The little woman in gym shoes and no stockings, with skirts driven horizontal by the snow, – never the weaker sex again.*[28]

They stopped on the edge of the plain and pitched what became Base Camp, immediately under the 20,300ft (6,180m) snow and rock pinnacle of Dongkya Rhi.

20th September was another day of acclimatisation. Noyce and Angtharkay went off to reconnoitre the route to the east and climbed slowly round Khangchung Chho Lake whence he could see the Pauhunri group, fantastic rock and snow spires and the great Tista Khangse Glacier. They thought that there was a possible way up eastwards and by 11.30 they had reached 18,200ft (5,540m). Camp I might be at 19,500ft (5,940m). They returned to camp at 13.05 and the daily snow started. By 15.00 the sun had come out and Noyce had a wash in a small lake nearby. The chilly wind discouraged him from a high-altitude swim!

The following day they set off with all seven carrying loads. The idea was for all to carry up to Camp I then four of the Sherpas would descend, leaving Noyce with Angtharkay and Namgar. Above Khangchung Chho Lake they startled a large herd of bharal, the Himalayan mountain goat, and watched them leaping across the formidable crevasses of the Tista Khangse Glacier. Noyce was much slower than the others and lagged very far behind the whole way *'which is a new sensation.'* and was annoyed that a descent of 100 feet was necessary to reach the camp that the Sherpas had already pitched:

> *But one thing is certain, in fact confirms my impression of things read, if Everest is ever climbed it will be on the shoulders of these chaps. They can instantly after a hard climb get down to making a fire, building platforms, etc. And all cheerfully.*[29]

Noyce found himself puffing when eating and drinking and getting in and out of the tent. Angtharkay and Namgar occupied the other small tent and the other porters went down with instructions to return on 25th September, in four days. Noyce discovered that the medicine box had been left at Base Camp and Namgar would go down to get it as the aspirin would be needed for headaches at high altitudes.

In the early morning light of 22nd September they could see the north-east face of Pauhunri. It was cold and even Angtharkay complained. The two Sherpas set off at 8.30 on one route and Noyce went off to the left and to go right later to hit the ridge higher, being much slower and wanting to have an easy acclimatisation day. There were views of Everest to the west and then Chomolhari and its satellites east over towards Tibet. Noyce reached 20,600ft (6,270m) and rested until the others joined him. They continued on up cutting steps in the snow and managed to reach 21,000ft (6,395m) where they dumped their loads and came back down to Noyce at 12.25. They all descended to camp at a run in forty minutes! Angtharkay produced butter tea with tsamba – a new and delicious taste for Noyce.

The two Sherpa were well acclimatised but Noyce was still puffing a bit and each day was an improvement. He washed his feet in the glacier stream nearby and reflected on his concerns and the number of imponderables. *'Is Angtharkay unwell? What will the weather do? How good is my acclimatisation?'*

On 23rd September Noyce started at 8.50 ahead of the others, as he was still slower, and followed the steps they had made the day before. Angtharkay and Namgar caught him up after 1,200ft. At 13.05 they reached the place where they had left their loads the day before. The snow was soft, the going had been difficult and the loads were big. In short order a snow platform was built and the tents were up. Noyce comments,

> *Angtharkay really is miraculous and Namgar an absolute tower of strength and helpfulness, took his turn at leading, unfortunately speaks no Urdu (none do except Angtharkay).*[30]

It was a sunny afternoon and the only thing they can see higher is Chomolhari. Kanchenjunga is blocked by Pauhunri. That evening there was a major culinary disaster: Noyce had brought up some sausages and Angtharkay tried to cook them. The cooker went on the blink and the sausages stayed uncooked. Noyce could not eat raw sausage!

It was a cold night and they rose to a lovely morning at 6.00. Angtharkay had the cooker going and produced tea and tsamba. Noyce also had frozen sardines and biscuits. They set off at 7.50 with Noyce leading for the first bit in laborious snow. The other two led through and went up the steep but easy slope to what they thought was a summit. Round a corner they saw the summit of Pauhunri *'looking very stately and distant'* about 1,000ft above. They stopped and had biscuits and food and saw Chomolhari like a fang rising out of the clouds. Namgar started to want to go back.

> *A. eventually said, "Do we go on?" Said I thought we might look over the edge, the time was 11.30 only and we could get as far as we could. A. stumped up and kept calling back, "We can do this next bit but not any further." Called back, "All right do the next bit," I being a Plazatoro in the rear. Of course the ridge did go*

on and on, and there were many summits. Couldn't go too slow, as chilly wind and I had left one of my sweaters to pick up rope which Namgar wrongly left behind. Tantalising to see the tops so near and be so terribly slow getting at them. Reached highest, a corniced-cone (23,385ft) at 1.15 breathless. Distributed biscuits but not hungry self.[31]

After ten minutes at the top they descended to Camp II in fifty-five minutes and packed up quickly and went gently on to Camp I where they arrived at 15.35.

The wine was opened, '*but like all celebration pieces not so good*', and they put the tents up in a snowfall. Tibetan tea then sunshine. Noyce went up to the moraine ridge and had a view over to Chomiomo to the north-west and the Tibetan hills in the distance to the north. '*This is the most perfect hour of the expedition.*' Noyce thought his main contribution was the route-finding and pushing the other two. Angtharkay felt the effort for Pauhunri was comparable to big climbs. Noyce comments: "And it was a bloody big effort." He concludes that it was not a difficult mountain and that the route they followed seemed to be the only one. The map that they had let them think wrongly that the Tibet side was easy. He also felt he might have estimated Camp II too low. He was surprised at Angtharkay's misjudgements; thinking it would be an easy climb and then that it would be impossible to do it in one day. He wondered if it was the difference in conditions or whether this lack of judgement distinguishes the best of the Sherpa from the Swiss guide. When he was pushed gently '*he stamped like a Trojan*'. Noyce had reached a 23,000ft (7,000m) summit within two weeks of leaving the plains of Bengal. His stamina and determination had been essential.

On 25th September they set off at 10.00 for Base Camp with big loads. Noyce went off to climb a hill on the Tibet-Sikkim border but the hail beat him and all he saw was a herd of bharal. They reached Base Camp at 13.15 in the sunshine. Angtharkay had a big sore on his arm which was worse in the cold, and it was probably this that made him unhappy higher up. Nonetheless,

A. produced self-baked bread. Unfortunately it's very heavy but it's hard to tell him so and one can't go on hiding it under stones. I'd much rather eat chappatties and tsamba, and I wish I hadn't brought so many tins.[32]

A storm had already broken over Pauhunri so they were very lucky with the weather and had managed their climb in time.

Noyce was now halfway through his leave and had achieved the main objective of his trip. However, he did want to explore further to the west towards Donkung and Chomiomo, 22,403ft (6,820m). Perhaps he was conscious of the journey of Joseph Hooker in 1849 when he travelled the same circuit, but in the opposite direction. Hooker's narrative and descriptions of the flora and fauna are amazingly detailed and precise and provide a running commentary of comparisons with similar regions.

On 26th September they set off at 9.30 under a sunny sky. It was easy walking down beside one of the feeder torrents that became the Teesta River. The cliffs of Khangchengyao were on their left and the mass of Chomiomo was in front of them. In Donkung, a *'funny little open village all over prayer flags'*, they were still debating what they should do – particularly in view of Angtharkay's arm and the threat of snows higher up.

There were some attractive peaks such as Chomiomo but Noyce did not wish to do too much without Angtharkay.

28th September was the best day. It dawned bright. Noyce left at 8.45, on his own, and set off over difficult scree. He was rewarded with a magnificent view of clouds beating up against the line of Chomiomo, Kanchenjangyao and Pauhunri. He reached the summit ridge at about 12.10, then followed a very long snow ridge against a bitter wind. He was reassured that their decision not to take on Chomiomo was correct. It was difficult to move fast enough to keep warm. From 40 paces at a time he was reduced to 25 and at 20,100ft (6,120m) his pulse was 102. He reached the summit, 20,330ft (6,192m), at 13.20 and had some sardines in the sun. He had found a cairn below the ridge, perhaps indicating the highest achieved by an unknown predecessor and went on to a second summit. He tried scrambling a little but the rock was rotten. He returned to the first summit and went down the névée, easy going with crusted snow and on to the camp.

On 29th September Noyce went off to explore the north-east glacier and to get some ice practice and climbed a short way up the north face of Chomiomo. As Angtharkay had warned, the snow was bad and he came down and returned to the glacier snout where he had lunch. He cut some more steps in the ice and found that he was getting better at it as he had felt very weak and unsteady before. He also had ideas about going up a small hill, 18,250ft (5,550m), near Donkung but his boat-like '*Kanchenjunga*' boots and the sunshine persuaded him to sit in the sun and enjoy '*watching sun and snow and wind in turn sweep over Chomiomo's face*'. He carried on down and reached Donkung at 16.35 just before a storm broke.

After this they followed the river valleys down to Thanggu and Lachen. At Yatang, three or so miles down the valley from Lachen, he changed from his unmanageable boots to gym shoes.

On 2nd October after a difficult trek through steep bamboo they reached Chungtang, where there was a great mass of mail at the post office.

They carried on down but Noyce's footwear caused him trouble. A gym shoe gave out and Noyce tried one boot and one gym shoe and this seemed to work well. Again the threat of civilisation – as manifest at Gangtok – made him nervous. They reached the Dak Bungalows at Gangtok on 5th October. The 'whole English population' was there and Noyce was lucky to get a room. He was about to go to the truck office when he '*got talking with a really nice chap setting off on trek – and that continued*'.[33] Trevor Braham, the author of three books on mountains, was the '*nice chap*' and recalled this occasion,

> *Later that afternoon I noticed a small party of Sherpas entering the Rest House situated alongside ours. Following them shortly after was discernably a climber, evidently English, wielding an ice-axe, wearing a battered felt hat, and shod with a climbing boot on one foot and a canvas shoe on the other. We met that evening when he introduced himself as Wilfrid Noyce. I was able to extract from him a hesitant account of his ascent, with Angtharkay, of Pauhunri 7127m. situated in N.W. Sikkim… Noyce modestly ascribed to Angtharkay almost all the credit for the ascent, hardly referring to the part he must have played in their success. I was immediately struck by his quiet and self-effacing manner, and his gentleness. He was then 28 years old, and he possessed a charismatic quality.*[34]

The passage from Gangtok to Siliguri was an obstacle course of torrents and mudslides and Noyce made the train back to Calcutta on 9th October.

Notes

1. Wilfrid Noyce, *Garhwal diary (unpublished)*
2. *Ibid*
3. Wilfrid Noyce, *Mountains and Men p.80*
4. *Wilfrid Noyce, Garhwal diary (unpublished)*
5. *Ibid p.33*
6. *Ibid p.36*
7. Wilfrid Noyce, *Simsaga diary (unpublished) p.4*
8. *Ibid p.19*
9. *Ibid p.26*
10. *Ibid p.57*
11. Wilfrid Noyce, *Mountains and Men p.99*
12. Letter to Ian Grimble 3.10.1944, Balliol Archive
13. *Ibid* 21.10.1944, Balliol Archive
14. *Ibid* 24.10.1944, Balliol Archive
15. *Ibid* 19.11.1944, Balliol Archive
16. Author of *More than Mountains,* George Harrap 1955
17. Letter to Ian Grimble 26.11.1944, Balliol Archive
18. *Ibid*
19. Lady Esmé Roy
20. Sir S. N. Roy
21. Sir John Tymms
22. Wilfrid Noyce, *Letter to Ian Grimble 26.11.1944*
23. *Ibid 7.3.1945*
24. Letter to Ian Grimble 21.3.1945, Balliol Archive
25. *Ibid* 15.3.1945, Balliol Archive
26. *Ibid* 20.4.1945, Balliol Archive
27. Wilfrid Noyce, *Mountains and Men p.111*
28. *Ibid p.122*
29. *Ibid p.124*
30. *Ibid p.126*
31. *Wilfrid Noyce, Sikkim Diary p.24*
32. *Ibid p.27*
33. *Ibid p.40*
34. Letter of Trevor Braham to the author 12.5.2010

CHAPTER EIGHT

THE YEARS 1946-50 – SETTLING IN

After three successful years in India, Wilfrid Noyce disembarked in England just before the end of 1945. He was twenty-eight years old and apart from his consuming desire to be in mountains he had no idea what he wanted to do. He had a reputation as an expert rock-climber on British crags, and had made a number of ascents in the Alps where he had earned the respect of leading guides for his skill and speed. He had also had four periods in the Himalaya, with considerable exploration and important ascents to his credit. He was on the committee of the Alpine Club and was also an editor of the *Himalayan Journal*. He had a broader and more varied experience of the mountains than most of his contemporaries.

Dividing his time between his parents' home at Grayshott, in Surrey, where he spent the Christmas, and Cambridge, where he was in lodgings at 7, Peas Hill, he spent most of the first two months visiting friends, including Frida Leakey, Menlove Edwards, Marcia Winthrop Young, George Trevelyan and of course Arthur Pigou, who was still in King's.

At Grayshott he was very stressed and moody and his father was annoyed that he was unkempt and did very little except work in the garden sawing wood. His family was very concerned about his unsettled state and realised later that a major contributor to this was his preoccupation with Marcia Winthrop Young.

On 5th February he went down to London to attend a meeting of the Alpine Club Committee. Following the meeting, in his desire to resolve the uncertainty he went to see Marcia and clearly they must have discussed marriage. I believe that he may have misunderstood Marcia's reply but this did not stop him from writing to Ian Grimble,

> *I think it can be said safely now, that I am engaged to Marcia. I think this will please you. It happened finally only last night, when I had to go down for an AC committee, and saw her a-bed with flu. She's coming up next week and I shall be able to tell you more plans...Anyway it's happened.*[1]

Noyce was seeing quite a bit of his sister Rosalind at this time. She was in her first year at Oxford, and he had tea with her on Saturday 9th February in Lady Margaret Hall. Two days later, he wrote to Grimble after that visit,

> *I can't write a thing, but I do want you to say not a word on our two selves, to a soul. I can talk but I can't think. Above all I don't know if I realise other people, and the doubts and agonies of their minds.*

The situation with Marcia was rapidly clarified. He wrote on 17th February,

> *I got back to find the letter I was rather expecting, from Marcia. She believes that she was wrong, when she gave way, and she believes that it cannot be love that is accompanied by so much agony and doubt & fear. She believes that 'no' is the answer. As you can think, it spun me round flatly for a bit. As far as I am concerned, and I really am not much of a bid for such as she, she may be right. But I think love with her is bound to be mixed up with true agonies and uncertainties until she learns to give herself to it, to whoever it might be.*
>
> *Poor Marcia. She has a high price to pay for her beauty and her fineness: it is very important to me that it should be no higher than it need be – and – well I still have the fundamental feeling that where there is genuine good will, things will not miscarry, however they come out. And for me, it has been and is a thing of beauty among sordidness, loving and having loved her.*

Shortly after he wrote,

> *I have had another letter from M., much happier (I think) now that the new relationship is assumed, for the time: because she*

was trying to make one relationship into another (as she said), for which she was not ready: and being faced with all the agonies and doubts Mummy says she had to cope with, even later. I must be patient, this little bit. As Frida says, I have dominated her thoughts so long, and I do need to become a background (she may easily find when she gets out in the world two dozen people far more suitable).

Marcia still continued to send him cakes![2]

He was still trying to work out what to do. He admits, *'No, I haven't got a plan[3]. Only exploring possibilities and doing too much. It is important for everybody that I should get somewhere with a career.'* From Kashmir he had written to one of the dons at his college, Bobbie Stopford, who had suggested some contacts but these were mainly in the economics field – which had little interest. He applied to the International Labour Organisation and received a barely encouraging reply that there may be *'something going if he can muster an economic capacity or a capacity for specialisation in one of their departments'*; again not quite what was required. He also put in an application to the Foreign Office: *'Seemed sense though I'm not used to the idea.'* This also does not appear to have had any result.

At Easter 1946 Noyce and Rosalind went up to the Lake District to stay at Gatesgarth, the house of Professor Arthur Pigou at Buttermere. Pigou had told Noyce that it was important to bring his ice-axe and Lady Noyce carried it to the station. As the train drew away and gained speed Rosalind noticed that her mother was waving goodbye with the ice-axe. From then on, when vital items are made ready and then left behind, these incidents were described in the family as,[4] *'waving goodbye with the ice-axe'.*

From Gatesgarth on 22nd April he climbed Pillar Rock, Savage Gully, the Nose and North Climb with John Hunt and Harry Tilly. He had not been with Hunt in the mountains since the Mountain Warfare course in 1942: Tilly had been with Noyce at the Aircrew Centre in Kashmir in 1944 and 1945 and had lent boots and equipment for Noyce's trip to Sikkim in 1945: he and John Jackson, another instructor at the Kashmir had collaborated with Noyce on the production of **Climber's Guide to Sonamarg, Kashmir** which had been published by the Himalayan Club, Delhi, in 1945.

On 24th April Rosalind, Noyce and Philip Noel-Baker were going on an excursion. The original plan was for Noyce and Noel-Baker to climb in the coombs and Rosalind would go over Grassmoor. Then Noyce decided that he would like to go on Great Gable. Later Claude Elliott, the Headmaster of Eton, who with his wife was staying at the Buttermere Hotel, turned up, probably at the invitation of Noel-Baker, and joined the party. They all went up and had a picnic just below Windy Gap. After lunch they went round Great Gable to Tophet Bastion so that the men could climb and Rosalind would meet them at the top. Noel-Baker decided the climbs were too difficult for him but Elliott wanted to climb. According to Rosalind, they were unable to understand what Wilfrid wanted to do. Rosalind and Noel-Baker watched the climbers for some time and as it was getting cold they went up to the top of Great Gable where the mist descended. They left a handkerchief to show that they had passed and went home by Base Brown, still in the mist and rain, and arrived at Gatesgarth late and completely soaked.

Noyce was leading on Tophet Bastion, which was not a difficult climb, according to Pigou, but it is subject to violent gusts in a storm, as the locals all knew well. He was blown off his holds and fell some thirty feet and broke a leg. When Elliott got down to him he was swearing volubly – at himself – for Elliott a good sign. The latter went off immediately to Seathwaite, where there was a telephone some three miles away to get help. He found two scouts, told them to get hold of some climbers, then went back to Noyce, all within the hour! Colonel 'Rusty' Westmoreland, a man named Filds, who knew about first-aid and tying people to stretchers, having participated in six rescues, and three hefty men followed Elliott up. It was a very difficult rescue. By the time the rescue party got to Noyce night had fallen and there was light snow. Noyce had to be strapped to the stretcher and pulled in an upright position to the top of the cliff before they could lower him rope's length by slow rope's length to the bottom and take him across country. They started to move him at 18.20. They managed to get Noyce down over the scree and difficult terrain to Wasdale by 6.00 in the morning in the mist, violent storm and, by then, snow. It was an heroic effort as afterwards it was said that fifteen to twenty men would be normally required for the task. From Wasdale the RAF ambulance took him to Whitehaven Hospital.

If the fell-walkers had reached Gatesgarth earlier, Noel-Baker could have gone with Pigou to Seathwaite and led the walkers, who had agreed to help, to the right place. In fact, those walkers refused to venture above

Sty Head as they said it was too dangerous. One of them said that he had seen Noyce and said that, "...*he was in a bad way*". This was quite untrue. If too Elliott had gone to Wasdale, where in fact there was no telephone, the rescue party could have gone up with him and got Noyce down quickly. Scott came back to Rosalind and Noel-Baker at Gatesgarth at 1.00 and said that Noyce was still up on the mountain and would not be down that night. Pigou spent the night at Seathwaite. At 7.30 on the following morning Scott took Noel-Baker to Seathwaite. Finally those at Seathwaite heard from a walker who had come from Wasdale that Noyce was down. There was no telephone at Gatesgarth so Rosalind went down to the Buttermere Hotel to await a call from Noel-Baker who called at 11.00 from Seathwaite to say that Noyce was at Whitehaven Hospital.

The Times of 25th April 1946 reported, with a strange indifference to the facts:

CLIMBER'S FALL IN LAKE DISTRICT

Two search parties were out in the Lake District last night in the hope of rescuing Captain Wilfred [sic] Noyce, son of Sir Frank Noyce, of Grayshott, Surrey, who fell 150ft. into Hellfire Gap while climbing yesterday with Mr. P. Noel-Baker, Minister of State, and Mr C. Elliott, head master of Eton. The climbers were on the bastion of Napes Ridges of the Great Gable at the time of the accident. Mr. Noel-Baker walked five miles across country in a blizzard to fetch help. Blankets, food, and tea were lowered into the gap, but Captain Noyce had not been found when the search was discontinued till daybreak.

Rusty Westmorland from Keswick was a well-known local mountaineer who after the accident founded and became the first president of the Keswick Mountain Rescue. He subsequently became President of the Fell and Rock Climbing Club and was awarded the OBE for his services to mountain rescue. He died in November 1984 at the age of ninety-eight.

Noyce's incredible resilience was again demonstrated: Philip Noel-Baker wrote shortly afterwards to Lady Noyce, Noyce's mother:

It is to my mind almost a miracle that he should have been so completely unaffected by shock, and that when he had been in hospital only an hour or two he had already written several letters with his own hand.... I have no doubt that he will make as remarkable a recovery as he did before.'

The above account is based on the correspondence of Rosalind Noyce, Noel-Baker, Pigou and Elliott to Wilfrid Noyce's parents immediately after the accident.[5]

This accident, the third in nine years, gave Noyce considerable opportunity for reflection. He wrote to Grimble,

How this happened — how the gust of sudden strengthening wind hurled me off that rock — I don't know still. And I must confess I still don't believe it really happened. It couldn't have.... But I did come to realise sitting on that ledge that this is the end of my playboy life: and playboy hills. My only justification to man or beast now is to cut off from that, and get down to a bit of the service that is waiting for me (if I can). It's my only hope of sanity. The direction is still clouded: but not for long.[6]

Later he wrote:

Fracture healing according to plan. On a crutch this afternoon. I'm really about round to predestination! The chain of events that led to this silliest of silly breaks, at the last moment — it was designed clearly to teach me — and perhaps that my lines have been all wrong, at any rate that I've got to give them up a while, and get on. The hard step is moving now, from the past and on to the first rung of a ladder.

The stitches came out on 17th May but he still had the leg in plaster for another two months.

In the epilogue to **Mountains and Men**, published in the following year, he recounts an imaginary conversation with his highly critical alter ego during a trip to the mountains. He reproaches himself for his pride and vanity in climbing.

Like the airman, I had never been able to visualise the crash. Could I disentangle my hurt from my vanity? The third accident — I must

therefore be the criminal condemned by his third conviction.[7]

However, it seems that he did not really want to acknowledge his own thoughts and the piece concludes: '*With my companion I scrambled on, across the scree. At the foot of Tophet Bastion and by the side of Great Hell Gate, we put on the rope.*[8]

In May 1946 Noyce was back in Cambridge staying at 7 Peas Hill and in King's. He took his MA in June, a necessary step if one is thinking of becoming an academic. At the end of July he moved from Cambridge back to Grayshott, near Hindhead and devoted himself to editing the 1946 edition of the **Himalayan Journal.**

He was still undecided what to do, but it is quite clear that he was still passionate about being in mountains and enjoyed writing both prose and poetry. He had enjoyed the periods of instructing others and sharing with them his love and appreciation of the mountains. It appears that he did not wish to follow up the success in cryptography that he had achieved during the war and ideally wanted a congenial job that provided enough scope for him to climb and to write.

It seems that Professor Pigou intervened to help Noyce obtain gainful employment. Pigou's circle of friends included Tom Gaunt, the Headmaster of Malvern College, near Worcester, and a King's man, and an introduction was arranged for Noyce. Shortly afterwards he accepted the offer of a teaching post at Malvern; this was an ideal situation in which he could earn a living sharing his scholarship in classics and modern languages as well as having plenty of opportunity to climb and develop his talent for writing.

He was in Lausanne from mid-August to mid-September. He observed to Grimble, '*The leg is fairly tranquil. Two letters from Marcia set me rotating a bit. It is appalling to think how unqualified one is to teach.*'[9] He returned to England to become an Assistant Master at Malvern College.

The College is in the centre of the Worcestershire town of Malvern on the east side of the Malvern Hills, the highest point of which is the Worcestershire Beacon at 1,395ft (424m) above sea level. It was founded in 1865 by a group of mainly local businessmen with some twenty-four boys and twelve masters on a 250-acre campus.[10] The school expanded rapidly, and from the initial two boarding houses has expanded to eleven houses and some 650 boys and girls. Between October 1939 and July 1940 the school, in reduced numbers, was moved to Blenheim Palace to make way for the Admiralty. It moved back to Malvern and then in May 1942 the government took over the school again, for the Telecommunications and Radar Establishment (TRE). From then until July 1946 the school was housed with Harrow School, a reverse evacuation. Harrow normally had a large number of pupils from overseas. This was considerably reduced owing to the war and the accommodation was made available to Malvern. A further naval connection was created when the Free French Navy ran training courses for their cadets in No. 5 house from 1940 to 1941. This association is still commemorated regularly by college and town together.

When the college returned to Malvern, Gaunt had the task of restoring the school to its former size and eminence. He was also active in government missions to assist in the rebuilding of educational systems on the continent and strongly encouraged an international outlook at the school. Masters who had been in the services returned and new ones were recruited. Some houses, known by numbers, had been in suspension during the war. No. 1 house, for example, was restarted by H. C. W. (Bill) Wilson, who had originally joined the school in 1937 teaching biology, served as a captain in the Gloucestershire Regiment and returned in 1946 after five years in a German prisoner-of-war camp. There, according to his diary, he had kept his hand in by conducting Biology classes for his fellow captives.[11] Those masters who had been with the school all during the war still carried on as before, but those that had been in the services and those joining after the war felt constrained and believed that the school should move with the changed times and have a more liberal approach to discipline and pupil-teacher relations.

Noyce taught the Classical Sixth[12] initially and later taught French to other classes. His lodgings were at Corneville in Albert Road, not far from the school, and later he lodged in the house of another master and his wife, Roland and Eileen Legrand. He was attached to No. 1 house as house tutor, and was an assistant to the housemaster.

The classroom may not have been the natural milieu for Wilfrid Noyce. He was mainly a teacher for the boys who wanted to learn. His voice was always quiet and, as a later pupil of his, I never heard him raise his voice. There always appeared to be a certain diffidence and this was increased by the traumatic effects of the accident in April 1946, which had deprived him of most of his teeth. He did, however, participate in the life of the school and in a number of local activities. Roland Legrand was Secretary of the local United Nations Association, and Noyce became treasurer of the association in 1947.

When he went to Malvern he was still recovering from his accident and spent the initial weeks looking at the Worcestershire Beacon before making cautious steps up it, getting farther each time. In October he was well enough recovered to get to the top and started a very long love affair with the Malvern Hills. Noyce was a great explorer of the local hills and later on he discovered that the *'rocks in the north tip of North Hill, in and out of the quarries, gave good solid climbing and demand a rope.'*[13]

At this time he was preparing his first book, **Mountains and Men.** It was first published in January 1947. It is a young and thoughtful mountaineer's autobiography with details of his early Welsh, Alpine and Himalayan trips. David Cox, a fellow mountaineer and Oxford academic reviewed the book in the **Alpine Journal** that year.

> *As a simple record of climbing achievement, were it written that way, it would have been remarkable,* and *in so far as stress is ever placed on mere performance, it is on the performance of the author's companions, never on his own.... . Fundamentally, he is writing on the relationship set up between the climber and the mountains, and as this relationship is never constant, but changes as the climber himself changes, the story is the story of his own experience of this development.*[14]

In the summer holidays of 1947 Noyce went on courses to improve his German in Zurich in Switzerland and Seefeld in Austria. He thought about not taking his climbing equipment, but was eventually persuaded to. In Switzerland the course had a weekend at Davos, '...*that pathetic city, half hospital and half pleasure palace*', and he managed to get away and climb the Weissfluh, already by then, '...*submitted to every indignity of poster placard and ski-lift.*'[15] He wanted to climb the Tödi and on his way from Zurich to Innsbruck by chance met Eddie Stalder, a leading figure in the Red Cross and the Pestalozzi organisation, and a mountaineer. Together they climbed the Tödi.

He had been warned that it was miserable in Austria and that food was limited – he would have to exist on the standard 1,500 calories per day. From the passport officer at the border to his hostesses at his lodgings and the people around him he saw nothing, nothing but smiles. He also enjoyed a great deal more climbing. Early on he visited the Karwendel Group with one of his fellow-students. In the hut afterwards there was a good crowd and he was delightfully surprised by the merriment, music and generous amounts of food. No 1,500 calories here! *'The Tyrolese were still the Tyrolese as I had always pictured them.'* He also had introductions through Dr. Paul Kaltenegger, the editor of the **ÖAZ**, the **Austrian Pharmaceutical Journal**, who directed him to Willi Rutscher of the ÖAV, the Austrian Alpine Club. With Rutscher he climbed the Parseierspitze, the highest peak in the northern limestone Alps. As they basked in the sunshine on the summit they surveyed the distant Orteler and Bernina and talked. Rutscher had clearly taken the German invasion of 1938 very badly, "*I comforted myself that our hills they could not take away.*" Noyce observes that, '*...they were out now on a pilgrimage of escape into the hills that was to preserve their laughter, to keep the cold from their hearts.*' On another Sunday he went up the Olperer 11,430ft (3,476m) in the Zillertal Alps in the company of an Austrian student and marvelled at the proximity of such high mountains. They could leave Innsbruck on Saturday morning, get up to a hut, climb a high peak or two and return home for supper on Sunday evening.

After the course he chanced to meet the Countess Irma Scheidegg, a very experienced mountaineer. He hoped through her to make a better acquaintance of the mountain people and '*...penetrate more deeply into the secret of that smile*'. They went up by bus to Ginzling, a village in one of the Zillertal side-valleys. A farmer guide and his wife welcomed them and they arranged for a huge rucksack to be carried over to the Berliner Hut, while they were to go there by the peaks. The wife brought from the cupboard what had become a rarity, an apple pie. "*Yes, we had everything,*" she said, offering it round and taking no refusal. "*Now we have nothing. We are very poor people.*"

The following day they visited a hunter and his family. There was little hunting and the only game available were marmots which were not in great demand. The hunter supervised the herdsmen and graziers in the high pastures and in winter went down to Ginzling and worked in a timber yard. The Countess thought that it was nice to keep him there, '*with his green jacket and enormous pipe. Besides he gives us milk and butter.*' When they reached the chalet, the Countess undid her rucksack and produced a metre of cloth. Immediately a slab of butter appeared. Then Noyce:

> *...offered the hunter a fill for his picturesque but tobaccoless pipe. As if by magic there stood before us two cupfuls of creamy milk.*

The little stone-floor room, bare boards and bare-legged children, seemed to radiate an increased warmth at us. I thought that now I understood how to do it. "It's no use thinking of money here," smiled the Countess. "Tausch (exchange) is the word."

This then was how these people of the valleys still smiled, still gave. Obviously the money system is absurd, a joke in fact, for no one could possibly be expected to live on that. To get to our mountains therefore we must think out what we can most reasonably exchange. Two metres of cloth equal one kilo of butter. An egg is worth two cigarettes. So the exchange goes on for the benefit of all, the Tyrolese still smile and their hearts are warm and their hands generous.[16]

There was the feeling also that in the mountains that they had escaped from a shadow as they walked the heights like *'truant but happy schoolboys'*. The mountains round the Zillertal, at about 11,000ft (3,350m) in altitude, with their bare rocks provided a good introduction for beginners.

The parties left late, at 6.30 and were able to climb up to three peaks in the day. The best of his expeditions was the Great Mösele by the fronting ice ridge, Schneedreieck, '*...a steep Brenva-like affair, but straightforward in crampons,*' and the Turnerkamp, going up by the harder west ridge and descending by the east, this time in mist and snow. The Countess did not enjoy the bad weather and Noyce told her, "*If you come to England, you will climb in nothing else.*" "*Then I will not come to England, I love the sun,*" was the reply. The ascent was very hard for Noyce and the passage of the ridge was by crawling astride. This 'Reitgrat' cost him the skin of two knees and his ice-axe. The score of humiliation was evened up when the Countess fell into a crevasse in the mist.

The variety of the people using the huts provided interesting contacts; the guides who were looking for a crashed aeroplane, the engineer in the small cabin near the Berliner Hut, the students who collected crystals, three Innsbruck bank-clerks. Of these to Noyce the engineer was the most extraordinary. He was unemployed and had taken over the cabin which was also close to the glacier snout. In this were some remarkable caves and he had made a living showing visitors round the caves and guiding parties over the peaks. However, by the time of Noyce's visit the glacier had retreated and the caves no longer existed so he cut wood for the farmers instead. He lived with his wife in this one-room shack and maintained an enormous international correspondence. His wife found it very dull and had nothing to do but cook the maize, their standby food, which by then the Austrians had come to dislike heartily.

Noyce was much taken by the jollity of the expeditions; the groups would start on the path quietly and then as they ascended the laughter would break out until, on the tops they would all be yodelling and singing. On the Countess's last day they joined the three bank clerks for a trip to the Schwarzstein, a flat snow promontory and continued to the Great Mörcherer.

Noyce still had two more days and sought again a climbing companion or two. The Austrians seemed much more relaxed about teaming up with new acquaintances than the Swiss. He joined up with the bank clerks, who were very pleased for him to join them. They crossed to the Furtschlagelhaus in the next valley and climbed the Great Mösele again, by an easier flank. At the top they looked over the South Tyrol.

> *"That should be ours," said the senior bank clerk, pointing. "It is always sunny there." I knew what he meant by this. Pamphlets had been showered on my head, by Innsbruck professors and students. The fascist Torinelli, said they, had been allowed by the Italians to remain in office. Italy continued her pre-war policy of fascist domination. And of course they were right. The cultural and social unity of North and South Tyrol was all too obvious.*[17]

After they had returned to the Furtschlagelhaus Noyce left them and hastened back to Ginzling.

The last two nights were spent in Innsbruck with the very generous and hospitable mother of one of his fellow-students. Noyce spent a long time trying to persuade his hostess to accept his rations. *"'We deserve it,'" she said. "Everyone despises us, because we did not stand up to the Germans and the Swiss did." I could not say no, for there was just the grain of truth in this confession, which might complete the answer to my question. "How can the Austrians still smile?"'* Whatever their boasts of independence the Austrians have retired to their mountains in the face of invaders and not wanted to make their peaks a battlefield. 'They prefer,' wrote Noyce, 'shrines to fortresses. It is not for nothing therefore that the paths are strewn with chapels, the alps with crucifixes that link their green pleasantness with the deeper meanings. This, at least, is the impression of a very fleeting visitor.'[18]

The Years 1946-50 – Settling in

From Innsbruck it was back to Malvern for the beginning of term. Perhaps influenced by what he had seen in Austria he became the assistant secretary of the Malvern Committee of European Relief.

As in most public schools, Malvern had its 'Corps', or Cadet Force. This was obligatory for all boys almost all the time they were in the school and until 1960 every able-bodied boy could expect to be called up for two years' National Service when he left school. The time in the Corps was regarded as a prerequisite to becoming an officer during National Service. Basic proficiency was recognised by the awarding of 'Certificate A', which required a certain standard in weapon-training, drill and tactics. However, the Corps was not to every boy's taste and there was a search for alternatives after 'Cert A' had been completed. In some public schools there were scout troops. There were, however, no scouts at Malvern until a group of renegades from the Corps made a deal with the headmaster in 1948 that if they formed a senior scout troop, they would attempt to become King's Scouts.

The Malvern College Senior Scout Troop was registered at Scout Headquarters[19] in May 1948 with a strength of fourteen senior scouts and two leaders. Ronald Born, the School Chaplain, was appointed Senior Scoutmaster and Noyce was recruited as his deputy. This suited him very well. Noyce's first task as Scoutmaster was to test Michael Boyd-Carpenter for his Interpreter Badge, which involved a walk up the Beacon and chatting in French. He then suggested that they try climbing a tricky bit in the disused quarry. This they did and after that three of the scouts, Boyd-Carpenter, Peter Holmes and Tim Colthurst *'spent numerous afternoons climbing in the hills with Wilf doing extraordinary things at great speed and encouraging us to copy him'.*[20] From then on the other scouts did more regular scout activities but Noyce and these three spent their time climbing. For them Noyce became less of a schoolmaster, but rather a friend. They visited him in his digs and in an undergraduate way made toast in front of the fire. On Sunday trips if they were too late for evensong in the college chapel, they would slip into a pub for a quick drink before returning to school.

In 1948 the Malvern Anglo-French Society was launched, as noted in the **Malvern Gazette**, and Noyce and Legrand were both active members.

He was elected Guidebook Editor for the Climbers' Club in 1948 and being responsible for the production of the detailed climbing guides particularly to the crags and cliffs of North Wales. With his experience of writing guides and his knowledge of the crags he was able to reduce the inconsistency of the standards applied to the various climbs. The challenge of standards is highlighted in this fragment from a pre-war **Climbers' Club Journal**:[21]

> Edwards and Noyce
> Differed in the Vertical Vice.
> Edwards thought it an 'almost mild severe,'
> Noyce said, "Nowhere near."

At Easter 1949 he was again in Snowdonia with the Malvern boys, Holmes and Colthurst and in the August the Malvern Senior Scouts camped at Capel y Fin, some ten miles into the mountains from Hay on Wye. During that time together they explored the mountains and trekked over to Llangorse Lake. Not long after that he wrote up their experiences in a long article for the **Malvern Gazette** on **Camping in the Black Mountains**. He describes them as the nearest mountains of any height to the Midland towns. The highest point which is Waun Fach; at 2,660ft is *'a respectable height by Welsh standards'*.

In the summer Noyce climbed in the Graian Alps with David Cox and Peter Harding; later David Cox wrote:

> *It was an ideally chosen district: few huts, no guidebook, only a borrowed map and a postcard of instructions from A. C. Pigou, to which we owed a memorable day of steamy heat traversing the Bec d'Invergnan and the Grande Rousse from a camp by a torrent in the pine-woods of the Val Grisanche. Even on this holiday, I discovered in quite trivial ways how different Wilfrid's standards were from my own. There was a little stretch of dry glacier which had to be crossed to reach a bivouac hut; the ice was perfectly easy, except that it was just steepening to spill over a big cliff a few yards below. Wilfrid walked across it without taking his axe from under his arm, then had to wait while I put on crampons. On a traverse of the Grivola, he drifted on ahead up the South face and only came back from the top when I shouted up to him asking to tie on. This was quite a long day, fifteen or sixteen hours, but next morning he made us walk most of the twenty-five odd miles from Val Savaranche round to Cogne and, a poignant memory, took it for granted when we got back to the tent, that as this had*

not been a climbing day, only one egg would be enough for the evening meal.[22]

Noyce was a good scout leader but happy to leave the more 'normal' scout activities to others.

In the Summer term 1950 there was a week-end camp at Ripple near Tewkesbury on the bank of the Severn. Very scouty! Wilf got bored so we went off to my then home at Gretton where we had lunch with my aunt, then Wilf took the dog for a long walk whilst I had a rest. I think that the Scoutmaster, who was a parson, was somewhat vexed as the rest of the troop went to church, woggles & all.[23]

Later on in 1950 the Scouts had another summer camp in the mountains but this was overshadowed by the prospect of National Service, which then meant the war in Korea, for the three Seniors at a time when Noyce was about to be married. The rejection of the Corps did not affect the service career of these three. Boyd-Carpenter was a career submarine officer before becoming a successful city figure. Holmes did National Service in the Royal Leicester regiment and won a Military Cross in Korea *'for heroic assaults on Chinese troops'.*[24] He went on to Cambridge, continued to climb with Noyce and became a distinguished member of the Alpine Club, the Royal Society for Asian Affairs and Head of Royal Dutch Shell. He is supposed to have said that he only joined Shell to pay off the overdraft incurred by two Himalayan expeditions after he left Cambridge![25] Colthurst did his National Service as an officer in the Royal Marine Commandos and subsequently became a director of a number of City companies.

Noyce enjoyed sharing his interest in rock-climbing and the mountains, particularly among young people and he often gave lectures on mountain topics to local organisations. He was a regular contributor to the **Malvern Gazette** on mountaineering matters and he continued to figure in the paper long after he had left Malvern and indeed long after his death.[26]

Noyce had broadcast a talk on the BBC Third Programme on **Tryfan: Rock Mountain of North Wales,** towards the end of 1948. It was subsequently printed in **The Listener**. 'Hillman' of the *Malvern Gazette* had commented on this in his weekly column, *'regretting that* similar publicity could not be obtained for our own modest mountain, the Worcestershire Beacon.*[27]* Noyce took up the challenge and wrote a delightful article that appeared in the ***Malvern Gazette*** of 18th February 1949 under the headings, ***The Beacon: A Friendly Hill. Mountaineer discovers a rival to Tibet.*** He describes how he has been on the Beacon in every weather and in all conditions. In the bad winter of 1947 he and his companion had great difficulty in getting to the top.

> *The only way my robust companion could get me up in rubber-soled shoes was by producing from his pocket a large bootlace to which I attached myself while he kicked the steps and did the pulling.*

He recounts that in November 1948 he was on the Beacon examining a Venture Scout for his Climber Badge and they were above the mist and fog that covered the surrounding countryside.

> *Over to the East and beyond the Severn the tip of Bredon Hill beckoned to us above a vaporous sea; between it and ourselves lay the shadow of the Beacon against cloud, and upon that shadow our own shadow, a "Brocken Spectre" surrounded by a very faint halo. Such a light effect I had only seen before in the Alps. I waved and my shadow waved, and his spectre waved back to him but I could not see it.*

He went on alone to North Hill and away to the west the tops of the Black Mountains in Wales were standing out as majestic as the Himalaya. 'My Beacon had justified itself as a mountain.' He ends, 'Perhaps then, height is relative, the Beacon is both higher and lovelier than the 20,000-foot Tibetan lump which stared disdainfully down at us hour after painful hour on the slopes of Pauhunri.'

A version of this article appeared in the 1949 ***Climbers' Club Journal.***

Not long after this adventure he gave a lecture on mountaineering at the Public Library in Malvern in support of the Malvern Scout District. As reported by the ***Malvern Gazette***[28] he said that he had seen the Brocken Spectre in the Alps, but it was not until two weeks previously that he had seen it in Britain.

In addition to the articles and talks he was preparing at this time another book, ***Scholar Mountaineers,*** which was published just after he left Malvern and it reflected the range of his mountaineering, linguistic and literary interests. Noyce was climbing with his colleagues from the Climbers' Club in Snowdonia and with P. R. J. Harding, on 22nd January 1949 they put up a new 'Severe' route on Craig Ddu in the Llanberis Pass, 'The Crown of Thorns'. He also climbed regularly with the Senior Scouts and the following month in the Malvern Hills he was with Peter Holmes on the 'West Buttress'. They could still find new routes in the disused quarry and they were not without hazard.

> *The rock needed very careful handling and was complicated by vegetation. In the centre rises a formidable looking nose. They put up two routes, one just to the left and one to the right of the nose, on 11th and 17th February. The second zig-zags and is well over 200 feet. The standard is probably about Difficult, with a flavour of mountaineering given by the general uncertainty of the material. The other outcrop of special merit overhangs the green, smooth top of a water reservoir, only a few minutes up the valley from the North Malvern clock tower.*[29]

At the end of his last term at Malvern an article in the **Malvern Gazette** of 28th July 1950 records Noyce and the Malvern Scouts demonstrating rock-climbing on the Ivy Scar outcrop of the Malvern Hills to distinguished local figures, among whom were Tom Gaunt, the Headmaster of Malvern and the Rev. Ronald Born, Assistant District Scout Commissioner, Byam Grounds, a local climber and Professor Micklem, the Principal of Mansfield College, Oxford. On that occasion the Malvern College Troop Leader, Boyd-Carpenter, was presented with his King's Scout Badge. Peter Holmes should have been presented with his King's Scout badge on that day, but was unavoidably absent. Holmes later recounted that Noyce used to say, "*Christopher Columbus!*" when a boy caused him some surprise in class! I too can remember him exclaiming thus at Charterhouse. He also recalled that Noyce used to fill his rucksack with rocks and go up and down Russet Gill to maintain his fitness.

Appropriately Noyce was one of the founder members of the Malvern Writers Circle which not only encouraged young writers but also set up its own library for the benefit of its members and others.[30]

Noyce's father, Sir Frank Noyce died in 1948 and neither of the sons was at his funeral at Grayshott, both being abroad, as **The Times** notice of 12th October 1948 observed. Ronald was in Nyasaland in the colonial service, but it is unclear where Wilfrid was. However, in appreciation of his father he wrote:

> *He never once sought directly to influence our plans for a career, our ideas on marriage or religion. Yet he was deeply concerned with them all, and would often have been in a position to criticize. He never even tried to avert, and indeed assisted, my early passion for mountaineering, although it caused him acute terror and three times, unhappily, an ill-merited anxiety. Such was his love for us. If it is the duty of a good parent to encourage by example, not direct reproof and admonition, I know none so worthy of the title as my father.*

In the July-September 1948 edition of the **Adelphi Magazine** the poem 'Cholderton in Wiltshire' was published. It had originally been written in 1941 when Noyce was stationed nearby, at Perham Down.

He became less and less comfortable at Malvern and in addition the death of his father gave Noyce some concerns over his mother and had now moved to Hurstmere, another house at Grayshott.[31] As his brother was in Africa and he was the elder son he felt some responsibility for her. In March 1950 he was offered a post at Charterhouse to start in September 1950. It was an attractive offer financially and he would be in an environment with which he was familiar and some of the masters who had taught him were still there. It gave him great pleasure to accept as he would be nearer to his mother who was then well into her sixties.

Roland Legrand used to produce plays in Malvern and in 1949 he was putting on **Our Town** by Thornton Wilder with a certain Rosemary Davies in the cast. She was teaching French at Malvern College for Girls, and was a keen and talented actress. Rosemary had been at Oakfield School at Arnside and fruit-picking camps at Colwall were organised by the school. On these occasions she would stay with Stephen and Eveline Ballard who were farmers. When she was at St. Anne's College, Oxford, reading Modern Languages she continued to come and brought friends from Oxford, continuing the friendship with the Ballards. After graduating in 1947 she was introduced to the headmistress at Malvern Girls School and she joined the staff in January 1948. Initially, she stayed with the Ballards and subsequently the Noyces and the Ballards became very close.[32]

Wilfrid Noyce was persuaded to join the cast and took the role of the milkman Howie Newsome. Rosemary recalls, *"I remember he used to say his lines and was very funny about it, and I was in the play and that is virtually how we met". ... "And we all joined in the Anglo-French Society in the town. So that was another contact."*[33]

Their engagement was announced in the **Daily Telegraph** on 12th April 1950. Rosemary was the only child of Mr. Harry Campbell Davies and step-daughter of Mrs. Davies of Heswall in Cheshire.

Noyce's last act as a bachelor was to climb the Worcestershire Beacon on the morning of his wedding day, 12th August 1950. This wedding, by all accounts, was a considerable event in the relations of the Malvern Girls School and Malvern College. The extent to which the girls were shielded from the boys was remarkable. '*The girls had to open any letter with a Malvern postmark in front of the house-mistress.*'[34] *The jokes were all about the first person to get near someone from the Girls College.*'

Wilfrid Noyce and 'the dainty, fair-haired'[35] Miss Rosemary Davies were married in Malvern Priory. Harry and Hilda Davies were present and Roland Legrand was best man. The bridesmaid was Pat Ballard and the page was Julian Legrand, who subsequently became one of Tony Blair's economic advisers. The ushers were three colleagues from the College, James Bolam, H. J. Farebrother and A. N. Willis. The service was conducted by the Rev. R. B. Lunt, the vicar of Malvern Priory, assisted by the Rev. Ronald Born, of Malvern College. The reception was held in the College and afterwards the couple left by car for the honeymoon.[36] This was intended to be spent entirely in the Lake District, at Lower Gatesgarth on Buttermere, the house belonging to Professor Pigou. They were the only ones there and Rosemary recalls being well looked after by '*the Prof's housekeeper Miss Jackson, known as the Queen of Gatesgarth*'. The weather was terrible and not conducive to much outdoor activity, although the weather never bothered Noyce. However, they went down to Stratford-on-Avon to see some plays then continued on down to Godalming to settle in ready for the new term at Charterhouse.

Notes

1. Wilfrid Noyce, *letter to Ian Grimble 6.2.1946 Balliol Archives*
2. *Ibid 10.3.1946 Balliol Archives*
3. *Ibid 22.2.1946 Balliol Archives*
4. Conversation with Rosalind Brain, 6.10.2008
5. Prof. Arthur Pigou, *letter to Sir Frank Noyce, 26.4.1946*
   Rosalind (Noyce), *letter to Sir Frank and Lady Noyce, 28.4.1946*
   Philip Noel-Baker, *letter to Lady Noyce, 1.5.1946*
   Claude Elliot, *letter to Sir Frank and Lady Noyce, 2.5.1946*
6. Wilfrid Noyce, l*etter to Ian Grimble from Whitehaven hospital, 25.4.1946 Balliol Archives*
7. Wilfrid Noyce, *Mountains and Men p.158*
8. *Ibid p.160*
9. Letter to Ian Grimble, 26.8.1946
10. Malvern College website, 13.6.2010
11. Old Malvernian Newsletter, April 2009
12. Malvern College Red Book for 1946
13. *Malvern Gazette* 18.2.1949
14. *Alpine Journal*, November 1947, A. D. M. Cox
15. Wilfrid Noyce, *Austrian Impressions, Alpine Journal 1947 p.221*
16. *Ibid p.225*
17. *Ibid p.226*
18. *Ibid p.227*
19. Scout Association Registration of 11.5.1948 (Cancelled 1963) Other Senior Scouts mentioned were Mcready and Brentnall
20. Michael Boyd-Carpenter, *note to author 13.7.2010*
21. *Climbers' Club Journal*, 1939
22. David Cox *C.W.F.N. Obituary AJ 1963*
23. Note from Michael Boyd-Carpenter, 14.7.2010
24. The *Guardian*, obituary by Anthony Sampson, 15.3.2002
25. Trevor Braham, *Himalayan Odyssey,* p.45
26. *Malvern Gazette*, 1993
27. The *Listener*, 6.1.1949
28. *Malvern Gazette*, 11.12.1948
29. *Climbers' Club Journal*, 1949 pp 113, 114
30. *Malvern Gazette* 11.3.1949
31. Rose Binney, 'Binns', an old friend was living with the Noyces
32. Eveline Ballard died in 1961. Rosemary Noyce married Stephen Ballard in 1963
33. Conversation with Rosemary Ballard 16.11.2008
34. Note from Michael Boyd-Carpenter 13.7.2010
35. Malvern press August 1950
36. *Herald* for Farnham, Hindhead and Haslemere 18.8.1950

CHAPTER NINE

THE YEARS 1950 TO 1954 – GETTING ESTABLISHED

Wilfrid and Rosemary Noyce came from their honeymoon directly to Godalming. They had rented a house, Little Barn East, in Mark Way, just outside the Charterhouse grounds, from Pippa Butt, widow of a retired Charterhouse bursar, Commander Butt. To help pay the rent they took in as lodgers two staff from Priorsfield, the girls' public school, some two miles from Charterhouse along the Puttenham road. One was a French girl doing a thesis in English on E. M. Forster which Rosemary typed for her and later on Rosemary joined the staff at Priorsfield and taught French there.

Noyce also celebrated his wedding with the publication of **Scholar Mountaineers.** The local newspaper, among several newspapers and journals, reviewed it and also reported his wedding as a 'local' boy.[1] In the book he has chosen to analyse the feelings toward the mountains of twelve writers in English, French and German, across some 600 years, starting with Dante and Petrarch, including the Lakeland poets, men of action such as Leslie Stephen, one of the early presidents of the Alpine Club, and Robert Falcon Scott, of Antarctic fame. The definition of 'mountaineer' was wide and sympathetic. A reviewer wrote: '*We can unhesitatingly place his present collection of agreeable essays among our good mountain books of the older order.*'[2] At Christmas that year Noyce sent a copy of the book to his mother: '*To Mum for a very Happy Christmas from Wilf.*'

The scene at Charterhouse was not too different from that which Noyce had left some fourteen years before. The school had recovered from the war and was up to its strength of some 650 boys. George Turner, had been headmaster for three years of the five he had agreed to serve until a definitive appointment could be made. He had been a pupil of Frank Fletcher at Marlborough, and had recently retired as Principal of Makerere College, Kampala, now the most important university in Uganda. There had been very little new building, the austere interiors of the boarding-houses had not changed and a number of the masters whom Noyce had known as a pupil were still there. Among them were Frank Ives, by then housemaster of Noyce's old house Weekites, Vincent 'Peter' Russell and Brian Lee.

By the end of his period at Malvern Noyce was no longer teaching classics and had switched to French. At Charterhouse he taught French to the fifth forms, those who were taking Ordinary Level School Certificate at the end of the school year, and the Modern Language Specialists in the sixth forms.

Almost immediately he became involved in the Senior Scouts. The Charterhouse Scout Log records:

> *The Senior Scouts were reformed in October 1950. Mr R. C. Fletcher welcomed the first members at a special ceremony; and handed the section, then consisting of 5 members, to Mr C. W. F. Noyce.*

For the record the members were I. T. Macleod, E. M. W. Robinson, J. P. Harwood, L. W. Morrish and M. C. Melchisa. Inevitably Senior Scout activities focused on mountains and climbing skills. The first Senior camp was 19-27th April 1951 led by Noyce in which MacLeod, Morrish and Robinson participated. They were based at the Climbers' Club Hut at Ynys Ettws, in the Llanberis Pass.

The role of Assistant Master at Charterhouse was ideal for Wilfrid Noyce. He was able to develop his two main interests of mountaineering and writing and the school was pleased to have a distinguished mountaineer and scholar with his connections and experience to inspire the boys. He was granted leaves of absence for his longer mountaineering trips and in the holidays he could concentrate on his writing. This took a number of different forms, articles for magazines and newspapers, a novel, plays, poetry and biography. Not all his work was published but it was during his time at Charterhouse that Noyce began writing in earnest and he spent a great deal of time researching in the London Library.

He enjoyed very much being in the mountains on his own. He shared this preference for solitary activities when he described his solo descent, in February 1942, of the Devil's Kitchen, in the Ogwen Valley, in a talk on the BBC Home Service in June 1951. He had planned a second talk in which he described his great climb on Curving Crack on Clogwyn d'ur Arddu in May 1942, but this does not appear to have been broadcast. He was nonetheless a very good 'team player' and always did his fair share and more of the chores in camp or the hut. Of him in the Pamirs Hunt wrote; *'Derek [Jones], Robin [Smith] and of course, Wilf are wonders of selfless labour in the common weal.'*[3] He was content to accept a supporting rôle in the interest of the expedition and also take a leading role if necessary, as he would demonstrate on Everest, Machapuchare and Trivor.

Italy continued to be a major interest and in the summer of 1951 Rosemary and Wilfrid had a camping holiday in Italy. Inevitably, climbing was on the programme and they ended up in Arolla, in Switzerland, where Arthur Pigou was staying, and Noyce and he climbed together. The breadth and depth of Noyce's knowledge and appreciation of the country is shown in his review of Lady Sydney Morgan's recently republished ***Italy*** that she had written following a journey in the country in 1820.[4] At Charterhouse he taught Italian to a wives' group: Italian, however, was not on the school curriculum until much later.

He was also working on a mountaineering anthology with Edward Pyatt, a fellow mountaineer and writer. Pyatt had written a number of books on the British hills as well as a history of the National Physical Laboratory at Teddington. In addition he was editor of the ***Alpine Journal*** from 1971 to 1982. The result of their collaboration was ***British Crags and Climbers,*** which covered almost all aspects of climbing in Britain. After an introductory history of climbing in Britain by Pyatt it included selections of writing from the early pioneers such as Tyndall, Stogden and Spencer and described climbs in North Wales and the Lakes in 1850-1870 as well as more recent ascents in Scotland, Cornwall, the Surrey hills and even the spires of Cambridge. It is a delightful collection about the British hills and mountains and first appeared in 1952.

As Guidebook Editor of the Climbers' Club he was very much in favour of guidebooks so that the adventurous, and prudent, might not be dependent on finding an experienced climber to assist them and might also be helped to determine a destination for an expedition. There were, however, those who decried guides and the need for them and set their views out in the ***Climbers' Club Journal.*** Noyce felt bound to answer their criticism:

To the Editor, Climbers' Club Journal.

Dear Sir,

I have read with interest the letter of J. N. Mills in the 1951 Journal, and feel that perhaps it behoves me, as Editor of the Club's Guide-Books, to say something in reply.

The evergreen controversy of guide-book versus non-guide-book has flourished ever since the days when Geoffrey Winthrop Young inspired the first guides, with the feeling, as he says, that they had become a regrettable necessity. Most writers and editors of guidebooks probably agree that in an ideal world their existence would be doubtful. They are, however, the best arrangement in a bad world; since there is a demand for them which should be satisfied in a sensible rather than misleading way, and since they provide information which can show newcomers and others where they may most safely and profitably go.

There is one point which is often lost from view in this controversy. Nobody is compelled to use the new guide-books. Either, if you like to have a description like "…An easy line follows an obvious groove …" you may enjoy very pleasant and instructive climbing with the 1910 series of guide-books, which in their own way are masterpieces. Or you can throw guide-books to the winds, and climb over the cliffs of Cader Idris or Moel yr Hydd with all the élan of the early pioneers in Snowdonia. Guide-books are written for those who want them, not for those who don't.

*The phrase which seems especially to have filled Mr. Mills with foreboding is that in the author's Preface to 'Outlying Crags of Wales' (1950 Journal): 'Complete and exhaustive works in the latter style (of the present series) can follow in later years.' They can follow, but by no means need. It depends entirely on the policy of the Club at a future time. So far as the present goes, **my own** feeling and that of some others was that a guide to the outlying areas would be useful, not because it led to a complete working out of all cliffs, but in the hope that it might draw away just some of those nail scratching crowds from Idwal, which Mr. Mills appears to dislike. In furthering this hope E. C. Pyatt has done an excellent and useful work. For up to date it has always surprised me, **how** many frequenters of the C.C. huts seemed to* *be unaware that there was climbing at all south of Siabod or west of Beddgelert.*

The climbers of the next generation, if they are drawn by the guide to visit outlying districts, will be in a position to choose whether or not any further guide to these districts is needed. And I for one feel very happy to leave the choice to them.

Yours, etc.,
Wilfrid Noyce.

Noyce encouraged the production of guides and developed the coverage considerably over the years that he was editor. Originally the guides covered only the Snowdon District but from 1955 they included Cornwall in the title of the series. Eventually with the inclusion of the rocky outcrops in the South of England the series covered England and Wales from 1956. Noyce edited and produced some twelve guides during the period 1948 to 1961.

The Noyces by this time had moved from Mark Way to Badgers Hollow, a small block of flats belonging to the school, in Peperharow Road, at the bottom of the copse which covered the hill on which the school stood. At the back, running the length of the block was a stone retaining wall some four metres in height. This also turned out to be a very good climbing-wall and the Senior Scouts spent many hours clinging with their fingertips to the stones or practising various mountain first-aid and rescue techniques, sometimes to the consternation of the neighbours. It was said that George Leigh Mallory climbed on this same wall, when he was teaching at Charterhouse.

On 29th June 1952 Michael Noyce, their first child, was born. Noyce, from all accounts, undertook his new rôle as a father very seriously. He would push the pram up the hill from their flat to the school making a virtue out of his fitness training. It made a change from pushing an old pram full of stones. Ian Grimble, Noyce's comrade-in-arms in India was godfather.

After a different kind of summer holiday Noyce started his third year of teaching at Charterhouse in an ordinary way. However, he was aware that there were discussions about an Everest attempt and the activities of the Swiss on Everest were being watched carefully. The invitation came in the October and Noyce's part in this expedition and the follow-up is covered in other chapters. The preparations started at the end of 1952 and with the lecture tours that followed Noyce did not get back to full-time teaching until 1954.

He was, however, living in Godalming when he was not lecturing and later in 1953 to commemorate his participation in the Everest expedition the Godalming and District Youth Committee established **The Wilfrid Noyce Personal Achievement Trophy**. This is awarded annually for the most outstanding feat of courage, leadership, fortitude or enterprise by a young person under twenty-one who lives in the Godalming Youth Committee area.

He was also broadcasting, in a variety of programmes for the BBC. Soon after their return from Everest Sir Edmund Hillary, as he was by then, Griff Pugh, the physiologist on the Everest expedition, and Noyce did a twenty-minute schools broadcast on *The Conquest of Everest*.[5]

Nationalism in Mountaineering featured in a talk Noyce did in German for the German Service of the BBC on 17th May 1954 and ten days later he did a BBC Schools broadcast on *Life in the Himalaya* in the Geography series. With Pugh again he discussed the use of oxygen in mountaineering on the German service of the BBC in 1955.

The poem *Michael Angelo* which had developed from Noyce's very strong interest in the sculptor when he was at school was being prepared for publication in the autumn of 1953. It is a long poem, in twelve parts recounting important episodes in the sculptor's life. He was very apprehensive about its reception by the public. He wrote, paying tribute to Frida Leakey's encouragement and support for the writing of the poem,

> *The actual publication date is Oct 26th. It will perhaps but not be reviewed much – I don't know – but I feel terrified for the poor thing, as if it were my child going out into the world. "Mr Noyce climbs better than he writes…. He would do better to stick to mountain books." I am prepared for that though I hope some may get it as meant.*[6]

He need not have worried:

> *The straightforward method of Mr Wilfrid Noyce will be found agreeable by those who do not look for subtlety and his honest enthusiasm is invigorating. To read this poem is, in some ways,*

an exhilarating experience for it expresses the enduring spirit of the human race.[7]

At the same time he received further encouragement for his poetry: he had sent some of the Everest poems to the, then new, literary magazine **Encounter**, which was run by Stephen Spender a friend of Frances Cornford, who herself had inspired and encouraged Noyce over the years. Spender responded with an invitation to lunch to discuss a plan to include Noyce's poems as a regular feature of the magazine.

Noyce returned to his teaching duties for the summer term in 1954. The teaching of French to the fifth forms was a renewed challenge as the boys were very happy to side-track him into more adventurous discussions.

He was also working on his own chronicle of the Everest expedition. This was published in the autumn of 1954, after he was back full-time teaching, and he intended it as a personal view of the expedition, complementary to the formal record of **The Ascent of Everest.**[8] It was widely and well reviewed and he clearly succeeded in his objective. Trevor Allen wrote;

> *He achieves his purpose with honour, in a prose spare, strong, sinewy, warming at times to a magical beauty.*[9]

And **The Times:**

> *He describes, as well as the intimate details of the expedition and the characters and idiosyncrasies of the members, the emotional impact of the mountain recollected in tranquillity.* **South Col** *will be as much at home on the shelves marked "literature" as on those marked "travel and adventure."*[10]

F. Spencer-Chapman, the explorer and writer, wrote,

> **South Col** *is not only a book of great enchantment and revelation but it is a most admirable complement to John Hunt's official narrative.*[11]

In October 1954 **Trade News** published an article by Noyce, 'War, Escape, Travel, Crime – No Comics or Science Fiction – or what do boys read now?' In this he admits that he is woefully ignorant of what girls read and compares the evidence of an earlier publication, 'What do Boys and Girls Read?' It was written by A. J. Jenkinson in 1940 with a snapshot of the tastes of the 1950s. Surprisingly, science fiction was hardly looked at by that generation. Somerset Maugham, Sapper and Leslie Charteris with his seemingly endless Saint novels though were very popular. Adventure and war stories were also popular but Noyce did not think that comics, horror or otherwise, were a menace to a school library.

> *The road from comics to Virginia Woolf is a long one; but a boy might just take the step between say,* **Sound Barrier** *and the novels of Saint-Exupéry, in which the action goes on in the adventurer's mind.. Whether he does or no, the adventure itself should be the genuine article, because only that will stimulate him to a like activity.*
>
> *Let him read the good science stories and then go back to his own experiments. Let him read Shackleton and Shipton and Cousteau (not potted versions) and then go to the ends of his own earth. Let him read, if Shelley no longer pleases, a poetry that takes him to places and introduces him to people.*[12]

The following month he was reviewing Maurice Herzog's epic **Annapurna**, which had had a very popular following in Britain since it appeared in 1952, comparing it with **The Ascent of Everest.**

> *It moves out of the field of normal mountain literature, that is the reason for the non-mountaineering public. ... At first reading it carried me through the night like an exciting novel of impossible daring...I gasped at the speed of the final action, hurried through before the oncoming monsoon. F. S. Smythe had pronounced it all but impossible to reconnoitre and climb a major Himalayan peak in the same season. The French did it; at a cost. And the spirit of Herzog went beyond that suffering to write an account coloured by it and never dimmed; an unparalleled glimpse back into the inner mind of men, when they climb the highest mountains of the world.*[13]

In December he published an article 'Cruelty to Snowmen', recounting a tale, that he and others had heard from the Deputy Abbot of the

Thyangboche monastery, of the visits and depredations of the legendary *yeti*, or 'Abominable Snowman'. It did not settle any arguments about the yeti and it did preserve the mystery.

He was also writing articles for various periodicals, such as the **Cambridge Review** and the **Spectator**. His article on 'Sherpas at Home' appeared in both these journals in 1954. Among the Noyce circle of friends was Odette Tchernine, whom Noyce used to refer to as the 'Russian Ball'. She was a small lively woman who had been writing poetry and books on mountains and the Abominable Snowman for many years and she wrote a novel at the age of 92. She lived at that time in a small flat in Bayswater and used to receive visits from climbers such as John Blashford-Snell and Chris Bonington. Of Noyce she wrote:

> *He was one of the finest persons I have ever known, and friendship with him and Rosemary, his wife, was a privilege. Apart from being considered the finest mountaineer of his generation, he possessed such understanding, and nobility and kindness of character, that this had to be experienced to be realised, and these qualities are reflected in the books and poems he wrote.*[14]

In the same year that he was on Everest he became one of the founder members of the Alpine Climbing Group (ACG). Noyce more than most spanned at least two eras of major mountain exploration. He had made a name for himself as a rock-climber and Alpine mountaineer in the late 1930s when the Alps and the more distant ranges were frequented only by those with sufficient time and funds – or sponsorship. After the war we have seen how he participated in the new wave of enthusiasm for mountain activities by his encouragement of the young and in communicating his enthusiasm to the members of the much wider public who were now excited by the mountains. In the late 1940s and the early 1950s rock-climbing had become very popular in Britain and the number of mountain clubs had grown. Increasing leisure time and wealth gave encouragement to go into the hills and mountains and take up the challenges of the British cliffs and crags and the mountains on the continent of Europe.

Activity in North Wales, the North of England and Scotland had increased enormously. The Ramblers' Club, the Fell and Rock Climbing Club, the Northumbrian Mountaineering Club, the Manchester Gritstone Club, the Midland Association of Mountaineers, the Rock and Ice

Club, the Rucksack Club and the Northern universities' climbing clubs, among others, nurtured this interest and dramatic advances in climbing technique and proficiency were being made. Leading edge activity was moving away from the older clubs such as the Climbers' Club and the Alpine Club to these newer groups.

Joe Brown, a Manchester plumber, was typical of this new generation of climbers. He developed new techniques and made a number of remarkable first ascents including Cenotaph Corner, in Llanberis Pass. He and the celebrated Don Whillans, his companion on many first ascents, were both members of the Rock and Ice Club.

In 1953 leading climbers such as Whillans and his colleagues from the North, Scottish climbers such as Bill (W.H.) Murray, a number of Oxford and Cambridge University mountaineers, such as Alan Blackshaw, Tom Bourdillon and George Band and one or two from the Alpine Club, such as Wilfrid Noyce and Roger Chorley, came together to form the Alpine Climbing Group, modelled on the French Groupe de Haute Montagne (GHM) based in Chamonix. Membership was restricted to men *and women* under forty years of age who were 'of the requisite standard of mountaineering competence, which is determined according to the discretion of the committee'. Tom Bourdillon was elected the first president. He had made the first summit attempt on Everest in 1953 with Charles Evans and was president until his death in the Alps in July 1956.

An annual Bulletin was 'published, containing news of important mountaineering in the Alps and other great ranges of the World'. Guide books were also produced for Mont Blanc, the Pennine Alps and the Dauphiné. Initially there was no formal connection with the Alpine Club, which had the air then of being an elderly gentlemen's club, resting somewhat on its laurels. The Northern climbers were not anxious to be 'caught in the cob-webs of the Alpine Club'. Members of the ACG were elected, usually without hesitation, to the Alpine Club and brought a new vigour to its activities and membership. The ACG finally became part of the Alpine Club in 1967. This fusion created a good combination of the skills and technical prowess of the 'young tigers' with the access to funds and support of a network of resources of an established institution.

When Noyce returned to teaching at Charterhouse in April 1954, he found an increased interest in rock-climbing and mountains. The Senior Scouts were the main practitioners and on 22nd to 25th May, with the school doctor, Jo Waycott, Noyce took a group to explore a new group of rocks at Stone Farm, not far from Tunbridge Wells, and then on to the better known Harrison's Rocks. Stone Farm Rocks was a particularly good find and subsequently the rocks were regularly visited. For the author of this book, who had by then moved up to the Senior Scouts, this was his introduction to climbing.

On 17th May Noyce gave a talk on the German Service of the BBC on **Nationalism in Mountaineering.** Earlier he had already written a piece on Everest for the journal of the CUMC. There were men from both Oxford and Cambridge on the 1953 Everest expedition and consequently the Oxbridge and Cambridge mountaineering journals for 1954 were both reviewed together:

> *Inevitably, the two journals overlap, not only in the Alps, and it is interesting to note the parallel lines along which they run in many of their pages. For example, Noyce for Cambridge and Westmacott for Oxford each describe a personal chapter in the Everest story, whilst Nicol for Oxford and Wrangham for Cambridge describe their combined ascent of the North-West ridge of the Charmoz – in marked contrast to the leisured luxury of the Himalayan sleeping-bag.*[15]

The next major event was the arrival of the Noyces' second son, Jeremy, on 11th July 1954. Stephen Ballard was invited to be godfather. Noyce celebrated this with a Sunday outing on 18th July with the Senior Scouts to Harrison's Rocks!

In August there was a trip with John Hunt, David Cox and Michael Ward in the Alps. They were based mainly in Chamonix. The weather, however, was bad and they were forced to turn back from their objectives on several occasions. Hunt recalls:

> *We were forced to bow to the elements just beneath the summit ridge after climbing the frontier ridge from the refuge on the Col de Fourche: all hell prevailed on the crest above us, and there was nothing for it but to return. Wilf was totally serene. Before we turned back for the refuge, as we stood in their steps with our noses pressed against the slope, he pronounced it was time for breakfast.*[16]

Noyce, as ever, unperturbed by the precariousness of the situation just thought that it was time to eat.

On another occasion they were within a few 100 feet of the summit of the Aiguille du Peigne by its north-west ridge and were forced to turn back. The major success of that season, however, was the double traverse of the Rochefort Arête from the Dent du Géant and back. The weather further deteriorated and they had to content themselves with less ambitious routes such as the Clochers Clochetons and the Aiguille Belvédère. Later on that trip, to the consternation of his companions, Noyce proposed that they do what he always did, squeeze in another peak or two before going home.

> On the last day but one he and John Hunt were caught in a fierce electric storm and heavy snow three-quarters of the way up the frontier ridge of Mont Maudit. The retreat down the ridge must have been a nightmare for some hours as two of us who were on the ordinary route on the Midi could judge; yet when we met up in the late afternoon and were walking down, it was Wilfrid who suggested that we should stay on at the Montenvers so as to snatch a quick traverse of the Petits Charmoz and the Aiguille de l'M next day before we left for home.[17]

There was a short holiday with the newly enlarged family and it was then back to school in September, for teaching, and scouting. This term he planned outdoors activities for the Senior Scouts, which would form the basis of a guide-book for the district around the school. This never actually came to fruition. There was also an outing to Stone Farm Rocks on 31st October. The year ended with Noyce appearing at the *Schoolboys' Exhibition* in London and signing copies of his book **South Col** for an enthusiastic audience.

Notes

1 Herald for Farnham, Haslemere and Hindhead, 18.8.1950
2 Geoffrey Winthrop Young, *The Spectator 29.9.1950*
3 John Hunt, *Life is Meeting* p.192
4 Wilfrid Noyce, *Cambridge Review 31.5.1952*.
5 *BBC Home Service (Schools)* 23.9.1953
6 Wilfrid Noyce, *letter to Frida Leakey 17.10.1953*
7 *Times Literary Supplement 15.1.1954*
8 John Hunt, *The Ascent of Everest, the official story of the expedition*
9 *Everybody's* magazine, November 1954

10 *The Times* 10.11.1954
11 *The Broadsheet,* World Books 1.9.1955
12 Wilfrid Noyce, *Trade News, 30.10.1954*
13 Wilfrid Noyce, *The Broadsheet, World Books Nov 1954, p.2*
14 Odette Tchernine, *Surrey Advertiser 3.8.1962*
15 *Reviews* CCJ 1955 p.165
16 John Hunt & David Cox, *Wilfrid Noyce 1917-1962: Some Personal Memories* AJ 1993 p.69
17 David Cox, *Wilfrid Noyce Obituary AJ 1963*

CHAPTER TEN

EVEREST 1952-53

The Preparations

In September 1952 Col. John Hunt, Noyce's mountaineering friend from the war, was asked by the Joint Himalayan Committee to lead a British Everest expedition proposed for 1953. The project was still not firm because the Swiss were at that time making an attempt to get to the summit of Everest, and looked like succeeding. If they succeeded, this British expedition might have to find another objective such as Kanchenjunga. This, however, would reduce the media appeal and the prospect of generous sponsorship. Nonetheless, an expedition to Everest had to be planned.

Immediately, John Hunt set about selecting a team. The winter term at Charterhouse in 1952 started in the ordinary way for Noyce. On Saturday 11th October when he arrived home from school for lunch, with thoughts of the christening that afternoon of his son Michael, his wife said that there had been a telephone call from John Hunt. Three days later he and Hunt finally made contact. Noyce came out of the classroom to answer the call, having enjoined the class *"...to look at the irregular verbs on page ninety-six for a few minutes"*. Hunt asked him to meet him in London as he wanted his opinion on a few things about Everest and asked him if he would be free to join the expedition. In his book, **South Col** one has the feeling that at the bottom of his heart Noyce wanted to be invited. Although he had had more Himalayan experience than most at that time and had made bold and distinguished ascents in the Alps, in the recent years he had done more modest climbs and his activities had been largely confined to taking boys climbing. *"I have done little more than being led up 'Very Severes'."*

He wrote later:

> *So it had happened, as I suspected, and perhaps it came as more of a shock to me than to any other member of our party. I had planned no such thing. I thought I had seen my last of the high Himalaya, and for the summer I hoped to visit Italy and finish a book about some of the nineteenth-century travellers there. Nor did I know how fit I was. But now – into all plans this utterly new idea had intruded. And I think my wife and I felt there was something of fate about it. A choice, yes, but how could it be made otherwise than by consent?'*

These were some of the thoughts when Noyce reflected on the invitation from John Hunt. After discussion with Rosemary, his wife, and with her full support he accepted. Happily, Charterhouse gave him considerable leave of absence. This was necessary for the planning, preparation and training period before the time in the Himalaya, but what was not so clear then was that following the success of the expedition there might be lectures and events in Britain and on the continent which would take him away from family and school until the summer term in 1954. There was another reason for reflection; the only person on the expedition that Noyce had climbed with was John Hunt. He had met only two of the others while several had climbed together recently in the Himalaya, on Cho Oyu, on the Everest reconnaissance in 1951 and on British hills. Noyce was conscious of being somewhat of an outsider and he was the third oldest at thirty-four. John Hunt and Alf Gregory were older and Alf had been on Cho Oyu in 1952.

Immediately Noyce started to work on his fitness. The Noyces now lived in Peperharow Road which ran along the bottom of the hill on which the school stood. There was a private road up to the school with a fair gradient. We schoolboys used to see him pushing a pram with his baby son, Michael, and stones in it, putting in progressively more stones. At other times he had Michael in his rucksack.

In his considerations when choosing the team, Hunt wanted each member to be a '*potential summiter*'[2] and when set against the other criteria, '*age: temperament: experience: physique*',[3] Wilfrid Noyce became an obvious choice. Edmund Hillary wrote of him:

> *Wilf Noyce was a tough and experienced mountaineer with an impressive record of difficult and dangerous climbs. In many respects I considered Noyce the most competent British climber I had met.*[4]

Alf Gregory, the photographer on the expedition, also said that Noyce was the strongest contender for the summit party.

In the early 1950s, expeditions to climb major peaks in the Himalaya were almost affairs of state and matters of national prestige. This was not an Alpine climbing meet; it was a project of national importance and the full range of national resources, from government, the armed services, and from industry were mobilised in support. Royalty was also involved.

Hunt, who had been Chief of Staff to General Montgomery at Supreme Headquarters, Allied Powers in Europe, before his appointment as leader, called the first meeting of the team in London on 17th November 1952. He planned the expedition as meticulously as any military operation. The organising secretary was also a soldier, Major Charles Wylie of the Gurkhas. There were eleven climbers in the team, including Hunt, and two others, a physiologist, Griffith Pugh, assigned by the Medical Research Council and a cameraman, Tom Stobart. These two also had mountain experience. The numbers were made up to fourteen by the addition of Sherpa Tensing to the climbing party.

Hunt organised the group so that each member was responsible for an aspect of the organisation. George Band, for example, fresh from National Service in the Royal Signals and still an undergraduate at Cambridge, was in charge of wireless communications and equipment and Tom Bourdillon was in charge of the oxygen equipment. Noyce was in charge of mountaineering equipment. He worked with Anthony Rawlinson, a reserve member of the expedition, on this in the UK and had the complete responsibility on the mountain. This involved discussions with many suppliers in the UK and on the continent, quite a number of whom were developing equipment specially for the expedition. As part of this responsibility Noyce even went on a boot-repairing course at Robert Lawrie Ltd.

The second gathering of the party and reserves was at the Climbers' Club hut, Helyg in North Wales in mid-January 1953. This enabled the members of the party to get to know each other better and to test items of equipment such as the oxygen apparatus developed by Tom

Bourdillon and his father. As Hunt wrote: '*Altogether, the occasion was a very happy one.*' It was a good augury for the weeks to be spent together on Everest.

Preparations included the more tedious and equally vital tasks of listing, sorting and packing the provisions and equipment for dispatch on their varied journey to Base Camp. Noyce was the only one of the team who saw and oversaw the entire process of the gathering of the equipment and the packing of it and its delivery to Kathmandu where it was all united with the full team. Various other members of the team assisted at various times, but Noyce was there from beginning to end. This was an adventure in itself.

During January 1953 Noyce, with Charles Evans and Ralph Jones, a reserve, spent considerable time at the Wapping warehouse with the packing. They executed the carefully prepared plan so that the right items were packed together and were marked up. The cases were made up into coolie loads of about sixty pounds (twenty-seven kilograms) and marked with the place on the journey where they would be opened. The precise execution of this task was a vital contribution to the success and smooth running of the expedition.

Climbing insurance was not usually taken out at that time but when Charles Wylie said that the Sherpas were covered by insurance, the 'sahibs' made enquiries and received an offer of insurance of £1,000, payable in the event of death, for a premium of £100, just for the period of the expedition. When the odds were understood, one in ten chance of death – and there were ten of them – there was amazement. Griff Pugh, the physiologist looked up the statistics and concluded it was not far wrong! Noyce, with a family, felt that he should be covered and got a reduced premium of £50!

Public interest in the venture was growing; broadcasts on radio and television, lectures and interviews were requested and articles had to be written for **The Times**, whose correspondent, James, later Jan, Morris was to join the expedition. The six, including Noyce, who went to Tilbury on 12th February to embark for India on the SS *Stratheden* were grilled by the BBC and the press for one and a half hours. John Hunt, who had had to go into hospital, and the others flew out to India later in the month. Among the well-wishers who saw them off at Tilbury was Frida Leakey a loyal supporter of the Noyce family, with whom he maintained a correspondence throughout the expedition.

Tilbury to Kathmandu

The two-week voyage had two advantages; it provided a welcome rest from the frantic preparations and it enabled the party to get to know each other better. It also provided an opportunity for Charles Wylie to instruct the others in Nepali as well as some time for reflection for Noyce:

> *To come on such an expedition a man must make sacrifices, even if he does not think about most of them. I myself must forfeit salary at Charterhouse over these months; also, far more important, for five months the company of wife and small son. Not only that, I am condemned to give them anxiety which I could avoid, if I stayed at home. The boldest would not claim that climbing Everest is as safe as walking over green fields. To the average person it is a dangerous occupation; however much he may have confidence in the skill of the climber, objective dangers loom large. All this the family will not like to say, for fear of harassing the already harassed. But the terrors are there, and at the back of the climber's mind too. He does his best for them by paying insurance premiums, a useless precaution since nothing can replace that loss if it comes; and yet these pledges he must give, as an insurance for his own peace of mind.*
>
> *I could not claim that I was going to Everest for pleasure. Lesser mountains, yes, lesser ranges, where the hiss of the axe, the swing of the thigh uphill, the balanced body upon rock are the physical music of the mountaineer. But on Everest these pleasures are swirled away with the dust of Tibet, in the pain of the rarefied air, numbed limbs and storm-bound nights. I was not expecting to enjoy myself (and that I did enjoy myself after all is quite irrelevant). Therefore I was not going for pleasure.*
>
> *I was going, it seemed to me, because this adventure was one of the fine things of life, an exciting thing. During the broadcasting on the boat before we left, an Italian commentator asked Michael Westmacott whether he felt a great thrill at going to Everest.*
>
> *"Oh It'll be good fun," Mike said, or something equally unenthusiastic.*
>
> *"E molto emozionato", the commentator translated into his microphone. And of course he was right. We **were** very excited, though being English we disliked intensely admitting as much*

in public. This adventure was apart from ordinary experience, a great compulsory heaving away out of a rut. Normally, modern men have little chance to take part in anything that can be called 'great'. Everybody must have an urge to break out, just once, from the comfort as well as the monotony of day-to-day; to do it by the proxy of books if the reality of escape is not possible; to live hard and to live fully these few days of life. Further the sharing of such an enterprise with others will come to mean as much as the original challenge. The idea of Everest as an unclimbed mountain must first be present to the adventurers, and Everest must be climbed 'because it's there', in Mallory's phrase. Then to the individual there presents itself the idea of a great common effort, an adventure in the company of others. Finally, there may be added to this conception the thought of Fame. She is, no denying it, a lady who sometimes takes us by the shoulders and spurs such part of our spirit as we can call 'clear', away from our inhibitions and laziness. In this case she sets the seal of Everest on a climber's career; to gain the seal she goads him to unpleasant efforts over which he might hesitate if left to himself.

Before he left home he managed to get an article off to the **Spectator** under the very apposite title, **'Why Mountaineer?'**[6]

Noyce passed the time playing deck tennis, reading and eating enormous meals.

I used to wonder occasionally: is it better to make the most of food while one has it, or start tightening the belt in preparation? Or perhaps never tighten it at all, that may be the answer.

On one occasion he went down to check his trunk in the baggage room and discovered that the boot-repairing glue had leaked all over his one respectable suit. Lawrie replaced the glue but Noyce does not record how successful he was with the stain removers.

They reached Bombay on the morning of 28th February and were met by Professor George Finch of the National Physical Laboratory of India, who had climbed to a record height of 27,300ft (8,315m) on Everest in 1922, A. R. Leyden, the local secretary of the Himalayan Club, Basil Goodfellow of the Himalayan Committee, and George Lowe who had come from New Zealand to join the party. After lunch at the Taj Mahal Hotel Finch talked to them about oxygen then Noyce, as the only member of the Wapping Working Party to go out by boat, found himself as Baggage Master and had to go down to the station to supervise the loading of the baggage into the special goods-wagon for the next part of the journey.

> *It was the first time I had seen it all together, and I stood with the representatives of Mackinnon and Mackenzie, watching the strangest assortment of oddly-shaped packages descend on to the back of porters, be carried across and dumped in apportioned places on the wagon floor. The procession seemed endless. Some packages were short and small, like the photographic box, some long and awkward like the sections of the duraluminum ladder, some robustly square like the cookery boxes. There were kitbags containing personal clothing, and an enormous round sackcloth package, the bane of all who tried to handle it, containing the New Zealand sleeping-bags. The loading took two and a half hours; we reckoned nearly eight tons of equipment in over five hundred packages (including personal kit). The wagon was then locked. I pocketed the key and went off, hoping fervently that it would meet us safely at Lucknow.*

They were splendidly entertained by Leyden and others at Pali Hill, the very smart suburb of Bombay, then Noyce, Band, Lowe and Westmacott left on the train at 23.00 heading for Cawnpore (Kanpur) and thence to Lucknow. The train broke down on the following day and after waiting for the relief engine they reached Lucknow at 9.00 on 3rd March. The baggage was not due to arrive until the afternoon, so they had to spend the night in Lucknow – a considerable relief. That afternoon they went back to the station to check that the baggage had arrived and get it trans-shipped on to the narrower gauge line running to Raxaul, on the borders of India and Nepal. This time they were assisted by Burma Shell employees and it was a much quicker operation than in Bombay. The baggage, they were assured, would depart in the course of the next few hours. During their brief visit to Lucknow they managed to visit the zoo and the historic Residency, scene of battles during the Indian Mutiny.

They took the afternoon train on 4th March and had a memorable night on the train. One is surprised that Noyce, with his experience

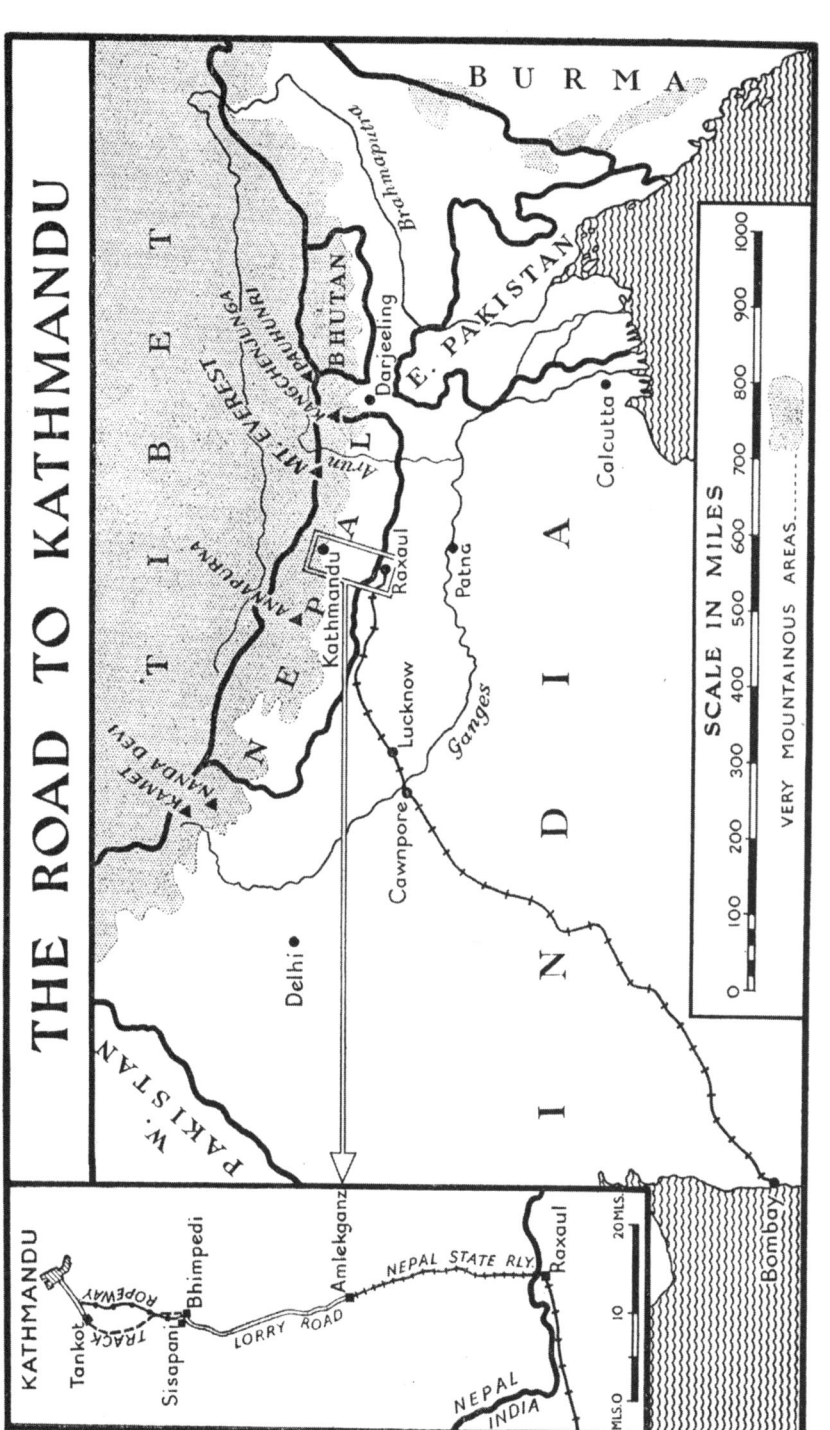

This shows the political boundaries as they existed in 1953.

of trains in India ten years before was not prepared, but this is how he recounts the night up to Samashtipur:

As the evening wore on we became rapidly filthier, although rather cooler (Lucknow was suffering a heatwave). During the night I disgraced myself. At about 2 a.m. I heard thumpings on the door. I remember thinking through my dreams: 'Ah, ticket-collector.' I clambered out of my bunk half-awake and opened up. Alas, in an instant and before we could get the door shut, the total population of India seemed to have dumped itself screaming on the floor of our carriage. In vain George Lowe gesticulated and threatened. Families, bearers, merchants, they were all coming on "only for one station more". Occupation, like possession, is nine-tenths of the law, and that was the end of our sleep for the night.[7]

They had breakfast at Samashtipur with Mr. Chatterjee of Burma Shell and left at 8.30 on another train. This time they did not open doors, even for food! They reached Raxaul at 15.30 and before they could get refreshments Noyce, Lowe and Westmacott were taken off through the rice-fields to the Indian border post. Here they were given the documents for the mortar bombs which had been brought up by the Indian Army and collected more kerosene from Burma Shell.

The Nepal State Railway, as it was then called, ran from Raxaul on an even narrower gauge some twenty-five miles up to Amlekganz (Amlekhagunj). To-day it has been superseded by a road. In this further trans-shipment they were assisted by *'a curious little Nepali, distinguished by a stammer and a topee, who styled himself "runner to the British Embassy"'*. He did not manage his men well and the loading took three hours, and even then nine loads had to be stored overnight in a locked warehouse. Finally Westmacott and Noyce joined George Lowe at the dak bungalow in the trees and had the first real meal of the day, chicken, vegetables and chapatti. When Noyce asked for bread, the bearer was surprised; they were no longer in bread country.

The following morning, 6th March, they were at the station soon after 7.00. They received the mortar bombs from the Indian Army, collected the nine loads and chugged off to Nepal. *'A dirty little stream'* was said to be the border and no passports were demanded. At the first station in Nepal, the runner, dubbed 'Henry' by Noyce, went off and came back with a grubby piece of paper, their pass for Nepal. The journey of twenty-five miles took two and a half hours and they were sleepy and hungry when they arrived. While the train shunted and Henry wandered at a loss among the coolies and chickens, the British settled down to breakfast of the two chickens, potatoes and tomatoes that they had brought with them from the bungalow.

At Amlekhagunj they trans-shipped the loads again on to four lorries for the twenty-four-mile journey to Bhimpedi. The porters who presented themselves to do the loading were a ragged bunch, broad-featured and yellower-skinned than the Indians, with high cheek-bones and slanting eyes. The loads were transferred to the lorries and they got away at 12.30 installed on the tops of the loads. At 14.50 Noyce arrived with the first three lorries at Bhimpedi in a shower of rain, for the last trans-shipment before Kathmandu. George Band and Lowe had a puncture and arrived later. The transfer this time was to a rope railway that would take the 807 loads on the penultimate stage to the stub of road where lorries would take them into Kathmandu. It was going to take three hours to get the loads on to the ropeway and work stopped at 17.00 – there was not enough time that day. The following day was a holiday. So far they had been keeping to the overall expedition schedule planned by Greg. According to that they were due to load at Bhimpedi on 6th March – that day – and get to Kathmandu by 7th March so that the expedition could start the march on the 9th. All they were faced with was the piles of luggage that the lorries had dumped on an uneven sack-covered floor. What to do?

They found two telephones, neither of which appeared to work. Then it was suggested that perhaps the Indian engineers who were building the road from India to Kathmandu might help. Mike Westmacott volunteered to walk up to their officers' mess and had not got far before he was picked up by Col. Grant, the Commandant, in a jeep. He generously agreed to put them up and put guards on the baggage and checked it for them. The following day, a Saturday, was a Nepali holiday so nothing could start until Sunday. As there was no point in all of them staying Mike Ward and the two Georges continued after tea to walk to Sisapani. Noyce and Westmacott, the treasurer for the baggage party, stayed to supervise the loading and pay any expenses. Although others tried to learn Hindi and Nepali for the expedition these two, Charles Evans and John Hunt were the only ones who knew Hindi, as they had all had previous service in India. They appreciated their stay in the officers' mess.

The experience of two nights with Indian Army officers is worth having for itself. The mess is a fine white stone building, situated on a bluff near the head of the valley a mile and a half from the rope railway. It was once the pleasure palace of the Prime Minister, a notably more spacious one than the King's palace nearby. The living-rooms are on three sides of a square, about a central courtyard in which the dining-room stands as a separate upper storey supported on wooden pillars. Here, that evening over dinner, we met the officers in charge of the road, the first road to join India and Kathmandu; and next morning, up at unit headquarters, we saw a model of it as it will be when completed, winding many miles over the westward hills. Colonel Grant hoped that this very autumn it would be 'jeepable' and finished by the end of next year. The sentimental traveller must regret that Nepal's isolation will be of the past; no longer will this land be the mystery of a few. But that consummation, we must admit with a sigh, was bound to come. The best we can hope is that the invaders will be merciful.[8]

John Hunt wrote, '*Despite all efforts to speed it up, our luggage reached the far terminal of the ropeway only on 8th March, one day before we planned to start our march.*' He was up against local tradition and holidays were sacrosanct!!

The following morning Noyce and Westmacott attended a Durbar at which the men, sitting in rows in front of the Colonel, could voice their concerns and grievances. One ingenuous suggestion was that the period of service on the road should be shortened so 'that others may have the wonderful experience of this great work'. They rested at Bhimpedi and explored the village reflecting that when the road is finished and the rope railway becomes obsolete the village will be 'finished' too. An elderly member of the Rana family, the ruling family of Nepal, lunching with them, observed,

"*The good old days are gone.*" *He thereupon bared his backside to show a scar left by the knife of an Indian whom he had defeated at wrestling, in the times when men were men.*

On 8th March at 0.45 a jeep from Col. Grant took them to the rope railway terminus where they started to load. Each load had to be checked and the trolley number noted. There were eighty-six loads and all except the odd ration-box arrived virtually undamaged at the other end. The task took five hours. Fortunately, the main body of the expedition was at the other end and they arranged for the collection and transfer of the loads to an Indian Army depot at Bhadgaon, eight miles west of Kathmandu. This enabled some of the lost time to be made up.

Noyce and Westmacott then set off to walk the rest of the way to Kathmandu. There was eighteen miles of track to the roadhead at Tankot then another five miles into Kathmandu. It was their first real exercise since leaving Britain. They had all walked round the deck of the *Stratheden* countless times but this was really the start of their trek to Everest. The track went up from Bhimpedi to a ridge where they could get a good view of the rope railway. It was worrying to see a box of high altitude boots swinging over a 1,000-foot gorge. Any slip would have been disastrous for the expedition. It was, however, a most agreeable walk in this springtime; the rhododendrons were in flower and the almond trees were covered in pink blossom. Noyce notes, '*Once, resting on the wayside grass and eating their second chapatti, Mike said, "Whatever happens on the expedition, I really am **happy** today." We both felt that.*'

They went over two 6,000-foot passes and on the second saw traces of a bulldozer, and wondered how it could have negotiated the track. They passed dismembered motor-cars; it took thirty coolies about a week to get a car body over the hills to Kathmandu. From the second pass they looked down on the plain of Nepal, with great relief. They descended a zig-zag path through cedar and pine passing wealthy Nepalese travelling in sedan chairs who eyed them curiously.

They reached Tankot and clearly enjoyed the hospitality of the tea-shop. Rather than wait for the transport that John Hunt had said would meet them, they started walking down the road. After two miles a gleaming chauffeur-driven limousine drew up. It was the British Ambassador, Christopher Summerhayes who had come to meet them in person. The gesture was enormously appreciated and when they arrived at the embassy, the expedition was finally all together. It was still 8th March and it had been a very long day for Noyce and Westmacott.

The March to Thyangboche

The rest of the expedition had been in Kathmandu for a while, some over a week, and were very anxious to get at their kit. Noyce was once again working with Charles Evans, the quartermaster, and on 9th March went out to Bhadgaon where it had all been lined up on the parade ground by Evans and Wylie. Each member checked his own department's equipment and it was divided into manageable loads. One item that was very heavy was the coin to pay the porters. They would not accept notes so twelve porters were required to carry these funds.[9] This was also when Noyce first met Tenzing, who was the Sirdar of the expedition. He was responsible for the Sherpas, the high altitude porters, and had brought most of them with him from Darjeeling. Although natives of Sola Khumbu in Nepal, they tended to be based in Darjeeling as that was where expeditions were accustomed to start at that time and the twenty Sherpas for this expedition had been selected by the Himalayan Club. Tenzing was very experienced as he had started his climbing as a porter on the British Everest reconnaissance expedition in 1935 and had been on nearly all the Everest expeditions since. In 1952 he climbed to within 1,000 feet of the summit of Everest with the Swiss guide Lambert. He was a world-class mountaineer. Noyce renewed his friendship with Angtharkay, with whom he had been in Sikkim in 1945. This time, however, his personal Sherpa, or orderly, was Ang Dawa I, whom the French had nicknamed Benjamin, as he was so small. He appeared in cloth cap, plus-fours, red stockings and gym shoes. Some of the Sherpas had brought their women-folk, the Sherpanis, who added colour and joy to the group. They worked as porters and were capable of carrying loads almost as heavy as those of their menfolk.

> *Some of them were very pretty; rose-red upon the dark bloom of their cheeks, flashing teeth, straight black hair and bright eyes that narrowed to slits when they laughed. There was Daku, "La Plus jolie de nos Sherpanis," as the Swiss called her, and "Ang Temba's girl-friend," tall and straight, with clean-cut features and the grave gentleness of a Madonna.*[10]

350 porters were needed to carry the loads up to the Base Camp at Thyangboche a seventeen-day march away, and these were recruited through a local contractor by Wylie. They came from the valleys around Kathmandu and assembled on the parade-ground at Bhadgaon.

After a very grand farewell reception on 9th March at the Indian Embassy graced by Nepalese Royalty and enlivened with a Military band, the main party left the following day with 150 porters. Wylie, Ward and Pugh followed a day later with the other 200, assisted by five

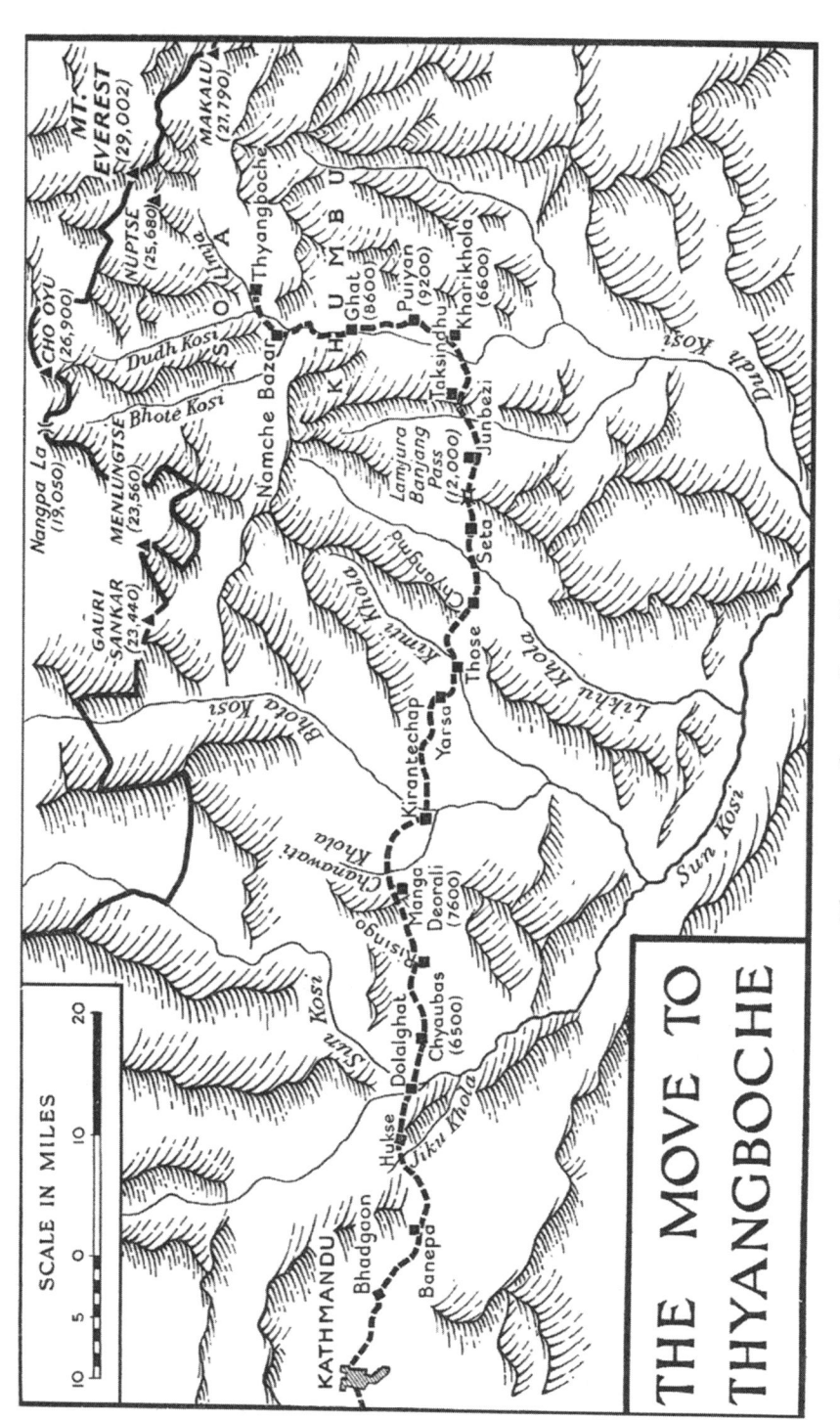

The approach march to Everest.

N.C.O.s from the Gurkha Brigade of the British Army. It was a busy road for the first six miles to Banepa and thereafter for most of the way it was a track, wide enough for only one person. The twenty-first century tourist would scarcely recognise it. Each member of the team carried a pack of about fifteen kilos and the orderly carried his and his Sahib's other personal kit.

Noyce carried:[11]

> 3 diaries, 9 books, the most important being *Il Purgatorio, The Brothers Karamazov,* and *Les Misérables II and III,* Camera and Compass
>
> Sponge bag and two small towels, Two pairs thin cotton pyjamas
>
> Gas cape, Vidor torch, Tablets from Mike Ward: Multivite and Water Cleansers Iodine & Mylol Insect Cream, Oxygen mask, Sticky tape
>
> Two pipes, one packet pipe-cleaners, Five pairs socks
> Gym shoes (worn sometimes instead of boots)

Ang Dawa carried for Noyce:

> Li-lo, Two sleeping-bags
>
> Polythene bags, one containing extra silk gloves, Thick sweater
>
> Spare pants and vest, Spare shirt, Climbing breeches

The books were the most difficult choice – and the heaviest. They are indispensable and the temptation was to take too many, as there would be many periods of inactivity, probably lying in a sleeping-bag, in what came to be known as '*The Everest Position*'. The diaries were very important for Noyce. John Hunt wrote, in his musing on how the expedition members spent their spare moments, '*Wilf Noyce, no less unobtrusive, would undoubtedly be scribbling page upon page of closely written manuscript in one of his several large notebooks.*' For the march he preferred an old pair of climbing boots rather than the gym shoes favoured by most of the others. Gym shoes had caused him pain and grief in Sikkim in 1945.

The oxygen masks were a source of irritation and amusement. They had been strongly advised in England to wear them on the march to get used to them. Some were more diligent than others. Noyce would sneak off and practise with his in the cool of the morning. Others would wear them all morning for a long walk uphill and arrive '...*in an aura of sweat, virtue and exhaustion at the top.*'

The normal routine on the march was to rise early with the orderlies producing mugs of tea just after 5.00 and they would set off at about 6.00, walk for two hours then have breakfast. Thondup, the Sherpa cook, would make a fire and very often cook the full English breakfast. It took a little while, but it was worth waiting for. Then they would continue until early afternoon and set up camp .This gave them time for their own pursuits. On the second day they had their first uncertain view of the Himalaya from the pass just after Banepa. This was the longest day and they reached Dolaghat at 2,500ft (760m) on the Sun Kosi River. Here they started to sleep under the stars. In such remote areas there is no light pollution and the skies appear to be full of stars – not just the bright ones that can compete with the street-lights. It is awe-inspiring.

> *I glimpsed again the less mundane feature of the expedition. Poetry, she had to hide her head, with all the flurry of oxygen masks, equipment sorting, baggage worries and the like. Now she peeped out with the drone of distant voices over innumerable camp fires, inviting me to measure the starry sky, lulling me asleep to the river's tune.*[12]

The rivers in Nepal flow south and their track took them eastwards. It was uphill and downhill with a succession of valleys and passes, each higher than the last. After six days they reached Kirantechap. Noyce gave some ideas to Hunt for the first dispatch on the march for **The Times.** He himself was writing reports for three schools, Charterhouse, St. Edmunds and Malvern. That day they had passed through Jiri, to where now the bus runs from Kathmandu. Two days later they climbed up to a pass at 9,500ft (2,900m) and entered the Sola Khumbu, Sherpa country. Here the people looked different to the other Nepalis. They were round-cheeked and slit-eyed and dressed in a homespun cloth robe and high felt boots. The men had pigtails and the women their hair in buns. The Nepalis they had seen until then had worn Indian clothes or the tight pyjama-like trouser under a full coat. On that day too they had their first glimpse of Everest: through a gap in a tangle of rhododendrons they could just see the summit of the mountain.

It was a very happy journey, although not necessarily carefree. Westmacott and Noyce left with the last of the coolies in the morning to make sure that the loads were safe and these and other worries saw to that. One could walk alone or with others, friendships were being cemented and interests were discovered and pursued. Some collected butterflies or flowers and Noyce participated in these activities with those who had a particular interest. He records the richness of the rhododendrons and other flora and spent an afternoon with John Hunt looking at the bird life along the Yarsa stream. He notes that the prettiest bird on the march was the scarlet minivet, a forest and garden bird that is seen mainly in the Indian sub-continent and the countries of South-East Asia. Sometimes he just sat and reflected:

> *I lazed and dreamed on a primula slope. I found myself asking: What makes a poet? Surely, in his poetic self, a certain inability to do things. I had neither inclination nor will-power to capture that butterfly for John, that beetle for George Band, or pick this primula, however rare, for anybody else. I lay and absorbed and wondered. Where the real poet comes in, is in turning this luxurious absorption into words.*[13]

His poem 'Walking to Everest' is the product of these reflections.[14]

On the twelfth day, 21st March, they arrived at the Taksindhu Monastery and the Dudh Kosi Gorge. Here they started to head north. They were now in 'Everest Country', the mountain was visible and Noyce wrote:

> *Everest hung for me like a school test over the school holidays: a trial to be looked forward to apprehensively, but which nothing in the world would make me avoid.*[15]

For the next three days they were in or above the Dudh Kosi Gorge and on the fourth day on 25th March arrived in Namche Bazaar, the Sherpa capital, set on a hillside at an altitude of 11,286ft (3,400m). Here they were greeted by the relatives of their Sherpas with a barrel of *chang*, the Sherpas' favourite tipple. They camped above the village to avoid infection. In 2010 one can fly in a small aircraft to Lukla, a few miles south, and if the walk is too much at that altitude one can be helicoptered in to Namche. The following day they went up to the

Buddhist monastery at Thyangboche, and established the first Base Camp in front of the monastery at over 12,000ft (3,600m). On the last part of the walk up, Noyce, to his dismay, felt out of breath. They did need to be more acclimatised.

Everest was visible ten miles away to the north just above the serrated ridge joining Nuptse and Lhotse, with the fang of Ama Dablam, at 22,700ft (6,900m), on the right. They were surrounded by peaks of 20,000ft (6,000m), none of which had so far been climbed. This is where they would get used to their equipment and become acclimatised.

The three days in Thyangboche were busy: Noyce and Evans sorted and distributed the mountain equipment and clothing. Noyce recorded,

> *Before breakfast. Walked out and observed musk-deer and ram chikor (like brightly coloured partridge). These are quite tame as the lamas forbid taking life.*
>
> *Gave out crampons to sahibs and Sherpas. Fitted and adjusted. Straps not perfect.*
>
> *Sat with John over Times report. Drew map of acclimatisation areas.*
>
> *Helped Tom to test oxygen cylinders.*
>
> *1 p.m. Lunch. Salmon and veg.*
>
> *Helped put up tents for airing.*
>
> *2.45. A break. 50 minutes up hillside above, and felt very different from yesterday.*
>
> *Back 4 p.m. Packed up spare ice-axes and dud oxygen cylinders. Washed teeth in rather dirty water-hole. Wrote letter home.*
>
> *Helped organise boxes in big tent for supper, to sit on.*
>
> *Very crowded supper of sheep (killed by George L. this a.m.) all of us in tent.*
>
> *Talk by John on acclimatisation plans after supper.*

The blacksmith came up from Namche to help Noyce fit the crampons to the boots. He thought that perhaps the blacksmith's less than tender treatment may have contributed to some of the later breakages. Tom Bourdillon was teaching how to use the oxygen equipment, while George Band got the radio sets to work and provided instruction. He also managed to pick up the Radio Ceylon report that Cambridge had won the boat race. The loyalties in the group were fairly evenly divided, with representatives of both universities. In between times they paid a visit to the Deputy Abbot of the monastery and called on the mother of the Abbot.

Acclimatisation

John Hunt divided the group into three teams for acclimatisation and each went off in to a different area. The first group, Evans, Band, Bourdillon and Westmacott went off on 29th March to the area round Ama Dablam. The others spent 30th March preparing for their trips. They climbed a 15,500ft (4,700m) rock above the camp for practice and tried out the walkie-talkie sets. It was like a British scramble, but for irritating thorns and dwarf juniper in many places and they had the new experience of talking to the camp, clearly visible, 2,500 feet below.

Noyce had taken on the responsibility for Sherpa food and when he went to work with Tenzing, the task was complicated as Tenzing could neither read nor write! They had to calculate what was required for the acclimatisation period and how the loads should be distributed. There seemed to be an infinite number of variables: the number in the party at any one time, the duration of the trip and the appetites. The Sherpas' first attempt to plan their food required three coolies to carry it. They were told to reduce it to two pounds per man per day.

Finally the requirements for the eight day acclimatisation for this group were:

Cookers	31 lbs
Sherpa food	70 lbs
4 Tents	45 lbs
Oxygen apparatus etc.	58 lbs
3 oxygen cylinders	70 lbs
Food	120 lbs
TOTAL	**394 lb**

Included were two days' high-altitude rations for everyone, as a trial. There was also kerosene, Li-los, sleeping-bags, personal gear and the other indispensables, altimeter, compass, glacier cream, binoculars, goggles and anti-mist, matches, candles, lantern, torches, cigarettes for Sherpas, camera and film, eight karabiners and 300 feet of nylon rope.

The second group was led by Hillary and was composed of Noyce, Ward and Wylie. Unfortunately, Hillary had a temperature and sore

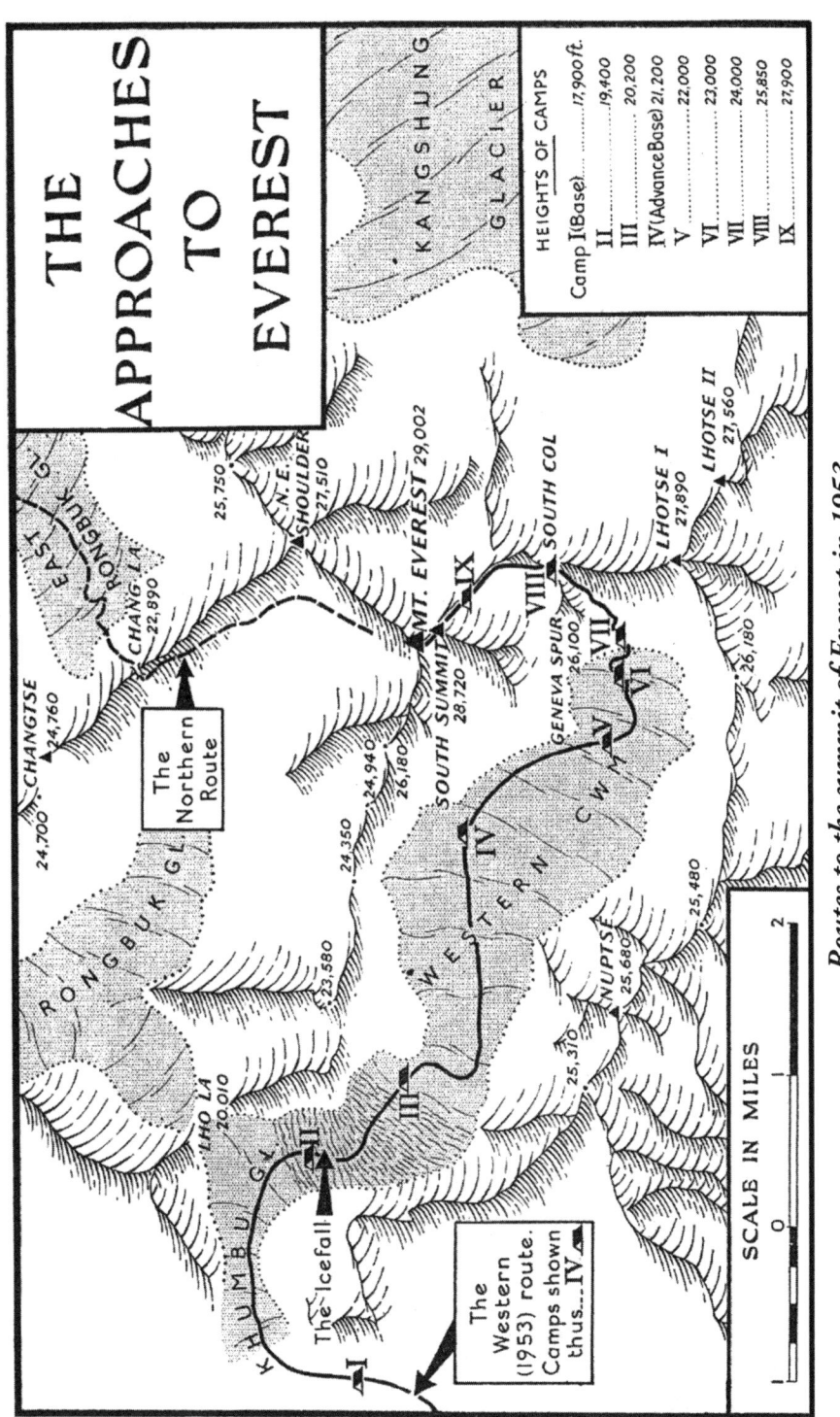

Routes to the summit of Everest in 1953.

throat and stayed in camp for two more days. Noyce took over as leader. The third group consisted of Hunt, Gregory, Lowe and Tenzing and set off at the same time to go up towards Everest itself.

Each party would have some four Sherpas and four coolies initially. When they loaded up they discovered that the Sherpas, Sherpanis and coolies were all carrying seventy pounds each and were very unhappy. They themselves were carrying some forty to fifty pounds each. The track led them through forest then along the Imja gorge. At the first village, Pangboche, some three miles out, each party recruited two more coolies and redistributed the loads. The Hunt party continued up the Imja Valley and Noyce's party went off north-west up into the valley of the Chola Khola, so far unexplored. Noyce was much happier now that he was in a smaller group. '*We had been a too unwieldy a party for real converse, for the real companionship of the hills.*'

The first night they camped at a small village of shepherds, Phalong Karpo at 14,500ft (4,400m), almost all the way round Taweche, 21,390ft (6,500m). Noyce and Ward climbed a stony hillside for the view. He notes,

> *I wished I was not puffing so much. At this stage one spends so much time comparing one's own puffing with that of companions. How much of the mountaineer's time is taken with such thoughts of trivial everyday; hopes of tomorrow, worries about cut fingers, breathlessness and above all, food. Perhaps it should not be so, but so we are made.*

The following day they made their way up the valley and by a frozen lake '*that groaned and creaked like a bad floor*'. The Sherpa Angtharkay had grazed his sheep here as a boy. They camped at 16,000 feet below the glacier of Pointed Peak. From here the two coolies went down but the Sherpanis stayed, to the joy of the Sherpas. This meant that they had to get nine people into two Meade (two-man) tents! At this altitude mountain sickness can strike and Wylie suffered a fair headache for which he took aspirin. Noyce himself suffered from a very dry throat and catarrh blocked his nose at night so that he had to breathe through the mouth. His remedy was to suck lozenges.

This was the time for practising with their oxygen and to become properly acclimatised. Wylie and Ward put their oxygen on while Noyce did not and they all reached the snout of the glacier together; Noyce was puffing a bit, he admitted. They then had a gentle snow walk up to a col where Noyce put on oxygen – not an easy process.

> *In fact it is a clumsy business. A bulky black cylinder must be pushed and wriggled into its carrying frame; nuts must be adjusted, mask fitted and the weight swung on to the back. But when at last it is set and the switch turned on, all is different. A god has somehow wriggled between you and the outer scene, persuading you, on no evidence, that life is good after all. And one effect that we all found, even at this low altitude, was that we enjoyed the scenery. Instead of breathing hard and keeping eyes on the next step, we looked round and admired the view. The world appeared rosy rather that a dun grey.*[16]

They continued on up and eventually reached the col at 18,500ft (5,600m), where Mike Ward had been with Tom Bourdillon in 1951. From here there was a view of unnamed peaks and unknown valleys, only previously explored by Eric Shipton; for Noyce, who was fascinated by shapes, ever since he had tried to mould the Welsh hills in plasticine, this was a collection of entirely new forms. Cho Oyu was very visible over to the north-west and Everest towered over everything to the east. The excitement was replaced by horror when he saw a brand new crampon swing loose on the descent. Another crampon had already broken and this was not to be the last.

Sleeping was still not so easy, Noyce found he had to sleep on his left side to keep one nostril clear. '*But I often turned in sleep, and that clogged me up. Apart from this, with Li-Lo inflated and sleeping-bag drawn tight under the chin, I slept well.*' Right from the earliest days Noyce has shown indifference to physical comfort and shown himself able to sleep anywhere. This attribute was invaluable on Everest. Domestically it made life difficult as Rosemary liked the warmth and Wilfrid always liked the windows open!

The following day Ward, Wylie and Noyce climbed Pointed Peak, 19,200ft (5,850m): they had a happy three-quarters of an hour there watching Hillary pitching their camp on the col 500 metres below them. They saw another peak to the north-west, Kang Cho, and decided they would go on down into this valley, which they did not expect to find, climb Kang Cho and go down the Dudh Kosi River back to Thyangboche. One snag, they had Assault Rations for each member of the party for only two days and the detour would take longer than that. Each day-pack consisted of:

> 14 oz. Sugar, 1 pkt Bovril Pemmican (for soup), 2 oz. Cheese, 2 pkts. biscuits – 1 sweet, 2 oz. Jam, 1 pkt. Boiled sweets, 1 pkt. Grape-Nuts,
> Tea, coffee, small pkt. Porridge to go with soup, 1 pkt. powder milk,
> 1 2-oz. bar Kendal Mint Cake, or chocolate, or Frubix, or banana bar,
> 1 pkt. Lemon or orange powder

It was tough for those who did not like pemmican or Grape-nuts and not a lot for ravening appetites just off the mountain. Each 'day' would have to be spread over a longer period.

Noyce shared a tent with Hillary and really got to know him for the first time.

> *We discussed his great problem of killing time at high altitude; his "battle against boredom". My own very simple method is reading, a long novel for preference. One of the pleasanter tasks of this whole period was that of getting to know each other, and here I got to know Ed; his straight frontal attack on every problem; his restless energy; his cheerful deep laugh and sense of humour; his staunch feeling for friends.*[17]

On the following day, 3rd April, they all felt off-colour, with colds, indigestion or headaches, the effect of altitude, but set off down across the valley towards the glacier at its head. They camped under its snout. In the morning they formed two ropes and set off. Hillary, Noyce and the two Sherpas Da Namgyal and Ang Dawa were on one and Ward, Wylie, Gompu and Shepalay on the other. On the way up to the glacier Wylie's crampon broke and, like Noyce and Gompu, now only had one and a half crampons. They continued and found some very useful ice-climbing up to the ridge to the right of the peak. A mushroom-shaped lump of ice nearly defeated them on the ridge. Two of them made attempts to get by it but finally Noyce spotted a route, *'a honeycomb shelf upon which, with a few chips from the axe, one could walk'*, which he proceeded along to discover he was only 300ft from the summit which they reached at 13.00 at an estimated altitude of 20,300ft (6,200m). They returned to camp. The following day, 5th April, they continued down the newly discovered valley of Chugima, recovered the compo rations they had cached on the way up and continued down the valley.

> *We were enjoying the most exquisite pleasure of Himalayan mountaineering: a small party of friends, we were exploring new country among the greatest scenery in the world. We had just climbed a new peak, and were descending an uncharted valley. There was much to talk about, to point out, to ask our loyal companions, the Sherpas. Moreover we had the easy sense of having done our duty to the expedition; we were acclimatised, and knew more about oxygen and rations.*[18]

They camped by the junction of the Dudh Kosi and their valley, in a meadow from which the toothless owner dug up a huge dish of potatoes – the first fresh food for a week. Noyce had never eaten or seen eaten so many potatoes at a sitting.

On 6th April they were back at Thyangboche by 13.00 and listening to the accounts of the other groups. Again this was a busy time for all and for Noyce especially as he was the expedition cobbler and there were boots to repair, in addition to organising the food for the Sherpas, and the other tasks of distributing loads and equipment. In the second phase of acclimatisation the groups were composed differently. Hillary, Band, Lowe and Westmacott went straight to the Icefall to start work there. Hunt, with Ward, Noyce and Bourdillon would go up to the top of the Imja glacier, using open-circuit oxygen then climb Ambugyabjen, 19,500ft (5,940m), which they did twice, on successive days using closed-circuit oxygen taking it in turns to use the one set they had.

Pokalde, 20,000ft (6,090m), adjacent to the pass between the Imja and Khumbu valleys was irresistible. Noyce, Ward and Bourdillon climbed it. Hunt was not able to be with them as he had breathing difficulties, later diagnosed as pleurisy. The following day they arrived at the Lake Camp, on the moraine of the Khumbu glacier, which the Swiss had used as their Base Camp in 1952. Noyce was still quartermaster until they joined up with Hillary's group on the Ice-Fall, which had taken up the stores for them. They still had three-course dinners with mushroom or tomato soup, meat and potatoes, and cake and coffee. The fruit cake never lost its appeal during the whole expedition. And for Noyce there was always a pipe afterwards.

Noyce had to prepare a report for Hunt and ***The Times*** on the work of the Ice-Fall party and so he and Ward went over the moraine and after a morning's walk arrived at the Base Camp which Hillary's group had set up close to the base of the Ice-Fall, on the site of the Swiss camp I. Westmacott was there suffering from 'Basecampitis', an unhappy combination of diarrhoea, cough and sore throat. The less than completely hygienic habits of the cook, Kirken, and the proximity of the Swiss sanitary arrangements may not have helped.

The Ice-fall

The Ice-Fall, a jumble of heaving, groaning snow boulders on a steep part of the Khumbu glacier that took them from the lower glacier at 18,500ft (5,630m) to the lip of the Western Cwm at 20,100ft (6,120m). This was a major obstacle, but it had been climbed twice before. The ice moved and slipped and they had snow most afternoons which obliterated their hard-made tracks. Each time they climbed it was a new experience. Hillary, Lowe, Band and Sherpas had gone up to Camp II to explore a route for Camp III at the top of the Ice-Fall. It had already taken several days hard effort to make a way up to Camp II, just halfway up, and it would require more effort to make it safe for laden Sherpas. Noyce had 100 marker flags on bamboo sticks which would help but the movements of the ice and the frequent snowfall reduced their effectiveness.

The following day, 17th April, Ward and Noyce climbed Pumori, 'Daughter Peak', named after George Leigh Mallory's daughter, from which they could look down on the Western Cwm, the valley that stretched from the top of the Ice-Fall to the base of the Lhotse face and view conditions there. They could also see the whole of the Ice-Fall and Camp II in the middle of it. An additional pleasure that day was the arrival of the first mail since Kathmandu. '*There is no comparable joy to the traveller; we spent the afternoon reading and re-reading.*' Hunt also appeared from Camp II with the news that Hillary's group had reached the top of the Ice-Fall.

On 19th April Noyce, Ward and Westmacott went up to move Base Camp and spent considerable time finding flat stones to make the base of the big tent. They appreciated the skills of landscape gardeners! The new Base Camp was a model of organisation and hygiene at the beginning, but was a little different when they vacated it in June! At this point Noyce handed over his responsibility for Sherpa food to Nimmi, a Sherpa, whose heart would not let him go high, with all the requirements for thirty-four Sherpas for six weeks.

The same three with Sherpas set off on 20th April, Noyce ahead to fix flags to the sticks at the old Base Camp and they worked on the route up to Camp II. Westmacott, the engineer, had two six-foot lengths of ladder, which they used to bridge a wide crevasse. The Sherpas were nervous at the beginning and went across on their hands and knees, but later on walked across quite happily even with crampons. Noyce found the flag-placing a good opportunity for photography – and the others were happy to stop too. They reached the top of a steep wall and decided to return and improve the route so far. They were back in camp by 15.40 with snow falling. It was a cold night and Noyce had defective Li-Los: they had two Li-Los, one next to the ground that was inflated hard and the one on top soft. In his case he inflated both hard in the hope that both would be reasonable in the morning. He still ended up inflating them at 1 o'clock in the morning, reflecting that '*this won't be much fun on the South Col*'. The following day they continued the work and at one particularly deep crevasse, which was too wide to jump, they needed a ladder. Noyce trod gingerly over a thin sliver of ice that was wedged and reached the other side. They dug a platform for the ladder on both sides of the crevasse and fixed it with ice pitons. 200 yards farther on they came to the orange and yellow tents of Camp II.

Noyce writes: '*At this time Camp II (19,400ft) still seemed a high mysterious place. We had not yet come to scorn it as a disagreeable night halt low down the mountain.*'

Hillary and Band and their Sherpas had arrived, Lowe had gone down with severe 'Basecampitis' and Hunt and Westmacott were staying. Ward and Noyce saw them all settled in and began to descend before the snow became too heavy.

> *As we walked along the last stretch of trough* [above Base Camp] *I said to Mike, "If anyone asked what we've been doing to-day, I certainly shouldn't feel like saying 'Climbing Everest.'" We agreed that it had never occurred to us that we had been spending the day on Everest. We concluded that perhaps it is because climbers are short-sighted creatures, and can never see beyond the next handhold, ledge, or at most, camp.*[19]

Base camp had been fully constituted by then. Jimmy Roberts had arrived with the main stock of oxygen and Bourdillon was building stacks for the cylinders; the kitchen had been built. Charles Evans' party had brought up all the stores and the group had been joined by James Morris the correspondent of ***The Times***. Noyce described him as a '... *very parfit gentle journalist,*' and said that, *"Nothing could be pleasanter than pouring experiences into a sympathetic placid ear, and knowing that they would be turned into good English."*[20] Fair praise from such a word-artist as Noyce! In addition Morris relieved Hunt of the need to write the dispatches for ***The Times***. A minor irritation at this time was the rate of breakage of spoons and forks. Morris found it odd that the leader of the expedition should be eating his porridge with a fork. Noyce even found Wylie at Camp VII feeding himself Grape-Nuts with a spanner.

The following day, 22nd April, was a rest day for Base Camp. However Ward and Noyce had noticed an 'irresistible' variation to the particularly difficult crevasse-crossing named 'Hillary's Horror' just below Camp II. They went off and found a crossing lower down, cut steps on the ice-wall above it and put a hand-rail – making a very acceptable staircase. They returned to Base Camp and spent the afternoon sunbathing. That evening Hunt and Band came down with the good news that they had found a site for Camp III at the top of the Ice-Fall at 20,200ft (6,150m).

Hunt then divided them into two teams; the Low-Level ferry would carry loads up to Camp III and the High-Level ferry consisting of Noyce, Gregory and seven Sherpas would be based at Camp III and take them on up the Cwm. After a rest day on 23rd April, when boots were repaired, letters written and masses of Thondup's excellent scones eaten, the ferries started operating on 24th April.

The Ascent

A week's camp at altitude demanded considerable preparation, and Noyce as an Urdu speaker had to explain to the Sherpas of both teams their tasks, organise their loads and distribute their rations before he took the High-Level team up to Camp II. Gregory was bringing up the Low-Level team. Crampons continued to break and even disappeared mysteriously from outside tents. They were certainly not comfortable objects to have inside the tent. Finally the climbers departed at 10.30. Noyce wrote in his diary;

Progress slow. Hot and sunny at first but clouds banking. Gompu's crampon broke (another gone), but tied up. 11.30 snow started and increased. Arrived at first bridge now replaced by two poles. Sherpas found great difficulty and were nervous. Tashi Phutar on belly and the loads had all to be slung across. Load of flags very awkward. Greg not pleased with his lot, who certainly weren't efficient. Much shouting. On we went. Two hours to Hillary's Horror, which is better our new way. On, with hood up, visibility nil, Sherpa loads coming off, crampon buckles slipping, and my following Sherpa fell at the icy traverse. However, slowly on, four ropes of us, and reached Camp II at 2.50 p.m. Four and a half hours!

At Camp II they found Hunt and Hillary: falling snow had stopped them going up to Camp III. That night Noyce after a sally out into the cold decided to cease being the only member of the expedition not to have taken a pill, and took one for his diarrhoea. This and one on the Lhotse face to help him sleep were the only two he took on the mountain.

The first day of the High-Level carry, 25th April, when Noyce would lead a team of Sherpas up to Camp III, as he confessed, he had *'the grumps. Every climber must have such days; thank Heaven they are rare. On them it would give the greatest pleasure if all his colleagues fell into the largest crevasse available.'* Nonetheless, he got his Sherpas loaded and moving. There was one item that was difficult. Two six-foot sections of the aluminium ladder had been brought up to Camp II joined together. There was no spanner at Camp II and so the ladder, while not particularly heavy, was exceedingly awkward to carry in and out of the seracs of the Ice-fall. The Sherpa Tashi Phutar tried carrying it various ways and even Pemba tried but it always snagged on some protruding piece of ice. They even tried one person at each end but going round corners one of them ended up over a crevasse! However, it did enable them to measure the crevasses fairly accurately! John Hunt wrote.

> *It was easy to imagine the nightmare which this proved to be, in the labyrinth of ice boulders above that crevasse and at many points of the way. Indeed it called for all the great reserves of Wilfrid's patience to finish the journey.*[21]

Mike Westmacott, on his way down to Camp II met them and handed over a spanner and they arrived comfortably at Camp III at 14.25 to join Hunt, Tenzing, Evans and Hillary.

Hunt was very anxious to investigate the big crevasse that the Swiss had found above Camp III. Noyce set off with the others at 15.30 and headed up the Cwm and with Tenzing put three sections of the ladder together at the 16-foot crevasse and they all went across. At 16.45 Hunt asked Noyce to return to Camp III to make the daily radio link-up, '… *the nightmare of all dialogues*'. The others came back at 18.00 satisfied that there was little difficulty in getting to the head of the Cwm and what would be Camp IV. The following day Hunt, Hillary, Tenzing and Evans went up the Cwm and found the Swiss Camp IV – and a supply of stores left behind, including *'the most delicious of all imaginable drinks'*, a tin of half-frozen Swiss orange juice. Nearby they established Camp IV.

The following day Noyce and Gregory started the nine days of High-Level Carry. The first day was the hardest and it was very hot at 13.30 so they made a dump of their loads and went back down to Camp III. On the way down Noyce, still a quartermaster, made a list of the stores left at the Swiss Camp III half-an-hour above their own. They were joined by Evans, Tenzing and Hunt who had established a route to Camp V that day and with their after-supper coffee they discussed marriage and climbing. Hunt was certain that marriage was the only way to happiness even for a mountaineer. Evans gave the reasons why he was not married and Noyce and Gregory sided with Hunt!

In nine days the Low-Level Ferry transferred some ninety loads of about forty pounds each from Base Camp to Camp III. Of these half were taken up to Camp IV and on the last day, 30th April, Noyce took up a final carry and listed the stores at Camp IV and went down to Camp III. On 1st May Hunt, Bourdillon and Evans went up to establish Camp IV.

The ferrying of loads from Base Camp to Camp IV operated like clockwork.

> *The Low-Level Ferry would leave Base at 12.00 – arrive Camp II 15.00 – spend night – leave Camp II 08.00 – arrive Camp III 09.30 – leave Camp III (down) 10.30 – arrive Base 14.00. The High Level Ferry would leave Camp III 08.00 arrive Camp IV 11.00 – leave Camp IV 12.00 – arrive Camp III 13.30.*[22]

After this strenuous routine the ferry teams went down to Base Camp for a rest on 2nd May. During this time Noyce changed his shirt for the first time in four weeks and worked with Tenzing on the Sherpa food needed for the rest of their stay. There was a problem; the budget had already been overspent! Then he went down a little farther to the Lake Camp at Lobuje for two days. He was joined there by Ed Hillary. There they were able to get the weekly mail direct from the runner who brought it from Kathmandu. How welcome it was! *'Photographs of my wife and baby son brought home very close to me.'*

The party which had been in the Cwm exploring the route across the Lhotse Face to the South Col eventually joined the group at Lobuje and Base Camp. They had been experimenting with the oxygen equipment. The results were varied and the merits of both systems were debated. The Closed-circuit was more efficient, enabling the climber to operate as if he was at sea-level. At thirty-six pounds it was nine pounds (four and a half kilos) heavier as it reclaimed the used air. The Open-circuit system released the exhaled air to the outside. Noyce himself favoured the Open-circuit, as in the event of failure, it would be less difficult to go from an oxygen and air mix, rather than pure oxygen, to the rarefied air experienced at very high altitudes.

Another period of ferrying started on 6th May, in order to establish an Advance Base with the whole party at Camp IV. Hillary and Noyce went up to Base Camp. Noyce was despondent; all he was doing was leading groups of heavily laden Sherpas. In a revealing paragraph he wrote,

> *I had already decided that, being a writer, that is one whose kink it is to transfer experience to ink and paper, I must write my personal tale of the adventure. Of what could I write? Perhaps it was the altitude that gave a dreary sense at that moment of the monotony of adventure. I remember a feeling of disappointment; sticking hands in my pockets, kicking at a stone, and saying: "I don't suppose I shall see any **new** ground." Like a small boy suddenly told to play goal. This thought was in my throat when I came down on the 7th and asked John, if there were any exploration to be done, to think of me. His reply was disarming. Charles Wylie and I were the two who could best handle the Sherpa up to the Col. And the unprecedented effort of getting eighteen (it later proved to be nineteen) loads to over 26,000 feet was of such importance*

that the final assault would be unthinkable without it. **Après ça que dire?**'[23]

Until then it was ferrying loads and all were involved. Noyce with Tenzing and Gregory were leading the lifts from Base to Camp III, which by now the Sherpas could do in one day. However, Noyce enjoyed the overnight stops at Camp II as he was usually on his own with the Sherpas and enjoyed sharing their life with them. *'At close quarters (three in a tent on one occasion) and with no other sahibs present, they came forward with their happy selves.'* The Ice-fall was changing its nature. Cracks and crevasses widened and narrowed and large blocks became more precarious. On 10th May Hunt spoke to Noyce, who was at Base, from Camp III; there were a couple of new danger points on the Ice-fall route; a large block of ice about to fall in the part they called Hell Fire Alley and the crevasse between II and III had widened. Would Noyce and his Sherpas attend to these on the way up!

The morning was as hot as any, we were in shirt-sleeves. Panting towards the top of Hell Fire Alley I soon made out the offending serac. It was indeed a block, perhaps as big as a small bus, mushroom-shaped and perched on a flat stalk. It was joined by a massive neck to the green, bulging cheek of ice next door. The first step was to separate it from the side wall. The Sherpas disliked the whole job. It was clearly far better to rest when one did halt. Why waste energy on child's games? However they consented to hold me on the rope. I clambered up awkwardly. It was easy to cut away the neck, but not at all easy to get at the mushroom stalk in such a position that the block could not possibly fall on myself. I pecked and pecked, bent double. At this height it was hard work; I panted, paused, twisted the axe and went on. I shifted position, but that did not help as my blade hit the side wall at each swing. At last the stalk looked dangerously small, the whole structure something like the Bowder Stone in Borrowdale. We brought the battering-ram into action, an eight-foot pole brought up for bridging. One Sherpa consented to ram with me. We stood together, heaved back, then lunged forward. At the second ram the thing tottered forward, heeled over and crashed on to our tracks below. Broad grins from the Sherpas. There it lay, with its fellows of every day. We had assisted Nature and possibly saved ourselves.[24]

The following day on the way down they tackled the widening crevasse. The ladder which bridged it had six inches of overlap on both sides, rather than the original two feet. The pole they had brought with them had to be lashed to the ladder. Noyce '*sighed for a better knotsman*' and with a stiff, partly-frozen rope he was less sure of his lashings. With the assistance of Chotaray tying a series of granny knots, his Sherpa colleagues grinning the while:

> *I advanced anxiously to inspect the knots, till we were both sitting opposite one another over nothing. Poor Chotaray was as unscoutly as any Sherpa.*

The bridge was lengthened and secured. Westmacott subsequently tied a pole on each side to make a regular gangway. Noyce records:

> *Reading my diary that evening, I thought how commonplace the day had been, and how completely I had forgotten the noble purpose of climbing Everest. I might have been out for a day's bridging with the Charterhouse Scout Troop. Even the magnificence of the scenery my eyes spurned from familiarity. No great venture can keep going, I suppose, at its top level for very long; hence the banality of everyday conversation, to avoid straying too far into the depths. The tinge of morning rose on the pale infinite sky before dawn; and the twinge of tooth cracking on hard biscuit. The burst of song before a scene that sings the glory of Creation; and the bursting crampon which sends a man swearing down to fumble with ice-cold fingers. High sentiment alongside straight farce and the comedy of day-to-day. The plays of Shakespeare rather than Racine.*

At Camp IV in heavy snow Hunt already had concerns about the arrival of the monsoon and when he heard about the heavy snow on 11th May at Base Camp, it only added to them. A call was made to All-India Radio for a special report. However, he had asked Noyce and Ward to go up and help Lowe who was route-making on the Lhotse Face. It was new ground for Noyce. On 13th May Noyce, with Evans, Bourdillon and Gregory moved up to Camp IV in very difficult conditions, sinking in several times up to the armpits. Camp IV was now Advance Base and the expedition settled in there. Far above them

George Lowe and Ang Nyima could be seen working on the Lhotse Face.

At this point Noyce began to find himself on 'new ground'. Ed Hillary had described him as 'the most competent mountaineer' and his stamina and ability to keep going was being brought into service for some of the crucial parts of the climb. He himself was anxious to meet his own and his fellows' expectations. To this end he would improve on the precept that the key to acclimatise is to sleep at the altitude. During the afternoon he would go a few hundred feet above the camp where he was to spend the night, as he appeared to have had the same level of energy on Everest that he used to exhibit in Wales and the Alps. At the end of a hard day's climbing in the Alps or North Wales he would quite often go off and do a walk or climb a peak on his own.

By this time George Lowe, *'the master of ice-craft',*[25] and Ang Nyima were established at Camp VI (23,000ft, 7,000m) on the site of the Swiss Camp VI and had been up to the site of Camp VII at 24,000ft (7,300m). Hunt had decided that Camp V was to be the depot for the stores required for certainly two, if not three, attempts on the summit.

> *The exact amounts and their weights were already known, and consequently the number of High Altitude Sherpas required was established. At least 12 men were needed, each under the leadership of a member of the climbing party. The two leaders chosen for this most important part of the Assault plan were Charles Wylie and Wilfrid Noyce; both had a quite exceptional understanding of our men.*[26]

They were now issued with high-altitude boots which gave them all an elephantine appearance. The ice-steps were a challenge and the boots were easily ripped by crampons, but the advantages of lightness and warmth outweighed the disadvantages. On 15th May Hillary and Noyce left Camp IV at 6.45 and reached Camp V at 7.55, a climb of some 800 feet. There they found Westmacott who had a terrible cough and had tried to reach Camp VI. He was still ill with 'Basecampitis' and decided to go down. They continued on to Camp VI and joined George Lowe there at 12.25. There was only room there for one tent and they stood around. Hillary and his party took the tent, cooker and other equipment up to Camp VII and returned. George Lowe had taken five and a half hours on the first ascent from Camp VI to VII. It was a long way, even assuming it becomes easier each time one does it. Hillary did it that day in one hour and fifty minutes – a time that remained a record – and returned to Advance Base afterwards.

That night was the sleeping-pill episode. Noyce, to ensure that he slept well, took a sleeping-pill – for the only time, Lowe did the same. They planned to establish Camp VII the next day. Noyce woke at 6.00 on 16th May and tried hard to wake Lowe. He got up and knelt – then fell asleep again. By 9.00 Noyce had had breakfast and Lowe was beginning to come together. They set off at 10.30 and Lowe led at first, as he knew the way and '*could set the pace most suited to his own somnambulatory needs.*'[27] Lowe was still fighting sleep and Noyce took over the lead as there were still tracks to break.

> *We were moving very slowly, and twice George said: "Wait a minute. I must stop." The first time he took off his boots, and we both rubbed the cold feet grown sluggish, I suspected, with the dope. At 11.30, the second halt, he relapsed upon his rucksack – and slept. Another huge, half-moon-shaped wall reared over us. We wound under it to the right. By the time we had reached the steep fixed-rope, in a snow-slope swinging you back leftward towards its top, we were ready to sit down again. "Perhaps I'll have something to eat," George said, "That'll make me feel better". He was seated on the snow, propped once more against the rucksack. I pulled out a tin of sardines and opened it. But things were looking black indeed when George actually went to sleep with one of these delectable fishes in his mouth! An unforgettable picture, I felt in my heart then a horrible weight of apprehension, no doubt exaggerated by the altitude: we would not see Camp VII today.*

After further attempts to make progress and Noyce's increasing anxiety that Lowe might not have the strength to get back to Camp VI even, they reached Camp VI at 14.00 and Lowe was asleep by 14.05. That evening halfway through the cooking, the Primus ran out of fuel. As he went out to get the kerosene Noyce stopped in the door of the tent.

> *It was a miracle, after the tedious care of stove-lighting. Little Pumori, darkened with sun shadow, had decked her shoulders with cloud fleece, but she could not this time wipe out her larger background. The long, irregular ridges of Cho Oyu and Gyachung*

> *Kang sparkled, shifted and beckoned against a paling, silver-blue sky. The sun shone whitely still into my face, still whitened the dazzling linen of the valley at my feet. What matter kerosene, stoves, sleeping-bags, even the ascent on which our every thought had been concentrated? Something here beyond me, outside me, "far more deeply interfused" than my muddled brain would care to know, lent a magic to the air that made human effort meaningless. I was for a moment, again near to Nirvana.*
>
> *Heartened, yet not knowing why, I went back to cooking sausage-meat in soup.*[28]

The following day they packed up and got away by 8.30, leaving a note for Ward and his Sherpas who would bring the kit up later in the day. Lowe took the lead, setting a cracking pace and Noyce carried the rucksack. It took forty-three minutes to get to the point where they turned back after two and a half hours. Noyce was now higher than he had been on Pauhunri in Sikkim in 1945 and being conscious of this made him feel more breathless than he really was. Lowe seemed to go on and on, a machine, an automatic hill-climber, while Noyce's pace slowed considerably. Earlier they had climbed without pause; now at 23,800ft (7,250m) it was twenty steps and a breath, leaning gasping on the ice-axe. Then ten breaths and stop, then six. They reached the dump of packages that marked the site of Camp VII, at 24,000 feet, at 10.45. They had to stamp down a platform in the snow, drag the Meade tent across and erect it. It took them an hour and then they went inside the tent and slept. '*At 1.15 George opened an eye and said: "Well." I said "Well," too, and we dozed off for a few more minutes.*' At 13.30 two very sleepy men emerged from the tent trying to come to terms with the idea that they still had to reconnoitre the route to Camp VIII that day. Camp VII was by a wide crevasse which separated the serac, on which the camp was sited, from the main body of the mountain. While it protected the camp from falling ice and rock it was the first challenge on starting. Fifty yards along Lowe found that some snow had come down a couloir and had lodged in the crevasse. Belayed by Noyce, he led gingerly across the bridge and in to the couloir. Noyce then led through and after another fifty feet of step-cutting he was on the upper slope and Lowe joined him. They continued up to nearly 25,000ft (7,600m) and at 15.00 as they could see no further difficulties, they turned to go down. At Camp VII they found Ward and four Sherpas, very dehydrated and tired after their rapid climb from Base Camp. Noyce and Lowe were also dehydrated: '...*a dipsomaniac passion to drink several oceans of liquid before I took another step*'. Despite his desire to stay with Ward and Lowe and explore farther up to the South Col, he went down to Camp V as Hunt had asked him to bring the first lift to the South Col. The following day, 18th May, he went down with Evans to Camp IV. '*The walk from V to IV was one of the pleasantest half-hours of the expedition.*'

The Assault

At that point, a number of them, including Hunt, were gathered at Camp IV, Advanced Base, preparing for the Assault. Ward and Lowe were still at Camp VII and with Da Tensing and were trying to continue on the Lhotse Face where Lowe and Noyce had left off. Their progress was being watched closely by all the eyes at Camp IV. They were higher than Noyce and Lowe had been the day before: then they turned round and went back to Camp VII. Consternation in the camp! Tom Bourdillon who had been at Camp VII came down later that day explaining that they had been battling with frostbite in a bitter wind and that Da Tensing was bothered with the conditions. Ward and Lowe stayed at Camp VII and rested the following day.

On 19th May Noyce took up his team of eight Sherpas, accompanied by Hunt as far as Camp V. There Hunt said to Noyce:

> "*In case George and Michael don't manage to prepare the Traverse before they come down tomorrow, you will have to decide whether to carry straight on to the Col with the Sherpas the next day, or whether it will be better to go up there yourself first and prepare the track. If this is necessary, then your party will have to spend a second night with Charles Wylie at Camp VII and you must go up together on the 22nd. You can only judge this on the state of your chaps and the going as you will hear of it from George*"[29] "*Get to the Col if you possibly can, Wilf, that's the most important. We're depending on that.*"[30]

Lowe and Ward made another attempt to get up, they managed to push the route still higher, but after nine days working on the route across the Lhotse Face, exhausted and frostbitten, finally came down on 20th May to recover at Lobuje.

Noyce had sent his biographical poem on Michaelangelo to his publishers, Heinemann, before he left and from Camp V he wrote to them that '*...he was getting a good deal of writing and when was he going to see the proof of his poems?*'[31]

On 20th May Noyce left Camp V with his Sherpas. He was using an Open-circuit oxygen set.

> *I always found climbing with Sherpas three times more tiring than with Sahibs. As I dragged along I was heartily envying those lucky ones like Tom Bourdillon, who from the nature of their jobs had less to do with bear-leading. At the time I had no pity for what others might miss. And now the moral tug on the rope was so strong that it almost pulled me from my steps; a dead weight of doubt, dismay and reluctance which the Sherpas could never have explained, had they been blessed suddenly with the gift of tongues. We climbed very slowly; the halts were very frequent. "Aram (rest), sahib", and the whole caravan would plump panting down in the snow. I found the whole business so much more tiring than the ascent with George without oxygen, that I risked all and increased my flow rate to four litres a minute.*[32]

After an hour and three-quarters they reached Camp VI. They were there an hour. He had told the Sherpas that they would have light loads and would collect more at Camp VI. They still had loaded themselves with more than they had been given and were appalled when asked to take the additional loads! Just below Camp VII they met George Lowe, who said that the main problem at VII was the shortage of kerosene. Noyce detached two of the Sherpas to go down to Camp VI to collect some. They reached Camp VII at 13.45. They still had to pitch a couple of tents, '*...a shuffled, jumbling job, thankfully disposed of by all, so that all could flop exhausted inside.*' Noyce found the remains of a thermos of lemonade in his tent and shared it with the others. They revived. It was the heat, thirst and heavy loads that had tired them. It was the first time loads of fifty pounds had been carried to 24,000 feet. After lunch and a rest Noyce started to prepare for the next day. He had six Sherpas selected by Charles Wylie as the most suitable to carry up to the South Col. They would operate as two ropes with Anullu leading the other rope. If the other Sherpas were not able to continue, Anullu and he would go up on their own. Noyce set about arranging the oxygen equipment.

He tested the cylinders one by one and they all appeared to leak. He looked in vain for a spanner and at the appointed hour spoke to Tom Bourdillon:

> *"I've turned all the cylinders on and they all seem to leak." Alas it was a capricious creature, our wireless. At this critical point a 'break in transmission' caused a sleepless night for Tom Bourdillon, down at IV. The mechanic in him had spotted that I had omitted to say that I had switched them off. Knowing me to be far from mechanically inclined, he suspected at once that I had failed to do that operation. I was told later that John spent the rest of the evening hopping around with the wireless set. "Come out from behind that serac, Wilf!" – and doubtless stronger expressions such as my informant was too kind to repeat. Fortunately they were not justified.*

There was panic elsewhere but Noyce enjoyed a very good supper of soup, lemonade, biscuits, cheese, chocolate and condensed milk. He was able to write up his diary and even poetry but as the sun went down it became too cold and he retired to his sleeping bag.

At 5.00 Noyce tumbled out of his tent to answer the call of nature. He was so taken with the magnificent '*wild golden light already splashing upon Pumori and the peaks down the valley*'. He returned to the tent to stoop and wrestle and find his camera and record this splendid view. Back to sleep as he had told Anullu they did not want to start too early because of the risk of frostbite and then at 6.30 tea appeared.

> *Then another lie, in that suspense which precedes the tearing of a man from peaceful horizontal ease to the painful gasps of the vertical. I must kneel, must pull off the sleeping-bag, must wriggle lumpishly on all fours into the cold air. The eye wandered round the tent roof, seized every excuse, a scrap of paper to be read, a film to be looked at or even the stitching of the tent; anything to delay the moment! It was long before I was out, feet clumsy in the big boots whose laces seemed to catch at every step. The time was 7.45. One or two Primuses were going, but there were no other signs of life, except a number of groans and Pasang quietly being sick. Everything was **not** well and I pushed in more medicine.*

Most of the Sherpas were suffering from the altitude and the effort of the day before. Two were sick and had to be sent down. It was Anullu and Noyce left to continue. At 9.30 they set off, Noyce leading. In three-quarters of an hour Noyce reached the point Lowe and he had reached on 17th May. They rested then continued until they found the rope fixed by Lowe's party. They got to the bottom of it but found themselves in deep snow. They reached the top of the rope and a wall of snow confronted them. They tried a slope up to the right and it led nowhere. They came back, thankful that they did not have Sherpas with them. Then went up to the left which led to a minor steep wall up to easier slopes. They found an aluminium piton and a coil of rope left by Lowe's party and marked their highest point reached. They were keeping to the left-hand side of the Lhotse glacier and in heavy snow found the bottom of another rope – left by the Swiss. This they did not dare to use and when they reached the other end one tug was sufficient to unseat the piton to which it was attached!

Noyce cramponed up beside the rope and reached a small platform which was the beginning of a narrow ledge that ran across the face. The plateau was *'bounded by space on the Cwm side, and a crevasse on the other'*. Going to the right Anullu pointed out where the crevasse narrowed to three feet due to two 'lips' that pushed out from each side. Noyce recounts:

> *I signed to Anullu that he should drive his axe well in and be ready for me. Then I advanced to the first unsupported ledge. I stood upon this first ledge and prodded. Anullu would have held me, had one ledge given way, but he could not have pulled me up. As the walls of the crevasse were undercut to widen the gap, I would have been held dangling and could not have helped myself out. It would be silly to face such a problem in the Alps without a party of three. But I cannot remember more than a passing qualm. Altitude, even through oxygen, dulled fears as well as hopes. One thing at a time. Everest must be climbed. Therefore this step must be passed. I prodded my ice-axe across at the other ledge, but I could not quite reach deep enough to tell. I took the quick stride and jump, trying not to look down, plunged the axe in hard and gasped. The lip was firm. This time the Lhotse Face really was climbed.*
>
> *Only lying in my sleeping-bag that night did I realise the implications of one step.*[33]

They continued across a bridge over a small cleft then halted at 12.15 to eat, drink and for Anullu to smoke a couple of cigarettes! At 12.50 they started again with Anullu in the lead up a slope where a few steps needed to be cut. After an hour they reached the wide gully in the shadow of the Geneva Spur and found the first rock since Base Camp. It still was not clear how they would get on to the Spur. They spied a gangway slanting up to the crest. It was steeper than it looked, a few pecks with the axe necessitated a rest. They reached the crest, Noyce leading, but no view – still farther to go. There were boulders over which they stumbled and snow but then they were at the top. Only Everest and Lhotse were above them. It was a further 200 feet down to the South Col. Before they descended Noyce belayed the end of a rope to a piton and ran it down to the Col.

John Hunt wrote of this achievement:

> *I was able to watch them* [from Camp IV] *for some time longer; then after an interval, I caught one more fleeting glimpse, this time a point of blue – the colour of a windproof smock – against some rocks just below the skyline; it quickly merged into the background of sky. It was 2.40 p.m. Wilfrid Noyce and his companion Anullu stood at that moment above the South Col of Everest, at about 26,000 feet. They were gazing down on the Swiss drama, and they were also looking upwards to the final pyramid of Everest itself. It was great moment for them both, and it was shared by all of us who watched them. Their presence there was symbolic of our success in overcoming the most crucial problem of the whole climb; they had reached an objective which we had been striving to attain for twelve anxious days.*[34]

Forty years later Hunt wrote:

> *It would be difficult to exaggerate Wilf's contribution to our success on Everest in 1953. None of us, watchers at that anxious time at our camp in the Western Cwm, will ever forget our excitement as he, with Annullu, climbed the upper part of the Geneva Spur on one of those critical days in the second part of May. We raised a cheer as their blue anoraks blended with the sky, framed by the rim of the South Col. It marked a psychological breakthrough. It heartened us all and gave our Sherpas the courage to complete the carry of stores to the camp site on the Col.*[35]

There they found the tattered remains of the Swiss camp and stayed long enough for Noyce to take photographs and for Anullu to pick-up a rucksack and boots left by the Swiss. When reproved by Noyce, Anullu said that Tenzing had told him he could have first pick of the 'spoil'! Noyce comments on how warm it was on the top of the Spur, warmer than the Col. He was wearing a string vest, flannel shirt, thick sweater, thick pyjama trousers and windproof suit overall – at over 26,000ft (7,900m).

They descended with light hearts. '*The perilous crevasse we jumped merrily from its upper lip.*' They took the couloir by Camp VII very slowly and fixed ropes to facilitate the crossing of the bridge in the crevasse for the Sherpas and the others. By 18.00 they were drinking tea with the group that had now arrived at Camp VII, Charles Wylie and seven Sherpas, Ed Hillary and Tenzing. Noyce's Sherpas had stayed there acclimatising to be ready to join the group with Wylie.

Noyce felt that his job was done, for the moment, having had '*one of the most enjoyable days' mountaineering I've ever had*'[36] and there was nothing else to do but talk – and talk he did with the patient Wylie with whom he shared a tent that night. Moments of retrospection on the crevasse and the loose piton gave him qualms but these were eclipsed by the enjoyment of the achievement. In addition the Open-circuit oxygen system left him with a feeling of elation long after he had taken it off.

The following day 22nd May Noyce and Anullu went down to Advanced Base in some ninety minutes and had a hero's welcome. The rest of Camp VII headed upwards in a great 'carry' to the South Col. After lunch at Camp IV binoculars were turned up towards the Col. There was a line of figures edging up the Spur and then they reached the sky-line led by Ed Hillary and Tenzing. Charles Wylie was shepherding the fourteen Sherpas. One did not make it to the spur, Wylie took over his load and despite his own failing oxygen supply, took it on to the Col. Then he made sure that the loads were secure then they descended to Camp VII. Some Sherpas, Hillary and Tenzing continued right down to Camp IV, quite a day! The supplies were now in place to start the summit attempt. The following day Charles Wylie and his Sherpas came down to Camp IV and George Lowe prepared a second carry up to the Col. After tea Noyce went up to Camp V alone to do an oxygen check for George Lowe.

> It was my first experience quite alone on the mountain, and I looked forward to it. To be sometimes alone is to me almost

a physical necessity, for then the imagined shapes of the hills seem to speak, as they cannot do when another person, however sympathetic, is present to blur the contact. Solitude enlarges the nervous personality, heightens perceptiveness. Terrors are then more acute, so also is the sensation of being a part with hills, and through them with all natural forms. I could never be frightened of ghosts among mountains, as I am often in mid-night woods and towns.[37]

On the way back down Noyce visited the grave of Mingma Dorji, the Sherpa who was killed on the Swiss expedition and was buried in the moraine.

On 24th May sitting in the sun and writing a report to send down to James Morris for **The Times**, Noyce looked up at the Lhotse Face. Hunt and two Sherpas were on one rope; Tom Bourdillon and Charles Evans, the summit pair, were travelling slowly with heavy loads. Lowe had another five Sherpas. They all reached the Col and established Camp VIII in the face of terrible winds. Exhausted by their efforts 25th May for them was a rest day, if trying to survive on the South Col, can be called restful; the second summit team, Tenzing and Hillary and their supporters moved up to Camp VII.

Ward also at Camp IV asked Noyce if he would help with alveolar tests. This involves breathing the air from the bottom of the lungs into glass tubes, which would be sealed for subsequent examination. Ward was anxious to take samples at 24,000ft (7,300m). Noyce was concerned with the organisation of a possible third attempt for the summit, but as he enjoyed climbing with Ward he decided to go with him up to Camp VII on 26th May. The following day they did various chores, including the alveolar test, and, as they both had been to the same preparatory school they had the highest St. Edmund's Old Boy dinner on record, albeit of *'pea soup and Ryvita smeared with condensed milk'*.

On 26th May Evans and Bourdillon set off for the summit, supported by John Hunt and Da Namgyal. The latter dumped their loads at 27,350ft (8,328m), some 100 feet higher than the tent occupied by Lambert and Tenzing on the Swiss expedition of the year before and returned to the South Col. Evans and Bourdillon reached the South Summit 28,700ft (8,739m)) at 13.00. They were now on the highest peak ever climbed. However fatigue and a possible shortage of oxygen convinced them to descend and they reached the South Col absolutely all-in at 16.30.

They had, however, had a view of the final ridge which they were able to describe to Hillary and Tenzing, who, as the second assault team, had arrived with Lowe and Gregory.

On the South Col on 27th May it was blowing a gale and after consultation Hillary and Tenzing decided to spend another night on the Col. Hunt, who had planned to support the second Assault felt that he should escort both Bourdillon and Ang Temba, who were both in a bad way, as well as Evans down to Camp VII. John Hunt writing again:

> *To our relief and delight here we were met by Wilf Noyce and Mike Ward, who helped us in. Just as we were coming down the ice pitch above Camp, Temba slipped and fell into the big crevasse. He was held by Charles, and Wilf managed to get his sack off (he was upside down) and get him up. It is indicative of my state of exhaustion that I could not find strength to lift a finger throughout this incident.*
>
> *Wilfrid Noyce's presence at Camp VII was very fortunate. Without him, Tom Bourdillon, Ang Temba and I could not have managed for ourselves that evening; he looked after us like a nurse and prepared our supper. Moreover he was half-way to the Col and unbeknown to him, I had told Hillary before leaving there that I would send up Noyce and three more volunteer Sherpas with further stores, in order to enable them stay out yet another day of bad weather if necessary. I also had in mind that Noyce and one or more of these men might replace any casualties up there and thus take part in the second Assault.*[38]

On 28th May Lowe, Gregory and Ang Nyima set off from the South Col at 8.45, each carrying over forty pounds and using oxygen. They were to cut steps to make the climb less demanding for Hillary and Tenzing, who were following them. They all reached the South Ridge at noon and reorganised the loads going on up to the dump left by Hunt and Da Namgyal and adding those stores to their loads, now fifty to sixty-three pounds. They all continued along the ridge until 14.30 and decided to pitch camp, at 27,900ft. Lowe, Gregory and Ang Nyima dumped their loads and descended to the Col.

On 29th May Noyce set off with three Sherpas from Camp VII for the South Col. It was a difficult carry. One of the Sherpas, Ang Dorji became too weak and most of his load was taken up by Phu Dorji.

Noyce realised that Ang Dorji should go down as quickly as possible to Camp VII and sent Phu Dorji with him. Pasang, the third Sherpa, and Noyce split Phu Dorji's load so they were carrying fifty pounds and forty pounds respectively. Noyce's small oxygen supply had given out by this time and was discarded. Pasang had one sack, Noyce had a sack over each shoulder. They started again:

> *The first few steps: that showed how slowly we were going. At very first my impression was, "Well, I've defeated it. Here am I chugging up all right." But that was only for a few steps. A dead weight, two long leaden arms, began dragging at my two shoulders. Curious things were beginning to happen to my breath, to my mind. As in a dream I was back at the end of a cross-country course at Charterhouse. I was spattered with mud, breathing hoarsely, exhausted. Now somebody was asking me to run the thing again. No, it was too much!*
>
> *Looking up I kept comparing my slope with the approach to a rock buttress of Tryfan in North Wales. Say it was five hundred feet to the top. That was just about the height of a Tryfan buttress, and here it was, snowed up. It would take at good speed, quarter of an hour. Would I ever reach "a good speed" again? The idea of walking fast, ever, up a hill was ridiculous. Yet the top rocks looked near, very near. Suppose I tried a trick: cheat the breath by taking seven or eight steps at a time, then pause for longer if necessary. The breath I must check almost completely, just breathing in and out lightly on the top layer for the time, instead of trying to be deeply rhythmical with every step.[39] For a while this ruse against the body seemed to work. Pasang, surprised at the change of pace, changed his own manfully. But alas, my lungs perceived the deception and compelled me to revert to the old rhythm. Three...slow...steps and a pause. Life held no more than that, for the time being.*
>
> *It is usual with me, as I think with many climbers, to be two people at once on a climb, particularly when I am alone. Here I was in several senses alone. One half watches and criticises the fumbling of the incompetent other, and is itself removed and remote from the physical conflict. In high climbing this schizophrenic condition becomes more pronounced, as I noticed on Pauhunri in 1945. I believe that such a state led to Smythe's strange act on Everest in 1933, when at 28,000 feet, alone, he broke a piece of*

mint cake and turned to give half to his supposed companion. On the Spur one half of me hovered airily above the slope, wondering why in the name of everything it was tied to this grinding, panting creature.

As they reached the top of the Geneva Spur they could see two small figures descending from the South Summit:

So clear is the air, they seemed no smaller than such climbers on such a day from near the top of Snowdon's P-y-G track. And so bemused was I, that the dramatic suddenness of this sight, with all its possibilities stirred only a very small layer of me. "That's good, they may have done it," and I pushed on for the next three steps.

They went down to the South Col and there joined Lowe who was preparing for the return of Hillary and Tenzing.

The same morning of 29th May at 6.30 Hillary and Tenzing crawled out of their tent, heaved on their oxygen and started up toward the South Summit which they reached at 9.00, having noted where Evans and Bourdillon had left oxygen bottles. They might need them on the way down. After another hour they reached the rock step, the crux of the ridge. After a search for a route, Hillary led up a chimney between the rock and the cornice and came out on the final ridge. Hillary continued to cut steps and was tiring. They then realised that the ridge was dropping away – and that they were on top. It was 11.30. After the photographs and flag-unfurling, Tenzing buried some food items in the snow, as gifts to the Gods and Hillary a crucifix. They looked down the north ridge and sought signs of Mallory and Irvine. Then they started to descend, tired but cautious, conscious that there was nothing between them and the Kanshung glacier, 9,000 feet below. They arrived at the couloir above the Col and found that the wind had obliterated their steps; Hillary cut steps to start, then Tenzing took over. 200 feet above the camp George Lowe met them with soup and emergency oxygen. Noyce was brewing tea for them and took it up to them. They were down.[40]

Once they were settled, Noyce wondered how he could keep the promise he made to Hunt to let him know at Advance Base whether the summit had been reached. They would use sleeping bags as signals. At 5.30 Noyce turned out Pasang and they each took a sleeping-bag up the Spur to a stretch of snow facing the Cwm. They lay in the sleeping-bags, making a T. Pasang was the cross and Noyce the upright. They lay there for ten minutes, hoping that a gap in the clouds would let them be seen at Advance Base but they began to get very cold so they returned to the Col. At the crest Noyce halted, '...*watching Pasang's strong figure moving down the frozen crust between the rocks, expressive in its every jolt of the conviction that all sahibs are off their head*'.[41]

Another wind-blown night on the South Col, when the events of the two days were recounted and retold and the atmosphere in the tents became a thick comfortable fug. Noyce wrote in his diary,

> *Ed and George very generous on me, say bad luck I can't do third assault and fittest to go high. But after it all I think my feeling is of great relief, the thing is done and I have had a good run.*'[42]
> He wrote later, '*At the time all I knew about the third party was that I believed I would be on it. Only afterwards John confided his secret hope that he and I might make the last attempt.*

The Return

On 30th May the talk continued on the South Col but now the thoughts were more of home and wives and families. They gathered what they could with pangs of conscience at leaving the Assault Rations, and Noyce and Pasang set off first, without oxygen, and were pleased to see the handrail Noyce had placed on 21st May with Anullu. Hillary and the other followed and caught them up on the Geneva Spur. The route across the Lhotse face was now a highway and *'There was a holiday feeling about it all, as if this were the last day of term'*. They cast off the down clothing as they descended. No one was expected to be at Camp VII but Wylie was there with two Sherpas, Ang Dorji who was still recovering from his exertions on the South Col and Phu Dorji. Hillary and his party wanted to get down to Advance Base to reassure Hunt but Noyce, in no particular hurry, stayed with Wylie and with Pasang and Phu Dorji took down the tents and packed them up. These had been pitched for two weeks and the pegs were frozen hard into the snow and ice and had to be chipped out with ice-axes. Eventually they were all packed up. Noyce took the still listless Ang Dorji on his rope, walking like a sleepwalker, and Wylie took the other two. The Sherpas asked for a rest. Noyce and Wylie continued down as the Sherpas were out of harm's way now.

I shall not forget the walk back to IV. The afternoon battled at the lower buttresses of Nuptse interposed wreathing veils that thickened and dispersed, and thickened again between ourselves and the burning sun; which burned nonetheless fiercely. We walked in shirtsleeves, crampons in hand, with a weight on our backs. We walked down upon a trail now beaten by many feet: one trail through a white loneliness, and that too would soon be covered up.

We reached V, now desolate, and paused only to admire for a moment the great slanting ice plunges of the West Shoulder, with their metallic shine as if a myriad jet aeroplanes were speeding down to destruction. I have never asked Charles what he felt here, but I sensed that he too was tired with the thought that it was 'over,' with the weight on his back and the looseness of muscle in descent. Tiredness took strange forms. We were going on together for ever, through this loneliness, among magical personalities around. One of them was friendly. The shapes of the hills, half-hidden and magnified by mist, were watching us. And the mist, a diaphanous green through my sun goggles, laughed in and out of them and played with the outline of their faces. Mingma Dorji might any moment step out from his grave, over there on the right, to greet us. The ghosts of Mallory and Irvine themselves were not far round the corner; it seemed even that the Swiss would climb up to meet us. **Would** *anyone bother to come?*

John Hunt came up to meet them as they arrived at Advance Base.

Even under the white smear of glacier cream, under a white hat and sun-glasses, it was clear that he was very moved. With the warmth of his pressed hand the spell of tiredness was broken.

or as Hillary wrote,

To see the unashamed joy spread over the tired strained face of our gallant and determined leader was to me reward enough in itself.[43]

They still had to pack up and get themselves down through the Icefall to Base Camp. They could not take everything with them and Noyce regretted not having one of his high-altitude boots as a souvenir. The main party went down on 31st May and Noyce stayed with Wylie to help with the loading and the Sherpas. He also managed to copy out the article he had written earlier and some poems. On 1st June Noyce went down to Base with Stobart, Pugh and Ward.

2nd June was Coronation Day and James Morris had managed to get the news through for the newspapers on that morning. This added to the euphoria of the crowds that lined the procession route. The author remembers as a scout programme seller along the procession route, marching past the Bank Tube station at 5.00 that morning and seeing the headline '**Everest is conquered**', thinking how great it was that my scoutmaster was part of that success. I did not realise how much he had contributed until long after his death.

There was a celebration dinner at Base Camp and toasts were drunk to the Queen, the Duke of Edinburgh, the expedition's patron, the Prime Ministers of Britain and New Zealand, and Eric Shipton. The Sherpas continued their revelry well into the night.

The following day the coolies were assembled to take their loads back to Kathmandu. It was a motley crew from the nearest villages, grandmothers, young Sherpanis, old men, young men, big men and small men. It would be eighteen days before they all reached Kathmandu. The Sherpas had an infinite capacity for merry-making and were frequently given to this on the way. There was entertainment at the monasteries and receptions in the villages. There were still the valleys to cross and unending ups and downs. Noyce writes: '*Tiredness. It must be confessed that the legs do not face a slope with the same zest, after they have been doing nothing for three months but climb similar slopes.*'[44] They treated themselves to bathes in the cool rivers and luxuriated on the grassy banks. All the time the Sherpas looked after them and eventually they reached the pass above Banepa where they were met by Col. Proud, the Defence Attaché at the British Embassy '...*and two smooth young gentlemen recognised with difficulty as Mike Ward and Charles Wylie*'.[45] The others were still very hirsute and they all continued in procession down to Banepa. Hillary, Hunt and Tenzing were covered in garlands and prepared to give voice on a dais that had been set up for them. Noyce and George Lowe were picked up by Macmillan, the embassy architect and his wife and brought them the tumultuous twelve miles to Kathmandu. The Nepalese were determined to celebrate Tenzing's achievement and they passed banners 'THE UNPRECEDENTED HERO TENZING' and 'Poor Mount Everest', and there were triumphal arches in many streets.

Still in the clothes they had arrived in they were all went off to the

Town Hall where there were speeches of welcome then they were whisked off to the Royal Palace where the King and his ministers awaited them. Tenzing was decorated with the Star of Nepal, first class and Hunt and Hillary both received substantial medals and photographs were taken. To quote Noyce: *'After 7.30 in the evening a group of very tired men with grateful hearts was taken to the British Embassy; to food, to a bath, to sleep between the sheets of a bed.'*

They went down to Calcutta, as it was called then, to a great welcome and hospitality, to Delhi where there were receptions with the President of India, Sri Rajendra Prasad, and presentations of decorations and a meeting with the Prime Minister, Sri Jawaharlal Nehru.

Then it was on home to the welcome of heroes at London's Heathrow airport on 3rd July.

Notes

1. Wilfrid Noyce, *South Col* p.3
2. John Hunt, *Ascent of Everest* p.24
3. *Ibid.*
4. Edmund Hillary, *Nothing Venture, Nothing Win* p.172
5. Wilfrid Noyce, *South Col* p.37
6. The *Spectator* 13.3.1953
7. Wilfrid Noyce, *South Col* p.42
8. *Ibid* p.45
9. George Band, *Everest* p.133
10. Wilfrid Noyce, *South Col* p.53
11. *Ibid* p.57
12. *Ibid* p.59
13. *Ibid* p.67
14. *Ibid* p.292
15. *Ibid* p.64
16. *Ibid* p.78
17. *Ibid* p.81
18. *Ibid* p.84
19. *Ibid* p.110
20. *Ibid* p.111
21. *Ascent of Everest* p.112
22. *Ibid* p.117
23. Wilfrid Noyce, *South Col* p.145
24. *Ibid* p.148
25. *Ascent of Everest* p.140
26. *Ibid.*

22 *Above*: With Gunturia in Garhwal, 1943
23 *Right*: Aircrew Centre, Kashmir – Noyce going up to dig out ponies on the Zoji La, 1944.
24 *Below left*: Aircrew Centre – Noyce with a pupil on the Kazim Glacier, 1944.
25 *Below right*: Srinagar, Kashmir – Picnic group Florence Castle, Wilfrid Noyce, John Hansbury, Gordon Macdonald.

26 *Wedding Day 12th August 1950, l. to r.: Pat Ballard, Wilfrid, Rosemary, Julian Legrand; behind: Stephen Ballard, Lady Noyce, Prof. Arthur Pigou, Mrs Campbell Davies, Eveline Ballard.*

27 *Left: Tenzing Norgay with Rosemary, Wilfrid and Michael Noyce, Godalming, 1957.*

28 *Above: Jeremy and Michael Noyce Badgers Hollow, Godalming, 1960.*

29 Family group at Hurstmere 1957, Rose Binney, Lady Noyce, friend of Lady Noyce, Rosalind, Jeremy, Rosemary, Michael.

30 Above: Noyce on Mount Everest, 1953.

31 Right: Noyce with Anullu at Camp IV on Everest, 1953.

32 Below: A scene of desolation, the Swiss tents on the South Col, 21st May 1953.

33 *Noyce and the Sherpas on the Lhotse Face, 1953.*

34 *Charterhouse Climbing Meet, Cwm Glas, April 1955, l. to r.: John Hansbury, David Cox, Dick Marsh, Alistair Gourlay, the author, Roy Davey, Peter Norton, Jon Moore, Richard Hills, Donald Percival.*

35 Displaying mountain equipment at a village fête, 28th June 1959.

36 Signing an autograph for Stephen Pearne at a Young Persons' Literary evening, Guildford 1954.

37 Right: With Carthusians on Tryfan, January 1957. From left to Right, D. Mallock, A. Roberts, A.Rabeneck, A. Young and D. Meggs with Wilfrid Noyce and Angus Graham on Adam and Eve.

38 Below: Noyce on the scree with John Hunt, Pik Garmo behind.

39 The Wilfrid Noyce Memorial bench at Grayshott.

40 Robin Smith (l.) and Wilfrid Noyce on the summit of Pik Garmo, 24th July 1962.

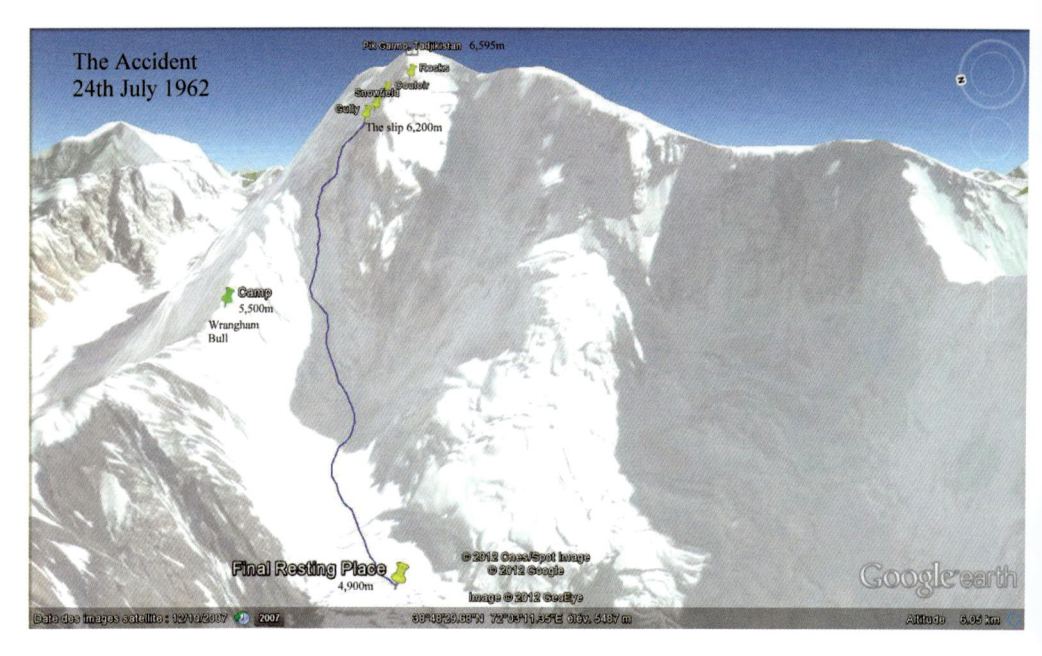

41 The Accident.

42 Jeremy Noyce at the memorial to his father and Robin Smith, Garmo Valley, Tajikistan, 29th September 2009.

27 *South Col p.165*
28 *Ibid p.168*
29 *Ascent of Everest p.157*
30 Wilfrid Noyce, *South Col p.183*
31 *Heinemann Archives,* Reading University Library
32 Wilfrid Noyce, *South Col. p.187*
33 *Ibid p.193*
34 *Ascent of Everest p.166*
35 John Hunt & David Cox, *Alpine Journal 1993 p.70*
36 *Ascent of Everest p.166*
37 Wilfrid Noyce, *South Col p.203*
38 *Ascent of Everest p.195*
39 See also John Hunt, *Ascent of Everest p.185* for his attempts with this method
40 See Edmund Hillary, chapter sixteen in *Ascent of Everest*
41 Wilfrid Noyce, *South Col p.233*
42 *Ibid p.237*
43 Edmund Hillary, in *Ascent of Everest p.209*
44 Wilfrid Noyce, *South Col p.275*
45 *Ibid p.278*

CHAPTER ELEVEN

EVEREST AFTERMATH

The expedition flew back to Britain vaguely aware that the Everest expedition was not fully over.

'*The Other Everest*'[1], in Noyce's words was still to climb.

> *Not one member of the party can have anticipated one-tenth of the excitement which the ascent caused. It would be an amusing task, perhaps that of a cynic, to picture the news had the forty-foot rock step proved just that fraction harder. The happy coincidence of the announcement that was made on Coronation Day itself, the feeling that in this year especially Britons can do it after all, the correlated feeling that British prestige abroad would be enhanced: all these factors now contributed to the aureole now thrown round the ascent of Everest.*[2]

On the flight home they stopped at Zurich and had a session with the Swiss Alpine Club, some of whose members had been on Everest ten months earlier.

Shortly after his return, in fulfilment of a promise made before Noyce left for Everest he went to see Frank Ives, the housemaster of his old house at Charterhouse and a master when Noyce was a pupil. Although it was late, Ives roused the House and Noyce gave his first public account of the trip to the boys, some in pyjamas, in the housemaster's drawing room.

Andrew Douglas-Bate wrote in **The Carthusian**, the school magazine,

> *After the expedition he quietly returned to his home. I do not think that he meant to arrive back at Charterhouse in the way*

that he did. It was a fine afternoon for cricket…I was keeping out of trouble away in the deep field. Suddenly in the distance I heard the sound of cheering. It grew louder and louder and then I could see "Wilf" Noyce walking down the avenue. He seemed a little embarrassed by the noise as he walked with his wife and wheeled his baby in the pram which he had used to get fit a few months before. As he went by our game we all cheered and cheered. He waved a thank you and when he passed we took up the game again.[3]

He was formally received back to Charterhouse at the School Assembly at the end of the summer term. He was greeted with tremendous acclaim, and in response to headmaster Brian Young's congratulatory remarks, was characteristically diffident and modest about his achievements on Everest.

Noyce was a well-known local figure in Surrey and Worcestershire and through his local and literary connections he received his first invitations before the formal lecture organisation was in place.

A Mr. Van Wyck with Charles Evans seem to have been the lecture tour organisers and on 22nd August 1953 Noyce wrote to Evans,[4] *'I don't want to do too many because of writing'* – and asked if Smiths, the instrument makers, wanted them to return the watches with which they equipped the expedition. He also said that he would be, *'Very busy in September with school starting'*. He was also very concerned about the promoter's need to go for the high-paying lectures:

If a local Youth Club or Scout Body really wants to hear me, and can't pay, I shall certainly not say no for that reason.

He talked to the scouts in Godalming on 27th July and it was reported in detail in the **Surrey Times**. At Charterhouse he addressed the reception for 200 Queen's Scouts on 26th September 1953 when Lord Rowallan, the Chief Scout, presented Royal Certificates, including one to the author.

The Royal Grammar School, Guildford, which had produced the Himalayan explorers, Godwin-Austen and Durand, was an early audience and Noyce was the guest speaker on their Speech Day on 20th November and presented the prizes.

Arranged early on was a public lecture at Chichester, 17th October, which apparently was at George Turner's instigation. Turner was Noyce's headmaster at Charterhouse when he first arrived to teach. Then it was Malvern College on 22nd October, where he was still remembered as a popular master. David Murray-Rust, the Charterhouse master who had been with Noyce in the Lakes, Wales and the Alps in the 1930s, was now headmaster of the Quaker Sidcot School in Somerset and he invited Noyce there on 25th October. This was followed on 26th October with a Public Lecture at Malvern and another two days later at Worcester.

He was back home in Godalming, if not back to teaching at Charterhouse, and was able conveniently to lecture at Priorsfield School, where Rosemary was teaching, on 6th November. He never forgot his earliest days in England and gave a talk to the local Women's Institutes at Grayshott, where the family home was. On 7th November there was a grander occasion, also at Grayshott, to raise funds for the Village Hall. The hall was packed and there was great interest shown in the items of equipment. They charged for entry one shilling for Noyce's autograph. Seventy-five pounds was raised for Village Hall funds. In thanking him the chairman of the Parish Council, Major Whitaker,

> ...recalled that the first time he had met the speaker was some years ago, when Mr Noyce, then an undergraduate at Cambridge, had come to him when he himself was ill in bed and had asked if there were any jobs on the farm that he might tackle. "I said that certainly there were, and for the next fortnight I had him spreading dung. I should like to take this opportunity of making him a public apology."[5]

On 10th November he was at Cranleigh School.

Noyce had provided assistance to John Hunt working with him on the dispatches to *The Times* from Nepal and was helping with the official book of the expedition. On Coronation Day 1953 the only two names the public were really aware of were Hillary and Tenzing and in the excitement the rest of the team was barely visible. There was some pressure to publish the official book to tell the full story and pay tribute to the entire team and amplify the original impression. Noyce provided the draft of the foreword to which Prince Philip put his signature and sent it off to Balmoral in August. *The Ascent of Everest* with John Hunt as the author, but with considerable contributions from other members of the team, came out in November 1953.

Noyce was also preparing his own book on the climb, which would be a more personal record as well as readying his full-length poem on ***Michel Angelo*** for publication at the end of the year. An article for ***The Climbers' Club Journal*** was clearly a must and the *Central Council for Physical Recreation (CCPR)* asked him for an article for their journal.[7] He also penned a wide-ranging canter through mountaineering literature for the ***Journal of the National Book League*** in October 1953 entitled 'A Mountaineer's Bookshelf'. Extracts from his diaries appeared in the ***Encounter*** in January 1954 together with some of the poems he had written on Everest. He claimed that they were the highest ever written.

The premiere of the film, ***The Conquest of Everest***, on 21st October 1953 was a glittering occasion on which the expedition members and their wives, including Lady Noyce, Noyce's mother, were presented to the Queen. The film was received with acclaim:

> *The camera records what it saw, a team working together to make the impossible possible. Indeed when the story is told what one remembers, beside the enormous hungry presence of Everest, is the working together, the companionship of men intent on a job dangerous to the point of suicide.'*
>
> *'The Conquest of Everest' is not that boastful either. But again there was no temptation to boast; the images on the screen make clear enough how appalling were the perils and how miraculous was the victory.*[8]

The 'Everest effect' was a popularisation of mountaineering and adventure activities far beyond the fairly small, at that time, mountaineering fraternity. To respond to public demand the official lecture programme got under way by the end of October. To accompany the lectures Noyce produced a short brochure with a foreword also by Prince Philip, details of the team and a concise account of the climb.[9] The lecturers received a £25 fee and their expenses, and after the payment of costs, the proceeds went into the expedition fund. Noyce addressed the English Speaking Union on 29th September and The Rotary Club in Bristol on 24th October. He appears also to have addressed the Royal Grammar School at Worcester, not far from his old stamping ground at Malvern.

The Commonwealth Section of the Royal Society of Arts and the East India Association invited Noyce to give their Thomas Holland Memorial

Lecture on 15th December 1953; the President, Sir Harry Lindsay was an old colleague of Noyce's father in India.

His colleagues were equally busy: in Manchester there were seven public lectures instead of the one originally planned, and it was said that George Band, still an undergraduate at Cambridge, gave more lectures than his dons!

Then there was the demand from the US and the Continent. He wrote, *'I am painfully aware that I have seen only a minor part of the reception of Everest lectures abroad.'*[10]

His fellow-climbers were in Holland, Belgium, Scandinavia, Yugoslavia, Singapore, the United States and Canada. John Hunt received the Christopher Columbus Trophy in Genoa and the Hubbard Medal of the National Geographical Society from President Eisenhower. A replica of the medal was also presented for each member of the team.

The European tours for Noyce started in November when he, Hunt, Gregory, Lowe and Hillary went to Paris. They had receptions '...*on an enormous scale which filled the days*'. He and Lowe addressed 300 enthusiastic young people at a lycée for an hour, in French, without notes or pictures and the evening lecture given by Hunt, Hillary and Gregory in the presence of the President, Vincent Auriol and General Juin, seemed a push-over by comparison.

The warmth of the reception was a tribute to the spirit of the team that had been able to put two men on the top of Everest. The French, who are never great team players, found it difficult to believe this and in fact one said to Noyce, *"How nice it was of John Hunt to say in his book that you all got on so well. Now what did really happen?"* On another day they were taken to the rocks at Fontainebleau, where Paris climbers assemble on Sundays, and guests of every country are always invited to test their skills.

Noyce started 1954 with a lecture to the British Society, in Eastbourne on 4th January. He then appears to have had leave of absence from Charterhouse for another term to lecture on the continent. He was off to Switzerland, standing in for John Hunt who was ill, with Howard Somervell, who had been on Everest in 1924. He was, however, not without misgivings, as the British had benefited from the Swiss experience and had succeeded on Everest where the Swiss had failed only a few months before, and there might be a feeling of envy. However, there was nothing but good-natured interest as befits a mountain people and an increased respect for British climbing. Noyce was still a little diffident about lecturing in German; he had written to Ann Debenham, the secretary in the Mount Everest office asking if his lectures in Switzerland could be in French rather than German. In the event he appears to have overcome this diffidence, although there were some comments on his German!

At Basle it was said from the platform that the British deserved to get to the top of Everest as they had tried so many times already![11] And Noyce felt strongly that this nation of professional mountain men had greatly raised their opinion of British climbing. This impression was endorsed at a lunch party in the British Embassy in Bern, where Noyce had lectured in the big hall of the Casino, in a not always easily understood German.[12] Nonetheless the audience felt they were with him on the mountain sharing his tribulations.[13] His final phrase, "*We did not have the feeling that Everest was conquered, but much rather that she had been kind to us,*" clearly made an impression.[14]

On 12th January he was in Zurich addressing the crowded Large Hall of the Kongresshaus, at the invitation of the Swiss Alpine Club and the Swiss Foundation for Alpine Research. The press reported[15] that Noyce had spoken impressively, in German, and with typical British humour, of the expedition, and modestly of his part in it. They appreciated the phrase: "*We conquered not Mount Everest but the unruly bits of ourselves.*" There was no trace of sour grapes. Afterwards there was a meeting in the Music Room with the president of the Swiss-British Association, Dr. Wildi, and members of the Swiss Foundation.[16]

They were in Geneva at the Salle de la Reformation on 13th January. This time Noyce delivered his anecdotes and gentle humour in French. The press described it as a meeting '*en famille,*' only 600 attended, as it had been cancelled when they heard that John Hunt would not be able to give it. However it was an audience that gasped as one, '*when the picture of the ruined Swiss tents on the South Col appeared*'[17] and applauded generously at the photograph of Tenzing on the summit. Great affection was felt at these sights of Tenzing and the tents and they enabled the audience and the Swiss climbers, of whom Chevalley, Lambert, Ditter, Hofstetter and Asper were present, to share the joy of the British success. The lecture finished to long applause.[18] The recognition of the assistance that the Swiss expedition had afforded to the British was also very much appreciated.[19]

Noyce finished in Mürren, where the lecture was in English, with two days skiing as the guests of the Swiss Foundation. He records,

> *T. H. Somervell and I disgraced the name of Everest by coming down a run which should take 5 minutes for women, 4½ minutes for men, in one and a half hours.*

There were lectures in Italy in February 1954. In Milan there was a great deal of interest in the Himalaya and the shops were full of Everest books. The Italians were preparing their K2 expedition under Professor Desio: one of the members said, *"Your expedition inspired ours."* Noyce thought this was one of the most intelligent audiences as many Milanese are mountaineers with Monte Rosa not very far away.

In Innsbruck they were welcomed with 'very informal friendliness'. The two lectures were in the Upper Hall of the British Council and to very keen audiences. The parts most appreciated were the technical points, the ice-fall, the top crevasse, Lhotse face and the final ridge. In between times the Innsbruckers took him skiing,

> *…with that fine and generous abandon which makes it a sacred law that a man (or woman) must have the afternoon off from the office if it looks fine and good snow on the Hafelikar. And Sunday is devoted to the sport.*

On 26th February Noyce and others had been in Munich for a Press Conference and he returned there for a lecture on 3rd March in the great Kongressaal with 2,500 seats. It was, however, Ash Wednesday and there were fears that the effects of 'Fasching' would have seriously reduced the potential audience. The people of Munich are hard mountaineers and did not disappoint and the hall was sufficiently full to ensure a good audience. Paul Bauer, the greatest Himalayan mountaineer of his day, introduced them and in the audience were Hermann Buhl, who reached the summit of Nanga Parbat on his own, and Dr Herrligkoffer, who led that expedition and did not want Buhl to summit on his own. Here also they were very interested in the technicalities and in the British casual humorous approach; *'a light-heartedness which I believe is a factor welding a party together, and ours particularly.'*

Noyce had met some of the older German mountaineers earlier, heroes of his boyhood and veterans of the early Kanchenjunga expeditions and after the lecture he retired to the Ratskeller with the younger element. Rebitsch was planning an expedition to the Karakoram in 1954, Ertl and Buhl who both had been on Nanga Parbat and others who regarded the Eiger north face and other terrifying spots as friends.

They told Noyce, *"that the impressive part of the Everest tale to them was the team spirit and affectionate loyalty for the leader"*. German mountaineering had been seriously divided after the ructions on the Nanga Parbat expedition in 1953. In 1954 the quarrels were out of the courts but there was still competition between groups and no unified national approach.

From Munich it was up to Regensburg, where they are rock-climbers rather than mountaineers. They took Noyce climbing on the limestone rocks near Kelheim, which he *'wormed up painfully'*. He felt that there was a great deal of escapism in the climbing. Some, like Ertl, took up residence in South America.

> *Others earn just enough at a low-grade to allow the week-end among the rocks, the summer vacation in the Dolomites. But it seems a more moderate escapism now than the Nazi-Nietzsche mountain-madness between the wars. The young men might still echo the German who said before a dangerous north wall, "We Germans have nothing more to lose."*[20]

At this point the audiences seem to have become smaller, at any rate in Nuremburg and Fürth and Noyce wondered despondently if the German public had already had enough mountain lectures after Nanga Parbat. However after these two towns the audiences seemed to increase progressively in Karlsruhe, Wurzburg, Darmstadt and Cologne. In Kiel and Lubeck they were more just satisfactory but in Kassel there was again a good audience. This is in the middle of a flat plain where there is not a mountain in sight! Noyce remarks that:

> *The Press continued to be interested, as much as anything in the common effort of Everest, which one paper contrasted with the unhappy and almost national consequences of the Nanga Parbat ascent.*

Then it was on to Berlin, where there was great interest and delight in the adventure as opposed to the technical details. The Berliners felt very much enclosed within the Soviet Zone – it was a two to three hour drive to the Western Zone. Travel books were very popular and visitors were encouraged. Noyce did a broadcast for the Eastern Zone in which he was particularly asked to stress the pleasure of the West Berliners in welcoming foreign lecturers, because their neighbours in the Eastern Zone clearly did not have this facility.

It was Athens next and into a phase of Greek Anti-Britishness over Cyprus. However, Noyce found the Hellenic Alpine Club perhaps the most congenial of all. He wrote:

> *At Munich I had felt something of a weakling, not being able to bicycle off at week-ends and do the Matterhorn North Face or the rock walls of the Badile. There was a sense of strenuous urgency about. At Athens I felt exactly in the picture, pottering over the ridges of Parnis, Hymettus and Pendele; and when, with Jocelin Winthrop Young, I tried some bouldering by the wayside, the Club's charming secretary turned up an amused if tolerant eyebrow at us, much as my elder Swiss guide had done.*

The political situation forced the cancellation of the lectures at Thessaloniki and Patras. However,

> *the lecture at Athens was saved by the presence of the Royal Family. But even then the hall was packed with more security police than I could have believed it would hold alongside the audience. An excellent audience too, and particularly the very gracious Royal Family. The peaks of Greece may not be as high as the Alps; and it may be an event to be talked of when anybody reaches Olympus; but there are no truer-hearted or more hospitable mountaineers.*[21]

Noyce was in Vienna at the end of April 1954, for the last of his lectures. It was a sad city still in the hands of the Russians and the Western allies – although without the rigid demarcation of Berlin. There may even have been Russians in the audience in the big Konzertsaal, '…*gleaning information for attempts on the North side of Everest*'.[22] The audience was perhaps the most expert of them all. They needed no explanations of terms, they were all familiar with crampons and karabiners and paid close attention to all that was said. Noyce wrote, with characteristic diffidence, that he felt a fraud in Austria and Switzerland. '*How can a poor schoolmaster from the Home Counties, with nothing nearer to him than Snowdon, presume to lecture on the highest mountains?*'

The Everest lectures strengthened the bonds between British

mountaineers and their continental colleagues and increased their appreciation of the substantial contribution being made by British mountaineering. The interest in Everest was sustained for a considerable time and the lectures continued for several years. There were at least six lectures in the Royal Festival Hall and in the larger concert halls they, *'were able to charge the same ticket prices as if Barbirolli were conducting the Hallé Orchestra.'*[23] With the receipts from the lectures, the film and John Hunt's book, enough funds were raised to establish the Mount Everest Foundation which continues to support research and exploration in mountain regions.

At the end of April Wilfrid Noyce returned to his task of teaching French and German to unwilling adolescents who were quite happy to side-track him into tales of other fields of endeavour.

Notes

1 George Band, *Everest* p.177
2 Wilfrid Noyce, *South Col* p.285
3 *The Carthusian*, December 1962
4 Noyce's Letter to Evans 22.8.1953, RGS archives
5 *The Herald for Farnham... 13.11.1953*
6 *Climbers' Club Journal 1954*, p.282
7 *Physical Recreation Oct-Dec 1953* p.8, with *Mountaincraft* (same article)
8 Dilys Powell, *Sunday Times* 25.10.1953 p.19
9 Wilfrid Noyce, *Ascent of Everest 1953*
10 Wilfrid Noyce, unpublished *Mount Everest Walks Abroad*
11 *Mount Everest Walks Abroad*
12 *Der Bund, January 1954, RGS Archives*
13 *Neue Berner Zeitung, 16.1.54 RGS Archives*
14 *Der Bund, RGS Archives*
15 *Neue Zürcher Zeitung, 14.1.54 RGS Archives*
16 *Die Tat, 16.1.54 RGS* Archives
17 *Mount Everest Walks Abroad*
18 *Journal de Genève, 14.1.54 RGS Archives*
19 *Tribune de Genève, 14.1.54 RGS Archive*
20 *Mount Everest Walks Abroad*
21 *Ibid*
22 *Ibid.*
23 George Band, *Everest* p.181

CHAPTER TWELVE

HIMALAYA AND KARAKORAM 1957-60

Part 1 Machapuchare 1957

In the autumn of 1956 David Cox, Charles Wylie and Wilfrid Noyce met at La Belle Etoile restaurant in Soho to start preparations for the Machapuchare expedition. Their respective employers, University College, Oxford, the War Office and Charterhouse had given leave of absence. Jimmy Roberts, the instigator of the expedition, was leader and being in India was making arrangements for permissions, getting Sherpas and working out the details of quantities and loads. He had been studying the mountain for some considerable time and his last Alpine season had been ten years earlier. Noyce was responsible, as on Everest, for equipment, Cox was the treasurer and Wylie, again as on Everest, the secretary. Noyce, however, was the leader on the mountain. These responsibilities were the background to their other activities over the next six months. Roger Chorley joined the team shortly afterwards and organised the food. They benefited from the experience of the recent Muztagh Tower expedition and Roger Chorley drew heavily on his experience on the Rakaposhi expedition in 1954.

The end of term came and on 1st April Noyce left London to climb Machapuchare with the good wishes of the school and of the borough of Godalming as shown in the Council minutes:

28.3.57 Monthly Meeting Mr Councillor Noyce

> *On behalf of the Borough the Mayor wished Councillor Noyce good fortune on his journey to climb a peak in the Himalayas.*

The Borough would look forward to welcoming Councillor Noyce back, safe, sound and victorious.[1]

It was an expedition with difficulties. At every turn they were met with frustrations and sometimes misfortune. The route up the mountain was not at all clear. Roberts' reconnaissances had not provided enough information for them to plot the route to the top. The twelve hours enforced wait of Cox and Noyce at Düsseldorf made them miss their connection at Karachi and they just managed to find places on a later plane to get them to New Delhi. Noyce, however, managed to write a chapter of his 'Adventure' book on the plane.[2] Wylie had gone on ahead, and Chorley joined their plane when it touched down at Istanbul. They all finally arrived at the Gurkha Depôt at Lehra, in Northern India, not far from Gorakhpur, on 4th April. They spent four days there, enjoying the hospitality of the Depôt Officers' Mess and becoming increasingly anxious. There was still no sign of the kit they had sent by sea. On 8th April, they left Lehra and went across the border into Nepal to the airfield at Bhairwa, now called Bhairahawa, to take the plane to Pokhara and Kathmandu. They spent four days in Kathmandu, sightseeing principally but made a number of contacts including their liaison officer, Dikshya Man.

Like every expedition to Nepal, they had to pay the government a fee, the cost of which depended on the mountains they planned to climb, or the maximum altitude they were hoping to reach. In return the government provided a liaison officer whose main objective was to ensure that the expedition did not exceed their stated plans.

Then they flew back to Pokhara, within sight of the mountain they wanted to climb, waiting for the kit which finally turned up on 17th April. Pokhara was of a certain interest but it did not help with acclimatisation as it was at only 3,000ft (920m) and Machapuchare was 22,958ft (6,894m). This was not the way they planned to spend Easter and they all were thinking about home. Noyce wrote letters to his wife Rosemary and each of his sons and to his mother. He was very appreciative of his mother's support to his family.

How wonderful of you to be having the family over this Easter. You know how it is appreciated and what a difference it will make to Romie. There is an Easter tradition about us and Hurstmere.[3] I do say a big thank you on behalf of us all.[4]

On 18th April they left Pokhara for the seven-day walk to Base Camp. They were accompanied by the Sherpas and the fifty coolies that Roberts had arranged. Each coolie had a load of sixty to seventy pounds (twenty-seven to thirty-two kilos). Another companion was John Nicholls Booth, an American Unitarian Minister who was in Nepal filming. The day they left Pokhara the town was all decorated – for a visit of the king. The route they were following was the westerly trade route into Tibet, which later turns north and passes between Dhaulagiri and the Annapurna massif. The weather on the march was varied; it usually started off fine but deteriorated in the afternoon so they could get into camp before it became unpleasant.

At Biretante, nearly halfway, Booth departed, with cordial farewells, to return to Pokhara and the party turned north following the Modi River to Ghandrung. This was the largest place they went through and there the headman made a point to Noyce that they should not go up the mountain until the barley was in. The headman visited the camp and told Roberts not to annoy the gods of the mountain. They promised to be as tactful as possible with the gods and to respect their sanctuary.

Dikshya Man was clearly out of his depth. He asked Noyce what he thought he should do and they all tried to be helpful. He did not enjoy the march, attired in shorts, carrying a rolled umbrella, and asking questions in his laboured English. He could not understand the locals either.

From Ghandrung they had three days in the Modi River gorge. The first day was the most pleasant consisting of a gentle walk up to camp on a grassy patch at Kuldighar at 7,500ft (2,250m). They dined off a roast Indian tragopan pheasant[5] that had been caught in a trap. The other two days were tramping through difficult forest and on the third day Noyce recounts:

> The 'path' used by venturesome shepherds during the monsoon, had all but disappeared. David, suffering badly from dysentery, missed it and must have found himself almost in the Modi's bed. He and I ended by bringing up a depressed rear – trip, stumble, umbrella catch, climb over fallen rhododendron, trip again, and the broken bamboos as sharp as knives. How they got sheep through this stuff![6]

To add to the discomfort Noyce was also suffering from dysentery. On the third afternoon they reached the shrine that marked the edge of the Annapurna sanctuary. Beyond this point they could not take eggs or chicken and at the last village nearby, Chomrong, they had to dismiss their low caste coolies. Pressing on in the rain, in very low spirits, they reached Hinko, beyond the end of the gorge, where they pitched camp at nearly 10,000ft (3,000m). Half the coolies did not want to go any farther. The following day, 24th April, was brighter and they waited to see the sun in the valley before starting with the twenty-seven coolies who had volunteered to carry up to Base Camp. Soon after leaving, they were in avalanche snow but the Pokharis, bare-footed, coped very well with the snow in blocks and drifts. On the way Roberts pointed out his 1956 Base Camp down on the left: then it began to snow and after midday they reached a patch of bare snow under the moraine of the South-East Annapurna Glacier at 13,000ft (4,000m). The coolies had a quick smoke and rest then went down to Hinko, having agreed for a handsome fee, to return the following day with the other loads. The big mess tent, supplied by Chorley was pitched and tea and warmth were soon being purveyed. The least happy person was Dikshya Man. This was not what he expected; his only solace seemed to be a very worthy book, ***Hope for the Troubled: A genial warm-hearted guide to those who are psychologically disturbed.*** He studied it in his tent making notes and compiling a list of words he did not understand.

> *"What is schizophrenia, please?" Unanswerable question – at any rate in words of one syllable. That night after a snowy supper of soup and our usual rice mixture, he was receiving some instruction from Charles about the soldier's qualifications.*
>
> *"You have to be practical too."*
>
> *Dikshya Man was impressed with this. "Yes, one must be practical." He stumped off to bed, and that night badly burnt the entrance flap of the tent he was using, by upsetting his lighted candle.*[7]

From Base Camp they could see Machapuchare, but not all of it. From the River Modi, 700 feet below them at Base Camp, to the top was the same difference in height as from Base Camp to the summit on Everest. The mountain was guarded by vertical cliffs broken only by a wide gully which ran away in front of them, nicknamed by Roberts Gardyloo Gully, and it appeared to go up towards the North Col. Beyond that on the other side there were snowfields that could take

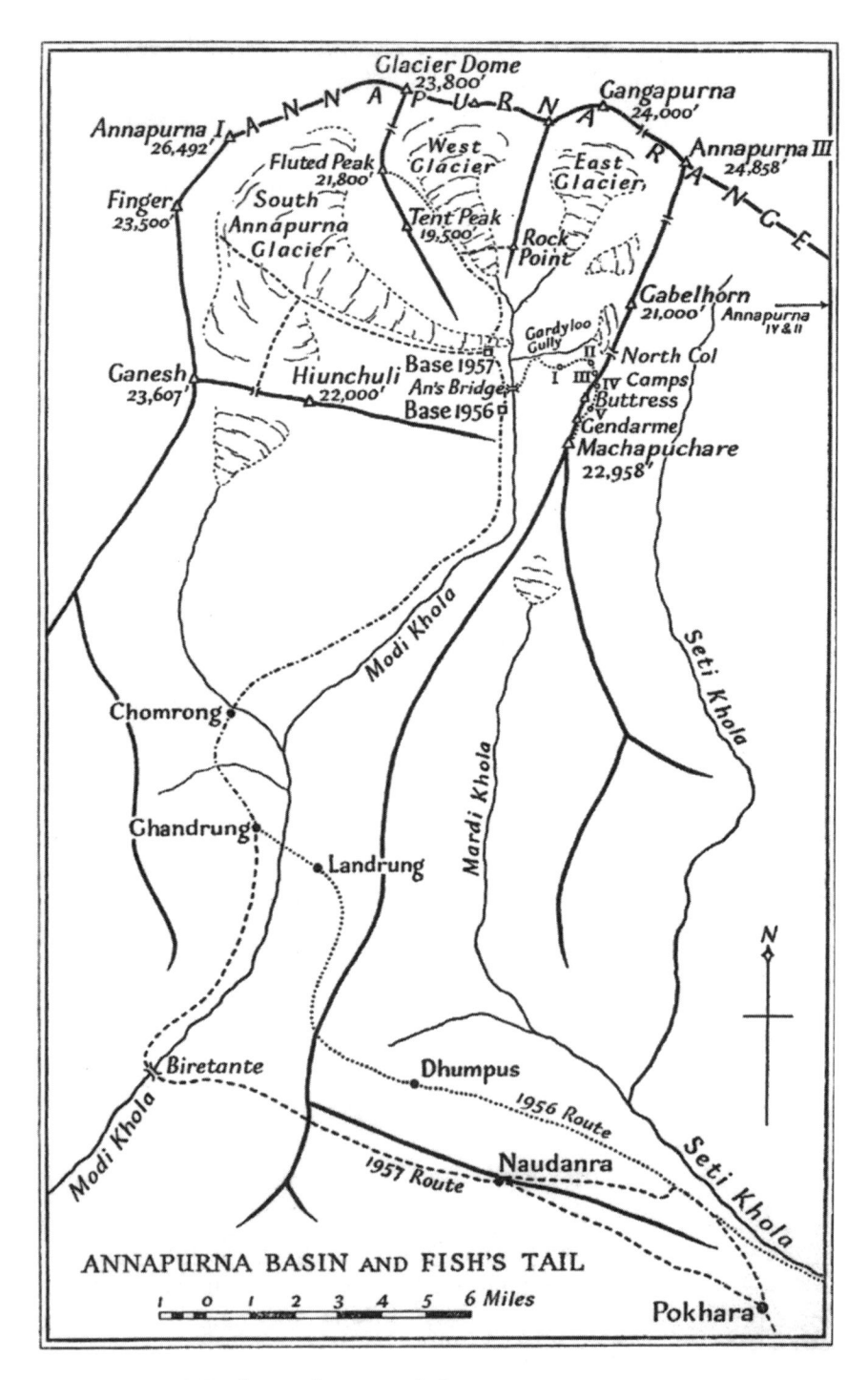

Machapuchare and the Annapurna Basin.

them up to the final steepness. Roberts had taken pictures of these from Annapurna II in 1950. They would have to go up to the Col to see how they could get to the summit. In addition they needed to become more acclimatised.

On 25th April Roberts stayed in camp to await the coolies bringing the second part of the loads up from Hinko and the others went off towards the west where the peaks of Hiunchuli and Ganesh overlooked the Annapurna Glacier. The morning had started fine but at 15,500ft (4,700m), in heavy snow and with Chorley's ice-axe sizzling from the thunder storm, they decided to return to camp.

The climbing started in earnest on 27th April when all except Wylie, who had a stomach bug, went down to the Modi River, across the wooden bridge that Ang Nyima had built the year before and entered Gardyloo Gully. They continued on up and reached 15,000ft and found a site for Camp I. The weather had by this time turned and after a miserable wet packed lunch they went back to Base Camp.

In order to justify the grants and sponsorship that the expedition had received they had, rather against the grain of purists such as Noyce, to make a contribution to science or the appropriate cause. The Mount Everest Foundation required them to correct a major error on the Indian Survey map of the area. Roberts was the most expert in this field and with Wylie during the period 28th April to 4th May did a reconnaissance in the west, under Ganesh and Hiunchuli. They produced a very good sketch map from their measurements and photographs. Noyce's contribution was the daily recording of the weather.

On 29th April Noyce, Chorley and Cox set off with four Sherpas at 8.40 to take loads up to the site of Camp I. Chorley was slow, surprisingly, as he had a reputation for carrying heavier, higher and faster than anyone else, and they eventually reached the site of Camp I and set up the tents. Chorley said that he felt chilled, although the sun was very hot.

The next day Noyce and Cox with the four Sherpas pressed on from Camp I, departing at 6.40. In heavy snow they reached the top of the 'Rognon', a rock feature 1,000ft (300m) above Camp I. From there, leaving Chorley to come on slowly, they continued in knee-deep snow and it became gradually steeper. They reached 18,000ft (5,400m) at 11.00 and reckoned the Sherpas had endured enough. They dumped their loads and went back to Camp I where there were no signs of life. Chorley was asleep in his very hot tent, still with his boots on. They still believed that Chorley was suffering only from altitude sickness. He stayed at Camp I for another two days while Cox and Noyce went up to 18,000ft with a couple of Sherpas and pitched Camp II. The Sherpas returned to Camp I and Wylie and Roberts in the meantime managed to get up to the col between Ganesh and Hiunchuli at 19,500ft (5,850m). On 2nd May Cox and Noyce pressed ahead with their reconnaissance on very difficult, steep ice and snow up to what was the main ridge of Machapuchare. The North Col at the head of Gardyloo Gully was down to their left, at 19,500ft:

> *It seemed a long pull, our bodies weary and our breath short, before we reached a crest which, quite suddenly, had nothing at all beyond.*[8]

There was a snow cornice overhanging a sheer cliff. This vivid moment Noyce recorded:

> *But it was the view southward, slowly being swallowed by mist, that held us. No mountain scene has ever awed me with a greater sense of the beautiful and inaccessible. Even Ama Dablam near Everest looks heavy in comparison with the feathery ridge that raced away from under our feet, over the Snow Hump and then, twisting in its course, along to two soaring triangles of ice.*[9]

They then started the difficult descent having selected the Snow Hump as the next day's objective. They descended to Camp II where Sherpas had brought up more loads as well as a message from Chorley saying that he had wanted to go up but thought it wiser to go down to Base Camp.

On 3rd May Cox and Noyce followed the tracks they had already made and then cut across up steepening snow which became difficult ice until they reached the main ridge. A very unpleasant half-hour of rotten cornice on one side and steep cliff on the other, brought them, quite exhausted to the top of the Hump at 13.00. There they left 200 feet of manila rope. Another difficult and nightmarish descent where they could not risk slipping brought them back to Camp II at 17.30 after ten hours on the mountain. They were very conscious that they were not sufficiently acclimatised and this meant that they were more tired than normal, with consequent effect on performance.

The next day, 4th May, they went down to Base Camp where all the team were by now gathered, and were greeted by Dikshya Man who was relieved to see them. They were anxious about Chorley and he met them hobbling on an ice-axe and his left leg did not function. The following day Chorley could not get up: he had suffered a high temperature and his legs would not obey him. Amazingly, he had come down from Camp I on his own. The conclusion was that it was polio. His arms and right leg were getting weaker and he had difficulty carrying out his natural functions. The entire team, Sherpas and Dikshya Man included, worked most of the day building the most luxurious latrine for him, so that he could spend all day on it, if necessary. However, the main concern was to get him down to where he could receive more expert care. Roberts was probably the best person anywhere to take charge. He sent Da Temba, the Sherpa, on 7th May, to order carriers from Chomrong and then to go to the British Women's Hospital at Pokhara. He also decided to go down with Chorley and the porters on 9th May, a considerable sacrifice, as the expedition was, after all, his inspiration.

Meanwhile two of the Sherpas, Tashi and Ang Tsering carried loads up to Camp I, followed on 8th May by Wylie, Noyce and Cox, the latter two continuing to Camp II on 9th May. They hoped that it would take a week to get up to the ridge at 20,700ft (6,300m). It took nine days. The first day, 10th May, Cox and Noyce tried a route to the right of the camp but found that they would need to cut across to the right to get beyond the Rock Buttress on the ridge. They returned to Camp II where Wylie had arrived with three Sherpas who went straight back down to bring more loads the next day.

On 11th May the three climbers were by now becoming excited with their progress and at 6.30 started up the gully to the left of Camp II. Wylie threw himself into his role of official photographer and set his tripod at impossible angles, at great personal risk, to film the other two in their ascent of the steep slopes. Then they crossed some ribs characterised by very hard steep ice and saw a large ice-cave on the other side of the gully, approached by a line of easy snow. However, before that they had to cross a vertical band of ice, where even Noyce found difficulty with his balance. They were greatly relieved to reach the cave, but it was no place for a camp and they went out to behind a sérac where there was some flat snow, ideal for Camp III.

On the way down they were fixing ropes to ease the passage of Sherpas up the more difficult stretches and Wylie was filming them, when a storm caught them. It drove in hail that went everywhere. It filled the steps in the snow and ice before the next man could put his feet in them. It almost seemed that the whole slope was slithering down. They got to the tents of Camp II and made some tea and started to eat some bread and honey: it was 16.00. The slithering hail washed on to the tents and began to smother them. They used anything they had, mugs, plates, shovels, to dig out the equipment, the more they dug, the more it came, until 18.30 when the storm eased off. Wylie dug a channel in an effort to divert the flow of hail. They had a very damp and uncomfortable night in the one tent as the other was buried. In the morning they set to again and dug out the buried tent. It started to hail and snow again mid-morning but by 13.00 had stopped, and they decided to move camp to a place half-an-hour away. However, the snow was waist-deep now and it would not be possible to move until the morning, when some of snow would have melted.

By midday on 13th May they were installed in the new site between two large crevasses which would protect them from anything that came off the mountain. They then waited until Tashi, Ang Nyima and Ang Tsering joined them with more loads. Enough supplies were now in position for the team to make a serious attempt on the summit.

Tashi and Ang Tsering set off down to Camp I on 14th May with a piton and 100 feet of rope to secure the route round the ice-bulge. Ang Nyima went with Cox and Noyce and Wylie to see how a Sherpa would cope with the icy traverses. The original Camp II was completely obliterated. They went up the Great Gully and reached the bottom of the fixed rope. Noyce reflected:

> *I had never before had the experience of climbing fixed ropes up a place previously climbed without. It is very agreeable. Gone the worry as to whether steps will hold, the forebodings at the green glint of ice. Easily and happily we swung upward, admiring the view, enjoying so much the final airy pull that we named it Jacob's Ladder, since it clearly led to heaven. Blissful ourselves, we could not understand Ang Nyima's slowness. He came on doggedly, but seemed to disapprove.*[10]

They reached the grotto at 10.30 and Wylie and Ang Nyima went up to 20,000ft (6,100m) to dump high altitude rations and a tent, while Noyce and Cox installed 600ft of fixed rope between Camps III and II on the way down. Noyce continued:

> *Here let it be said that none of us considered himself an expert pitoneer in the modern sense. Before 1953 I had only struck one piton into rock, and that more in fear than anger, in the Central Gully of Lliwedd, North Wales. Indeed with Menlove Edwards, I had removed two, from the Munich Climb on Tryfan because we thought it so silly of these foreigners to need artificial aids. Times change. I have since struck one or two more into rock, still with an uneasy conscience, and with some pleasure into ice. The pegs that we drove into Machapuchare were for attaching a protective handrail, for belay and for bringing up Sherpas, not for overcoming steepnesses we could not otherwise have attempted. In that sense this was an ascent by the old school; although we did also use them later for getting down places which we could have climbed neither up nor down without.*

On 15th May sahibs and Sherpas all went up to where Wylie and the Ang Nyima had made a dump the day before and levelled a platform for Camp III. The Sherpas went down for a further load. The sleeping bags had been put out on the tents to dry when Wylie's slipped off the tent and swooped 2,000 feet down to within 300 yards of Camp II. Frantic signals to the descending Sherpas were of no avail and the sleeping-bag very shortly disappeared forever under the snow that arrived in the afternoon. From then on, Wylie spent his nights wrapped in his and the others' down clothing and even said that he slept well!

To go beyond Camp III on the following day they had to go left up an ice chimney and then left up a snowy gully with a steep ice rib at the end. 200 feet more brought Noyce to the crest:

> *The view made me for a moment forget the others, forget everything. To the north the corniced crest sprang wildly away, over turret and pinnacle, to swing leftwards to the Snow Hump and North Col. Beyond the col, in an even fiercer series of giant ice leaves, vertically fluted, I could now see the ridge continue over minor summits, before it flattened finally against the broad bosom of Annapurna III. Looking south, all I could see was a steep pyramid of snow, our ridge being one of its edges: the so-called Rock Buttress, with not a speck of rock visible. And to the east, over the cloud-filled Seti, the smooth rocky head of Annapurna II peeped for the first time over the flattened shoulders of IV, giving the impression of a new and separate range.[11]*

There was no way along the ridge. A few steps forward in the interests of photography convinced them of that. However, Noyce did see a gully that descended on the other side of the ridge and this might be a way to the flat area of snow on the far side of the Rock Buttress that could host Camp IV. Noyce hammered in a birch stake and attached 100ft of rope on which he descended 'into the void'. He dropped his ice-axe – fortunately it jammed a little lower down – and at the end reached reasonably solid snow. The other two followed and they went to the end of another 100 feet of rope and reached the bottom of the gully and a drop to the glacier. The only way was now across a steep snow traverse of 400 yards, which took them over an hour. A rock-step gave them a bad moment but by 12.30 they were resting on the snowfield. A short break for biscuits, apricots and chocolate and then back, the traverse only taking twenty-five minutes this time. It was an effort to climb back up the rope to the crest and when they got there the full force of the wind hit them. Noyce attached 100 feet of rope to the birch stake for the western side and the snow chased them down the gully. Soon they were drinking hot sweet tea with the Sherpas.

The weather was depressing them. Every evening there was snow and the tracks made and steps cut were covered and the fixed ropes would be hidden. They made 17th May a rest day and planned the final approach. Wylie, as ever, worked out the logistics. The Sherpas would be carrying fifty pounds and the sahibs forty pounds. Some of the day was given to photography, for the benefit of the purveyors of provisions such as the soup and biscuits until the snow and thunder set in.

Despite the thick snow the entire party set off at 8.25 on 18th May. An additional rope was fixed in the west gully and it was now very safe for the Sherpas. They were all through the hole in the cornice in the ridge, named The Nick, and they all descended the east gully. They crossed the traverse and it had already begun to snow when they reached the site of Camp III. They pitched the tents and set up camp in a scene of 'determined misery' just short of a snow ridge, about thirty feet high, that would be easy enough to go round. Later the snow stopped and the mist cleared and they were able to see a possible Camp V near a shoulder shelf below the last steep 1,000 feet, and a way to the summit.

In the morning they started at 7.00 in high spirits with big loads and ten minutes later they reached the shoulder of the snow ridge. There they stopped. In front of them was a precipice straight down to the valley. It did not lead to the upper glacier as expected. Noyce and Cox took off their loads and the Sherpas went back to Camp III and pitched a tent. Wylie filmed the other two trying a traverse in soft and rotten snow, and then he tried to make a route over the Bergschrund with the Sherpas. It was all to no avail. They retired to the tents and reflected. Cox suggested that if they had 400 feet of rope, they might be able to lower themselves down to the glacier shelf. So far, when they had hit a problem, they had eventually found a solution and this was to be no different. The following day, 20th May, Wylie and Cox anchored themselves and let Noyce down to the full length of all the available rope, 220 feet. He estimated that the total drop to the shelf was less than 400 feet. From the shelf they could walk on to the glacier from there. '*Then for practice, I climbed back up the rope on my hands, my legs arched against the loosening slope.*' He was an indefatigable man, with huge reserves, who led, when he needed to, from the front. He could now see the way to the top, but they needed to get some more equipment from Base Camp.

The following day they were off early and Noyce led the very strenuous first part up to The Nick. It was too soft to take a piton and too steep to allow him to stand in balance so with one hand wrapped in the fixed rope he cut steps with the other. At The Nick it took a very cold half-hour in the vicious wind to bring the others through and then they were down the fixed ropes to Camp III. They needed to cut some more steps at the top of the Great Gully and they spent a short time looking for Wylie's sleeping-bag at Camp II. They reached Base Camp to be greeted by Roberts who was back up from Pokhara.

It had taken five days to get Roger Chorley down to Pokhara, where he spent a month in quarantine. Miss Steel and Dr. Turner had come up to Khuldigar in record time to examine him and then sped back to Pokhara.

We owed a lot to the lonely British hospital of Pokhara. Back in England Roger, who is a very determined person, very soon took to crutches, then to two sticks, then to one. By October he was doing a severe rock climb in North Wales.[12]

The three days in Base Camp were not as pleasant as they should have been for Noyce. He had a painful gumboil that did not give up its poison until the last evening. In the meantime an article for the **Daily Herald** and letters had to be written. Ang Nyima, Da Temba and Ang Tsering spent most of the time playing dice but Tashi was busy making a twenty-five-foot rope ladder. This consisted of split birch threaded in manila rope and weighed a remarkably little six pounds (2.7 kilos). Dikshya Man had endured a very boring time and had finished ***Hope for the Troubled.*** He then started on Noyce's copy of George Orwell's ***Nineteen Eighty-Four.*** He also sat in on their plans for the final assault.

They started on 24th May with Roberts going up first to Camp I then to Camp II with Tashi where he could spend a day taking survey photographs. Dhanbahadur and Da Temba took extra food up to Camp I and returned. Noyce wandered among the flowers and birds of a nearby valley and fell to composing poetry. The following day Wylie, Noyce and Cox explored in the area of Hiunchuli and had the joy of a 2,000-foot glissade. On 26th May leaving Dikshya Man at Base, the rest of the party went up to Camp I. The following day they all congregated at Camp II. On 28th May Tashi, Roberts and Ang Nyima went up to Camp III with loads and came down again. The other three sahibs stayed at Camp II and went up to Camp III the following day. Da Temba, the Darjeeling Sherpa, did not go up as he felt giddy on the steep section so Roberts took him down to Base.

Next day Cox, Noyce and Wylie went up to Camp IV and established it. Cox and Noyce fixed the rope ladder to the crest of the ridge above Camp IV and tried to drop another fixed rope to the glacier. The completion of this exercise had to wait until the next day, 31st May. Cox, Noyce and Wylie set off at 7.30 laden with rope and at the ridge Noyce anchored 220 feet of nylon rope to an ice-axe and sent it down. He then knotted two 100-foot lengths together and went down these. At the bottom he went down a seventy-degree couloir, clutching the rope, still trying to cut steps. Close to the end of the rope he found a small piece of rock on which he could stand. Another length of manila rope was tied on and this reached a point some thirty feet of easy snow from the glacier shelf. Noyce climbed back up by the rope and they reached camp again at 9.30 and spent the rest of the day 'panting like tired dogs'. There were six now at Camp IV. Ang Nyima and Ang Tsering went back to Camp III. Wylie and Tashi would stay at Camp IV while Noyce and Cox would carry on to make Camp V as high as possible.

Climbing down the ropes on 1st June was more complicated as they had considerable loads. At one stage Noyce had to reduce the rope between them to eighty feet to provide an extra twenty feet for the fixed rope. The whole operation took two hours and now the glacier shelf was steeper than they had expected. They kept going, changing the lead every half-hour, then every twenty minutes, driven by the anxiety that perhaps the shelf would go crashing down and very conscious that there were two crevasses to be crossed. They went along the rim of the first until it petered out and nature had provided a bridge over the second. However, the mist was gathering and after a short distance they camped at 12.30 at about 21,000ft (6,400m). The mist gave way to a light snow that stayed with them until well in to the evening.

On 2nd June Noyce and Cox lit the Primus at 2.45 in the candle-light. They had tea and Grape-nuts for breakfast and a long discussion whether they might not get some money from the makers for having selected their product for their summit breakfast. At 4.20 they set out and the tramp over the glacier was delightful. The snow was ankle-deep but this gave way, as the slope became steeper to snow up to their knees. They changed lead every twenty minutes and at 7.00 stopped for food and thought that they had less than 1,000 feet to go. The time passed slowly as they were moving continuously, cutting steps in the snow and ice. At 9.00 the snow started; they tried to hurry, but the going was not easy. They worked up a steep ice chimney with intermittent step-cutting, and the chimney walls were crumbling. Then Noyce recalled:

> *Just before 11 a.m. I rounded a rib, very near the top of everything as I thought, and saw four or five columns of blue ice, like the claws of some great dragon, thrusting up each to its place on the summit ridge: it was the summit itself, perhaps a little under 150 feet above our heads. The claws were swept and dusted of snow. David came up, I hacked two more steps. Each took many blows. It looked as if the Goddess had drawn her firm line here, at least for these her two respectably married suitors. With that we must be content.*
>
> *If it had not been snowing so hard, we could have eaten and considered what might have been, in good conditions, a two- or three-hour job. As it was we made our decision almost without speaking, and David turned imperturbably to the important ritual of lighting a pipe.*[13]

Noyce produced 500 feet of nylon line and tied it to a piton and they descended the chimneys in the thickening snow. Fresh steps had to be cut as those they had made on the way up had been obliterated. They had left one marker flag and back on the glacier, with just a few yards of visibility, they thought they had missed their tent. In the half-light they found the tent and at 14.30 they were getting their crampons off and getting out of the snow into the relative comfort of their tent.

Noyce's emotion at that time was not disappointment, but irritation at not knowing whether they would be said to have climbed the mountain. However, they were satisfied that they had achieved all they could *'without having to gamble our safety on the gods' further pleasure'*. Cox slept well that night, unlike Noyce who shivered occasionally. Then they descended the glacier and reached the 'cut-off', where they had to climb 350 feet to get on to the ridge, where Wylie and Tashi had been waiting for them. The latter had dug a cave some twenty-five feet below the ridge and this provided a very good refuge and relief from the beating snow outside. The snow continued to pursue them down the mountain, clearing briefly at Camp II where they spent the following night.

They got down to Base Camp on 5th June and although tempted to prolong the pleasures of this idyllic spot other attractions beckoned. Wylie and Roberts were going to take a slow walk down through the Gurung villages so that Wylie could film Gurkha festivals. Cox and Noyce had at least a week before they had to take the plane out of Pokhara on 21st June and thought a postscript to Machapuchare would be interesting. They had observed Fluted Peak, 21,800ft (6,640m) during their climb, up to the north-west of Base Camp and they were both attracted to it.

On 9th June they bade farewell to Dikshya Man, who was very happy to be released from his duties as 'keeper'. He had, however, served a purpose. He was the cause of much good humour, unsuspecting largely on his part, as his comments and unusual questions were recalled. Noyce and Cox took with them two Sherpas, the third, Tashi, would follow, bringing the delayed mail. They followed the Modi River up then crossed the snout of the South Annapurna Glacier. Noyce built a cairn to show Tashi their route and immediately Ang Tsering built a much bigger one *'for the cairn-building madness (and skill) is endemic among Sherpas'*. In the afternoon just short of the snout of the West Glacier they arrived at an enormous rock overhang, the Cave of which Roberts had spoken. There was wood there as the shepherds used it when they brought their flocks up in the summer. They continued their reconnaissance the following day and selected a site for their Camp I. The selection of campsites was always subject to the approval of Tashi who had a complete lack of faith in the ability of sahibs to choose campsites. They went back down to Base Camp, then the following day moved up in the drizzle to camp

I and Tashi made sure they moved it up under the ridge, a better site than they had chosen. They spent the afternoon re-reading the letters and absorbing the news from home. When the rain stopped Cox and Noyce reconnoitred the West Glacier and they decided that the route they found through the séracs was the only route up.

In the morning they were off to an early start with two Sherpas and with the minor inconvenience of one or two ice-chimneys they arrived at a plateau which seemed very suitable for a camp. Not, however, for Tashi who took them to a better site. There the tents were pitched and tea provided and the Sherpas descended, promising to return the following day. Noyce and Cox again overestimated their altitude, a common occurrence. They thought they were at 19,000ft but were in fact closer to 18,000 (5,490m).

After a restless night they started at 3.15 in the '*blinding silver light*' of a full moon. They kicked and chipped steps up the steep snow and ice of one gully after another. Then they saw a broad shelf out to the right and went along it. They continued to climb, changing the lead frequently, and then at 8.00 they were out finally on the ridge. There was still some 300 yards to go. However, it was not that simple. There was a large block of ice, over 100 feet on each side, dumped on the top of the mountain. It was steep and difficult. They had one attempt on a left traverse and lost an hour. Then they tried a frontal assault.

> *We should have known by now that things seen end-on are not as bad as they look. All the same, twenty feet near the top were as steep as anything on the expedition: a hard little facet where the ridge abutted, hard enough to take cut handholds when the angle threw me right out of balance. A few steps, and I could get a left leg far out on the snowy crest. A shift of balance, carefully so as not to disturb the handhold, a body poised in a tableau of silver and blue – and we were up.*[14]

The summit was a few yards along the ridge and they were on it at 9.30. What a view!

> *I shall never forget the scene, for it impressed itself on that subconscious, untroubled memory which has power to push its images to the surface in later days. The whole Sanctuary lay revealed, and round it every peak: Hiunchuli and Ganesh, and*

the long ridge to Annapurna I, whose south-east face seemed almost to be hanging over us. Then along over the Glacier Dome to Gangapurna and the great bulk of Annapurna III, and beyond that the flattened rise of IV, sharply topped by the neat cone of II. In front of these the bristling, broken ridge that led southward, to the fairy delicacy of Machapuchare queening it for all her slighter stature over every giant around. She was incomparable. Postscript chapters may be frowned upon; but for me this was the true climax of the expedition: a summit, and the sight of that supreme pyramid, the goddess-haunted, under whose very crest we suppliants had been allowed to stand.[15]

The weather was worsening and before they had descended far it started to snow. They descended with snow cascading down beside them and reached the tent and were drinking tea with the Sherpas Tashi and Da Temba at 13.15. By 16.00 they were all back at Camp I. From there it was a wet walk down to the grassy meadows above Naudanra.

Noyce appreciated no less the calm of the comfortable green meadows and reflected on the pleasure of the contrasts after the battles with the elements high on the mountain. The Himalaya, for him, provided these stimulating contrasts, from the tropical forests through the various temperate zones up to the frozen peaks where all his powers were called into play. He explores this theme further in the book he was writing on 'adventure'.

Back at Hinko the coolies met them and they walked on down to Pokhara and on to the comfortable quarters at Lehra where Roberts was a very welcoming and agreeable host. Noyce and Cox returned to England at the end of June.

Part 2 *Trivor 1960*

Towards the end of 1958 Colin Mortlock, the President of the Oxford University Mountaineering Club (OUMC) and two members, Jack Sadler and Dick Burgess, both American Rhodes scholars, were planning the exploration of a new and unclimbed peak in the Himalaya – or Karakoram in 1959 – or 1960 – and they invited Noyce to lead the party. For this **Anglo-American Karakoram Expedition** Noyce was not just the leader but initially the secretary and main co-ordinator. Michael Ward as the doctor and Don Whillans joined them. Burgess dropped out so they invited Geoffrey Smith to join them in his place. Smith had climbed already with Noyce and had been in the Karakoram in 1957. They still had not found a mountain to climb.

Over the next few months the search for a mountain to climb went on. Various peaks were considered and old maps were scoured. They did, however, decide to have a season in the Alps before they went to the Karakoram, so the big expedition was planned for the following year, 1960.

Noyce was responsible for the clothing of the expedition and Kagan Textiles offered their Gannex and Ganlette cloths, made famous by *'the 14th Mr Wilson',*[16] a British prime minister of the 1970s.

By the following summer the question of which mountain was still preoccupying them and the mountains available were slowly becoming fewer in number, either by being the target of other expeditions or by constraints on access to Nepal and Sikkim. Finally, a study of the map made by Eric Shipton in 1939 from the Royal Geographical Society archives showed Trivor at 23,370ft (7,118m) in the North Hunza country of Pakistan. This was it. They were going to Trivor. However, when permission to climb it was requested from the Pakistan Government, they were asked to identify it in full detail, as it was unknown to the Surveyor-General of Pakistan. Map references were given and permission was duly granted. Fortunately, in all these discussions with Pakistan they had the support and assistance of Mohammed and Soghra Ikramullah. 'Ikram' was the head of the Pakistan Foreign Service and had been a friend of Wilfrid Noyce during his time in Delhi 1942-45 and of Sir Frank and Lady Noyce in the 1930s.

By now two others had joined the party, Sandy Cavenagh, who replaced Ward as the doctor, and Oleg Polunin, botany master at Charterhouse, who had botanised in almost every part of the world and was anxious to go to the Karakoram. Sadler was taking over more of the administration and at the end of the year he asked to take on a secretary. *'Jack authorised to get pretty secretary'* appears in the notes.

At the beginning of 1960 Noyce was in North Wales trying out the equipment with Smith and Whillans. Noyce himself spent a cosy night of 10th January in a Gannlette sleeping-bag cover on the top of Snowdon in a blizzard. They worked closely with the manufacturers and eventually had exactly what was required. To be quite sure, Noyce ran the school cross-country circuit several times wearing a Gannlette suit!

Before Noyce could depart for Trivor he was still busy setting exam papers in French, German and Italian, making arrangements to write articles for *The Times*, sending letters to the political agent in Hunza and making contact with the various people in Pakistan who would help them such as the brothers Goodwin in Rawalpindi.

Then there was a problem with the goggles they had received; they were not snow goggles. New ones had to be obtained. All the details of the frenetic days before Noyce and the main party left were recorded in the note-book which provides a history of the expedition from its inception. Don Whillans had decided that coming back by sea or air would be too boring so he put his motor-cycle on the ship with the expedition equipment to ride back solo from Pakistan. He and the equipment left Liverpool on 16th May.

On 1st July 1960 Noyce was writing school reports and teaching; the following day he and Polunin joined Cavenagh and Smith to fly to Karachi.

Don Whillans and Colin Mortlock had gone upcountry to reconnoitre. Polunin and Smith went straight on to Rawalpindi to organise porters' food, and Noyce and Cavenagh did the essential rounds in Karachi of paying calls and getting permissions.

Two days later, Noyce and Cavenagh went to Rawalpindi where they joined the other two staying with 'Buster' Goodwin, a retired colonel, and his brother. The only way they could get up to Gilgit from Rawalpindi was by aeroplane. This was an erratic service as the planes, Dakotas, flew up the Indus gorge, some 12,000ft (3,600m) below the summit of Nanga Parbat making it a 'white-knuckle' flight even in good weather. They were four days in Rawalpindi, *'four of the dreariest days of my life'*, but the Goodwin hospitality and Buster's fund of stories kept their spirits up. The diary records days of frustration with going to the airport and finding the plane had eventually been cancelled. There were walks around Rawalpindi and visits to Flashman's, the bar within walking distance. The rain was a constant feature of the days.

Still in Rawalpindi, they received a letter from Mortlock dated 28th June. He and Whillans were at a temporary Base Camp some three days walk from Nagar. They had reached Gilgit, where they had left the kit and they had managed to get the jeeps up to Minapin. They had walked up to Nagar and there recruited coolies to take the kit to Base Camp. The Nagars were very difficult and went on strike on two occasions. They seemed to be living up to their reputation. There was another row when they tried to pay them off and this had to be settled by the Mir of Nagar. Mortlock also said that the south flank of the mountain was out of the question and that they should look at the head of the glacier. During this time they met their survey officer from the Field Survey Department of Pakistan, Sahib Shah. He had already done seven trips to the Karakoram and was a very useful addition to the party.

On 12th July they eventually flew into Gilgit and encountered another set of frustrations. The jeeps they had ordered to get up to Nagar would not take the loads they had said they could. It was difficult to get more jeeps as they were about to go to Rawalpindi for their annual refit. Eventually more jeeps were found but then they had to get more fuel for them. '*Their tyres shone smooth as waterworn pebbles, a pink hernia of inner tubing showed from time to time round the edges.*'[17] Brigadier C. H. B. Rodham, the President of the Pakistan Army Sports Committee at Rawalpindi had arranged for the supply of the jeeps and he was able to come up with the extra fuel and engine oil that the drivers insisted on, Mobil oil 50. They needed the very viscous oil as their pistons were that worn! There were still a few local arrangements to be made including the hiring of Q, a young Hunza, as interpreter and to look after the equipment. Noyce did not wish to identify him publicly for reasons that will become clear later. While the others were organising the equipment, treating the sick, doing the accounts or botanising, Noyce spent his days chasing round the Northern Scouts, the Police, the Gilgit Scouts, the Assistant Political Agent, Humayun Beg with the invaluable help of Sahib Shah, the imperturbable fixer. Geoff Smith and Q went with two jeeps on 15th July up to Minapin. A small consolation was the Chenar Bagh, the bungalow that the Commandant of the Gilgit Scouts had lent them with its riverside garden and familiar flowers. This provided a quiet place for Noyce to write one of his articles for *The Times*. They managed to get away from Gilgit finally on 17th July.

The first seventeen miles to Nomal took an hour through the dry, sandy, flat Hunza River valley. After that the valley narrowed and the road, barely wide enough for a jeep, clung to the cliffs until they came to Chalt, some thirteen miles farther on. Noyce could only admire the skill of these drivers who managed to bring the little convoy to the rest house at Minapin by the early afternoon.

Mortlock and Whillans had by this time found a possible route up the mountain. They had been up to the north-west col and thought that the ascent was possible from there. They were awaiting the rest of the party. After tea the leader and a member of the Austrian party who had just climbed Dastaghil Sar, 26,000ft (7,885m) walked in to the rest house. One of them took Noyce's photograph as the author of **Die Götter Zürnen,** the German version of *The Gods are Angry.* The Austrians hoped to make use of the jeeps that had just come up with Noyce. Likewise Noyce hoped to take the Austrians' ponies and porters. Although the return journeys of the jeeps had been paid for by the Noyce party, the drivers wanted 200 rupees each. Sahib Shah suggested that they get fifty rupees each as an advance and the rest at the police station in Gilgit. The drivers fell for it! The Nagar porters on the other hand did not negotiate. It was their terms and Sahib Shah could do little. Consequently, the horses and donkeys apparently were not available.

On 18th July Noyce and Cavenagh set off, with fair loads, for the walk to Nagar. As they walked through the village early in the morning they saw their porters loading a donkey. A donkey can carry at least twice as much as a man. Two porters would take their loads and put them on a donkey. At the end of the journey, as happened at Nagar, the donkey is hidden and one porter staggers in with two loads, saying his companion has fallen ill. It made for interesting discussions at the end of the day!

It was an agreeable walk. Rakaposhi towered over them to the south, then they crossed the Hunza River on a wire bridge that could ferry even jeeps across and entered Nagar country, following the Hispar River to the town itself. At the rest house to greet them was Don Whillans, Captain Yusuf and the Mir, or ruler, of the independent state of Nagar. Colin Mortlock was still up at Base Camp.

> *The first approach to a high peak is exciting. Four days march from Nagar and no one had even been up to Trivor. My own excitement was strongly tempered with anxiety. One hundred and fifty Nagar coolies to manoeuvre along the vertical road about the Hispar, then up a strange glacier, known only to be rough. This seemed the worst stage of all.*[18]

There was a major issue of porters. The Mir said, "*My people do not like to be just servants, they will also be high-altitude. It is their country and they say why do people come here and use us only as servants?*" The party already had five high-altitude porters, Hunzas, who had a good reputation, unlike the Nagars. Noyce agreed finally to take two Nagars. The Mir would supply 100 porters on 19th July and 50 on the 20th. Polunin and Sahib Shah caught up with them on 19th July. One of the

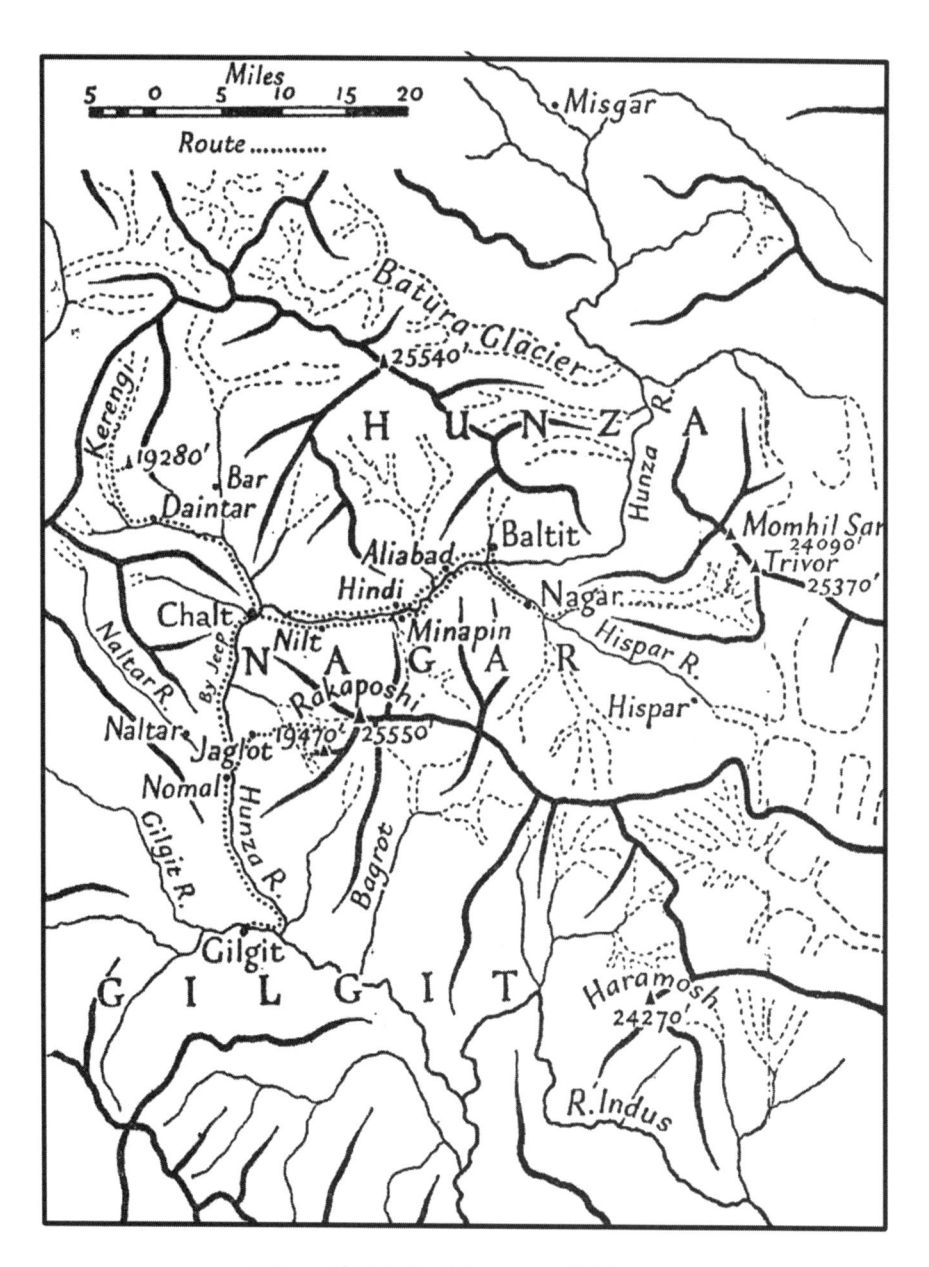

Map of Gilgit, Nagar and Hunza.

drawbacks with a large group in barren country is the need to carry all one's own food. Half the porters were carrying food for porters!

On 20th July Whillans and Ali Gohar, a Hunza, set off soon after 5.00 with ropes, stakes and pegs to install them at critical points on the track to ensure the safety of the porters. The party of Noyce and Sadler, with 100 porters, had to wait until the Mir appeared and said his farewells then they set off. At first they went up the Hispar Valley and then turned in to the gorge of the Gharesa or Trivor River and reached a clearing just above the river, the Gharesa Camping Ground.

After a night under the stars they continued up a gentle path in the gorge to a stream that ran beside the snout of the Gharesa glacier that ran up to Trivor. Here they camped again and Jack Sadler needed to pay off two more porters. Then the trouble started. Each group of twenty-five porters had a foreman or *lambadar*. These men had little authority and merely relayed the demands of the porters for more than the four rupees a day that had originally been agreed. The argument went on all evening and eventually they settled for six rupees a day for good work.

The following day started well. Whillans led the route he had reconnoitred earlier and the climbing party reached Temporary Base Camp on a flowery rise some 200 feet above the glacier at 15.00 where Mortlock was waiting for them. The Nagars arrived some two hours later. The food distribution passed off quietly but not the cigarette handout – they wanted ten cigarettes each and not the five that they had been given, as agreed. They came up and threw them at the sahibs' feet – later they came and retrieved them.

A peaceful night under the stars then there was more trouble. The Nagars wanted extra money for the glacier and they needed snow-goggles. Yusuf dealt with these problems and certainly *'earned his keep as liaison officer during these days'*. Eventually the party reached the small grassy plateau by a stream above the glacier. The tent on the higher ground had been pitched by Mortlock and Whillans on their reconnaissance. This was Base Camp at 14,700ft (4,477m).

The Nagars dumped their loads by the tent and Sadler and Yusuf paid them off there and they went down to the camp-site by the stream and back to Nagar. They were bidden to return at the end of August. The second group of porters arrived the following day and returned to Nagar. The set-up of Base Camp was completed with the establishment of the Polunin marquee and Yusuf's wireless aerial. This meant that they had continuous music – of all kinds – and the weather forecasts from the Meteorological Office in Rawalpindi.

By then it was 24th July and they were on the mountain with five Hunza and two Nagar high-altitude porters. Two of the Hunzas had already been on Rakaposhi, Ali Gohar and Akbar. Akbar and Hidayat had been on K2. Dadur, Zarayat Khan and Sharief were beginning their apprenticeship. Akbar was the only one who had an idea of how the sahibs camped and had still much to learn. The two Nagars were less successful. After three days absence one was dismissed on his return. The second was dismissed after being insolent to Yusuf. He descended in his underpants as he had to give up his special expedition clothes.

Smith checked the stores. Without counting the high altitude rations, they had sugar for four and a half days, meat for thirteen, cheese for seven, soup for twelve days and porridge for fifty-seven!! Thefts had occurred all the way along, at Karachi, in the trans-shipments and by the porters. They had lost 100 pounds of sugar! An urgent request was sent to the Political Agent at Gilgit.

The management of this heterogeneous group was not easy. Sickness, shortages and support for the surveyors and botanists had to be considered in addition to that of the climbers. Noyce was harassed. *'Many problems, had a wash and felt better.'*[19] And on 24th July he went up the steep glacier side for half an hour's walk and got his first full view of Trivor. He contemplated the mountain and noted the mighty dragon's back culminating in a great white spire. He descended to camp, encouraged and content.

The weather had so far favoured them. It now started to be stormy and rainy at night. They were still some five miles (eight kilometres) from the base of the 'Unknown Mountain'. Over the next five days they carried their loads up to Camp I at 17,300ft (5,300m). This was very good training and acclimatisation. On 25th July, Whillans and Mortlock led off at 5.30, while it was still cool, going up over rocks and then they rested. They then had a grassy descent to the glacier on which they had a gentle walk up to the small ice-fall. Noyce, who was following, paused for photography and a breather. He felt he was as breathless now at 17,000ft (5,200m) as he had been at 21,000ft (6,400m) on Everest. The leading pair had already cut steps but it was a steep climb and when he got to the top the others were sitting on packing-cases, Camp I, at just after 9.00. The descent was now easy and they reached Base Camp before midday to find Cavenagh distinctly unwell.

Q, the Hunza with very fluent English, was pulled in to help with the portage and on 28th July Pervez, who had been taken on to help Polunin, appeared with two Nagar porters. He joined the portage parties and the Nagars were now engaged as mail runners.

Whillans and Mortlock with the four best Hunzas, Akbar, Ali Gohar, Dadur and Hidayat were at Camp I in a light snowfall on 27th July ready to go up to Camp II at 20,680ft (6,300m). On 28th July Noyce held a meeting at which a plan was made by which Whillans and Mortlock would continue to spearhead the assault, while the others would move up to Camp II on 29th and 30th July. The ferries would continue to Camp I then carry on to Camp II to be completed by 31st July.

Noyce, Smith and Sadler with Zarayat Khan, Sharief, the Nagar Yusuf, Q and Pervez went up to Camp I on 29th July and pitched one of the four-man tents. They met Mortlock descending – with toothache – from Camp II. At Base Camp Cavenagh managed to extract the tooth, a little shakily, and then wondered if a wisdom tooth was not the reason for his own discomfort. He entrusted the extractors to Polunin and began to recover after the offending tooth had been removed. Noyce records this as '*the major tour de force of the expedition*'.[20] At Camp I Noyce was finally able to focus on the main task, to get two men to the top of Trivor.

On 30th July Noyce and his companions at Camp I ferried loads up the glacier to Camp II: Noyce admits he was slower than the others and needed to recite nursery rhymes to control his breath. By the end of the day he was fed up with *See-saw Margery Daw!* They descended to Camp I where Sahib Shah had arrived. The following day Sahib Shah and Noyce went up again to Camp II, which it was decided would be Advanced Base, and food and equipment should be ferried there. Sahib Shah estimated Camp II to be at 20,680ft (6,300m) and the North Col, between Trivor and Momhil Sar at nearly 23,000ft (7,000m). From Camp II they could see Whillans working with Ali Gohar fixing ropes on the Col. Whillans had already been up there earlier when he and Mortlock had reconnoitred the route. Sahib Shah and Noyce descended again to Camp I.

Sickness struck again. Jack Sadler had an ulcer in the throat which made it painful to swallow and it was necessary, very often, to vomit. Cavenagh was still poorly at Base Camp.

On 1st August Sahib Shah and Polunin went off to the Hispar Valley, Noyce, Smith, Mortlock and Akbar moved up to Camp II. Noyce notes that:

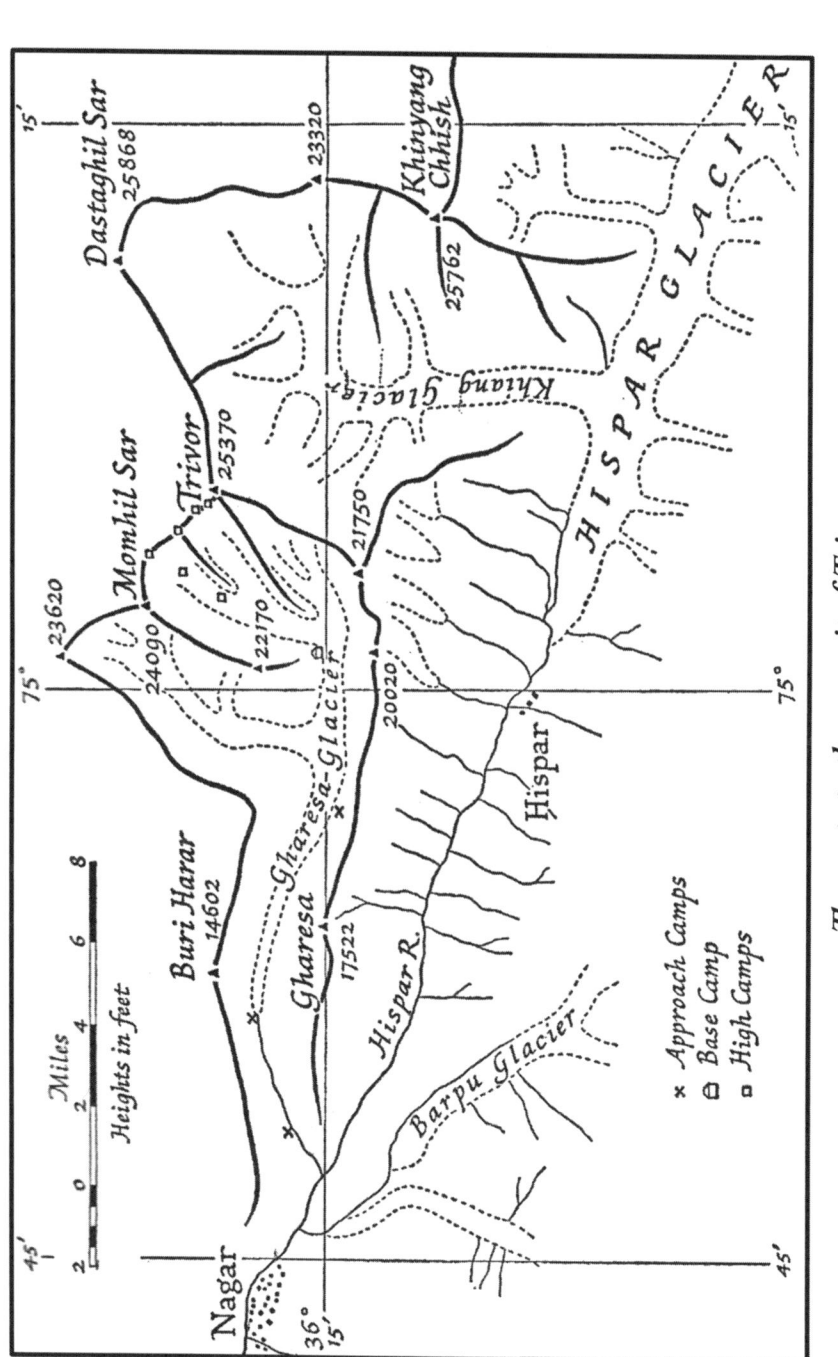

The route to the summit of Trivor.

One pleasure of Himalayan climbing lies for me in doing with ease what has, some days before, been done only with great pain and groaning.[21]

It must, however, be observed that Noyce very rarely gave the appearance of doing anything with pain and groaning. Everything, as has been observed on numerous occasions by his climbing companions, seemed to come easily and effortlessly.

They were shut in for two days at Camp II by the snow, although Sadler, in spite of his ulcer, continued to ferry loads up to Camp II. It was as well as it enabled the acclimatisation to improve and Noyce planned and re-planned the next few days and the approach to the summit. His diary contains several permutations of the plan. On 4th August Smith, Mortlock, Noyce, Whillans and Akbar set off for the Col hoping to establish Camp III there. The climb took five hours with Noyce and Whillans taking it in turn to lead, with Whillans ferreting out the ropes he had fixed. When these two reached the Col they stamped out a suitable place for a tent and waited for the others. The others did not come so the two descended and found the others with a tent pitched in a very suitable place they had noticed on the way up. Akbar had encountered problems and Smith had not felt acclimatised. They struck the tent and all went down to Camp II, where Cavenagh, who had recovered sufficiently, joined them. Advanced Base was now complete.

They lost another day, 5th August, due to snowfall. Cavenagh improved his strength by making an igloo. They read the airmail **Times** from end to end in turn and re-read their mail.

On 6th August at 3.40, with difficulty, the Hunzas were persuaded to get started. Whillans already had two primuses roaring. At 4.55 they left, with Cavenagh returning to Camp I to pick up more loads. At 8.45 they were on the Col. They dug the big tent into the slope to protect it from the wind to establish Camp III. It was a very clear day and in the lee of the ridge the view north was splendid. From there they could see the Momhil Glacier a long way below, Karun Kuh 22,891ft (6,972m) and Dastaghil Sar. They descended rapidly to Camp II arriving at the same time as Yusuf and Pervez. Yusuf brought a human problem with him. Q at Camp I had locked and sealed his kitbag and asked the mail-runner to take it down to Base. Yusuf and Sahib Shah both suspected something and opened the bag. They found in it twenty-nine articles belonging to the expedition or its members. These ranged from the only decent tin-opener they had, through cigarettes and batteries to Noyce's spare rucksack – already bearing the new owner's name!

They debated all afternoon what to do. Noyce went over to see the Hunzas. Q poured out a story of ill-treatment at the hands of Yusuf. The discussion continued into the following day and it was finally decided, at the appropriate time, to send a note with Q down to Polunin – another one was sent via Sharief – asking him to confront Q with the stolen property and dismiss him unpaid. Q opened Noyce's note and deleted the '*not*' in the sentence '*He shall not keep sleeping-bag…*' He protested that the items were gifts from members of the expedition. The following morning the Base Camp party found the stolen articles had been scattered around the kit-bags of the Hunza and Sahib Shah noticing that Q had a fly button undone saw that he was wearing a pair of Smith's jeans underneath. Q left in disgrace and with Pervez went back to Hunza, but this was all yet in the future. The Q discussion was a considerable distraction.

On 7th August they were able to observe the progress of Mortlock and Whillans who had gone up to Camp III on 6th August and were now exploring the flat ridge above the Col and a possible site for Camp IV. After the flat bit there was a difficult half-mile of up and down sharp edges and cornices along which they fixed ropes. Noyce had some anxious moments when the two disappeared from view and was very relieved when he saw them return to Camp III.

On 8th August Sadler, Noyce, Smith, three Hunzas and Q ferried loads up to Camp III. There they met Whillans and Mortlock. The Hunzas descended to Camp II. Noyce said his farewell to Q, who so far appeared to have suspected nothing.

At this point Noyce reflected on who of the team should constitute the summit party. His original idea had been for Whillans and Mortlock to be the summit pair as they were the best acclimatised. Whillans was a natural, on grounds of stamina, skill and speed. However, Mortlock was not so confident on snow and ice and was concerned that he could not keep up with Whillans; he preferred not to be 'spearhead'. Smith was not yet acclimatised, while Sadler was still troubled by his ulcer. Cavenagh was supervising the ferries up to the Col and finally there was Noyce himself. Characteristically, he was content to lead the team to put men on the summit. That was the overriding objective, so he did not have to go himself.

It looked as if I must go myself after all. I had not meant to go. I had reckoned the place of a middle-aged leader to be in the middle. But now I felt like the small boy who refuses the biggest piece of cake, and then has it handed to him on a special plate. Scribbling figures of what we would need I felt pleased and nervous; pleased because I had wanted to climb with Don, nervous because he was going like the proverbial bomb and might take some keeping up with. But on balance distinctly pleased.[22]

His diary puts it more tersely. '*Put myself in place of Colin and scheme for a 7-day climb – if weather holds.*'

On 9th August Smith, Sadler and Mortlock, the carrying party, left Camp III at 8.20 and went along the ridge. Noyce followed ten minutes later leaving Whillans still brewing tea. They negotiated patches of ice and rock and went down to a col some 1,000ft lower, a trying descent – as they had to climb it again to return to Camp III. They reached the Camp IV site. Smith was exhausted and he, Sadler and Mortlock had still to get back to Camp III, some 3,500ft higher. It took the indefatigable Whillans two and half hours to dig a platform for the tent, of which, when they pitched it, a pole was missing.

The following day Noyce and Whillans did the reconnaissance for Camp V. They set off at 9.05. It was a descent of 400ft to another col, the last they hoped before the summit. Noyce led along the ridge on to a small rock knob then Whillans took over with some step-cutting in ice, eventually moving out on to rock. There was a flat part of the crest at which point they saw the major obstacle, the Two-headed Tower. Noyce took over the lead and went along the ridge astride grateful for his '*untearable Ganlette trousers*'. Then Whillans suggested that they abseil to a lower level to where the rock ran into the summit ridge. '*I retreated and we performed the operation. Don had a way of being right, and it proved much simpler than my method.*'[23] After this they had some flat rock, a few steps on steep ice and they were on the top of the Two-headed Tower. From there they could see their entire route to the summit of Trivor. Only the weather and their own frailty could stop them now. They returned to Camp IV.

They were surprised that the others had not been up that day, but they must have been very tired after the efforts of the day before. 11th August brought bad weather and Noyce and Whillans were tentbound. Noyce read Proust and snoozed. They could not progress until more stores had been brought up. On the 12th Whillans extended the platform for the other tent they were expecting and Noyce improved the steps on the tricky approach slope and went on up to the Black Rock whence at 10.15 he could see some specks descending. He returned to camp, telling Whillans that they would arrive in an hour. The hours passed and no one appeared. At 15.30 Noyce and Whillans set off in the direction of Camp III. They reached Black Rock an hour later to see two figures heading back to Camp III. It was getting late but they decided to go down to the col and see if there were any loads. They picked them up and climbed back up the 700ft to Camp IV.

In the evening Whillans complained of the cold and was up several times in the night. He complained of cold the following morning as well as of 'growing pains' and weakness in his legs during the night. '*Polio!!*' is in the margin of Noyce's diary. They planned to leave a dump at the site of Camp V. They set off at 6.25 and Whillans appeared to have recovered from his growing pains. The route lay over rock and ice and they took turns in leading. They could see eventually a length of crenellated rock-crest, which they called The Castle, in a dell in the lee of this they could perhaps pitch Camp V. However, there were several hundred feet of smooth slope to negotiate and they each led this in spells of twenty minutes. Whillans was leading and almost at the top when his spell was up. He insisted on continuing for the last couple of hundred feet, then promptly collapsed on the snow, his legs had given out. It was 11.10. Fifteen minutes later they started back. The downhills were possible and Whillans pulled himself up with his arms on the abseil. The hardest part was the slog up to Camp III from the col, which took them an hour. Sadler met them halfway with cups of lemonade.

There was a need to take stock again. Cavenagh and Smith were not fully acclimatised and were making slow progress from the North Col. They would arrive the next day. Mortlock had been groggy the day before. Sadler, in spite of his throat, was the strongest now. Mortlock and Sadler agreed to go down for the gear required for the final push. They left at 15.00; Whillans went to bed, his temperature was 101°F. Later Whillans asked Noyce what Chorley's symptoms had been when he contracted polio on Machapuchare in 1957. With senses dulled by altitude he described them casually, then suddenly realised that this was the third case of polio on one of his expeditions – and he had insisted that they should all be inoculated against it. It would be difficult to get a helpless man back along the ridge.

Perhaps they were not getting enough salt so Noyce saturated the soup that evening with salt. Whillans felt better but his legs were still weak. The following morning, 14th August, Noyce was coaxing the primus into life at 5.30 and noted that Whillans' temperature was down to 100°F. At 7.15 Mortlock and Sadler appeared with the loads from Camp III. The doctor, Cavenagh, and Smith were expected later. Noyce knew that with polio the patient had to spend at least forty-eight hours on his back to see if other symptoms occur.

The weather was promising, which suggested that there was a window for the summit. They could possibly do it in three days. It was safe to go on. The question, however, was who would go with Noyce to the summit? Could Sadler make it? Did he want to? Yes he would, but he would have to borrow Whillans' sleeping-bag and mattress. Those would be replaced by Sadler's, which would be brought up during the day. Sadler and Noyce then repacked for four days, leaving Mortlock to look after Whillans:

> *It had been arranged that, if Don were pronounced fit in a day or so as we expected, he and Colin Mortlock would come up in support to Camp V; and we had an elaborate system of torch signals to be used between IV and V, which were clearly visible to each other... . We confidently expected both good weather and that "push from the rear" which is so comforting to a summit party. Neither were to materialise.*[24]

They left Camp IV at 9.15 and negotiated the Two-headed Tower with the aid of the fixed ropes. Noyce left his heavy load at the bottom to pull up afterwards. He tried to pull it up but it jammed and, still holding it with one hand, he brought Sadler up with the other. He then had to climb down and get the load. He observed, *"There is no escaping one's burdens."* The going became easier in the tracks that Whillans had made earlier and at 14.00 they were pitching the tent in the dell under the Castle at 22,300ft (6,790m), Camp V. Noyce made a list for the next three days. His diary records: '*Tent, Personal, Primus (full) plus dixie, Biscuit tin, Sardines, Cheese, Tea, Raisins, ?Apple?, Kendal M Cake, Oatmeal Blocks, Soup, Sugar.*' He then made supper of oxtail soup with POM, the potato powder mix, with much salt, then lemonade and honey – which soothed Sadler's throat. At 19.00, ten minutes after the sun had set, Noyce went out to signal to

Camp IV. After ten minutes he gave up. Later Mortlock said he started signalling at 19.20.

> *I know of absolutely no certain good weather signs, and would rather believe, with Wordsworth, that it is all a matter of caprice,*
> > "*Not seldom, clad in radiant vest,*
> > *Deceitfully goes forth the morn,*
> > *Not seldom evening in the west,*
> > *Sinks, smilingly forsworn.*"[25]
>
> *Never did an evening sink more smilingly forsworn than that of August 14th. A straight brown haze overlay each horizon, a red sun kissed the clear outline of Momhil Sar opposite. We went to sleep confident.*[26]

They were grievously disappointed. At 6.00 when they looked out, to the south-west, from where their weather came, there were dark clouds. In addition Sadler was still not well. He was still vomiting. The time dragged, they waited until 8.30 then Noyce said brutally, "*What about it? Perhaps it might be a bit feeble not to go and look at Camp VI.*" '*Sadler replied "OK" with the kind of voice one dies in.*'[27] They packed and left at 9.35 with food for several days. There was a level stretch of ridge that gave way to a drop to a col. They continued, up a broad concave slope with a few crevasses. The crevasses became more frequent and the slope became steeper until they reached a deeper crevasse that cut well into the mountain just before 14.00. There was a flat patch a few feet down underneath an overhanging upper lip, just big enough, with a little enlargement for their tent. They pitched Camp VI at 23,200ft (7,066m). Noyce made tea and afterwards Sadler slept. At 18.00 Noyce looked out. It was clear. '*But what does it mean? How far to go? Can Jack do it? Can I? Looks a long way still.*'[28]

At 6.15 on 16th August Noyce climbed out of the crevasse and found himself in a blizzard. At 9.30 he wondered if they should go down, but it seemed safer to stay where they were. They spent the day in bed. Noyce spent the time debating with himself the various elements of the decisions. Was Jack fit enough? Could they get across the rough ground in time? Could he justifiably do it on his own? In the evening the weather was clearer and the mountains around them were all visible. They were buoyant as they ate their supper of soup and biscuit.

Noyce woke at 4.00 on 17th August and looked out on a starry clear sky. '*The worst ordeal, as usual, was that of putting on crampons whose straps had been hanging out all night.*'[29] At 5.40 Noyce started up out of the crevasse, followed a few minutes later by Sadler. The snow was deep with holes in the real surface below. Sadler, not quite fully recovered, led for twenty minutes and then they rested. After an hour they reached the bottom of the first of two rock-ribs that divided the upper face. The first they tried to avoid but had to go back to it and found the rock much firmer than expected. This gave them 180 feet of good climbing until they came out on to a sunny snow crest and the top of the first rib. It was 9.00. They rested and Sadler took a boot off and they rubbed his toes. They were still cold when he put the boot back on. The sun gave surprisingly little heat. They went on up the second rib and along a broken crest, the hours went past. At 12.30 snow started again and a little later they sat and ate their last tin of sardines. The summit could not be more than 500 feet away. Should they turn back? They would at least struggle on to the great whaleback of the final crest.

They reached the crest at 13.15 and the sun filtered through and they had '*…glimpses in every direction down strange valleys and of unknown peaks*'. They trudged on, twenty steps and a pause, twenty steps and a pause; then ten steps and a pause, and at 14.40 they were on the summit. Noyce sat down and photographed Sadler climbing the last few feet. He also took photographs in all directions, thinking the while how inadequately they would recreate the scene:

> *I have never felt gladder, nor more happy at a view. Cloud billows hid the distant Baltoro, but nearer at hand the noble rock pyramid of Khinyang Chish (25,762ft)* [7,846 m] *seemed to dominate the still shapeless Dastaghil Sar. Two other pyramids, beyond, must be Pumarikish (24,580ft)* [7,487m] *and Kanjut Sar and below to the right we had a fleeting glimpse of the great Hispar Glacier. The eye followed round a golden horizon to Rakaposhi again then to the Baltoro ridges and far beyond, above Momhil Sar, and strangely moving, fairy castles of the Pamirs and Russia.*[30]

At 15.00 they set off down. Getting off the ridge gave them difficult slopes to descend. It was hard work kicking steps on to the traverse of a steep ice slope. It was 17.00 and they headed for the rock ribs and struggled down. Sadler took off his crampons, Noyce kept his on. At 18.15 they were at the bottom of the top rib. They had only another thirty minutes of daylight. Despite the pressure to descend quickly, Noyce could not help stopping:

> *Over a Rakaposhi golden in the late sun, great lemon-coloured bars stretched far into a sky of pale turquoise. Momhil Sar stood out stark before us, while to its left the sun itself, hidden by a black jigsaw piece of cloud, flamed out round the edges in long crimson streaks. I thought: 'If only I were not tired, and thirsty, and pressed, if only I could hold this moment until it became part of me, if only I had time to understand how good it is.' Then I looked at my watch and went on.*[31]

As darkness fell they found their track which led them to their crevasse and Camp VI at 19.30.

The hours following the ascent of a great summit, and particularly one as fraught as this one, provide the release of tensions and confusion in the mind of the mountaineer. Noyce wrote later:

> *It was a confused night. So keyed is the mountaineer to the pursuit of the mountain that when he has achieved his grail, the object of his desire, when at last his muscles are relaxed and his nerves no longer feel like fine elastic stretched to breaking point, he is quite incapable of appreciating what has happened. He has come to a full stop. That, perhaps, is why many accounts of a plain ascent end at the summit, or very near it. For what is that summit after all, when you get there? A piece of rock or snow, nothing very much. A view, a photograph, perhaps a flag. Climbers are ashamed that so little must justify so much toil and time. Yet they know that what really justified the summit was not the standing upon it, but the reaching it. Just as to the divine Michael Angelo the finishing of a statue could leave a sense of disappointment so that he rushed on, in titan fury, to hack out more and more great works that never knew completion, so to the climber, in his humbler mission, the climbing is more important than the top climbed. All those months and weeks of preparation and now at the top, it is over. Provided he can return safely there is nothing now but to return to everyday, and perhaps to pipe-dream of a new climb.*
>
> *But first he will try to remember, so that he can understand, hold, grasp, complete that summit. It is impossible to ask, of course,*

> when his only allies are memory, which is faulty, and the sense of contrast between effort and rest. However he tries his best to prick the day, like a butterfly in his collection, with a pin of durability that will make it last just that little bit longer than the others. In the hope of doing this, on that 17th of August, I refused the sleeping pill that would have brought oblivion.
>
> Tossing about I lived the climb again, each stage of it: the first rock rib, the false promise of the upper slopes, the second rock rib and the miraculous clearing of the weather that turned a day that looked as ominous as one could find into an evening of sheer beauty. Over and over it went, twisting and turning in my mind just as my body, cramped against the tent wall by Jack, who had slid into the trough now formed by the tent floor, twisted and turned to find easier lying, and found it nowhere.[32]

The following morning at 6.00 Noyce had the primus roaring away, but there was just enough fuel for a small drink. The new snow prevented them from digging out the tent, even if they had had the courage to carry it. They packed and left at 8.00. They hoped to find someone at Camp V. However, they did find a primus and, most importantly, found something to drink. They were there for two hours collecting the stores, but leaving the Gannlette tent, and pressed on with heavier loads. The last bit was an hour-long slog up the slope up to Camp IV where Mortlock was with a brew ready, lemon and honey thickened with lumps of Complan. He was on his own as the others had all gone down.

Cavenagh had been up to Camp IV to see Whillans on 14th August and thought he could have polio. He told him to spend two to three days lying down. On 17th August Whillans, now feeling quite all right and 'fed up with waiting' set off down to Camp III under his own steam. On the way he met Cavenagh and Smith improving the track. Cavenagh took Whillans' pack and had great difficulty in keeping up with him.

On 19th August Mortlock, Sadler and Noyce moved gently along the ridge savouring the views and descended to Camp III. There they were greeted by Cavenagh who provided them with lemonade and tinned peaches. Noyce reflected later that:

> ...the most wholly enjoyable moments of Trivor I would put them on that windy little col, during the afternoon and early morning of the 19th and 20th.

They decided that Sadler and Mortlock should go down immediately to Camp II. Noyce and Cavenagh would organise the packing and the Hunza porters who had had quite a long rest appeared early on the morning of 20th August to do the carry-down.

They loaded up and, heavily laden, started the descent. Helped by glissades and tobogganing the loads, they reached Camp II where Smith was. Leaving Cavenagh to start the final carries-down the following day, Noyce and Smith went on down to Base where they were welcomed to a splendid meal cooked by Yusuf, such '...*as I would never have suspected an Army officer of having the skill to cook*'.[33]

For several days they were able to rest and recover at Base Camp. The Hunzas were bringing the loads down and would have finished by 28th August when fifty Nagar porters were expected to arrive. The entire expedition, with the exception of Noyce and Mortlock, were suffering in one way or another, so there was little appetite for further strenuous activity and Mortlock was busy with preparation for his term at Loughborough. There was still a little time in hand. Noyce was able to catch up with his mail and letter-writing and finished typing his second dispatch to **The Times**, which appeared in the edition of 15th September 1960. There was still a little time for some exploration on his own. He had his eye on a col just south of Trivor, suggested by the map but which nobody had seen. On 24th August Noyce set off up the branch of the Gharesa Glacier coming in from the right into a valley that ran down from Trivor, with the cliffs of the Peak 21,750 on his right. It looked like a good route to the col until he turned a corner. The route became a mass of broken blocks of ice and avalanche débris. The puffs of smoke warned of rock and snow falls, the wisdom was to descend. On the way a great chunk of hanging glacier fell off from Peak 21,750 and seemed to come uncomfortably close. The following day he went up the branch of the glacier that goes north up towards Peak 23,620 and after a long and hard climb had a splendid view of the entire cirque of peaks and cols. There were sound effects as well with rocks and boulders falling and avalanches roaring down. He wrote, '*I lay again, on a boulder, and smoked a pipe. Animate, I felt almost an intruder in the inanimate yet moving world.*'[34]

After he rejoined the group Noyce was able to delegate the supervision of the loads and the porters during the three-day march to the town of Nagar. Leaving them on the morning of 30th August he set off in the tracks of the botanist and the surveyor, Polunin and Sahib Shah to get a glimpse of the Hispar Glacier. He climbed a ridge to the south which took him up to 15,000ft (4,560m) then bore east to get a sight of the glacier. The glacier had been explored by Fanny Bullock Workman and William Hunter Workman at the turn of the twentieth century.[35] He could see Hispar, reputedly a convict village, just below the snout of the glacier. He then descended some 5,000ft and reached the River Hispar, hoping to find a track. In fact the way was by climbing over boulders in the river bed and eventually after ten hours on the mountain a flat stretch of sand provided a place to lay out the sleeping-bag and to sit and enjoy Proust. However, the grinding of the boulders in the river and the crashes of ice and rock around him broke the spell. It was only for a short time on the descent from the summit of Trivor and on this solo trip that Noyce felt free of the preoccupations of an expedition leader, or indeed any member, and was able fully to enjoy a free and very personal relationship with the mountains. There were no worries here with sickness, loads, porters, routes and the countless other concerns that he was forced to consider on a daily basis. The expedition had made contact with the country but only to obtain the few services it could offer. The objective was to get to the summit, not to understand or deal with the inhabitants any more than they needed for that specific purpose. Now they were free to get to know the Hunza and the Nagars very much better.

Noyce left at 5.45. He found some Vibram prints in the sand, those of Polunin and Sahib Shah and followed them until they petered out at a cliff above the river. He descended into the very cold river and then went up a cliff of hard mud. At the top there was a spasmodic track and finally, within sight of Hispar, there was a bridge, well, '...*a small, swaying wire and wood structure*', that took him over the river. There were signs of a camp nearby and Noyce filled his water-bottle. He was very thirsty after the descent and the weeks in the snow. As he got lower it became hotter and more humid. He had to stop and drink every thirty minutes and later every twenty minutes. The track became definite at about mid-day and he could see the town of Nagar. However, he still had to cross the Barpu glacier which came down to 7,000ft (2,130m).

> *I dropped down the moraine on to the dirtiest glacier I have ever had the bad luck to cross. It took a slithery, mud-to-the-ankles hour, and my last prudent resolve not to drink muddy water off a glacier faded finally with other good resolutions. At 2 o'clock I*

was over, climbing very slowly up the moraine on the Nagar side. I had arrived.

The independent traveller had enjoyed his fling and it was back to being leader. At 17.00 the others were still arguing with the Hunza about pay. Noyce did not find peace, nor the harmony of mountains with men at Nagar. Their relations with the porters were contentious. However, the Mir of Nagar was very hospitable and gave them a farewell dinner on the last night.

On 3rd September they set off down to visit Hunza at the invitation of the Mir of Hunza. At the capital, Baltit, they spent a few days and were able to make a great deal of local contact. They played volley-ball several times against the palace team and had a superb lunch with the very westernised Mir and his wife in his residence which was furnished in a style which brought together both East and West. He was progressive and wanted to see his country develop with proper roads and the introduction of modern technology to enable his people to rise above their economy which provided 'just enough'. Nothing was wasted and everything was used and recycled. There were no fat men or women to be seen. It was a lean society in every sense.

On 6th September they received mail and the newspapers. **The Times** of 26th August had Noyce's first article from the expedition and it was noted that the second had been received. Noyce was in harmony, for a short time, with the characters and credulities of the people around him. The metaphysical and the reflective sides of his nature were aroused.

> *On the mountain, being mountaineers, we had been tied to the ego-centric, to the self-fulfilling. That I had seemed to realise in the Hispar. Here we were introduced to the other and more elusive world, and that perhaps is why Hunza formed for me a fitting climax to the journey. It complemented Trivor, as the active is complemented by the contemplative life.*[36]

The expedition departed from Baltit on 8th September having said their formal goodbyes to the Mir and taken the requisite photographs. They passed by Aliabad where the Lorimers had stayed during their year in the Hunzakut studying the languages of the area,[37] and continued down the Hassanabad Gorge to reach Hindi in the afternoon. Then it was on to Chalt and they reached Gilgit on 12th September.

Gilgit at 4,800ft (1,460m) was much hotter and the area was barren, but they installed themselves again in the Chenar Bagh bungalow that the Gilgit Scouts had put at their disposal. The swimming pool in the garden was very welcome. They organised the dispatch of the loads by plane to Rawalpindi and beyond and Noyce wrote his report for the Political Agent.

The winding up of the expedition had started and the next few days were spent in getting everyone down to Rawalpindi. Whillans set off from there on his solo motorbike ride back to Lancashire. This journey was a saga on its own and Noyce has it '*as brilliant an appendix as any expedition could wish*', to the Trivor book. Then it was on to Lahore, where Noyce offered his services to Pakistan radio, and down to Karachi where he made a tour of all those who had helped the expedition. Finally some shopping and then on to the aeroplane to arrive in England on 22nd September ready for the beginning of his last year as a schoolmaster.

Notes

1. *Godalming Borough Council minute 28.3.1957*
2. Letter to Lady Noyce 4.4.1957
3. The family home at Hindhead, Surrey
4. Letter to Lady Noyce 17.4.1957
5. A brightly coloured pheasant characterised by a fleshy horn on either side of the head.
6. Wilfrid Noyce, *Climbing the Fish's Tail p.48*
7. *Ibid p.51*
8. *Ibid p.66*
9. *Ibid p.66*
10. *Ibid p.86*
11. *Ibid p.90*
12. *Ibid p.103*
13. *Ibid p.119*
14. *Ibid p.134*
15. *Ibid p.134*
16. Sir Alec Douglas Home, *Speech in the House of Commons*
17. *To the Unknown Mountain p.32*
18. Wilfrid Noyce, *Private note written at Base Camp*
19. Wilfrid Noyce, *Diary note for 24.7.1960*
20. *To the Unknown Mountain p.70*
21. *Ibid p.72*
22. *Ibid p.84*

23 *Ibid p.89*
24 Wilfrid Noyce, *Trivor Log*
25 Wilfrid Noyce, and William Wordsworth, *Trivor Log*
26 *Trivor Log*
27 Wilfrid Noyce, *Trivor Diary, Trivor Log*
28 *Trivor Diary*
29 *To the Unknown Mountain p107*
30 *Trivor Log*
31 *To the Unknown Mountain p.113*
32 *Ibid p.115*
33 *Ibid p.122*
34 *Ibid p.126*
35 See *The Call of the Snowy Hispar* and other books on the Karakoram by W. H. and F. B. Workman
36 *To the Unknown Mountain p.151*
37 See *Language Hunting in the Karakoram* by E. O. Lorimer 1939

CHAPTER THIRTEEN

THE YEARS OF FULFILMENT 1955-62

By the end of 1954 Wilfrid Noyce had worked his way back into life at Charterhouse and felt able to develop further his interests within the school and elsewhere in a number of ways. He was established as a writer and critic and during the next few years he took a much more active role in public life, spent an increasing amount of time with his growing family, and published a constant flow of books and articles. All this as well as organising and leading two expeditions, to the Himalaya and the Karakoram.

It was a very busy period and one can observe the mellowing of Noyce's personality over these years. Rather than follow the chronological order of events, as hitherto, it will be simpler to treat each area of activity separately, and to note how effectively he shared his passions and enthusiasms with all those with whom he came in contact

School, Scouts and Charterhouse mountaineering

The author had been taught French by Noyce before he went off to Everest and then after his return some eighteen months later, as a Senior Scout I had a great deal to do with him in planning the activities of the troop. Mountaincraft was high on the agenda and on 13th February there was a visit to Stone Farm Rocks. A month later George Lowe, the other New Zealander who had been on Everest in 1953, lectured to the school on the 1954 New Zealand Himalayan Expedition. On the same occasion he joined the Scouts on a walk on the South Downs. Noyce enjoyed sharing with the Scouts and similar-minded boys his friendship with other distinguished mountaineers and when they visited the Noyces they very often joined us in our activities.

The Climbers' Club hut at Cwm Glas Mawr, in Llanberis Pass, during 12th to 22nd April 1955, was the venue of the first of a series of what became regular school mountaineering meets. The nucleus was the school Senior Scouts. In addition to Carthusians and Old Carthusians we had Roy Davey, a master at Impington Village College, a Community College near Cambridge and three of his boys. Noyce's invitation to Impington Village College to participate was very characteristic of his 'bridge-building' ideals. The Chairman of Governors of the College was Frida Leakey, who was still very close to the Noyce family. We had some very good mentors. John Hansbury, who had been with Noyce at the Aircrew Mountain Centre in Kashmir in 1944-5, Jo Kretschmer, who had been an instructor in winter warfare in Scotland and had climbed with Noyce on various occasions since they first met in 1945. The imperturbable David Cox, and Dick Marsh, a trainee priest from Cambridge, who had a number of good climbs to his credit were also part of the group. The ten days, of unbroken good weather were a wonderful introduction to rock-climbing, the mountains and mountain-craft. We started with modest climbs such as the Parsons Nose and by stages were able to climb 'VSs'.

One morning at 3.30 Noyce and Cox set off to climb Central Wall in Cwm Glas because the sun was on it. The member of the group who went with them remembers vividly David Cox appearing round a corner of the cliff, puffing his pipe. *'It was so easy to follow him because at every belay there was a pile of ash and matches and the smell of tobacco told us where he had gone.'*[1]

Encouraged by the success of the meet at Cwm Glas, shortly after the new term started:

> *On Wednesday 11th May a meeting was held in Mr Noyce's hashroom,[2] and the Charterhouse Mountaineering Club was founded with Mr Noyce as President and R. L. Hills and S. J. Hawkins as joint secretaries. The names of 40 were taken, and afterwards it was decided to limit active membership to those over 16 on account of the risks involved. This rule, though, could be overlooked in certain cases. There was also to be no entrance fee or terminal subscription.[3]*

The Mountaineering Club and Scouts occupied a considerable amount of Noyce's spare time as there were regular weekly meetings of the Scouts and weekend outings to Stone Farm and Harrison's Rocks. One of the ideas he revived was the Climbers' Club game of Scouts and Outposts, described over 100 years ago in the ***Climbers' Club Journal***.[4] It was originally played in the Lake District. The Scout log records that it was played twice, once on a common and the second time in the Wey Valley: '*It was a qualified success but a very interesting experiment.*' It was difficult to transpose it to the more enclosed Surrey countryside. Summer term 1955 culminated in a camp at Stone Farm Rocks on 16th to 17th July, with climbs there and at Harrison's for some fourteen participants including Jo Waycott, the school doctor.

Noyce managed to fit in one trip with the boys of Charterhouse in the winter term, to Stone Farm Rocks, and on this occasion, Sunday 30th October, Charles Wylie, an Everest colleague, joined them.

The New Year 1956 started with the school Mountaineering Club Meet, at the Climbers' Club hut at Helyg in the Ogwen Valley during 4th-13th January. Jo Kretschmer and David Cox again joined the group of eleven current or former Carthusians and three others including a representative of the ***Cambridge Daily News***. It is recorded that, '*Mr Noyce dragged two boys up the Devil's Kitchen.*'[5] The climax of the meet was a camp under Snowdon on the banks of Glaslyn. Noyce and two others walked over the Glyders from Helyg and pitched two tents in two feet of snow. They spent the night there and climbed Snowdon the following day returning to Helyg in the car that five others had brought over. These five set off to find the camp, failed and returned to the Pen-y-Gwryd Hotel. However three of them, bold spirits, having been duly refreshed set off to find the camp and reached it at 23.00, and spent a miserable, huddled night in the one tent, the other, a 1928 Millets hike tent, described as a 'flimsy tattered ruin' in the ***Cambridge Daily News***, was unusable. The following day the three climbed Snowdon in thick mist and heavy snow then broke camp and returned to Helyg.

Noyce recruited his friend Charles Wylie again for school trips and on Sunday 18th March they each took a group, Noyce, with another master George Ullyott, to Harrison's Rocks and the latter to Stone Farm Rocks. It is interesting to note that during this period of four months Noyce attended twelve council or committee meetings – one per week. The Helyg meet, however, caused him to miss two meetings

At the beginning of the summer term there were thirty-four members of the Charterhouse Mountaineering Club and at a meeting on 15th May it was decide to change the name of the club to The Mallory

Group, in memory of George Leigh Mallory, who had been a master at Charterhouse 1910-1921 and had died while attempting the summit of Everest or descending from it with Sandy Irvine in June 1924.

This was to be a busy term for the group. There was a trip with Noyce to Harrison's Rocks on Saturday 2nd June followed, the next weekend by a memorable excursion for the two who had not been able to join the earlier trip owing to lack of transport, Peter Norton and the author. On Sunday 10th June, Noyce took us to Joy and John Hunt's house at Camberley, where Hunt was Assistant Commandant of the Army Staff College. Gaston Rébuffat was staying and over coffee Hunt, Noyce and Rébuffat signed copies of **Starlight and Storm,** the English translation of **Etoiles et Tempêtes**, which Hunt and Noyce had just published. Afterwards we all went to Stone Farm Rocks, where we met Nea, who later married Sir Charles Evans (Everest 1953), and Denise Morin. '*We were treated to a display of climbing we had rarely witnessed before. The apparent ease with which the experts scaled Catwall staggered us and almost discouraged us.*'[6] It was an intoxicating experience for aspiring mountaineers to be with such an inspiring – and delightful – group.

Once again at the end of term camp on 21-22nd July at Stone Farm Noyce invited Michael Ward (Everest 1953) and Nea Morin to join us on our trip to Harrison's Rocks and they entertained us with a dazzling display of technique, making the ascent of '*…Birchden Wall look easier than going up a flight of stairs*'. Charles Wylie and Jo Waycott, the school doctor were also with us. The group was brightened by the presence of Jo's daughter Alison and two other masters' daughters.

Back at school there were the Scouts and the Mallory Group. On 4th November Noyce took a party to Harrison's Rocks and Charles Wylie and George Ullyott took a party to Stone Farm. The gathering was enlivened by the appearance in full uniform of the author and former secretary fresh from National Service Basic Training in the Argyll and Sutherland Highlanders.

The petrol shortage at the beginning of 1957 meant that the Mallory Group January meet at Helyg was rather less well attended. There were only seven boys and again Noyce had invited Jo Kretschmer and David Cox. An Old Carthusian, Angus Graham also joined the party. The weather was good and considerable ground was covered.

The climbing activities in the term were confined to the local rocks round Godalming and at one group meeting Noyce shared his plans for Machapuchare. On 27th March there was a major assault on Ashtead

Farm Rocks by the Scouts and the Mallory Group and they *'established a successful aerial runway with a dressing gown cord and a snap-link'.*[7] The day ended with Noyce giving a talk to the company on the Sherpas, *'... beautifully illustrated with slides'*. He left for Nepal and Machapuchare on 31st March.

In spite of Noyce's absence the Group arranged a camping meet in the Ogwen Valley over the Easter holiday and maintained their enthusiasm and programme in the face of very wet weather!

After his return from Nepal at the end of June, Noyce's appearances at Charterhouse until the end of term were largely only social but he did join the Mallory Group on 22nd July at their end of term meet at Stone Farm Rocks. He also had time to meet a contingent of Canadian Scouts on their way home from the 50th Anniversary World Scout Jamboree at Sutton Coldfield and talk to them about the Himalayas and The Abominable Snowman. While confirming that he believed The Snowman, or yeti, existed, he thought that the American expedition planned for 1958, with one of its objectives to find the yeti, might well be disappointed.[8]

The momentum of the Mallory Group was maintained in the winter term. The following comes from a notice which was circulated in early October. It shows Noyce's approach to getting commitment from feckless schoolboys.

> MALLORY GROUP
> *(1) There will be a meeting at Ashtead Farm Rocks this Sunday Oct. 6. Meet at Charterhouse Road Post Office, 2.30 pm,*
> *(2) It is hoped a visit to Stone Farm Rocks will be possible the Sunday after, Oct 13. Please give names to me or to T.J. Mimpriss, Hon. Sec. If transport is short, priority will be given to anyone who appears at Ashtead Farm.*

The visit on 13th October was marked by the presence of Michael and Jeremy Noyce aged five and three, gaining an early introduction to their father's passion.

The Mallory Group members were the guests of the Climbers' Club again at the Ynys Ettws hut in Llanberis Pass for the period 12th-19th January 1958. David Cox and Jo Kretschmer came up to lend a hand for the last two days and John Hunt's family joined the party for a fine ridge walk over Siabod. The weather was generally cold and wet but the nine participants were able to carry out a number of good climbs. The presence of Noyce's distinguished climbing friends was a considerable encouragement to the young climbers and all gained confidence and skill more quickly as a result of the association with them.

In June there was another meet of the Mallory Group at Harrison's Rocks. By this time the number of interested masters from the school and the availability of Old Carthusian members, all with transport, was increasing so larger groups could participate in the visits to Harrison's and Stone Farm from school. At the end of that term there were twenty-three at Stone Farm for the final camp.

In the Easter holidays, 8th to 15th April 1959, the Mallory Group had their meet at the Climbers' Club hut at Ynys Ettws in the Llanberis Pass. Once again Noyce had invited Jo Kretschmer and there were twenty-five participants. Impington Village College again was represented and Martyn Berry, then an undergraduate at Oxford, who later contributed to *The Climber's Fireside Book*, was with the group for a short time. The popular routes were climbed and the walkers ranged widely. Berry recalls climbing with Noyce: '*I seconded him up the Devil's Kitchen – a great experience – and later on a climb on the Gribin Facet.*' He had been introduced to Rosemary and Wilfrid Noyce by Heda Munro, née Armour, who created pictures for a greeting-card company. She was a close friend of the Noyces and did a very fine portrait of the Noyce sons.[9]

From the end of the summer the Anglo-American Karakoram expedition was being prepared but the Mallory Group was not neglected and had two outings with Noyce in the winter term when they were at Stone Farm Rocks on 15th November and at Harrison's Rocks four weeks later.

The Easter 1960 meet of the Mallory Group at the Cwm Glas Hut enjoyed the company of Jack Sadler who had been with Noyce in the Alps in the summer. For the brothers John and Edwin Herington it was very exciting to be part of the preparations for a Karakoram expedition as they tested with Sadler and Noyce the walkie-talkies on the Glyders. It was, however, a sad gathering; on the Monday three of the participants joined the search party for three Royal Masonic schoolboys from 4.30 until midday. The bodies were eventually found on the scree just to the left of the Parson's Nose and the Carthusians assisted with the stretcher parties.[10]

The winter term at school included several visits with the Mallory Group to the local rock outcrops and on 6th November they were joined by Geoffrey Sutton. In the Christmas holidays, with John Herington, the Secretary of the Mallory Group, Noyce was exploring local rock outcrops for term-time activities. In the spring of 1961 there were more Mallory Group visits to the Rocks. In March Richard Brooke, who had been with Noyce in the Alps in 1955, talked to the Group about the Trans-Antarctic and Rakaposhi expeditions, in which he had participated.

In the Easter holidays there was a Mallory Group meet at Helyg from 5th-14th April. There were some thirteen participants, of whom three were Old Carthusians and two from other schools. They were active on Tryfan, Idwal, Lliwedd and in the Llanberis Pass. Noyce, as ever, insisted on his swim in the stream at Helyg and on 7th April '*Mr Noyce appears naked through loft door after early morning swim! Remarks: "wasn't too bad actually!" But Afon Llugwy v. cold.*'[11] Ian McMorrin, who had already visited the Mallory Group on their trips to the Rocks from school, appeared with his girl-friend. He was working with Noyce at this time on an atlas of mountaineering. A short time later that holiday Noyce again walked on his own over all mountains over 3,000 feet high in North Wales in one day.

Noyce's final term at Charterhouse included the regular Mallory Group meets and activities with the Senior Scouts. The Scout Log records in the words of Keith Simpson the Troop Leader:

July 30th Presentation to Mr Noyce.

This was the last meeting of all the Seniors together and the main purpose of this was to present to Wilf (as we all really knew him) something for all that he had done for us and so many Seniors in the past. After a little consultation with Mrs Noyce I was assured that a Parker 61 would be a very treasured present, so we gave him that, which was most appropriate as he was leaving us to write more books. He certainly seemed very pleased with it.[12]

Noyce's widow, Rosemary, wrote subsequently to Keith Simpson, '*Your pen wrote the last book which is coming out soon. It did not go to Russia, so I still have it as a treasured souvenir.*'[13]

Noyce was greatly missed at Charterhouse. Frank Ives, the housemaster of his former house, wrote,

His contribution to the Charterhouse community was priceless and unique. Who can say how many boys of all ages, in their surprise to find that a man could be both a scholar and a hero, were stimulated to some sort of emulation by his close and constant presence, and by the help and instruction so freely offered to the humblest and youngest? His achievements were a source of pride as well as pleasure to Carthusians, who were impressed, almost awed, by the remarkable combination of gentleness of manner and profound modesty with rare scholarship, sublime courage, when it was called for, and complete integrity. Even his colleagues in Brooke Hall[14] shared this feeling of being privileged to know one whose scale of values was superior, whose horizons were wider, and whose mind and body were more highly disciplined than their own.

And finally the testimony of one of the Hon Secs of the Mallory Group:

What do I owe to Wilfrid?
He was not just a rock climber, but a mountaineer: on completing the climb, we would walk or scramble to the summit of the mountain. In this way, I learned from him not just a love of climbing but also a love of mountains themselves. For some thirty-five years I have lived close to the Cambrian Mountains, and, although my rock climbing days are now over, I still indulge my passion for them by walking, scrambling and photographing. Also, having learned Welsh, I can now appreciate the music of Welsh names, especially the mountain names. I was a very weedy and unadventurous child: Wilfrid's enthusiasm and guidance led me to an activity that enabled me to develop a love for the outdoors and a measure of self-reliance. Later, during a busy and stressful professional life, the mountains proved to be a powerful means of recreation and recuperation. I am sure that others can tell a similar tale.

Literary Activities

At the beginning of 1955 Noyce was still working with John Hunt on the translation of ***Etoiles et Tempêtes*** and in the Easter holidays went across to Chamonix to see Gaston Rébuffat in order to put the final touches to the book. He was able to combine that with some skiing at Les Contamines. Two other books were also on the stocks. The first was an anthology of Snowdonia and was a collaborative effort with his old friend Geoffrey Winthrop Young and Geoffrey Sutton, another regular climbing companion. Noyce was also the editor. The second was a new venture, a novel. Both these books were committed to the publishers in 1956.

The Royal Geographical Society in 1957 asked Noyce to review a couple of books by Charles Evans, the deputy leader of the 1953 Everest expedition, one on the successful Kanchenjunga expedition he had led in 1956, the other **On Climbing**, and a book by Ronald Clark **A Picture History of Mountaineering**.[15] This was a very sympathetic review and one was encouraged to read all of these books.

David Cox was President of the Climbers' Club and Wilfrid Noyce was this year elected to be one of the Vice-presidents, in addition to his duties as Guidebook Editor.

In November the novel he had struggled with in the previous year, **The Gods are Angry,** was published. According to one review it came across as 'a warts and all' story of an expedition, with quarrels, resentful wives, and villagers unhappy about their sacred mountain being violated. One climber dies and they fail to get to the summit. The reviewer ends, '*I will not blame Noyce's fellow-climbers if, on his next expedition, they first check the plot of any story he has just written.*'[16]

This had all been written before Noyce went to climb Machapuchare in 1957.

As he and Cox were resting at Hinko, on the way down from the summit, he reflected:

> *That imaginative literature must be impossible up here. In that sense of relaxed, rather selfish well-being that comes after effort, I marvelled that I had only a year ago written a novel, and decided then and there that it had been an impossible task. What person accustomed to action has ever been able to write of characters he has not seen, experiences he has not had himself? Cook or Park, Stanley or Sven Hedin, Scott or Shackleton, Tilman or Shipton? Their own experiences, yes, splendidly told, but that seemed to me a much easier task. The sea fares best with Melville and Conrad, and the air with Saint-Exupéry. But it seemed to me also, as I looked back, that all that had happened in the last months had been so personal, so bound up with living friends, with Charles*

and David, with Jimmy and Roger, with the Sherpas, that the experience could never distil itself away from their known faces, any more than the mountain could forgo that great shape which had dominated our waking thoughts. If I should write now, it must be of what I have seen.[17]

In the same year **Snowdon Biography** was published. After an introduction by Noyce this volume falls comfortably into three parts. Geoffrey Winthrop Young, with his incomparable breadth of knowledge and experience gives an amiable account of travellers and climbers in Snowdonia up until the 1920s and Geoffrey Sutton discusses the expansion of the interest and appeal of the mountains, the developments in climbing and the great contributors to the increased skill and improved techniques of the period after World War II. Noyce himself provides the third section in which the literary history of the area and the heroes and myths of Welsh history are evoked. It is an ideal bedside book. The reviews, understandably, were very favourable.

In a newspaper article Noyce went further with Geoffrey Sutton's ideas and observed that nine out of ten of the world's highest peaks had been climbed in the recent past. Most of these had succumbed to 'national' expeditions in view of the support required. Mountaineering had been a competitive sport at the national level and various nations had abrogated to themselves almost a monopoly on certain peaks.[18] Following the International expedition to Lhotse in 1955, Norman Dyrenfurth, the leader, in a report in a British newspaper, had exhibited a competitive spirit and indicated that some of their times over certain parts of the mountain were faster than those of other national expeditions . Noyce had been moved to respond in a letter to the editor.

> *At the same time some of my Everest companions may feel, like myself, that the element of nationalism and direct comparison in mountaineering, which most hoped would die after Everest, creeps into the report. 'The British had taken so many days over the icefall, we took only so long.' And the same with the Lhotse Face to the South Col. The words 'records' too in your headline has a savour that most mountaineers deplore.*

He also suggested that Dyrenfurth might have been more humble in acknowledging the debt he owed to those who had been on the mountain before him. He also reflects in his last paragraph, with characteristic humility on the short life of heroes.

> *It may well be that, having only parts of the report out of context, I have mistaken its atmosphere. For that I would apologise. But this letter would still be worth writing, to relieve the minds of those readers who must now fear that we of the 1953 expedition are even more back numbers than we really are.*[19]

Early in 1958 **The Springs of Adventure** was published. Some time later this excellent volume was very favourably reviewed by Raymond Mortimer, one of the leading literary critics of the time. In it Noyce establishes a definition of adventure, '*novel physical adventure undertaken for its own sake*', and then observes the practitioners through the ages. The reasons given for exposing themselves to hardship and danger are frequently given as fame or fortune or the desire to extend the frontiers of science and human knowledge. However he strongly suggests that there are deep personal reasons for engaging in these adventures which have nothing to do with the stated reasons. In the book there are analyses of motives and achievements in most fields of adventurous endeavour. His comment on courage is significant:

> *Courage divorced and alone is not a great quality. It takes more true courage for a girl wittingly to choose to spend her life looking after sick parents, a traveller to forgo travel in order to finance a family, than it did for Hillary*[20] *to fly under the Severn Bridge.*[21]

He also reflects that what was yesterday's heroic adventure and achievement becomes tomorrow's everyday occurrence. This was made forcefully evident in 2001 when eighty-nine climbers reached the summit of Mount Everest on 23rd May.[22]

The book recounting the expedition to Machapuchare was nearly finished. Arthur Pigou, Noyce's mentor and sponsor of his visits to The Alps in 1937 and 1938 read the text and made 'constructive comments'. The book was dispatched to the publishers before the summer term began. It appeared as **Climbing the Fish's Tail** in the autumn. It was a shorter volume than **South Col** but equally enchanting as it describes an expedition free from the constraints imposed by size and national prestige. A reviewer noted:

The book is short, but this is because it is so well written that all is made clear in a very few words, and there is ample room in its few pages to convey the feeling of a full-length expedition, with all its challenge and rewards.[23]

The 300th Foyles Literary Luncheon was held at the Dorchester Hotel, London on 28th November 1958 in honour of Sir Vivian Fuchs to mark the publication of his book ***The Crossing of Antarctica.*** Wilfrid Noyce was by now recognised not only as a distinguished mountaineer but also as a man of letters of some eminence. He was one of the thirteen guests of honour which included Odette Hallowes GC, the war-time secret agent in France, Ella Maillart, who had traversed Central Asia with Peter Fleming in the 1930s, and Donald Campbell and Neville Duke, breakers of records on water and in the air. Noyce was the only Briton among the guests of honour who had not been decorated by the Monarch.

In March 1959, Prof. Arthur Pigou, died and the legacy Noyce received from Pigou enabled him to think seriously about giving up teaching and starting to write full time.[24]

He was also still adding lustre to fêtes and school events with an exhibition of his mountaineering equipment on 28th June at a village fête and speaking on 21st July 1959 at the speech day of Howard County Secondary School, Kirton in Lincolnshire. All this while he was preparing an anthology of his own poems for publication. Some of these had already been published in various books or magazines and encouraged by the success of ***Michel Angelo*** he brought together a range of poems written over a quarter of a century.

In 1960, after twelve years, Noyce resigned as Guidebook Editor for the Climbers' Club. He had piloted a number of guidebooks through the press and in his last year, being also General Editor for the Alpine Club, he had produced the first of the Alpine guide-books in which the Alpine Club and Alpine Climbing Group were collaborating.[25]

The Karakoram expedition, preparations and execution, preoccupied him for a considerable part of the year and Noyce returned on 22nd September just in time to start his final year as a schoolmaster.

Poems, the collection of his poems that had been written over some twenty years was about to be published. Some of the poems had already appeared in his books and various journals and this volume brought together poems written on the mountain, with others that told of daily events with great insight and sensitivity. Frances Cornford, in her foreword to **Poems** observes,

> *Wilfrid Noyce has written admirably about why men want to adventure in general, and to climb in particular, though with characteristic humility and lack of dogmatism he only leaves us with various enlightening suggestions. All these suggestions seem also to apply to the writing of poetry.*

He had now delivered to the public a wide range of literary output. All, with perhaps the exception of **The Gods are Angry**, was received with considerable acclaim.

Noyce had always maintained contact with Menlove Edwards. He had stayed with Noyce at Cambridge in 1946 and they had corresponded over the years. Edwards was elected an Honorary Member of the Climbers' Club in 1953 at Noyce's suggestion. When Edwards was badly injured in a motor-cycle accident at the end of 1957 on his way home from a weekend in North Wales, Noyce was deeply concerned and wrote to Edwards' sister Nowell to ask if he could help in any way. He also wrote to Edwards himself and received a long letter in return. Early in 1958 Edwards took his own life.[26] As a tribute to his very powerful influence in his early days on the mountains Noyce wrote **Samson, the Life and Writings of Menlove Edwards,**[27] in collaboration with Geoffrey Sutton, This was published privately in 1960. It is a slim volume and explains a great deal of the complexity of the character and personality of this outstanding climber and very able psychiatrist.

Noyce was busy with at least two books and sketching ideas for other publications when he left for the Pamirs. One of them, **The Alps,**[28] a magisterial coffee-table tome was already at the publishers. The photographs are from many sources, but the introduction and the notes on the photographs are all Noyce's. Karl Lukan wrote the descriptions of the mountains.

They Survived was also in the hands of the publishers and came out in October 1962. This was a series of studies of those who, despite all odds, have survived to tell the tale. The psychology, motives and spirituality of those who survived apparently against all odds are all analysed to see if there is in fact a common element or 'a secret of survival'. It is in some ways Noyce's final testament. In it he talks of faith in oneself, courage and of the occasions when each member of a group, in a difficult situation, feels that another person has joined them, thereby strengthening and encouraging the group. This consciousness of that extra person disappears when 'the critical moments have passed.'

Two years later a much more comfortable volume appeared, *The Climber's Fireside Book*, a delightful anthology of mountain writings from 400 AD. The author of this book was very happy to receive a copy of this as a wedding-present in 1965 from Rosemary Noyce.

An atlas of mountaineering was being planned with Ian McMorrin. This was an ambitious project, and the structure had been established. Noyce had written those sections for which he was personally responsible. At one stage after Noyce's death, it seemed that the project might be abandoned but in fact McMorrin took on what was the bulk of the work and brought it to fruition as his own tribute to Noyce as *The World Atlas of Mountaineering* published in 1969.

Alpine Adventures and Mountain Matters

This section covers Noyce's trips to the Alps during the period, and contributions to the world of mountaineering not covered elsewhere.

In July 1955 an article by Noyce entitled 'The Highest Mountains' appeared in the **Observer.** He noted that after many unsuccessful expeditions over some thirty-five years to Everest, K2, Nanga Parbat and Kanchenjunga, the summits of these had all succumbed to the human footprint within the previous three years. There were three main reasons, the first was that garments, boots, food and equipment had greatly improved and oxygen at very high altitude was recognised as very useful. The second is the development of human psychology and physique. *'Each height attained makes the next easier of attainment; each difficulty overcome smooths a path for those who follow.'* Everest has been climbed now a number of times without oxygen. The third was the weather. The weather over Everest in the 'fifties appears to have been better than it was in the 'thirties. In any of these ventures *'some co-operation from the weather is required'.* He reflects on the future, and with considerable prescience suggests that until oxygen can be manufactured in a light and easily portable form there may only be a need for big expeditions to high altitudes because of the cost of the equipment. National honour has now been satisfied with the major national expeditions having scaled 'their peaks' and there is no further requirement for these. On the other hand there may be, more likely, a future for small parties doing very ambitious climbs, living off the land, as Noyce himself did in the 1940s. Even Everest they might climb, but he did feel that:

> ...*at present the Creator seems to have drawn a physiological barrier line between 28,000 and 29,000ft. They will spend holidays in the Himalaya and Andes much as mountaineers spend them in the Alps to-day. ...one thing is certain. Men will look back on the 1950s as the Golden Age of Himalayan pioneering.*[29]

It has all come true.

In the August Noyce returned to the Alps with John Hunt, and David Cox. They were again based in Chamonix. On one occasion they went up past the Vallot Hut, at 4,362m '..*with its refrigerator smell of stale orange-peel and exhausted blanket-bound bodies*', to the summit of Mont Blanc and then went on across untrodden snow to Mont Maudit, at 14,280ft (4,342m), some 1,600ft (500m) lower than the summit of Mont Blanc then carried on down to the luxurious Torino Hut, complete with every comfort including a dance-floor. The following day they went gently down to Courmayeur on the Italian side. After spending the night in Courmayeur they took the cable-car back up to the Torino Hut with the objective of climbing Mont Blanc by the Red Sentinel route on the south-east face. After a good lunch at the hut they set off and only got as far as the Col de Fourche where they bivouacked as snow was falling. They returned to Courmayeur the following day. The weather cleared and two evenings later they were trying again. They were going up the Brenva Glacier and found a German encampment. Here they were welcomed with '...*warm drinks, with the equally warming remark that "mountains remove barriers"*'. They continued refreshed and, slowed by the mist that swirled around them, eventually bivouacked on a ledge somewhat short of the Sentinel. They tied themselves to the rock and tried to cook on a little petrol stove:

> *Security was a matter to which he appeared to attach too little importance. Both of us had occasion to remonstrate at different times about the need to put on the rope on crevassed glaciers. We remember him, too, unaware of the limitations of us lesser mortals, dancing blithely, unroped, across the first of the great avalanche-scoured ice couloirs between the old Brenva ridge and the foot of the Sentinelle on Mont Blanc one starlight night in 1955, when*

the security of the other three members of our party was essential.[30]

They continued past the Red Sentinel on to the ridge where Noyce once again gave evidence of his phenomenal stamina as he led them '... *up the steep and exposed face which leads from the Sentinelle ridge to the summit of Mont Blanc, kicking small toeholds for the rest of us hour after hour*'.[31]

When they reached the summit, it was misty again and they were deprived of the view: so the only alternative was a drink. They descended to the Vallot Hut. Noyce described it:

In the daytime the Vallot is like a scene from Hogarth. It is made of metal, and at night has the chill air of a mortuary. But in the day it livens up. A motley collection, male and female, from every country in the world come here to refresh themselves from the labours of climbing the highest mountain in the Alps. Costumes range from deerstalkers to gym shoes, turbans to frock coats, and the voices are Babel.[32]

From the Vallot they went on down to Chamonix. Hunt continues the narrative:

On completing that great route and descending via the Grand Mulets to the Plan de l'Aiguille, his companions were only too glad to complete the descent to Chamonix in the téléférique: not so Wilf. Apparently as fresh as when he had left our bivouac some 14 hours earlier, he hastened down on the path.[33]

A day or so later they met up with Michael Ward, to do the great double traverse of Mont Blanc massif, the Croix du Mont-Blanc. They had started at Les Contamines several days before and were making their way up towards the Col de Miage when they were,

...overtaken by darkness and dense mist during the long climb up to the Durier Hut, groping our way through the enormous crevasses in the Glacier de Miage with visibility only a few yards ahead. It was Wilf, with his uncanny intuitive sense and undiminished stamina, who guided us to the empty, unlit hut that night.[34]

He returned to Godalming in time for municipal committee meetings on 30th August and shortly afterwards he was off to the Alps again with Geoffrey Sutton, another climbing companion of long standing and they met up with Richard Brooke to do the Couturier couloir of the Aiguille Verte. This was another occasion when Noyce made a remarkable display of his technical skill and natural ability. Brooke recalls:

> *The bergschrund was difficult and we dropped a rope to help a young French couple to cross. They continued to follow us as we went up the couloir. We had straight ice-axes, ten-point crampons, and I had an ice-piton in my left hand. We had a rest 3/4 of the way up on an easement on the right. To reach the summit ridge Wilf traversed an icy runnel and then bade me follow. The rope was slack and I had to call him to take in the slack. Wilf was on the other side of the ridge, sitting in the sunshine, admiring the view. I'm sure he never recognised that the traverse of the runnel was quite delicate.*
>
> *We descended by the Whymper couloir, which is notorious for dangerous snow conditions early in the morning as it faces East and catches the sun. We were part-way down and the French couple were still following us. We moved to the side of the couloir. They slipped, passed us and fell to the glacier. Wilf unroped and 'danced' down the old steps to the glacier. They were both dead. Geoff and I, shaken by what we had witnessed, climbed down with great caution.*
>
> *When we started to go down the glacier, which had many crevasses, Wilf tied the rope round his waist and then coiled it round his body to shorten it, but failed to tie it off. If he had fallen down a crevasse he would probably have strangled himself. We remonstrated and he secured the rope.*
>
> *I had the impression that it all came very easily to Wilfrid Noyce and that there was little perception of danger or fear. He never tired, and his competence, technical skill and amazing balance enabled him to take everything in his stride.*[35]

In October Noyce spoke on the BBC Home Service about his summer trip on Mont Blanc with Ward, Hunt and Cox and the talk was printed in ***The Listener***.[36] He was also at this time busy with John Hunt on the translation of **Etoiles et Tempêtes,** in which Gaston Rébuffat describes his epic ascents of the six most challenging north faces in the Alps.

In 1956 there was a short time at home after the end of the summer term before Noyce went off in August to climb in the Alps with Gaston Rébuffat and Michael Ward.[37] John Hunt joined them at Chamonix. They had set their sights on the Innominata ridge route up the Mont Blanc de Courmayeur and then on to the summit of Mont Blanc itself. When they reached the Col de l'Innominata, the rocks were covered in new snow and it was raining hard. A change of plan was necessary so they headed across the Glacier de Frêney to the Col des Dames Anglaises on the Peuterey Ridge where there was a bivouac. From a distance they saw a crowd of climbers on the Brèche and realised that the bivouac would be full. They turned back to the Gamba Hut rather vexed. However, there they met up with Alan Blackshaw and Bob Downes who had just come down from the Torino Hut and all went down the following day to Courmayeur.

Alf Gregory, the photographer on the 1953 Everest expedition, who had just descended from making a new route on the Tour des Grandes Jorasses with P. Ghiglione, was in town, as was Roger Chorley, another member of the Alpine Club and the distinguished Swiss molecular biologist Alfred Tissières who was well known to British Alpinists as he had done a PhD at King's College, Cambridge and had taken part in the British Karakoram Expedition in 1954.

The Noyce party then moved up to the Requin Hut and thought to climb at a lower level for a bit. They wanted to try a route, pioneered by Vallot, of which they had a vague description in the guide-book, direct up the east face of the Requin. It was a beautiful day, that 12th August, but the gods did not favour even Noyce, who was climbing with as much stamina and gusto as he had twenty years earlier. There is said to be:

> *A photo of Wilf standing on a ledge halfway up the face at a point marked by twin pitons, above which even Wilf could discern no prospect of progress.*[38]

Noyce describes that moment:

> *David belayed, I climbed up what seemed to be an overhang, slipped a sling through and came down. A IVb? Oh dear, we must be getting very old! Up again, finger through the piton. Three*

feet beyond, above the overhang, was another. Now a piton, I am ashamed to say, I sometimes find very comforting; two pitons even more so. But beyond that not a hold in sight, and I am not a man to move without at least two points of contact. All the encouragement in the world could not get me farther, nor produce holds where there were none, and the others declined a pressing invitation to take over. We reassembled, defeated.[39]

They then traversed across to the Meyer-Dibona ridge on the right of the face. It was practically dark when they got to the top, and they had to spend a very cold night standing wedged on a tiny ledge in the Cheminée Fontaine to which they had had just enough time to abseil before it became totally black. They survived this ordeal on two prunes, a few lumps of sugar and a packet of glucose.[40] John Hunt recalls, "*...a slow and insecure descent next morning on the steep, frozen slopes, with no crampons and only one ice axe in the party."*

The summer holidays in 1958 started with a trip to the Alps with David Cox and Anthony Rawlinson. Peter Norton, another Old Carthusian, joined them for some of the time. They based themselves on Armand Charlet's farmhouse near Argentière. Charlet was the Chamonix guide to whom Arthur Pigou had introduced Noyce in 1938. The group climbed mainly in the Argentière area and from the Argentière hut did the ascent of the Aiguille du Tour. Noyce was leading up an icy couloir. He '*said over his shoulder, "What we need now is pickles." When asked for an explanation he said "eispickels"'.*[41] It was always said that the higher the altitude, the lighter was the Noyce humour. They continued on to the Aiguille du Pissoir and on the descent there was a thunderstorm and thick mist through which Noyce navigated back to the hut using his simple scout compass. They then went on down to the valley and Rawlinson, Noyce and Cox then went off to climb on Mont Blanc. It seems that Cox caught polio on this part of the trip and was eventually brought back to hospital in Oxford and the resulting disability was with him for the rest of his life.

1959 was the year when the Anglo-American Karakoram expedition was being planned and Jack Sadler, Colin Mortlock and Noyce went to the Alps in the summer and did a number of important climbs. Jack Sadler led them up the Welzenbach route on the Dent d'Hérens; later Noyce and Sadler did the north-east face of the Lyskamm and crossed into Italy. They returned by the Lagarde-Devies route on the Signalkuppe on Monte Rosa. The latter two being first British ascents. Noyce was still climbing as effortlessly and smoothly as he had been two decades earlier. He was very taken with Jack Sadler's imperturbability on these climbs.[42]

Colin Mortlock recalls:

1959 Summer. I arrive by train from Chamonix at Zermatt to meet Wilfrid Noyce, the Everest climber. His age and Alpine experience make me feel very young. I am fresh out of Oxford and it is the start of my second week of my first alpine season. My first view of the Matterhorn from Zermatt convinces me that it is the most beautiful mountain I will ever see. It looks impossibly high and remote. About a week later, after two grade VI snow and ice routes, Wilf and I bivouac near the rubbish dump by the Hornli hut at the base of the popular route up the Matterhorn. Not long after midnight we traverse to the foot of the Furggen ridge. Wilf has agreed that I can return to my world of rock, as distinct from the unfamiliar world of snow and ice. In addition I am allowed to lead the climb. The route has never had a British ascent. To add spice, the Direct Finish is around Hard Very Severe and supposed to be exposed. Few young climbers in those days could have had such an opportunity, in such company, in their first season.

It becomes one of the most memorable of days – all 20 hours or so of it. The ridge is loose, non-technical yet a little dangerous. The Direct Finish is wonderfully exposed, strenuous and well protected by in place pitons. The summit amazes me, devoid of human beings but the habitat of several alpine choughs, which I never expected to see so high in the sky. Black clouds and a strengthening wind say not to linger. Within half-an-hour a full blizzard rages. Wilf, now in the lead, is simply brilliant. He knows the Hornli ridge. If we pass one climbing party we pass hundreds. The blizzard continues to the Hornli hut. A brief respite then down to Zermatt. Somewhat shattered – it is around 11pm – Wilf smiles and says, "a quick shower and I will buy you the best meal in town."[43]

This was only the fourth ascent of the Furggen Ridge Direct. They also tried out the Gannex clothing in the Alps and found that particular cloth not really suitable.

Sadler, Mortlock and Noyce had a weekend in North Wales in the following October when they met Geoffrey Smith and Don Whillans. They were on Gallt y Wenallt and Mortlock, the rock specialist, was leading the party and Noyce, climbing down, fell as he was taking photographs of Whillans. The ledge he had stood on during the ascent came away with a chunk of mountainside and he fell ninety feet to the scree; He broke his collar-bone and cracked three ribs. '*He set off at once to drive to Godalming, "They might keep me two or three days if I look in at a hospital," he said.*'[44]

A further tribute was paid to Noyce: the rules of the Alpine Climbing Group were changed provisionally to permit him, although well past forty years old, to become president which he remained until his death. This was a great tribute to not only his mountaineering skills but also to his ability to get on with anybody and to lead a diverse group of individuals. *"He had the common touch"*, to quote a contemporary member of the ACG from Yorkshire. His term of office as vice-president of the Climbers' Club was coming to an end and he was expected to be elected as the next president.

Morocco

On 1st September 1961 Noyce went off to Morocco with Len Frank for two weeks for what seems to have been his only visit to the High Atlas.[45] They were able to be at Asni, a tiny village within sight of the high peaks, some seventeen hours after leaving London. Here, based at the Hôtel Toubkal, they equipped themselves with mule, muleteer and a local guide called '*Lahouisse, known as Larousse for his encyclopaedic, if sometimes uncertain, knowledge*'. They did a two-day exploratory trip to Tachdirt and Oukaimeden and then returned to Asni. On the way they ascended Angour, 11,864ft (3,614m).

Then they set off to the south-west, and went up the long grind to the Lépiney hut. It was quite an adventure and the mule fell off the track. Happily it was caught by a juniper tree and came to no harm. The following day, however, Frank was beginning to suffer from a bad leg and a rash and so while he went down and round the mountain to the Neltner hut, Noyce took a route over the top of Biiguinoussene, 13,130ft (4,000m). He also tried Larousse out with the rope and decided that going solo was safer. They continued over Taadat, 12,589ft (3,835m) where Larousse watched Noyce climbing a strenuous chimney to its pinnacle summit. From there they descended to the Neltner hut.

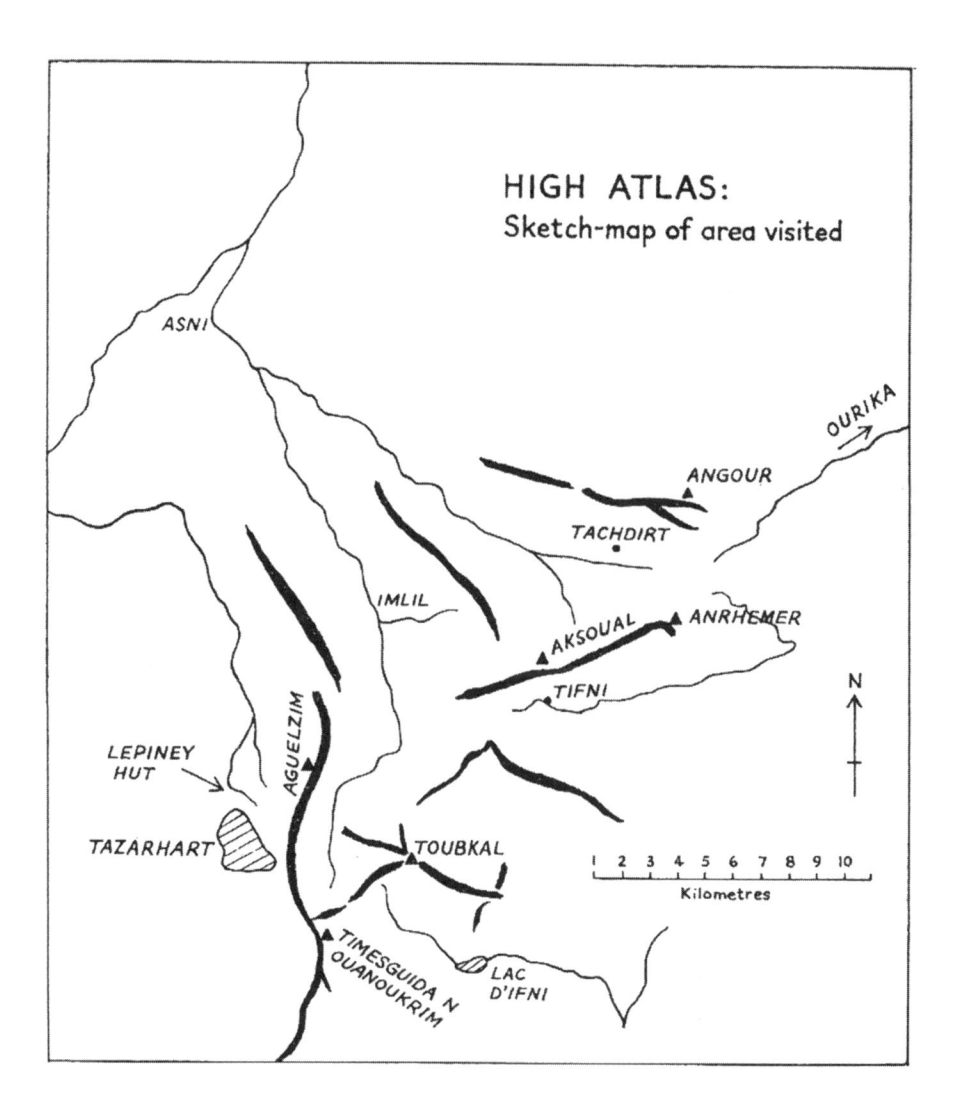

Sketch map of the High Atlas.

In the afternoon Larousse went to have a tooth pulled, Frank rested and Noyce strolled, his word, up the ordinary route to the summit of Jebel Toubkal, 13,666ft (4,163m), the highest in the Atlas – and fell asleep on top.

The following day, Frank rested, intending to try Toubkal in the afternoon. Noyce now was able to savour fully the joys of exploration and of being on the mountain on his own. His account[46] describes very few of the climbs as more than 'difficult' and he was able to indulge himself and climb a formidable number of peaks in the short time he had. He travelled light and moved fast and on one day climbed Afella n Ouanoukrim, 13,265ft (4,040m) then went along the ridge, down to a pass then continued up to Biiguinoussene again, on to Tadat on which he climbed four routes and wondered if any of them was a first ascent. He continued to the summit of Aguelzim, 12,369ft (3,768m) then found a pillar at the end of the ridge where he did two routes then '*dropped rapidly on the scree*' back to the hut.

Frank's condition had deteriorated and he walked back to Asni and went on to the hospital in Marrakesh. Noyce then sent off the guide and the mule round the mountains to Ifni Lake. This was another great Noyce day. He set off at sunrise towards Tadaft, 12,796ft (3,898m). The CUMC had thought that this was a mild Severe route and so Noyce became conscious of his age and became cautious. He had a long abseil down at one point. '*There is something faintly eerie about abseiling alone over a big drop, and mindful of accidents I left another sling.*' From there he went the top of the main bou Imrhaz group at 13,222ft (4,027m), then down to a col and up again to reach the second summit of the Atlas, Timesguida n Ouanoukrim, 13,416ft (4,087m) in time for a noon lunch. During lunch he mused on what a boring route to the top of Toubkal he had taken earlier and, rather than descend to Ifni Lake then climb up again on the morrow, he decided to do it in the afternoon. Unaware that it was supposed to take four to seven hours he descended the 400 metres to the Tizi d'Ouanoums and then after two and three-quarter hours he was on the top of Toubkal West! It was back to the Neltner hut before following the mule-track round to the lake, where they were to bivouac, and to enjoy a very welcome dip in the lake.

They left the lake in the morning and '*…crossed a high, toilsome and infinitely thirsty pass in company with a party of mules*' to descend to bivouac at Tifni.

A day later they were crossing the Aksoual ridge and Noyce left the guide and the mule at the pass, the Tizi n Lizkemt, and took in a couple of summits on the ridge, Aksoual 12,828ft (3,907m) and Iguenouane, 12,713ft (3,872m) and rejoined them later at the village Tachdirt, 7,550ft (2,300m).

With the continuous fine weather, Noyce could not resist the temptation to be voracious in his peak-bagging. On 12th September he thought he would follow a guidebook route up the north side of Aksoual, some 5,500ft (1,800m) above the village, but was seduced by a 600-foot buttress which provided a mild Severe climb to the ridge and a subsidiary summit, Tazegzaout n Louah. He thought that this might have been a first ascent. From there he '...*took another line of tempting clochetons*' to Azrou n Tamadout, 12,664ft (3,857m) and then carried on down back to Tachdirt where a band of musicians was leading festivities in the village for the second night running.

Noyce took in the one remaining major summit, Anrhemer, 12,773ft (3,890m) on the following day and descended to the small village of Timechi, near the Ourika Valley, where they slept on the verandah of the rest-house. On 14th September the party had a long, hot day's walk to another small village where they spent '...*a night as hot as any I have ever tried to sleep through.*' In the morning they left at 6.00 and in a temperature over 40°C (104°F) they walked the thirty miles (forty-eight kilometres) and were back in Asni by 13.00. He comments, '...*nowhere more keenly than in the Atlas have I enjoyed:*

The silence that is in the starry skies,
The sleep that is in the lonely hills.

He still took enormous pleasure in the same speed, stamina and rhythm of movement which he had enjoyed two and three decades before when, after a full day's climbing in North Wales, he would go for a long walk over Snowdon. Inside two weeks he climbed enough mountains to satisfy most of us for four.

Godalming Borough Council

In addition to his literary and school activities Wilfrid Noyce began to participate in civic affairs. The town of Godalming had already recognised his exploits on Everest in 1953 and he consequently presented himself for the local elections of 1955.

Wilf certainly had his arm twisted to take on this additional voluntary work while his heart was always in his writing. Brian Young was keen on maintaining a relationship with the town. Anyway, once he was persuaded, Wilf got on with the job.[47]

On 12th May 1955 Noyce was elected to Godalming Borough Council for a period of three years, polling 2,684 votes, the second highest that year, in a turnout of 45.55 per cent.

He was an active councillor and played a full part. He was appointed immediately to the Civil Defence, Health, Library and Public Grounds committees. On the first Council meeting of the new session on 23rd May 1955 he was confirmed as Vice-Chairman of the Library Committee and a year later was elected Chairman. Stanley Dedman, a Godalming historian wrote,

It was, like everything else he tackled, a matter of supreme importance that the interest of the Library service and the happiness of both borrowers and staff should be his personal concern; he took great interest in the individual members of the staff, being generous when one was married, and extending the hospitality of his home to Committee and staff alike.[48]

Noyce led this committee in its oversight of the County Branch Library in Godalming and the Godalming Museum fostering considerable interest in the museum. Both organisations continue to flourish and the volunteers in the archive section continue to be kept busy with enquiries from many quarters. Literary evenings for young people were started and Noyce would support these with readings, lectures and the presentation of prizes.

He became a member of the Youth Committee in 1955 and later advanced to membership of the Finance, Planning, Public Grounds and Selection committees – perhaps the key committees of the council, while relinquishing membership of Civil Defence and Health. Noyce attended regularly the meetings of all the committees of which he was a member and in spite of his absences in the Himalaya and the erratic demands made on a public school master he had a record comparable to those of his less peripatetic colleagues. It was a commitment of one meeting per week on average for eleven months in the year, not including the public appearances he made in support of civic events. He also used his position to strengthen the town's links with Charterhouse.

As part of this he established the Social Services Group at Charterhouse which carried out projects of benefit to the local Godalming and District community, one notable being the redecoration of St. Thomas' Hall in Godalming.

One of his first acts as chairman of the Library Committee was recorded by the Council.

31.5.55 Library Committee[49]
104 Library Association – Youth Libraries Association
On 6th July members would visit Godalming and Charterhouse and hear a lecture on Everest from Wilfrid Noyce in the school lecture theatre.

The meetings of the Godalming Borough Council and the various sub-committees continued to take a considerable amount of his time.

A measure of his conscientiousness, he came back specially from the Alps in time for municipal committee meetings on 30th August 1955. He himself chaired the Library Committee and was at the Civil Defence Committee when they discussed a recruiting poster for the organisation. Shortly afterwards he returned to the Alps.

The Public Grounds committee at its meeting on 7th November, when Noyce offered his apologies for absence, produced the memorable minute;

As it took one man with a fork three weeks to spike a bowling green, and with a spiking machine the same task could be done in one hour, the committee recommended the purchase of a machine for £120.

It was not only the youth at Charterhouse in which Noyce was interested but he adopted the young of Godalming as his constituency as a councillor. He was frequently to be seen presenting prizes and trophies and gave unstinting encouragement to the Godalming Boys' Club.

A little later a Godalming Borough Council minute records:

30.10.56 Library Committee Chairman Councillor Noyce
712. MODEL OF EVEREST EXPEDITION 1953

A model of Everest and its approaches constructed by boys of Charterhouse had been lent to the Library by the Chairman with a display of mountaineering books. The model would ultimately be kept in Charterhouse Museum.'

On their return from Nepal in 1957, in spite of Noyce's doubts about whether Cox and he could say that they had reached the actual summit of Machapuchare, they were greeted with considerable local acclaim. The school was given a half-day holiday for this 'notable achievement.'[50] The Borough Council welcomed him back with a very thoughtful Minute:

27.6.57 Monthly meeting
270. Mr Councillor Noyce

The Mayor told the Council that he had sent to Councillor Noyce on behalf of the Borough a cable of congratulations on his successful ascent of an hitherto unclimbed mountain in the Himalayas. The Mayor went on to say that in days when the spirit of adventure seemed to be dying a desire and love of discovery was something worthwhile. Added to that was the courage involved in climbing an unknown mountain never climbed before. There was, besides the courage of climbing, the courage in leaving a wife and two small children allowing her husband to go on the expedition.

and later:

25.7.57 Monthly meeting
408. Mr Councillor Noyce

The Mayor welcomed Councillor Noyce after his absence and presented him with an ink-stand inscribed as follows:-
Presented by the Mayor of Godalming Councillor Bernard F. Grillo, J.P. To Councillor C.W.F. Noyce to mark his ascent of Machapuchare, Nepal 1957.'

His great interest in young people and encouraging them to be both adventurous and of service to the community meant that he was always in demand at schools and youth clubs. He took considerable interest in the candidates for the Noyce Trophy and he always tried to be at the ceremony on 29th May, the anniversary of the first ascent of Everest, when the trophy was presented. He was regularly invited to present awards to young people who had distinguished themselves, and was always ready to add lustre to a school speech-day, particularly if any of his friends or relations were involved. His niece Joanna particularly remembers his visit to Tormead, the girls' school at Guildford. Noyce spoke with his usual enormous enthusiasm about the mountains. '*The lecture stood out above all the others.*'[51]

His devotion to the public service was recognised when he was re-elected to a second three-year term on 8th May 1958 on Godalming Council polling 2,109 votes – the highest number of votes that year with a turnout of 38.88 per cent. He remained Chairman of the Library Committee and was more active than previously with membership of the Finance and General Purposes, Highways and Sewers, Planning, Public Grounds and Selection committees. His membership of the Council and the various sub-committees was a considerable source of pride to his family, and some amusement at his participation in deliberations on sewers and drains in which he was not credited with enormous expertise!

However, the classroom continued to be where Noyce spent most of his time, any spare moments were taken up with council duties, speaking engagements and writing. At the Youth Revue, the climax of Godalming's 1958 Youth Week, Noyce presented the Noyce Trophy to eighteen-year old Peter Farrer, in recognition of his 1,750-mile cycle ride solo through Yugoslavia and Austria.

David Gould, Noyce's companion from basic training in the Welsh Guards depot and his first Himalayan expedition, was by now senior master at Mount Grace Comprehensive School, Potters Bar. In December 1958 Noyce was invited to present the prizes at the school. Comprehensive schools had recently been introduced and for many people the 'jury was still out'. After a speech from the headmaster, Mr. I. A. McBeath, illustrating the success of the school, Noyce, in presenting the prizes said that he welcomed the ending of the eleven-plus examination in Middlesex: *"I once tried to do it but got so hopelessly muddled up I dared not show it to anyone."*[52]

Towards the end of 1959 Godalming Council, on Noyce's initiative, set up a sub-committee to find a site for the new Godalming Youth Centre. Noyce inevitably was part of this. A site was chosen very close to the town centre and he was an honoured guest when the Centre was opened on 6th June 1962 just before he left for the Pamirs.

By the beginning of 1960 increasing financial independence was encouraging Noyce to think more seriously about becoming a full-time writer with perhaps just a part-time job. He would move away from Charterhouse and with the Karakoram expedition in view it was an opportune time to resign from the borough council, particularly as it would give time for a new candidate to appear in sufficient time before the next elections. He resigned from the council on 12th May 1960.

Family life

At the beginning of 1955 Wilfrid and Rosemary were settling in to family life. Michael was two and a half years old and Jeremy was six months. It meant that mountain trips would share the school holidays with family activities although as the boys grew older the two did sometimes coincide. Jeremy remembers that they went to North Wales in spring and to Cornwall in summer, after his father had returned from his annual Alpine trip.

Noyce's election to the borough council in 1955 appears to have precluded a summer holiday with the family that year. However, during Wilfrid's absences in the mountains Rosemary and the boys would spend some time with Rosemary's family in Cheshire, with Frida Leakey in Cambridge or they would take a house at Wittering in Sussex when Wilfrid's sister Rosalind would join them.

After Wilfrid's return from the Alps in August 1956, in the September, before term started, the Noyce family took the first of several holidays at Ardensawah farm at Porthcurno, near Land's End, owned then by Winnie and James Hocking. Michael and Jeremy enjoyed sunshine and sand-castles and there were outings to the dolmen, stone circles, St. Michael's Mount and the moors. Noyce photographed all these events with the same devotion as he did on the mountains.

As ***Climbers' Club Guidebook*** Editor he produced an updated version of the Guide to the Cornwall cliffs and the holidays at Porthcurno enabled him to keep up with developments.

It was a busy winter for Noyce with the preparations for the expedition to Machapuchare, reviewing books, council work and all the activities associated with school. At the end of March he departed for Nepal.

Following his return from Nepal at the end of June 1957 the family spent the summer together in Godalming and with Wilfrid's mother at her home in Grayshott. Tenzing Norgay, the Sirdar of the successful 1953 Everest expedition visited them in July and in September the family went again to the farm in Porthcurno for a week and Wilfrid's sister Rosalind again joined them.

The autumn of 1957 passed with council meetings, Scout meetings and a Mallory Group meet at Stone Farm when Noyce introduced his sons Michael, by then aged five, and Jeremy, three, to the delights of rock-climbing. Recent discussions with Jeremy suggest that this was the first of a rare number of times that the sons participated in the activity that impassioned their father. This is not an unusual phenomenon. The sustained absences that passionate commitment to a hobby might demand very often alienates the offspring and unfortunately Noyce was not to have the opportunity to reduce that distance as the boys grew older. He would certainly have become very conscious of this and his nature would have ensured that he restored close links with his children in their adolescence.

In the Easter holidays of 1958, rather than organising a meet for the Mallory Group or skiing in the Alps, Noyce's other great interest asserted itself and Rosemary and Wilfrid took a holiday *à l'amoureux* in Italy. They visited Pompeii and the Amalfi coast and together peered over the rim of Vesuvius. The trip concluded with a visit to Florence.

Noyce started his summer holidays in 1958 with the usual visit to Chamonix and in the September had a week with the family, including sister Rosalind, at Porthcurno. The boys have very good recollections of these holidays as they were able to spend all the time with their father and share his enthusiasm for the outdoors.

Towards the end of 1958 the planning of the Anglo-American Karakoram Expedition began to intrude. There was a hope that it should take place the following year but it took longer to set up than expected. It finally happened in 1960.

As a family they maintained strong links with 'The Prof', Professor Arthur Pigou, and would visit him in his house in the Lake District. Michael had been given Gatesgarth as one of his names in recognition of this very strong connection. In March 1959 The Prof died. This was a considerable blow to the Noyce family. He had been a loyal supporter and amiable mentor of Noyce's activities throughout his life, had given strong encouragement to Noyce's writing and had seen most of his books in draft. Noyce was appointed Pigou's literary executor and heir, and the legacy he received from Pigou enabled him to think seriously about giving up teaching and starting to write full-time.[53] It did take a little while for this idea to mature as the life in a big school was very captivating and

Rosemary was an active participant being involved particularly in the dramatic productions of both the boys and the staff.

In the summer of 1959 Noyce was in the Alps with the team for the Karakoram expedition and in September the family all went to Porthcurno. As the boys were getting older, they were able to do some gentle climbs on the cliffs that year. Then it was back to school and the preparations for the following year's expedition.

The family holiday in 1960 was spent in Snowdonia shortly after the school Easter climbing meet. Jeremy and Michael and some of their friends who had joined them on holiday were introduced to the lakes and hills that their father had adopted as his native heath. During this time Noyce took a few hours away from the family and walked on his own over all the Welsh peaks over 3,000 feet.[54]

Wilfrid and Rosemary were up in Wales again for the Everest reunion weekend in the May. On that occasion he was climbing with Geoff Smith when they met Dennis Davis who had been in the Karakoram in 1957. Davis warned,

> *Look out for the Nagar porters. They are bastards, that's what they are, bastards! Found one of them putting his hand in my rucksack pocket while I was having a rest.*[55]

July, August and early September were spent in the Karakoram and he returned to Godalming for his last year as a schoolmaster. It was a busy year with public engagements, lectures and the regular school activities and it was quite a wrench when they came to the end of the summer term in 1961.

On 16th August the Noyce family moved from Badgers Hollow to Hurstmere, the home of Lady Noyce at Grayshott, near Hindhead, the house to which she had moved when Sir Frank died in 1948.

At Hurstmere, the family were together. Michael and Jeremy were at the same preparatory school as their father had attended, St. Edmunds, which was within walking distance and it was an ideal base for Noyce's literary activities. He was in demand as a speaker and had a very busy programme of lectures. One that gave him particular pleasure was one he gave in November 1960 at Malvern Girls School.

At the end of September 1961 Sir John Hunt was invited to be leader of an Alpine Club – Scottish Mountaineering Club – expedition to climb with Russian mountaineers in the Pamirs, the highest mountains in what was then the Soviet Union. Hunt asked his old friend and long-term climbing companion Wilfrid Noyce to join the party. Noyce, at the age of forty-three, was very reluctant to accept. This was a considerable disruptive intrusion as he was working on a number of literary projects. He had hoped that the expedition to Trivor would be his last and Rosemary wanted him to give up serious climbing. However, his idealism and the prospect of fresh exploration added to Hunt's persuasiveness. It was at the height of the Cold War and thus presented an exciting challenge. Noyce eventually agreed to go and was heavily involved in the preparations of the expedition until he left for Russia and the Pamirs on 30th June 1962.

Notes

1. *Charterhouse Mallory Group Log 1955 (Charterhouse Mountaineering Club)*
2. Carthusian word for class-room
3. *Mallory Group Log 1955*
4. F. E. Ross, letter in CCJ vol. VII p.95 and E. A. Baker, *Scouts and Outposts* CCJ 1905 n°28 p.176
5. *Mallory Group Log 1956*
6. *Ibid*
7. Peter Norton, *Mallory Group Log*
8. *The Surrey Advertiser 31.8.1957*
9. Martyn Berry, *Note of 20.10.1996,* Balliol Coll Archives
10. Peter Norton, *Letter to Wilfrid Noyce April 1960*
11. *Mallory Group Log*
12. Keith Simpson, Troop Leader, *Senior Scout Log*
13. *Senior Scout Log*
14. Collective name for the Teaching Staff at Charterhouse
15. Wilfrid Noyce, *Untrodden Peaks, Geographical Journal March 1957 p.83*
16. *Sunday Times 10.11.1957*
17. Wilfrid Noyce, *Climbing the Fish's Tail p.138*
18. Wilfrid Noyce, *The Himalayas Since Everest, The Observer 6.10.1957*
19. Wilfrid Noyce, *letter to Editor of Manchester Guardian 11.1955*
20. Richard Hillary flew under the Severn Bridge, with inches to spare, during WWII, out of sheer bravado. He was not the first.
21. Wilfrid Noyce, *Springs of Adventure p.44*
22. George Band, *Everest, The Official History p.241*
23. *Times Literary Supplement 12.12.1958*
24. King's College, *Annual Review, Obituary of Wilfrid Noyce, November 1962*
25. David Cox, *Wilfrid Noyce Obituary AJ 1963*
26. See Jim Perrin, *Menlove ch 8* for a detailed account of Edwards last troubled years

27 Kevin Fitzgerald, *Review CCJ 1961 p.258*
28 MG Hughes, *Review CCJ 1962 p.385*
29 *The Observer 10.7.1955*
30 John Hunt & David Cox, Wilfrid Noyce 1917-1962: Some Personal Memories *AJ 1993 p.67*
31 *Ibid* p.68
32 *Wilfrid Noyce, The Listener 20.10.1955*
33 John Hunt & David Cox, Wilfrid Noyce 1917-1962, Some Personal Memories *AJ 1993 p.68*
34 *Ibid p.68*
35 *Telephone conversation with Richard Brooke 1.12.2008*
36 *Wilfrid Noyce, 'Mont Blanc Revisited', The Listener 20.10.1955*
37 John Hunt, More About the Fifties *AJ 1992 p.117*
38 John Hunt & David Cox, *Wilfrid Noyce 1917-1962, Some Personal Memories AJ 1993 p.69*
39 This whole episode is described by Noyce in his Night Life on High Hills, *Climbers' Club Journal 1957 p.40*
40 John Hunt, More about the Fifties *AJ 1992*
41 Peter Norton, *Email of 29.8.2011*
42 Wilfrid Noyce, *Trivor Log*
43 Colin Mortlock, *The Spirit of Adventure p111*
44 Talk *BBC Woman's Hour 25.2.1963*
45 *Wilfrid Noyce,* New Climbs *CCJ 1962 p.365*
46 Wilfrid Noyce, Climbing Solo in the High Atlas *AJ 1962 p.65*
47 Rosemary Ballard, *Note to author 3.7.2010*
48 *Godalming Borough Archive*
49 *Godalming Borough Council (GBC) Minutes of 30.6.1955*
50 *Mallory Group Log*
51 Conversation with Joanna Hewitt, 10.5.2009
52 *The Press and News* 6.12.1958 (North London & South Herts)
53 King's College, *Annual Review, Obituary of Wilfrid Noyce, November 1962*
54 David Cox Wilfrid Noyce Obituary *AJ 1963*
55 Wilfrid Noyce, *To the Unknown Mountain p.24*

CHAPTER FOURTEEN

THE PAMIRS 1962

A group of Russian mountaineers visited the United Kingdom in the summer of 1960 and climbed extensively in both Wales and Scotland. Out of this very successful visit emerged proposals for expeditions to Russia from both the Scottish Mountaineering Club (SMC), and the Alpine Club. The SMC and the Alpine Club each made separate approaches initially to the USSR Mountaineering Federation which eventually agreed to receive up to twelve British climbers in the Pamirs for sixty-five days from 30th June 1962. There were lengthy discussions on the composition of the British party and the expedition finally went forward under the aegis of the SMC, the AC and the Climbers' Club (CC). It was a difficult expedition to lead as some of the internal British relationships were not easy and there was the added dimension of working very closely with the Russians, who seemed to change at no notice the arrangements that had been agreed months before, creating unexpected delays and changes in plan. John Hunt was perhaps the only mountaineer with the experience, authority and approach who could have led the party.

The members of the expedition were:

Sir John Hunt, Leader	Director Duke of Edinburgh's Award Scheme		
		London	AC and CC
Malcolm Slesser	Lecturer	Glasgow	SMC
	Deputy Leader, British party		
Kenneth Bryan	Sales Executive	Glasgow	SMC
Joe Brown	Mountain Instructor	Buxton	Rock and Ice
Derek Bull	Insurance executive	London	AC
Ralph Jones	Asst Works Manager	Manchester	AC
George Lowe	Teacher	Derby	AC
Ian McNaught-Davis	Sales manager	London	AC and CC

Graeme Nicol	Pathologist	Aberdeen	SMC and AC
Wilfrid Noyce	Writer	Hindhead	AC and CC
Robin Smith		Edinburgh	SMC
Edward 'Ted' Wrangham	Farmer	Alnwick	AC
Anatole Ovchinnikov	Leader, Russian party Technical teacher	Moscow	
Nikolai Alchutov	Radio engineer	Moscow	
Eugene Grippenreiter	Foreign relations Commission, USSR Ministry of Sport	Moscow	
Vladimir Malachov	Hydro-electrical engineer	Moscow	
Anatole Sevastianov	Lecturer	Moscow	
Nikolai Shalaev	Carpenter	Moscow	

Slesser wrote:

> *"What is Noyce like?" I asked a fellow member who knew him. He replied using the idiom of the Sixties, "He's just not with it". When I later got to know this excellent man, I realised what was meant by this cryptic reply. He was a poet and a thinker. He could be close beside you, yet far away in thought, but when with you in thought, he was the most delightful of companions.*[1]

The Russians trained rigorously under strict supervision and as a result were very much fitter than their British colleagues. Their criteria for the success of an expedition were also different. A Russian expedition, to really succeed, had to get all the climbers to the summit. In addition several of the Russians were expecting to do climbs to qualify as Masters of Sport, a status of considerable prestige in the Soviet Union which also gave them the freedom to choose their own destinations in the mountains. The British expeditions, in contrast, operated as a team and achieved a successful expedition with the most suitable two, or three climbers, reaching the summit. The Russians were very happy that Hunt should be the overall leader of the expedition.

There were meetings of the British climbers every two months from September 1961 and in March 1962 they had a gathering at The Charles Inglis Clarke Memorial Hut on Ben Nevis. This was the first opportunity they had of climbing together and it was very successful. Noyce climbed the Tower Gap West Chimney with Slesser and another Scot, Graeme Nicol, the expedition doctor, who had recently finished his National Service with the Special Air Service (SAS).

Slesser wrote:

> *I was intrigued by Noyce's fitness and relaxed climbing technique. The next day I had another delightful climb with Noyce and I shall always remember his effortless technique and confidence as we came down the steep frozen slope at the end of the day. A slip could not have been checked. We wore crampons and there was Wilf, pipe in mouth, axe under one arm, nonchalantly walking down the slope as if it were his garden path.*[2]

Joe Brown and Robin Smith, the doyen of young Scottish climbers, a brilliant academic, and the youngest of the group, took immediately to Noyce. These three Hunt regarded as the best performers on the mountain.

Noyce played his full part in the preparations, obtaining maps and photographs of the area from Moscow and other sources. They were going to climb Pik Kommunizma, now named Ismail Somoni, 24,606ft (7,495m). Pik Garmo, 21,637ft (6,595m) had a vast unclimbed flank and there were other peaks above 19,500ft (6,000m). At the last meeting in May 1961 the objectives of the expedition were established and it was agreed that they would climb as many of the major peaks as possible, rather than try to put up new ascents on other summits.

In June 1961 Slesser left Britain taking the baggage and equipment by train and reached Moscow the day before the other British members arrived by plane on 1st July. At the Hotel Armenia the first members of the expedition he saw were Derek Bull and Noyce, '*…dressed in a tropical suit, was very much the Englishman abroad*', and the others arrived shortly afterwards. They had longer than expected to do their sightseeing in Moscow, then on 4th July flew to Dushanbe, the capital of the Republic of Tajikistan, where they met the Russian members of the expedition. The equipment was sent on up to Tavildara, a town on the edge of the Pamir mountains, from where they would walk for a few days up to the Base Camp at Avodara, some seven miles above the snout of the Garmo Glacier, at that time.[3]

They spent several days in Dushanbe during which time they visited the Lake of Communist Youth and several of them were tempted to enjoy a swim. As they did not have swimming costumes some of them swam wearing their underpants:

> *In full view of a rapidly swelling crowd such dignified figures as John Hunt, Wilfrid Noyce, Ted Wrangham and Ken Bryan would make for the water, covering the intervening fifty yards in a bunch, a process which had about as much dignity to it as convicts heading for a delousing chamber.*[4]

They also had a day with the Tajik Mountaineering Club when they visited a *kishlak* or collective farm where there were nine families.

The collaboration with the Russians had to be managed quite carefully and Hunt suggested that the Russian speakers, Noyce, Jones, Nicol, Slesser and himself should share tents with Russians. While a more spontaneous approach might have been preferred, this was accepted as the best way in the circumstances.

In Dushanbe they were told that they could not go to Tavildara. It was clearly a sensitive area. (In 2009 it was still a refuge of jihadis in from Afghanistan and the author of this book was asked by the British Ambassador in Dushanbe whether we had seen any security activity when we passed through at the end of September.) This was a blow as they had expected to see the country and people on the way in to the mountains to provide pictures and articles for journals in order to defray expenses. On 6th July they went by plane to Jirgatal, a town some 160 miles north-east of Dushanbe in the Vakhsh Valley. The same morning helicopters, at the limit of their performance, took them into the Garmo Valley, crossing the dramatic Peter the Great Range with its peaks of over 13,000ft (4,000m) and deposited them at the snout of the Garmo Glacier. This was some 2,000 feet below their planned Base Camp at Avodara and seven miles farther down the valley. They were not pleased at having to move most of their equipment up to Avodara in a series of daily carries. Hunt managed to arrange that helicopters bringing a large group of Spartak climbers should delay their return and drop some loads for them at Avodara and the first two camps above there. The three who went with the supply-drops to Camp III came back exhilarated with what they had seen and this boosted morale enormously.

In between carries Noyce was writing articles for the **Daily Herald**. He subsequently, on 15th July, pioneered the route up to Camp II with the Russian Ovchinnikov, who had been there before and marked the trail across the moraine, *'the foulest ground imaginable'* – to quote Slesser – with cairns. Noyce, although older than most of the party was still able to get up from Avodara to Camp II in four and a half hours, while other British were taking six hours!

The entire expedition moved up to Camp III, at some 14,000ft (4,260m) where they divided themselves into three groups for the first phase of the trip. Each group consisted of four Britons and two Russians. Hunt led one group consisting of George Lowe, Ralph Jones, Graeme Nicol, Eugene Grippenreiter and Nikolai (Kolia) Shalaev; Slesser led the second group consisting of Ian McNaught-Davis, Joe Brown, Kenneth Bryan, Nikolai (Kolia) Alchutov and Vladimir Malachov: Noyce's team, the strongest, consisted of Ted Wrangham, Derek Bull, Robin Smith, Anatole Sevastianov and Anatole (Tolia) Ovchinnikov. Hunt's group was going to climb a peak they named later Concord; Slesser's had peak Patriot as their objective, and Noyce and his team were going for Garmo, the west face of which was unclimbed and a considerable challenge, although Hunt had said to Noyce not to push too hard for this face as it was well covered in snow and formidable – the last words they exchanged.

On 18th July the three groups set off from Camp III agreeing to be back there by 27th July for the second phase of the trip. They had a simple method of signalling between groups; each had flares, green for 'everything OK', red for distress. Noyce's party in fact descended to Base Camp to rest for two days and then on 20th July moved up to Camp III at the bottom of the Vavilova Glacier. The following day this party moved up the glacier and went on up the icefall to establish a camp on the moraine below the flank of Mount Garmo. Smith, who had made a hit with the Russians as they appreciated his fitness – he was probably the fittest of the British – and his lively approach, was in a tent with the Russians and Noyce, Bull and Wrangham were in the other. Ovchinnikov noted:

> *The English had settled in with comfort – they had pyjamas and read English translations of Tolstoy and Dostoyevsky before they went to sleep.*[5]

The following day Ovchinnikov led them up through deep snow in very poor visibility towards the ridge. He asked Sevastianov to lead the last bit and when they reached the ridge they were exhausted and so pitched their tents. On 23rd July the weather had worsened and visibility was still very poor but they took down the tents and went along the ridge in the hope that the weather would improve. When they reached the end of the ridge they were on the edge of snowfields. Not wishing to risk avalanches or losing their way in the poor visibility they pitched camp at approximately 18,000ft (5,500m). At that time they thought they were 700 metres below the summit and it would be possible to reach the summit and descend in the same day. In the evening the sky cleared and it became colder.

On 24th July they were up early and Noyce was prepared to start before dawn. The Russians asked to wait until after sunrise to warm their boots. They did not want to risk frostbite. The British had felt-lined boots and did not have the same risk. The sun appeared about 6.00 and they set off. The two Russians had Noyce between them on the rope and Smith, Wrangham and Bull made up the second rope and followed slowly. The first rope stopped for a rest awaiting the others then Smith appeared on his own. The other two '...*were not confident enough to move together up such ground, and to have climbed it in pitches would have delayed the party too much*', and returned to their tent. Noyce undid one of his ropes and gave the end to Smith, so that Ovchinnikov was now climbing with Smith. There were now two ropes of two. The Russians led up the hard snow slope and they reached snow-covered rocks. The Russians took their crampons off as they had boots with tricouni nails. The other two, with Vibram soles, kept their crampons on. The Russians generously asked Smith if he would like to lead, which he did very capably on the rock parts but the Russians were concerned with the level of acclimatisation and fitness of Noyce and Smith and that they were not making fast enough progress so Ovchinnikov took over the lead. He gave the lead back to Smith for the last bit so that he could be the first at the top, his first 6,000-metre summit which they reached at about 15.00. Ovchinnikov noted at the summit that both Noyce and Smith were exhausted. It had been 1,300ft (395m) higher than they had expected. Sevastianov wrote that if they had known that they would have put in two intermediate camps from 18,000ft (5,500m).[6]

After a short rest when Noyce and Smith appeared to recover their strength they started to descend with Noyce leading Sevastianov and Smith leading the second rope. As they started to descend they could see their tents below. The first part was over rocks.

When they reached the end of the rocks and the beginning of the snow-slope, they stopped to enable the Russians to put on their crampons. Smith '...*suggested that to save time, he and Wilf should rope together and continue, leaving the Russians to follow.*[7] After Smith's suggestion they made a joint decision tacitly to descend in the way they did with a mutual responsibility to each other for the decision they took and its consequences. There was no discussion of how they would proceed although it was the first time that they were on a rope together. Noyce also did not want to rest.[8]

The following account of what happened at that point is based on several, at times, conflicting sources who have given 'eye-witness' accounts over a considerable period. Memories are unreliable and perceptions change with each telling over the passage of time. Hunt swore Ovchinnikov to secrecy about who had slipped first in the belief that he was the only eye-witness. This was

> *...for the benefit of the lay world, and in particular, the media, the back-biting and accusations that would have flown if it became known who fell first would have caused endless and damaging debate that would percolate far beyond the small world of mountaineers to the press and public.*[9]
>
> The pact of secrecy was designed to hush up details of the accident, not just from the Soviet authorities in Moscow but from the other expedition members and the British press. Only five others were "in the know:" the two Russians on the mountain that day, Anatole Ovchinnikov and Anatole Sevastianov, Ted Wrangham's climbing partner, Derek Bull, since deceased; Sir John (later Lord) Hunt, expedition leader (died 1998), and Eugene Grippenreiter, expedition member and Soviet Information Officer (died 1997).[10]

Ovchinnikov wrote thirty years later:

> *When we got down from the cliff* [presumably the summit rocks] *I saw Tolya* [Sevastianov] *doing up his crampons and Wilfrid continuing down the snow slope. Robin was standing by Tolya. That moment Robin untied himself from my rope and put him* [Tolya] *on to mine. He then tied on to Wilfrid's rope, telling us to follow. We were not in a hurry. I was doing up my crampons. Suddenly Tolya Sevastianov cried out, "They have fallen". I raised my head but couldn't see anyone on the slope. Sevastianov explained that he too was doing up his crampons and had raised his head and saw a rucksack hurtling down* [Wilfrid had a rucksack] *the*

slope, which was quite gentle and we were not anxious until we got to the brow of the slope and couldn't see anyone.[11]

Sevastianov told Cruickshank:

...I had put my crampons on before Ovchinnikov and as I stood there, I watched Robin and Wilf descend. The slope gradually became steeper and steeper and first of all one of them (I couldn't say who it was) disappeared over a crest on the slope and then the second one began to move out of sight. When I could only see the upper part of his body, something strange happened. If before the figure had been moving slowly and at an even pace, even now he disappeared in a flash from my field of vision. I can't say what happened. I can only say that I saw the figure hurtling downwards. Either he fell himself or he was sharply jerked by the rope. I don't know for sure. But, rerunning that scene through my mind again and again, I am more inclined to think that the upper figure was jerked sharply from below.[12]

Noyce and Smith, who were now on an almost fully extended rope, had continued to descend following the path of the ascent. The Russians had advised them not to descend by a certain snow couloir.[13] However, they did descend the couloir successfully, then crossed some rocks on to a snow slope. Then Noyce reached a gully which he began to run across;[14] Derek Bull, from 2,000 feet below saw him run and then called Wrangham:

Derek went out of the tent to check their progress and I heard his voice, "Ted, Ted, there is something terribly wrong; I think they have fallen." He had seen what he feared were two bodies flash past down a great gully of which a short section was visible to us. Hoping against hope that he was wrong, we scrambled across to a point from which we could just see the two bodies lying some 3000ft below. At the time we did not know which two it was.[15]

"One of them slipped, that's the answer," was John's analysis. A rope of two moves as one mind. If they moved together it would be a joint decision. The question of who slipped was not the question of who was to blame.[16]

Smith and Noyce were keen to descend as quickly as possible and belaying and pitching would have delayed them. They were, however, very tired, elated and probably relaxed having reached the summit and being on a not very difficult descent. It was also the first time they had been roped together. Each was one of the most brilliant mountaineers of his generation and both had also great promise in other fields of endeavour. They were both very experienced and highly competent with a confidence, agility, skill and endurance out of the ordinary. Under other conditions they might have taken such a slip in their stride. The combination of factors was nonetheless conducive to an accident.

John Hunt wrote afterwards:

It was 6.20 p.m. So died two outstanding British mountaineers.[17]

Jimmy Cruickshank wrote:

Gordon Greig, Robin's former lecturer in Logic (died 2006), referred to a poem as he recalled Robin – Browning's 'A Grammarian's Funeral' which they had studied together. "I quote the closing verse, slightly altered to embrace both the Climber and the Scholar," Greig wrote, "stressing the thought in the penultimate line, all too conscious of the real, not so gentle, irony that Robin and I had once carelessly, as academic exercise, weighed the poet's verdict in this honouring:

> ***Here's the top-peak; the multitude below***
> ***Live, for they can, there:***
> ***This man decided both to Live and Know—***
> ***Bury this man there?***
> ***Here – here's his place, where meteors shoot, clouds form,***
> ***Lightenings are loosened,***
> ***Stars come and go! Let joy break with the storm,***
> ***Peace let the dew send!***
> ***Lofty designs must close in like effects:***
> ***Loftily lying,***
> ***Leave him – still loftier than the world suspects,***
> ***Living and dying."***

Robin's fate ever to rest midst lofty heights might be poetically inspiring, but he – indeed Wilf – were victims of rotten luck when chance factors coincided to provoke the disaster. We know from the book that Wilf Noyce set off down the fatal slope on his own when the Russians stopped to fit crampons, and that he was a rope's length ahead by the time Robin reorganised the ropes. As Robin followed, Wilf ran across a gully, seemingly as Robin was still in the process of tying on to the rope previously attached to Wilf's Russian. At any rate, the sudden jerk on the near-taut rope pulled both men off the mountain during the briefest of windows when Robin was helpless to provide protection or save himself. Never before had Wilf and Robin been roped together. However, let's not dwell on that remarkable coincidence.

Rather, let's leave their spirits at peace, above the multitude, on heights which meet with Browning's and Greig's approval, where stars come and go, meteors shoot, clouds form, and 'lightenings' are loosened – a fitting resting place, we too might feel if seeking consolation for a tragedy in which extraordinary quirks of fate make reality so gut-wrenching.[18]

Hunt's team after climbing Concord Peak came down and set off to meet the Noyce party. On 25th July they climbed up to 16,000ft (4,870m) and to their relief came across a Russian tent. They also saw two figures on the ridge descending. Hunt and Nicol continued up through the ice-fall on the tracks made by the Noyce party. They saw the figures closer and tried to communicate. They waited and sheltered from the heat in an ice-cave. After a while they started to move up a rock rib and then saw Bull and Wrangham below them on the glacier. Bull shouted the news up to Hunt and Nicol. The two Russians in the Noyce party, Sevastianov and Ovchinnikov had arrived by this time, and they all descended together to the Russian tent to spend the night, where Jones, Grippenreiter, Lowe and Shalaev were waiting for them. That evening they debated whether to bring the bodies down to Camp III among other choices. Any decision was left until they found the bodies.

At 6.00 on 26th July John Hunt with Lowe, Nicol, Jones, Ovchinnikov, Sevastianov, Shalaev, and Grippenreiter set off. Wrangham and Bull stayed behind to prepare for the return. They went up into the upper cwm and through the ice-fall until they reached the bottom of the ice-slope. Lowe and Grippenreiter stayed down to collect the gear that Bull had thrown down from the ridge two days before while the others climbed the 750ft (230m) ice-wall on two ropes. Hunt with Jones and Shalaev and Nicol with the other two Russians. The climbing was difficult, over a really steep stretch they were on the front points of their crampons. Then after a short ice-wall below the big Bergschrund, which was less difficult than feared, they reached the terrace where Noyce and Smith had come to rest side-by-side, still roped, as if they had lain down to sleep. They both had extensive injuries. Noyce was wearing the same blue anorak that he had worn when he led Anullu up to the South Col nine years before. Hunt wrote:

We decided not to bring them down. Why not, as at sea, bury them where they lay in the glacier? There was a deep crevasse at the lip of the terrace and we put them in there. It was a painful act, which proved to be too much for my composure as I helped with Wilf. [19]

The Russians saluted with three volleys from signal pistols and they started the descent.[20]

It was also the express wishes of Rosemary Noyce and Mrs. Smith that the bodies should be left in the glacier.[21]

Noyce had written in 1953 when he visited the grave of Mingma Dorji, a Sherpa who died on the 1952 Swiss Everest expedition, and was buried in the moraine of the Western Cwm:

I have no hopes or anxieties about my body after death; but I confessed to myself at Mingma's monument that the thought pleased me of resting here, where the eye passes in an instant from the little stone erection, up the 8,000-foot precipice of Everest to its summit; where the only company is the mist, the snowflakes and the choughs.[22]

This tragedy caused considerable anguish within the expedition. The Russians were determined to carry on with the programme but at the same time showed great sensitivity to the dilemma facing the British members. Hunt said that he could no longer go on climbing there after the loss of his friend and that he believed he was the right person to meet Noyce's widow and Smith's mother and to explain to the British public why the expedition continued the programme. He asked Malcolm Slesser to take his place as leader. Lowe, Bull and Wrangham decided to accompany Hunt home. The other British members stayed and climbed the main objective of the expedition, the highest mountain in the USSR, Pik Kommunizma, 24,590ft (7,495m).

When the party returned finally to Base Camp, mountaineers of the Sports Society Spartak, led by Vitale Abalakov, who shared the area with the British-Soviet expedition, had built a memorial to Noyce and Smith a few 100 yards up the valley from the camp. It overlooked the glacier and was in sight of Mount Garmo.

> *Good as their word, Spartak had built a memorial to Wilf and Robin, and before sunset we went up to dedicate it. It was simple and its setting beautiful. At its base was a recess, which Mac likened to a fireplace, within which stood a small boulder. Abalakov explained to me how he had spent several days seeking one that truly resembled the shape of Peak Garmo. Round the cap-stone was a Union Jack, obtained from Russian stores, for we had none, and an ice-axe was bound to the outside by a white shroud which bore in blue letters the Russian words, "To Robin Smith and Wilfrid Noyce, from all Soviet Alpinists." Flowers and a small wreath ornamented its base, where Abalakov had carved the inscription in regular bold lettering. There was a surprisingly large turn-out. Borovikov, the meek-looking moustachioed president of the U.S.S.R. Federation of Mountaineering had turned up from somewhere, and I asked him to share the dedication.*
>
> *"Mr Slesser," he said quietly, "We know you are Christians, and you know we are Communists, but we should like you to know that if you wish a Christian service, we shall be happy to join with you."*
>
> *He took the first part, giving a sincere, but prolix address, attending to the facts. My own contribution was briefer. I gave thanks and spoke of the beauty of the little cairn and its setting. I spoke of the bond it established between the climbers of our two countries, and in dedication we observed a short silence.*[23]

Notes

1. Malcolm Slesser, *Red Peak p.37*
2. *Ibid p.79*
3. The Garmo Glacier had retreated seven kilometres between 1932 and 2005. Tajik Agency on Hydrometeorology
4. Malcolm Slesser, *Red Peak p.93*
5. Anatole Ovchinnikov, quoted in J. Cruickshank, *High Endeavours, The Life and Legend of Robin Smith p.305*
6. *Ibid p.307*
7. John Hunt, *Life is Meeting p.189*
8. Anatole Sevastianov, quoted in J. Cruickshank, *High Endeavours, The Life and Legend of Robin Smith p.309*
9. Malcolm Slesser, *With Friends in High Places p.109*
10. Conversation Wrangham/Cruickshank reported to the author by Cruickshank in a note of 19.9.2012. Robin Smith's mother died in 1981. Robin's sister Marion and sister-in-law Claudie chose not to divulge this information while Noyce's widow was still alive.
11. Anatole Ovchinnikov, *Alpinists of the Moscow School* cited in *With Friends in High Places p.109*
12. Sevastianov, J. Cruickshank, *High Endeavours, The Life and Legend of Robin Smith p.309*
13. John Hunt, *Life is Meeting p.190*
14. This information was passed in confidence to Jimmy Cruickshank by Ted Wrangham some years before his death in June 2009. Wrangham and his climbing partner, who witnessed the accident, were by a tent 2,000 feet lower down.
15. Ted Wrangham, cited in J. Cruickshank, *High Endeavours, The Life and Legend of Robin Smith pp.310-1*
16. Malcolm Slesser, *Red Peak p.151-2*
17. John Hunt, *Life is Meeting p.190*
18. Jimmy Cruickshank, *Extract from an unpublished piece dated 2001*, in a note to the author of 19.9.2012
19. John Hunt, *Life is Meeting p.192*
20. Anatole Ovchinnikov, quoted in Jimmy Cruickshank, *High Endeavours, The Life and Legend of Robin Smith p.315*
21. John Hunt, quoted in Jimmy Cruickshank, *High Endeavours, The Life and Legend of Robin Smith p.319*
22. Wilfrid Noyce, *South Col, p.204*
23. Malcolm Slesser, *Red Peak p.219*

EPILOGUE

Wilfrid Noyce was a man of peace, he carried an ambience of tranquillity with him, whether listening quietly and intently to what one was saying or because his thoughts were focused on distant peaks and far away. He was also naturally inclusive, indifferent to racial and social distinctions as he showed in his expeditions and in his approach to mountain training in the army.

In a document found in his papers in Russia after his death, Noyce had written:

> *To be with those who thought and spoke quite differently, yet on common ground and with common aims – this might be a bridge, not only of my understanding of other men's motives in the sport of mountaineering, but perhaps even in a small way, of the gap separating East and West over all other fields of thought.*[1]

It is said that Hunt never forgave himself for persuading Noyce to join the expedition as the Noyces and the Hunts were very close as families. When Hunt was releasing the news of the accident, he asked that Joy, his wife, should go to Rosemary Noyce to inform her of Wilf's death. The Noyce boys, Michael and Jeremy were ten and eight when their father died and have little detailed recollection of him. Jeremy remembers him as a very loving father and taking great pleasure in their company and achievements. Rosemary had lived through Noyce's three major expeditions and numerous trips to the Alps and was no stranger to anxiety but his death was a huge blow. She expressed her feelings in a letter to Susan Bradshaw, the secretary of the Pamir Expedition.

> *I want to thank you Sue for being such a tower of strength during that first ghastly week – do you find, as I do that it seems even more appalling in retrospect than it did at the time? I just don't*

know how we all got through it, except that it proves beyond doubt that one is given special strength to cope on these dreadful occasions.

and further on,

The best thing for me is to be forward-looking, and to forget the immediate past as quickly as possible – there are so many happy memories to treasure.[2]

Enid, Lady Noyce, like Mrs. Smith, had lost a son and this was hard and another sort of grief. For all of them a remote death made it even harder as there was no funeral or service as a final farewell or closure for the family. Rosemary stayed on with Enid at Grayshott and in August 1962 sent the boys up to Cambridge to stay with Frida Leakey, ever the comforter and support of the Noyce family. Frida had written on hearing the news of Wilf:

Wilfrid Aug 1962
for Enid
You said,
"Myself and not my yellow hair"
My dear – yourself complete
Needed no yellow hair.
Strength rooted deep in gentleness
Shared yet immaculate;
Humble in wealth of man-gifts, brave
The course from that under-worded all.
The search, life-long, in whitened light
a beauty beckoned you –
You who were part of all you loved
Sleep quietly in the snows.

Wilfrid and Rosemary's closest friends provided enormous support and Ian Grimble, as godfather of Michael, was very conscious of the now fatherless boys when he wrote to Colin Leakey,

He [Wilfrid] *left more than my deserts with me, but I wonder whether he left more with anyone than with you Colin, whom he*

> *accompanied all through the formative years. How to convey this gift of himself back to his sons?*[3]

There were tributes to Noyce from many quarters. There were the obituaries in the national newspapers; **The Times** had a long obituary which ended, '*He was richly endowed in mind and body. But what his pupils, colleagues and countless friends will remember is a character exquisitely blended of courage, gentleness, modesty and integrity.*' The mountaineering and exploration journals were generous in their tributes.

There was a deep sense of loss in Surrey and the **Surrey Advertiser** printed a number of eulogies on 3rd August 1963 chronicling the many aspects of Noyce's involvement in the community. However, his spirit lived on in Godalming. Fittingly the Centre he had helped to establish was called the Wilfrid Noyce Youth Centre in his memory in the same year.

In Godalming he was regularly remembered at the youth centre and the annual presentation of The Wilfrid Noyce Trophy.

> *His widow Rosemary and sons Michael and Jeremy were present at the 25th anniversary celebrations* [of the Centre] *in October 1987.*[4] *Also there on that occasion was Brian Souter, the Mayor of Godalming, Charterhouse master, and Chairman of the Management Committee of the Centre.*

His life spanned not just one generation of mountaineers but the succeeding generations of the twentieth century. He had associated with and later climbed with the pioneers who had been active before the first war, of the quality of Bruce, Winthrop Young and Bradley; he had done his apprenticeship with the most significant climbers between the wars, such as the Kirkus brothers and Menlove Edwards, northerners to a man, and had continued after World War II to climb at a high level with the leading practitioners of the younger generation such as Don Whillans and Joe Brown. He fitted well with all the generations and was appreciated by them. In 1992, he was still being remembered in the **Alpine Journal**. His endurance, stamina and energy, sustained into his forties, made him a formidable man on the mountain right up to the end. Even in an expert group he would emerge as the natural leader as seen with the Trivor expedition.

There have been questions raised about Noyce's approach to safety.

The combination of his natural balance, sure-footedness, agility, strength and confidence seemed to be of a different order to that of other mortals.

> *It never seemed to occur to him in his own mountaineering field that other men were incapable of his almost mythical feats of strength and balance and endurance.*[5]

When climbing with others Noyce was always very solicitous for their safety, particularly if he felt that they lacked skill or experience. He was a very patient tutor on the mountain.

David Cox who had climbed with Noyce over a number of years said that on Machapuchare Wilf was a very safe and careful climber, although on other occasions his companions had sometimes to make sure that what they thought were appropriate safety measures were taken. He always accepted their insistence on roping or belaying. John Hunt wrote:

> *To climb with him on a Welsh crag, an Alpine or a Himalayan peak, was an object lesson in rhythm and balanced movement. Sometimes he seemed to be oblivious to the limitations of lesser men; after surviving three falls, on one of which I fielded him, I wondered whether he was aware that there were limits even to his own exceptional powers. Wilf was without guile or pretence; he was an easy person to be with. Though we had shared many mountain and social occasions together, I knew his mind was often away on some far peak.*[6]

Noyce was a mystic with his poet's sense of the spiritual and his indifference to material comforts. Personal discomfort never interfered with the achievement of an objective. For him there were '*the two Verities, yourself and the hill you climb*'.[7] His solo climbing, free of the constraints of the rope and companions enabled him to enjoy the freedom of a continuous rhythm of disciplined movement and the exhilaration of being alone with the mountain and nature. He felt a greater communion with nature when alone in the mountains. He was not religious. He was able to nonetheless appreciate a beautiful church and a well-constructed sermon and the early Quaker influences had given him a formidable moral compass. He wrote:

> *In a tricky position on a mountain I have felt a prayer rising in*

my throat and had to beat it down, because I felt it was a request rather than a communion and that it made nonsense to ask for things in a crisis unless one's whole life was of a pattern into which such a prayer naturally fitted. But the urge was a normal and reasonable one. Those who have that type of faith believe that they are saved because of their prayer. He believed that, *…energy which but for prayer would be bound is by prayer set free and operates in some part, be it objective or subjective of the world of facts.*[8]

Robin Hodgkin, Noyce's friend from Cambridge, and fellow-climber, expressed an analogous view, which Noyce himself cited:

The Christian who utters a prayer in the face of danger is seeking no miraculous help; he is willing (asking) that whatever power is available in his small being may be free to flow, unimpeded, into his action.[9]

Wilfrid Noyce spent his life trying to understand his own motivations and testing his limits in the surroundings which gave him strength, inspiration and solace. Not only was he a great explorer and mountaineer but also he had the gift of putting his emotions and sensibilities into imperishable prose and poetry. His legacy is not only his writings but in the number of young people he has inspired with the love of adventure, the desire to challenge themselves in the hills and mountains and his quiet and reassuring example.

EPILOGUE

A Prayer for Everest[10]
(Written before the mountain)

*That I may endure
And love of friends confirm me
That I lend my ear
Kindest to those who vex me;
That I may be strong,
My will guide the faint footsteps;
That heart and lung
May learn, rhythm is conquest;
That in the storm
My hand may stretch to help,
Not cringe in the glove to warm;
That courage of mine
Bring to friends courage too,
As I am brought by them;
That in the lottery
(My last, my worthiest prayer)
No envy bleed,
When, as I know my heart,
Others succeed.
Here be content, the thought:
I have done my part.*

Notes

1 'The Last Words of Wilfrid Noyce', *The Sunday Times* 19.8.1962
2 Rosemary Noyce to Susan Bradshaw, Letter cited by Jimmy Cruickshank, *High Endeavours*
3 Ian Grimble to Colin Leakey, *Letter of 14.8.1962*
4 *The* (Surrey) *Advertiser 9.10.1987*
5 Talk BBC *Woman's Hour*, 25.2.1963
6 John Hunt, *Life is Meeting* p.192
7 Wilfrid Noyce, *Mountains and Men p13*
8 Wilfrid Noyce, *They Survived p.194*
9 R.A. Hodgkin, *Article in the Guardian 11.1961*, cited in *They Survived p.107*
10 Wilfrid Noyce, original version in *South Col p.290*

APPENDIX A

PUBLICATIONS AND DOCUMENTS

BOOKS

Mountaineering

A Climber's Guide to Sonamarg, Kashmir, Himalayan Club, 1945, with *J. A. Jackson, T. H. Tilly and G. Whittle*
Mountains and Men, Geoffrey Bles, 1947
Scholar Mountaineers, Dennis Dobson, 1950
British Crags and Climbers, *with Edward Pyatt*, Dennis Dobson, 1952
South Col, William Heinemann, 1954
Everest is Climbed, *with Richard Taylor*, Puffin, 1954
Snowdon Biography, J. M. Dent & Sons, 1957, *with Geoffrey Winthrop Young and Geoff Sutton*
Climbing the Fish's Tail, Heinemann, 1958
To the Unknown Mountain, Heinemann, 1962
The Alps, Thames & Hudson, 1963, *with descriptive essays by Karl Lukan*
The Climber's Fireside Book (Comp), Heinemann, 1964
World Atlas of Mountaineering, Thomas Nelson, 1969, *edited and completed by Ian McMorrin,*

Poetry

Michael Angelo, William Heinemann, 1953
Poems, William Heinemann, 1960

Biography

Samson: The Life and Writings of Menlove Edwards, Private publication, 1960, *with Geoff Sutton*

Novel

The Gods are Angry, Heinemann, 1957

General

The Springs of Adventure, John Murray, 1958
They Survived, A Study of the Will to Live, Heinemann, 1962

Translation

Starlight and Storm, *with John Hunt;* J. M. Dent & Sons, 1955
From the French of ***Etoiles et Tempêtes*** by Gaston Rébuffat

Climbers' Club Guidebooks

Tryfan Group (Volume II), Climbers' Club, 1937
   J. M. Edwards, C. W. F. Noyce
Lliwedd Group (Volume IV), Climbers' Club, 1939
   C. W. F. Noyce, J. M. Edwards

Climbers' Club Guidebook Editor

Climbing Guides to the Snowdon District
Llanberis Pass (Volume VI) *by P. R. J. Harding*, Climbers' Club, 1950
Climbing Guides to the Snowdon District and Cornwall
Cornwall: Volume V *by A. W. Andrews and E. C. Pyatt*, Climbers' Club, 1950
The Carneddau (Volume VII) *by A. J. J. Moulam*, Climbers' Club, 1951
Llanberis Pass (Volume VI), Climbers' Club, 1955 *with R. Moseley Appendix of new climbs*

Cwm Silyn and Tremadoc, Climbers' Club, 1955, *Interim Guide by J. Neill*

Climbing in Cornwall, Climbers' Club, 1955, *a supplement by R. Goodier, P. H. & B. M. Biven*

Tremadoc, *a supplement by J. Neill*, Climbers' Club, 1956

Climbers' Club Guidebooks Series III, grey with no spine number
Climbing Guides to England and Wales,

Tryfan and Glyder Fach by A. J. J. Moulam, Climbers' Club, 1956

South-East England: Volume VIII, Climbers' Club, 1956, *by Edward C. Pyatt*

Black Rocks and Cratcliffe Tor, Climbers' Club, 1956, *by P. R. J. Harding and A. J. J. Moulam*

Cwm Idwal by A. J. J. Moulam, Climbers' Club, 1958

Snowdon South by J. Neill, Trevor Jones, Climbers' Club, 1960

Llanberis North by D. T. Roscoe, Climbers' Club, 1961

APPENDIX B

FIRST ASCENTS BY WILFRID NOYCE

North Wales

Llanberis Pass,
1934 Colin Kirkus took Wilfrid Noyce up the Direct Route on Dinas Mot
Clogwyn-y-Grochan
1935	20th April	Scramblers' Gate	with J. M. Edwards
1935	20th April	Long Tree Gate	with J. M. Edwards

Carreg Wastad
1935	21st April	Dead Entrance	with J. M. Edwards

Craig Ddu
1949	29th January	The Crown of Thorns	with P. R. J. Harding

Tryfan
1935	22nd April	Soap Gut by Squint Start	with J. M. Edwards
1936	April	Main Long Chimney	with D. Murray-Rust
1936	24th August	Gashed Crag – Steep Bit	with J. M. Edwards
1936	24th August	Bubbly Wall	with J. M. Edwards
1936	27th August	North Side Route	with J. M. Edwards
1936	30th August	Girdle Traverse of Terrace Wall	with J. M. Edwards
1936	1st Sept	Yew Buttress	with J. M. Edwards
1936	2nd Sept	Scars Climb	with J. M. Edwards
1936	4th Sept	Soap Gut	with J. M. Edwards
1936	4th Sept	Hangman Gut	with J. M. Edwards
1942	9th May	Garden Path (Drws Neoddodd)	

	Craig Yr Ysfa		
1938	December	Truant Rib	with D. M. Craib
	Lliwedd		
1937	August	Cracks Rib	with J. M. Edwards
	Idwal		
1942	May	Cinderella's Twin (Holly Tree Wall)	

Himalaya

1953	15th April	Pokalde	with M. Ward and T. Bourdillon
1957	2nd June	Machapuchare	with A. D. M. Cox

Karakoram

1960	17th June	Trivor	with Jack Sadler

APPENDIX C

BIBLIOGRAPHY

Books

Allen, Charles (Ed), **Plain Tales from the Raj**, Futura, 1975
Arrowsmith, R. L. (Comp), **Charterhouse Miscellany**, Gentry Books, 1982
Band, George, **Everest – The Official History,** Harper Collins, 2003
Band, George, **Everest Exposed**, Harper Collins, 2003
Berry, Martyn & Brown, Hamish, **Speak to the Hills**, Aberdeen University Press, 1985
Bonington, Chris, **The Climbers, A History of Mountaineering**, Hodder & Stoughton, 1992
Braham, Trevor, **When the Alps Cast Their Spell**, The In Pinn, 2004
Brown, Joe, **The Hard Years**, Gollancz, 1967
Chapman, F Spencer, **Helvellyn to Himalaya**, Chatto and Windus, 1940
Chapman, F Spencer, **Lhasa: The Holy City,** Chatto and Windus, 1938
Charterhouse Governors, **Charterhouse Register 1925-1975**, Gentry Books, 1980
Connor, Jeff, **The Philosophy of Risk**, Canongate, 2002
Cranfield, Ingrid (Ed), **Inspiring Achievement, the Life and Work of John Hunt**, Institute for Outdoor Learning, 2002
Cruikshank, Jimmy, **High Endeavours, The Life and Legend of Robin Smith,** Canongate, 2005
Deacon, Richard, **History of the British Secret Service,** Granada, 1980
Deacon, Richard, **Super Spy**, Futura, 1989
Deacon, Richard, **The British Connection**, Hamish Hamilton, 1979
Deacon, Richard, T**he Cambridge Apostles**, Robert Royce, 1985

Dean, Steve, ***Hands of a Climber***, Ernest Press, 1993
Elphick, Peter, ***Far Eastern File***, Hodder & Stoughton, 1997
Evans, Charles, ***Eye on Everest***, Dennis Dobson, 1955
Fletcher, Frank, ***After Many Days***, Robert Hale & Company, 1937
Gibson, Ivor, ***John at Charterhouse and other Poems***, Elkin Mathews and Marrot, 1933
Hall, Vernon, ***A Scrapbook of Snowdonia***, Arthur H. Stockwell, 1982
Hankinson, Alan, ***Geoffrey Winthrop Young***, Hodder & Stoughton, 1995
Hillary, Edmund, ***Nothing Venture, Nothing Win***, Hodder & Stoughton, 1975
Hinsley, F. H. & Stripp, Alan, ***The Code-Breakers***, Oxford University Press, 1993
Holden, Wilfred (Ed), ***The Charterhouse We Knew***, British Technical and General Press, 1950
Hooker, Joseph, ***Himalayan Journals Vol II***, Routledge (Reprint), 2003, Scientific Travellers 1790–1877 Vol IV
Hunt, John, ***Ascent of Everest***, Hodder & Stoughton, 1953
Hunt, John, ***Life is Meeting,*** Hodder & Stoughton, 1978
Isserman, Maurice and Weaver, Stewart, ***Fallen Giants of Himalayan Mountaineering, A History***, Yale University Press, 2008
Jackson, John A., ***More than Mountains***, G. Harrap, 1955
Johnston, Alexa, ***Sir Edmund Hillary, An Extraordinary Life,*** Dorling Kindersley, 2005
Jones, John, ***History of Balliol College*** (2nd Ed.), Oxford University Press, 1997
Kaye, M. M., ***Sun in the Morning***, Penguin, 1992
Kaye, M. M., ***Golden Afternoon***, Penguin, 1998
Kerr, Philip, ***Esau***, Chatto & Windus, 1996
Kirkus, Colin F., ***Let's Go Climbing***, Thomas Nelson, 1941
Lemon, Elsie (Ed), ***Balliol College Register 1916-67***, Private Publication, 1969
Lowe, George, ***Because It is There***, Cassell, 1959
Macintosh, Charles, ***From Cloak to Dagger***, William Kimber, 1982
Macksey, Kenneth, ***The Searchers, Radio Intercept in Two World Wars***, Cassell, 2003
Mallory, George Leigh, ***Climbing Everest***, Gibson Square (Reprint), 2010
Masters, John, ***Bugles and a Tiger***, Viking Press, 1956
Milburn, Geoff, and Jones, ***Trevor Welsh Rock***, Pic Publications, 1986

Milburn, Geoff, Helyg, **Geoff Milburn & Climbers' Club**, 1985
Mortlock, Colin J., **The Spirit of Adventure**, Outdoor Integrity Publishing, 2009
Palmer, Bernard, **Willingly to School**, St. Edmund's School Trust, 2000
Perrin, Jim, **Menlove**, Ernest Press, 1993
Perrin, Jim, **The Villain**, Arrow Books, 2006
Quick, Anthony, **Charterhouse, A History of the School**, James & James, 1990
Shipton, Eric, **Upon that Mountain**, Hodder & Stoughton, 1943
Skillen, Hugh, **Knowledge Strengthens the Arm**, Hugh Skillen, 1990
Skillen, Hugh, **Spies of the Airwaves**, Hugh Skillen, 1989
Slesser, Malcolm, **Red Peak**, Hodder & Stoughton, 1964
Slesser, Malcolm, **With Friends in High Places**, Mainstream Publishing, 2004
Smith, Bradley E., **The Ultra-Magic Deals**, Airlife Publishing, 1993
Smith, Michael, **The Emperor's Codes**, Bantam Press, 2000
Stripp, Alan, **Codebreaker in the Far East**, Oxford University Press, 1989
Thompson, Simon, **Unjustifiable Risk, The Story of British Climbing**, Cicerone, 2010
Venables, Stephen, Everest, **The Summit of Achievement,** Bloomsbury, 2003
Woodruff, Philip, **The Guardians**, Jonathan Cape, 1953
Workman, Fanny Bullock, **Two Summers in the Ice-Wilds of Eastern Karakoram**, Fisher Unwin, 1917

Journals and Archives

Alpine Club, Alpine Journals, 1900-2012
Climbers' Club, Climbers' Club Journals, 1900-2012
Cambridge University MC, Cambridge Mountaineering, 1936-1946,
Himalayan Club, Himalayan Journal, 1945-1946
British Library, India Office List, 1938
              India Office Records
St. Edmund's School Archives
Charterhouse Archives
King's College Archives
Balliol College Archives
Army Personnel Centre, Historical Disclosures Section, 1940-1946
National Archives, The Army Lists

Royal Geographical Society Archives
The Archives of the Noyce Family
The Library and Archives of Godalming Borough Council
The Library and Archives of the Military Intelligence Museum
The Library and Archives of the Religious Society of Friends in Britain
Bedfordshire and Luton Archives and Records Service

APPENDIX D

WILFRID NOYCE AND POLIO

On three of Wilfrid Noyce's expeditions one of the members caught polio. Roger Chorley contracted it on Machapuchare in 1957 as they were starting the ascent proper and had to be carried down to Pokhara. David Cox was in the Alps with Noyce in 1958 and fell victim. Don Whillans was at high altitude on Trivor in 1960 when he showed symptoms of the disease. He recovered and was able to descend on his own and in fact to ride his motor-bike back from Pakistan to England. Both Chorley and Cox were less fortunate and were permanently disabled.

This gave rise to the suggestion that Noyce was a carrier of the polio virus.[†]

I am advised by the medical profession that:

- Polio is highly contagious and spreads easily by human-to-human contact. In endemic areas, wild polio viruses can infect virtually the entire human population.
- Polio can be transmitted by the faeco-oral route via contaminated food or water but can be oral-oral.
- The virus is spread probably from contaminated hands. Inanimate objects, such as eating utensils, may also spread the virus.
- Virus particles are excreted for several weeks following infection. It is most infectious between seven to ten days before and seven to ten days after the appearance of symptoms, but transmission is possible as long as the virus remains in the saliva or faeces.

[†] See Jim Perrin, *The Villain*, footnote p 212

- Polio was endemic in the Alps, Himalaya and Karakoram in the 1950s and early 1960s.
- It is possible a member of the party had caught the virus shortly before the trip and was asymptomatic (as most people were) and did not develop the disease, but passed it on to others in the party, only one of whom progressed.
- Given the close contact and cooking/feeding conditions of climbing it is most probable that everybody in the parties caught the virus but only one in each party eventually developed full-blown polio.
- The severity of their disease is exacerbated by the physical activity of climbing during the early stages of their infection, if, indeed, they did catch it then.
- Even if Noyce was the asymptomatic source of infection on the first trip to the Himalaya, he could not have been the source on the second trip to the Alps because he would have been excreting the polio virus for a few weeks only in 1957 but no longer the following year. Also, having had a mild form of polio in the Himalaya he would then have developed immunity and could not have caught it again a year later and could not have passed it on a second time.

The only recorded case of the silent carrier describes a very unusual and rather extraordinary situation that clearly did not apply to Noyce.

On 22 July 2002 BBC News reported the case of a European man in his late 20s, referred to as 'Polio Man', who is carrying the polio virus but has not developed the disease even though he is immunodeficient. It is thought that Polio Man originally received the weakened form of the virus in the Sabin vaccine and somehow this mutated in his body into the full-strength natural virus. Doctors were alerted to his case in 1995 when conducting a study into gastric problems associated with immunodeficiency. One test during the study involved analysis of the man's faeces and this revealed the presence of polio. It appears he may have been excreting the live virus for over 20 years. The Head of Virology at the UK National Institute for Biological Standards and Control said: "Although there is no official record that anyone has caught polio from him, it is a possibility. Doctors stress the man they now call "Polio Man" is not a serious health hazard.'

There would have been so many other opportunities for infection for his colleagues. In fact he wrote to his other two companions on the 1958 trip to warn them to watch out for any polio symptoms, with the suggestion that Cox may have caught the virus from dirty plates in a hut.

One has to conclude that Noyce was not the source on any of the expeditions.

APPENDIX E

A PAMIR PILGRIMAGE[1]

Having travelled and worked in Central Asia I had the desire to visit the memorial to Wilfrid Noyce and Robin Smith, partly as an adventure but also to express my debt to him. After discussions with Graeme Nicol and Ian McNaught-Davis, members of the 1962 expedition, I established the location of the memorial. It is in the Garmo Valley, one of the more remote and inaccessible valleys of the Western Pamirs and several miles from the nearest road or habitation. I discussed the idea with Rosemary Ballard, Wilfrid's widow and Jeremy, their younger son, and he agreed to go with me.

I had made contact through the website Pamirs.org with various people who had worked and trekked in Tajikistan but there was only one Tajik organisation that responded to my emails requesting assistance with arrangements. This was *Pamir Adventure,* run by Surat Toimastov, a biologist by training and an expert photographer. He knew the area and indeed most of the Pamirs and understood what was required. He had also tried several times to get into the Garmo Valley. His photographs appear in most of the brochures about Tajikistan.

I had planned to go in June 2008 but it turned out, after detailed analysis, that the Kyrgyz Ob River, which is across the entrance to the Garmo Valley might be impassable at this time as the glacier melt would be rising. It might have been possible to get across on horses but the return was less certain. The memorial is some twelve to thirteen miles up the valley from the Kyrgyz Ob. Jeremy and I decided to delay the trip until success was more assured when the glacier melt would be at its lowest and before the snows arrived. This window was the last two weeks in September and first week in October. We decided to go in 2009.

However, I felt that a reconnaissance might be useful and continued with the original idea and, with Surat, his son and a local guide, in June 2008 went over the route as far as the Kyrgyz Ob. Surat has a number of local contacts and our requirements for horses and assistance for 2009 were discussed with the Tajik farmers. In 2009 the party was completed with another pupil of Wilfrid's, Peter Norton, and a friend of Jeremy, Barry Cooper.

We arrived in Dushanbe, the capital of Tajikistan on 21st September and we stayed in the comfortable Taj Palace Hotel. The following day we left with Surat and Zaffar, an ex-wrestler, the cook/chauffeur in a big Mitsubishi 4 x 4 going from Dushanbe up the main road which leads via Gharm and Jirgatal through Kyrgyzstan to Kashgar in Xinjiang, Western China. The vehicle bowled along happily for first sixty miles or so through Kafarnihan to Abigarm on the good tarmac: thereafter the main road was spasmodically tarred until Darband. Shortly afterwards we turned off on to the *Pamir Highway*, a grand term for a mountain track, albeit marked in red on the maps.

The Highway follows the Khingow River for several miles and goes on south to the Afghan border which it follows to Khorog, the administrative centre of the Gorno-Badakhshan Autonomous Oblast (GBAO). It then goes east across the Central Pamir to Murghab, then north up to Osh in Kyrgyzstan. Access to The Eastern Pamir was frequently made from Osh, before the Pamir Highway offered an alternative.

There was a terrific storm, the rain was pouring down, and we had gone along the Pamir Highway for half an hour – about twenty miles – when we were diverted into a ravine. The bridge over the river had been washed away and two torrents had cut the road as well. Tortuous, steep, muddy bends led us to the bottom of the ravine and across the river and up in similar manner on the other side. The slope from the bottom of the ravine was blocked by a Chinese 18-wheeler which was stuck and not even with chains could it make more than a slither to give just enough room to pass. We spent the night a little farther along at a farm at Khur. The Tajik farmers are very hospitable and provide simple accommodation.

The second morning was still wet. We continued and shortly after Tavildara, 112 miles from Dushanbe, we turned off the Pamir Highway continuing up the Khingow Valley. Coaxing the vehicle over a ford, that we had to reconstruct, we travelled on broad cultivated terraces above the river which had cut in parts a steep-sided ravine. Sometimes it was one fast-flowing torrent, at others where the terrain was much flatter, it was a braided river, covering a wide area. Beyond the terraces the mountains rose to 4,000 metres and higher. We ourselves were already nearly at 2,000 metres. However we had not expected the mud-slide which provided a two-metre high barrier across the road. On one side was the mountain and on the other was a steep drop to the river – no way round. Fortunately some other travellers were behind us and we set to with stones and bare hands to make the lump safe to drive cautiously over.

The second night we were in an abandoned mining camp, in Russian ex-army caravans at Sangvor. This was now used as a rest-camp looked after by the village head-man, Hairatullah, who was a friend of Surat, and whom I had met the previous year. He accompanied us for the rest of the trip. It had taken two days to do what we had done in one last year.

Day three was more agreeable, although the road deteriorated. The scenery was impressive; at the top of the valley, where we could see into the Garmo Valley, we could see fleetingly Pik Ismail Somoni (formerly Pik Kommunizma 7,495m), and Pik Garmo.

Hairatullah had sent his son with two mares, and a filly, on ahead and shortly after midday we arrived at Arzing, the highest habitation in the Khingow Valley at 2,500 metres, some 180 miles from Dushanbe. The vehicle was unloaded. Two stallions and another horseman and a guide were provided and the four of us, Jeremy, Peter, Barry and I set off to walk to the deserted village of Pashimghar, five miles further on, where we camped with a splendid view into the Garmo Valley and stunning views all round. Last year I had seen bears just above the village.

Although there were just four of us, we now had, in addition to the two Tajiks who had come with us from Dushanbe, two local guides, their sons as horsemen, four horses, one filly which followed her mother all the way, and three dogs. It was quite a caravan. The Kyrgyz Ob was still fast flowing and we crossed comfortably on horseback behind the horseman and then we walked. There were no paths as only the occasional hunter ventured there. At one stage we did 1.75 kilometres in two hours! The primary forest was impenetrable. There was a little open parkland but we made best progress in the wide river bed. There was plenty of wildlife; we saw a bear, a golden eagle, a snake, ibex, hare and many traces of wild boar.

After two days we reached the Lower Base Camp of the 1962

expedition. Our Tajik friends recognised the camp from the pictures in *Red Peak*, Malcolm Slesser's book on the 1962 expedition. There we spent two nights. On the first night there we had another terrific storm and we wondered how long we would have to wait before the weather would let us do what we had planned. However, the morning of Sunday 27th September dawned fair and after breakfast our guide from Arzing, Abdul Sha'id, who had been up there once hunting, led us some 200 metres above the camp to the five memorials to Russian climbers who had died in the 1970s and then some 600 metres farther to the Noyce-Smith Memorial at 2,976m. It was in the same good state as in the 1962 photographs. Jeremy arrived first and he spent a little while on his own in front of the memorial. A final closure with a father who had died when he was eight years old. It was a moving moment.

Jeremy and his mother had arranged for a commemorative plaque to be made and we affixed this to the stone on which the two names had been engraved in 1962 using 1960s Rawlplug technology. Jeremy said a few words and Peter gave a short eulogy. Abdul Sha'id knelt and recited verses from the Qu'ran. Having taken all the necessary photographs we returned to the camp. The glacier that the memorial had overlooked forty-seven years ago has receded some two to three miles and all that remain are the slag-heaps of the moraine, '...*the foulest ground imaginable*`, according to Malcolm Slesser.

On the return, understanding the country a bit better, we stayed as much as possible in the Garmo River bed, leaping the small streams and using a horse to cross the main torrent, when necessary. The weather was exceptionally kind to us on the way down and we had the towering mass of Pik Garmo as our backdrop all the way back to the Kyrgyz Ob. We reached Arzing in two days, having walked over forty miles in the five days in trackless country. We returned to Dushanbe with very similar experiences as on the way out, but the weather was better!

In the three days left to us we visited one of the old cities of the Silk Road and called on the British Ambassador, Trevor Moore and recounted our exploits. The mission was well accomplished in the two weeks we were in Tajikistan.

Notes

1   A version of this account has already appeared in the *Climbers' Club and Alpine Journals*

INDEX

A

Alchutov, Nikolai 292; 295
Allen, Maurice 79; 82
Alpine Club xvi; 15; 67; 69; 125; 139; 145; 154; 269; 275; 288; 291
Alpine Journal 24n; 105; 133; 144n; 147; 207n; 306; 318; 326n
Amin, Idi 77; 85n
Angels ;47; 49; 50
 See also Apostles, The
Anthony, Michael 76
Apostles, The 48; 49; 50
 See also Angels
Arrowsmith, R. L. 24n
Ascent of Everest, Life is Meeting xi; 206n; 207n; 210
Ash, John Garton 12n
Auriol, Vincent 212

B

Bagot, Charles 108; 110
Ballard, Eveline 142; 144n
 Picture inset 26
Ballard, Pat 143
 Picture inset 26
Ballard, Stephen 142; 155
 Picture inset 26
Band, George xvi; 6n; 154; 160; 164; 167; 174; 175; 176; 181; 182; 183; 184; 212; 217n; 289n
Barry, R. V. M. 43
Bartrum, Geoffrey 23
Bauer, Paul 214
Berry, Martyn xvi; 263; 289n

Beves, D. H. 50
Bicknell, Raymond 46
Binney, Rose 144n
 Picture inset 29
Birley, Robert 19
Blackshaw, Alan 154; 275
Blair, Tony 143
Blashford-Snell, John 153
Blunt, Anthony 50
Boit, Anne xvi
Bolam, James 143
Bonington, Sir Chris 153
Booth, John Nicholls 220
Born, Reverend Ronald 137; 141; 143
Bourdillon, Tom 154; 160; 160–61; 175; 176; 179; 181; 184; 186; 189; 194; 195; 199; 200; 202
Boyd-Carpenter, Michael 137; 139; 141; 144n
Bradley, Major Gedley 27; 32; 33; 75
Bradshaw, Susan 304; 309n
Braham, Trevor xvi; 123; 124n
Brantchen, Hans 51; 52; 61; 62; 63
Bridge, Alf 74; 75
Brooke, Richard xvi; 264; 274
Brown, Joe 154; 291; 293; 295; 306
Bryan, Kenneth 291; 294; 295
Buhl, Hermann 214
Bull, Derek 291; 293; 295; 296; 297; 298; 300; 301
Bulley, Ivo 8; 9
Bulley, Rosamund 9
Burgess, Dick 234
Burgess, Guy 50

Burns, Robert 73
Butt, Pippa 145

C
Call of the Snowy Hispar, The (W. H. and F. B. Workman) 257n
Callimachus 68
Cambridge Mountaineering 61
Cambridge University Mountaineering Club 45; 50; 56; 61; 68; 72; 74; 114; 155; 280
Campbell, Donald 269
Castle, Florence xii
Cavenagh, Sandy 235; 236; 238; 241; 242; 244; 245; 247; 248; 252; 253
Chalmers, Helen xvi
Chantrell, Stuart 30; 110
Charlet, Armand xiii; 63; 64; 66; 67; 68; 276
Charteris, Leslie 152
Chorley, Lord Roger 154; 218; 219; 221; 223; 224; 225; 229; 275; 320
Clark, Ronald 266
Climbers' Club xvi; 23; 27; 33; 35; 45; 85n; 137; 141; 147; 154; 260; 266; 269; 270; 278; 291
Colthurst, Tim 137; 138; 139
Conquest of Everest, The 211
Cooper, Barry 324; 325
Cornford, Frances 47; 151
Cox, David 18; 43; 70n; 133; 144n; 157n; 218; 259; 262; 266; 274; 284; 289n; 307; 322
   IN HIMALAYA 219–234
   IN THE ALPS 138–39; 155–56; 272–73; 276; 320
   IN WALES 36–37; 259; 260; 261
   Picture inset 34
Craib, D. M. 68
Craig, Nares 36; 37
Cruickshank, Jimmy xvi; 298; 299; 303n

D
Daily Telegraph, The 143
Davey, Roy 259
Picture inset 34
Davis, Dennis 288
Dean, Steve xvi
Debenham, Ann 213
Dedman, Stanley 282
Dodd, F. D. R. 51
Dorji, Ang 200; 201; 203
Dorji, Mingma 199; 204; 301
Dorji, Phu 200; 201; 203
Douglas-Bate, Andrew 208
Downes, Bob 275
Doyle, Sir Arthur Conan 8
Duke of Edinburgh 205; 210; 211
Duke, Neville 269
Dunbar, Graham 20
Dyrenfurth, Norman 267

E
Edwards, Major Alan xvi
Edwards, Menlove xiii; 17; 19; 20; 23; 24; 28; 29; 31; 32; 33; 34; 35; 36; 37; 38; 39; 40; 42; 43; 43n; 48; 51; 52; 53; 54; 55; 110; 125; 227; 270; 306
Eisenhower, Dwight D. 212
Elliott, Sir Claude 46; 128; 129; 130; 144n
Evans, Sir Charles 154; 161; 167; 169; 170; 175; 176; 184; 186; 189; 193; 199; 200; 202; 209; 261; 266
Eyre, Richard 13

F
Farebrother, H. J. 143
Farrer, Peter 285
Finch, George 163; 164
Fleming, Peter 269
Fletcher, Frank xii; 15–17; 19; 24n; 27; 79; 146
Picture inset 10
Forster, E. M. 145
Frank, Len 278; 279
Friends Ambulance Unit xi
Fuchs, Sir Vivian 269

INDEX

G

Gaunt, Tom 131; 132; 141
Gillies, Sir Harold 56
Godley, A. D. 15
Gohar, Ali 240; 241; 242
Goodfellow, Basil 163
Gould, David 71; 86; 87; 88; 90; 91; 285
   Picture inset 19
Graham, Angus 261
   Picture inset 37
Greene, Richard 14; 17; 20; 22
Gregory, Alf ('Greg') 159; 160; 167; 170; 178; 184; 185; 186; 188; 189; 200; 212; 275
Gridley, Judith Sheila 76
Grimble, Ian 73; 74; 76; 80; 82; 85n; 92; 93; 95; 96; 100; 102; 105; 107; 108; 111; 112; 113; 114; 124n; 125; 126; 130; 131; 144n; 149; 305; 309n
Grippenreiter, Eugene 292; 295; 297; 300
Grounds, Byam 141
Guardian, The 144n

H

Hall, Dr Reginald xi
Hallowes, Odette 269
Hankinson, Alan xv
Hansbury, John 36; 105; 106; 259
   Picture insets 25; 34
Harding, John xvii
Harding, Peter 43n; 138; 141
Hargreaves, A. B. 35
Hartley, Sir Harold 27
Harwood, J. P. 146
Herald for Hindhead xi
Herington, Edwin 263
Herington, John xii; xvi; 263; 264
Herodotus 48
Herzog, Maurice 152
Heywood, Hugh 47
Hibbert-Ware, Alice 46
Hillary, Sir Edmund xiv; 115; 150; 159; 176; 179; 180; 181; 182; 183; 185; 186; 187; 190; 191; 198; 199; 200; 202; 203; 204; 205; 207n; 210; 212; 268
Hills, Richard xii; xvi; 259
   Picture inset 34
Himalayan Club 86; 93
Hinchcliffe, Jeremy xvi
Hitler, Adolf 22
Hobsbawm, Eric 50
Hocking, James 286
Hocking, Winnie 286
Hodgkin, Alan 50
Hodgkin, Robin 43; 308; 309n
Hodgson, Col. P. E. 20n
Holdsworth, R. L. 109
Holland, C. F. 74; 75
Holmes, Sir Peter 137; 138; 139; 141
Home, Sir Alec Douglas 256n
Hooker, Joseph 122
Hope, Richard 24
Hoyland, John 43
Hughes, Penelope Seth 36
Hunt, Sir John xiii; xv; 1; 6n; 18; 55; 70n; 72; 74; 75; 85n; 114; 127; 147; 151; 156n; 157n; 158; 159; 160; 161; 167; 168; 210; 212; 217n; 261; 265; 274; 288; 289; 290n; 291; 292; 303n; 304; 307; 309n
   IN HIMALAYA 1–2; 169–206
   IN SCOTLAND 292–93
   IN THE ALPS 155–56; 272–73; 275–76
   IN THE PAMIRS 293–302
Hutchesson, Mabel ('Hutch') 5; 6; 7; 21

I

Ikramullah, Mohammed 235
Ikramullah, Soghra 235
Iredale, Harry 21
Irvine, A. L. 17; 202; 204
Ives, Frank 146; 208; 264

J

Jackson, Eileen xii; xvi

Jackson, John 127
Jameson, Hugh 13
Jenkinson, A. J. 152
Jones, Derek 147
Jones, Ralph 161; 291; 294; 295; 300; 301

K

Kaltenegger, Paul 134
Kerry, Sir Michael 83; 84; 85n
Keynes, Maynard 49
Khan, Zarayat 242;
King Edward VIII 21; 37
King George V 37
Kingsmen of a Century (L. P. Wilkinson) 45
Kirkus, Cecil 3; 37
Kirkus, Colin 3; 25; 26; 28; 42; 43; 53; 75
Kirkus, Cuthbert 3
Kirkus, Guy 3; 10; 25; 28
Kirkus, Muriel 3
Kirkus, Nigel 3; 10; 25
Kirkus, William 3
Knowledge Strengthens the Arm (Hugh Skillen) 78
Knubel, Josef 51
Kretschmer, H. E. 43n
Kretschmer, Jo 36; 259; 260; 261; 262; 263

L

Leakey, Colin xvi; 47; 69; 85n; 305
Leakey, Henrietta Wilfrida 46; 47; 69; 125; 127; 150; 156n; 161; 259; 286; 305
Leakey, Louis 46
Leakey, Priscilla; 47; 69
Lee, Brian 22; 146
Legrand, Eileen 132
Legrand, Julian 143
    Picture inset 26
Legrand, Roland 132; 137; 142; 143
Leyden, A. R. 163; 164
Lindsay, Sir Harry 212

Listener, The 139; 144; 274; 290
Lloyd-Jones, Sir Hugh 78–79; 83
Longland, Sir Jack 28; 49
Lowe, George 163; 164; 166; 167; 175; 178; 181; 182; 183; 189; 190; 191; 192; 193; 194; 196; 198; 199; 200; 202; 205; 212; 258; 291; 295; 300; 301
Lucretius 68
Lukan, Karl 270
Lunt, Reverend R. B. 143

M

Macleod, I. T. 146
Maillart, Ella 269
Malachov, Vladimir 292; 295
Mallory, George xiii; 149; 202; 204; 261
Malvern Gazette xi
Man, Dikshya 220; 221; 225; 230; 232
Mardall, Margaret xvi
Marriott, James 20; 23
Marr-Johnson, Peter 78; 83
Marsh, Dick 259
    Picture inset 34
Martin, Peter xvi
Mason, A. E. W. 67
Maugham, Somerset 152
McCausland, Pauline xvi
McIndoe, Archibald 56
McMorrin, Ian 264; 271
McNaught-Davis, Ian xvi; 291; 295; 323
Melchisa, M. C. 146
Menlove, the life of John Menlove Edwards xi
Michelangelo 23; 40; 194; 251
Milburn, Geoff xvi
Mills, J. N. 148
Milner-White, Reverend Canon Eric 51
Mimpriss, Tim xvi
Moore, Trevor 326
Morgan, Lady Sydney 147
Morgan-Brown, Cyril 8
Morgan-Brown, Frances 8
Morgan-Brown, Reverend John 8

Morin, Denise 261
Morris, Jan (James) 161; 184; 199; 205
Morrish, L. W. 146
Mortimer, Raymond 268
Mortlock, Colin xi; xvi; 234; 236; 237; 238; 240; 241; 242; 244; 245; 246; 247; 248; 249; 252; 253; 276; 277; 290n
Munro, Heda 263
Murray, Bill (W. H.) 154
Murray, Jackson 69
Murray-Rust, David 19; 21; 24; 27; 35; 36; 37; 38; 39; 40; 44n; 46; 47; 54; 69; 210
Murray-Rust, Jeff 27; 46; 47; 69
Murray-Rust, Peter 43n

N
Nehru, Sri Jawaharlal 206
Nicol, Graeme xii; xv; xvi; 155; 292; 294; 295; 300; 301; 323
Nineteen Eighty-Four (George Orwell) 230
Noel-Baker, Philip 127; 128; 129; 130; 144n
Norton, Peter xvi; 261; 276; 289n; 290n; 324; 325
Picture inset 34
Noyce, Alfred 3
Noyce, Jeremy xii; xiii; xv; xvi; 155; 262; 286; 287; 288; 304; 306; 323; 324; 325; 326
Picture insets 28; 29; 42
Noyce, Jocelyn 5; 6; 17; 20; 25; 34; 37; 39; 40; 52; 61; 109; 110; 111; 141
Picture insets 1; 2; 3; 8
Noyce, Michael 149; 158; 159; 262; 286; 287; 288; 304; 305; 306
Picture insets 27; 28; 29
Noyce (*née* Kirkus), Lady Enid 3; 4; 5; 6; 7; 25; 79; 114; 127; 142; 144n; 145; 211; 219; 256n; 305
Picture insets 26; 29
Noyce (Ro), Rosalind xvi; 6; 7; 43n; 76; 126; 127; 128; 129; 130; 144n;
286; 287
Picture inset 29
Noyce (Romie), Rosemary xvi; 113; 114; 142; 143; 145; 147; 153; 159; 179; 210; 219; 263; 264; 271; 286; 287; 288; 289; 301; 304–05; 306; 309n; 323
Picture insets 2; 3; 26; 27; 29
Noyce, Sir Frank 3; 5; 6; 21; 48; 54; 55; 79; 129; 144n; 288
death of 141–42
Noyce, Wilfrid
and polio xi; 247; 248
See also Appendix D
books (as author, editor, contributor or collaborator)
See Appendix A
death of 299–300
IN ATLAS MOUNTAINS 278–81
IN HIMALAYA xiii; xiv; 1–2; 86–101; 115–123; 169–206; 219–234; 236–256; 321
IN SCOTLAND 292–93
IN THE ALPS 17; 24; 33–34; 40–42; 51–52; 61; 62–68; 133–36; 138–39; 147; 155–56; 235; 266; 272–73; 273–74; 275–76; 276; 276–77; 283; 288; 321
IN THE LAKE DISTRICT; 17; 27; 34–35; 46; 52–55; 127–31
IN THE PAMIRS xv; xvi; 147; 270; 289; 293–301
IN WALES 10–11; 19; 25–26; 28–32; 33; 36–37; 37; 39–40; 42–43; 47; 48; 51; 68–69; 75–76; 141; 259; 260; 261; 262; 263; 277–78; 288
marriage to Rosemary 143
memorial to 302
See also Appendix E
Picture insets 1; 2; 3; 4; 8; 9; 11; 12; 13; 14; 15; 16; 17; 18; 20; 21; 22; 23; 24; 25; 26; 27; 30; 31; 33; 35; 36; 37; 38; 40
Nyima, Ang 190; 200; 223; 226; 227; 229; 230

O

Orwell, George 230
Ovchinnikov, Anatole 292; 294; 295; 296; 297; 298; 300; 303n
Oxford University Mountaineering Club 234

P

Palamountain, Edgar 14; 17
Palmer, Bernard 12n
Paradise Lost (Milton) 52
Pearce, Hon. Mr. Justice 24n
Perrin, Jim xi; xvi; 38; 44n; 53; 70n; 289n; 320n
Pigou, Arthur 45–46; 48; 49; 50; 51; 63; 69; 111; 114; 125; 127; 128; 129; 130; 131; 138; 143; 144n; 147; 268; 269; 276; 287
Picture inset 26
'Polio Man' 321
Polunin, Oleg 235; 236; 238; 242; 245; 253; 254
Porter, H. E. L. 46
Prasad, Sri Rajendra 206
Proust, Marcel 246; 254
Pugh, Griffith 150; 160; 161; 205
Pyatt, Edward 147; 148

Q

'Q' 237; 242; 244; 245
Queen Elizabeth II 205; 211

R

Raeburn, Harold 46
Rawlinson, Geoffrey 92; 93; 95; 96; 97; 98; 100; 160; 276
Reade, H. V. 46
Rébuffat, Gaston 261; 265; 275
Red Peak (Malcolm Slesser) xi; xv; 326
Religious Society of Friends xi
Richard, Joseph P. 81; 82
Richmond, Wilfrid 8
Riddley, E. R. 84
Ritchie, Brenda 34

Roberts, Jimmy 184; 218; 219; 220; 221; 223; 224; 225; 229; 230; 232; 234
Robinson, E. M. W. 146
Rodham, C. H. B. 237
Rook, Arthur 47
Rothschild, Lord Victor 50
Roy, Lady Esmé 80; 85n; 110; 124n
Royal Geographical Society xi
Royal Signals Institution xi
RSI Journal xi
Runcie, Robert 47
Russell, Bertrand 49
Russell, Vincent 'Peter' 14; 21; 146
   Noyce's obituary for 14–15
Rutscher, Willi 134
Ruttledge, Hugh 115

S

Sadler, Jack 234; 240; 242; 244; 245; 246; 247; 248; 249; 250; 252; 253; 263; 276; 277
Saint-Exupéry, Antoine de 152; 266
Sant, Ivor 8; 9
Scheidegg, Countess Irma 134; 135; 136
Scott, Robert Falcon 145
Scottish Mountaineering Club 69
Sevastianov, Anatole 292; 295; 296; 297; 298; 300; 303n
Sha'id, Abdul 326
Shah, Sahib 237; 238; 242; 244; 245; 253; 254
Shalaev, Nikolai 292; 295; 300; 301
Shaw, George Bernard 8
Shelley, P. B. 152
Shipton, Eric 91; 115; 179; 205; 235
Shoesmith, Martin xii
Sills, H. H. 50
Simmons, Paul 17–18; 18; 20; 22
Simpson, Keith 264; 289n
Singh, Karak 87
Sinker, Charlotte 47
Sinker, Sir Paul 47
Skillen, Hugh 78; 85n

Slesser, Malcolm xv; 291; 292; 293; 294; 295; 301; 302; 303n; 326
Smith, Catherine xvi
Smith, Geoffrey 235; 236; 237; 241; 242; 244; 245; 246; 247; 248; 252; 253; 278; 288
Smith, Michael 81; 85n
Smith, Robin xii; xv; xvi; 147; 292; 293; 295; 296; 297; 298; 323
   death of 299–300
   memorial to 302
   See also Appendix E
   Picture inset 40
Smith, Wilfred 79
Smyth, Tony 86; 101; 102; 106; 108; 110
Smythe, Frank 115; 152
Somervell, Howard 212; 214
Spanish Civil War 47; 50
Speaker, G. R. 33; 39–40
Spencer-Chapman, F. 151
Spender, Stephen 151
Spirit of Adventure, The xi
Stalder, Eddie 133
Stephen, Leslie 62; 145
Stobart, Tom 160; 205
Stopford, Bobbie 127
Stork, Joe 22
Summerhayes, Sir Christopher 169
Surrey Advertiser xi; 157n; 289n; 306; 309n
Sutton, Geoffrey 44n; 70n; 264; 266; 267; 270; 274
Swiss Alpine Club 67; 208; 213

T

Tchernine, Odette 153; 157n
Technical Aid to the Commonwealth of Independent States xv
Temba, Ang 170; 200
Temba, Da 225; 229; 230; 234
Tensing, Da 193
Tenzing Norgay xiv; 115; 160; 170; 176; 178; 186; 187; 188; 198; 199; 200; 202; 205; 206; 210; 286
   Picture inset 27

The Ascent of Everest (John Hunt) xiii; 151; 156n
The Emperor's Codes (Michael Smith) xi; 81; 85n
Theocritus 68
Tilly, Harry 102; 104; 127
Tilman, Bill 115
Tiltman, John 73
Times, The 24; 55; 129; 141; 151; 157n; 161; 173; 182; 184; 199; 210; 236; 237; 244; 253; 255
   obituary to Noyce 306
Tindle News xi
Tissières, Alfred 275
Toimastov, Surat 323; 324; 325
Trevelyan, George Macaulay 49; 125
Tsering, Ang 225; 226; 229; 230; 232
Turner, George 24n; 145; 210
Turner, Rosalind 47
Tyndall, John 62

U

Ullyot, George 260; 261

V

Venables, Stephen xiii

W

Waddington, Conrad 47
Waddington, Jake 47
Ward, Michael 155; 167; 170; 172; 176; 178; 179; 180; 181; 182; 183; 184; 189; 192; 193; 200; 205; 234; 261; 273; 274; 275
Waycott, Jo; 154; 260; 261
Wedd, Nathaniel 68
Westmacott, Mike xvi; 155; 162; 164; 166; 167; 168; 169; 174; 176; 181; 182; 183; 185; 189; 190
Westmorland, 'Rusty; 128; 129
Whillans, Don 154; 234; 235; 236; 237; 238; 240; 241; 242; 244; 245; 246; 247; 248; 252; 256; 278; 306; 320
Whittle, Gordon 102; 104; 105; 112; 113

Wilder, Thornton 142
Wilkinson, Patrick 24n; 45; 73
Willis, A. N. 143
Wilson, H. C. W. 132
With Friends in High Places xi
Wittgenstein, Ludwig 49
Woolf, Virginia 152
Wordsworth, William 249
Workman, Fanny Bullock 254; 257n
Workman, William Hunter 254; 257n
Wrangham, Edward 'Ted' 292; 294; 295; 296; 298; 300; 301; 303n
Wright, Claud 22
Wylie, Charles 160; 161; 162; 218; 260; 261
   IN HIMALAYA 1–2; 169–206; 219–34

Y
Young, Brian 209; 282
Young, Geoffrey Winthrop 23; 30; 33; 37; 45; 46; 51; 111; 156n; 266; 267; 306
Young, Georgina 3
Young, Jocelin Winthrop 216
Young, Len Winthrop 45; 69
Young, Marcia Winthrop 44n; 45; 70n; 111; 113; 125; 126; 127; 131

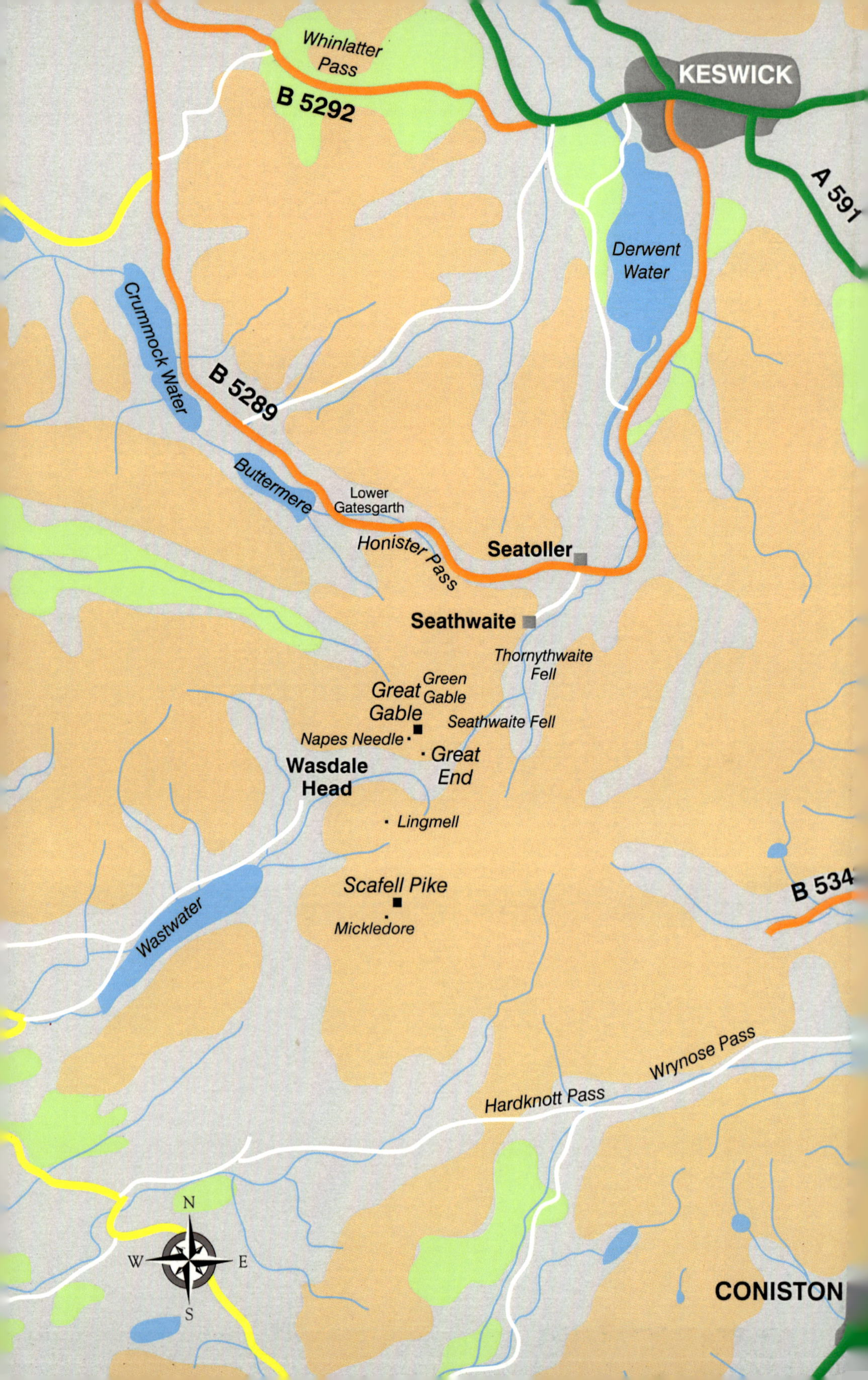

Whinlatter Pass
B 5292
KESWICK
A 591
Derwent Water
Crummock Water
B 5289
Buttermere
Lower Gatesgarth
Honister Pass
Seatoller
Seathwaite
Thornythwaite Fell
Green Gable
Great Gable
Seathwaite Fell
Napes Needle
Great End
Wasdale Head
Lingmell
Scafell Pike
Mickledore
Wastwater
Hardknott Pass
Wrynose Pass
CONISTON
N
W
E
S